*Glorious Bodies*

# Glorious Bodies

## TRANS THEOLOGY AND RENAISSANCE LITERATURE

Colby Gordon

THE UNIVERSITY OF CHICAGO PRESS
CHICAGO AND LONDON

The University of Chicago Press, Chicago 60637
The University of Chicago Press, Ltd., London

Published 2024
Printed in the United States of America

33 32 31 30 29 28 27 26 25 24 1 2 3 4 5

ISBN-13: 978-0-226-83499-3 (cloth)
ISBN-13: 978-0-226-83500-6 (paper)
ISBN-13: 978-0-226-83501-3 (e-book)
DOI: https://doi.org/10.7208/chicago/9780226835013.001.0001

The University of Chicago Press gratefully acknowledges the generous support of Bryn Mawr College toward the publication of this book.

Library of Congress Cataloging-in-Publication Data

Names: Gordon, Colby, author.
Title: Glorious bodies : trans theology and Renaissance literature / Colby Gordon.
Description: Chicago : The University of Chicago Press, 2024. | Includes bibliographical references and index.
Identifiers: LCCN 2023053680 | ISBN 9780226834993 (cloth) | ISBN 9780226835006 (paperback) | ISBN 9780226835013 (ebook)
Subjects: LCSH: English literature—Early modern, 1500–1700—History and criticism. | Transgender people in literature. | Transgender people—Religious aspects.
Classification: LCC PR418.T75 G66 2024 | DDC 820.9/353—dc23/eng/20231206
LC record available at https://lccn.loc.gov/2023053680

∞ This paper meets the requirements of ANSI/NISO Z39.48-1992 (Permanence of Paper).

*For Simone and Will,*
*for building something glorious with me.*

# Contents

[ INTRODUCTION ]

# A Trans Crux

In Holinshed's *Chronicles of England, Scotland, and Ireland* (1587), nestled away in the sixth year of the reign of Henry III between brief mentions of the most recent war with Scotland and a London riot instigated by disgruntled wrestlers, there lies a trans parable. Here, in the entry for this year (1222), Holinshed notes in passing the strange proceedings of a council convened at Oxford "for reformation of the state ecclesiasticall and the religion of moonks." Curiously, Holinshed fixates only on one minor and dubiously attested part of the synod: the trial and execution of a small but raucous assembly of frauds, deviants, and heretics. As the *Chronicles* records it, this is what happened. Stephen Langton, the archbishop of Canterbury, was presented with "two naughtie felowes" who had been taken into custody for pretending to be Jesus and, in this guise, "preaching manie things against such abuses as the cleargie in those daies used." To lend credence to their deception, the pair displayed "certeine tokens and signes of wounds in their bodies" like those borne by "our sauiour Iesus that was nailed on the crosse." These questionable stigmatics were apprehended in the company of two women, "of whom the one had taken upon hir to be that blessed virgine Marie," while "the other fained hir selfe to be Marie Magdalene." Condemned as "false dissemblers," it was the "doome of that councell" that the mock Christs should be "led foorth to a place called Arborberie," "nailed to a crosse of wood" and "there left till they were dead." If the archbishop of Canterbury presiding over a crucifixion were not sufficiently shocking, Holinshed punctuates the episode with a scandalous flourish. "One of them," he adds, "was an Hermophrodite, that is to say, both man and woman."[1]

Or maybe that's not what happened. It is as if this postmortem gender reveal makes the story glitch and triggers a hard reset. Holinshed backtracks and tells the story again, this time drawing on an alternate version of the narrative that he found in the chronicles of Ralph of Coggeshall, a report that adjusts its group of convicts. In this second iteration, two men and two women were indeed arraigned before the archbishop, but their roles have been recast, the gender variance of the first iteration redistributed but not erased. This time we are introduced to a "yoong man" accused of "contemning the sacraments of the church" who had "suffered himself to be crucified, hauing the prints of the fiue wounds appearing in his bodie." This fellow appears in court alongside two women whom he had recruited to "giue out and spread the rumour abroad, that he was Christ in deed." One of these accomplices was the self-crucifying youth's sister, and the other, "being verie aged," was subsequently convicted for "witcherie," having "with hir sorcerie and witchcraft brought that young man unto such wicked follie and madnesse." Finally, the company's ranks swell to include a deacon who, "for the loue of a woman that was a Iew," turned "apostata" and "circumcised himself." In this revised account, the punishments were parceled out differently. The elderly witch and self-crucifying youth were immured, "closed up betwixt two walles, where they remained till they died"; the sister was pardoned "because she had reuealed the diuelish practice of the other"; and the circumcised deacon was degraded, "committed to the secular power, & so burnt."[2]

Although it is not immediately obvious from the narrative Holinshed compiles, the solemn task of "reformation" undertaken at the Oxford Synod would engender momentous developments in the fraught relation between the religious and political spheres. The reason that the thirteenth-century Oxford council remained a matter of public concern some 350 years later was that the case had set an important legal precedent, one significant enough to be recorded by Bracton.[3] In the words of Frederic Maitland, this incident became "the main, almost the only, authority for holding that, without the help from any statute, English law can burn a heretic."[4] In point of fact, the circumcised deacon would be the only victim of judicial burning in England for almost two hundred years, when the practice was revived for the Lollards and expanded in the jittery aftermath of the Reformation. But it was not the ecclesiastical court that burnt the apostate, who appears in the hallucinatory shapes of a hermaphrodite, a witch, a mutilated youth, a false stigmatic, and a converted deacon. The immolation was conducted, as Bracton specified and Holinshed affirmed, by "the secular power."

The uneasy encounter between Stephen Langton's synod and the "secular power" of the mob that burned the heretic stages the problem at the center of political theology, which I invoke here in the senses adopted by Julia Lupton and Graham Hammill as a "recursive crisis" that accompanies the "coupling or entanglement" of the "ostensibly discrete domains" of religious and political life.[5] Characterizing the council as performing the work of "reformation" lends the event a forward momentum, affiliating it with the modernizing thrust of a secularization that cultural historians have long associated with the Protestant Reformation.[6] Even so, the relation of what transpired at the council throws into question the precise status of the secular sphere, which here serves as the enforcer of a violent, retrograde form of Christian particularism. In the wild excesses of the punishments meted out by the archbishop and his lay accomplices, which the chroniclers variously recorded as a burning, a beheading, a hanging, an immurement, and a crucifixion, we confront the indigestible remainder of a theology that has not been—and perhaps cannot be—wholly secularized. A curious temporal anomaly, an accretion of chimeric fantasies of religious violence circling around the transitional body of a "Hermophrodite," Langton's provincial council achieves in Holinshed's *Chronicles* the status of a primal scene of political theology.

*Glorious Bodies* begins with the question of what it might mean that Holinshed condenses this "reformation" to the trial and execution of a crucified hermaphrodite, a figure that I take as a cipher for transness.[7] This book asks how gender variance is bound up in the historical processes and epistemic shifts at stake in the episode Holinshed recounts, and further, what theoretical and historiographical tools we would need to tell the story of early modern trans history if we began not with boy players or *Twelfth Night* but with the "Hermophrodite, both man and woman" nailed to the cross by an archbishop in a pleasant grove in Oxfordshire.[8] To speak of transness having an early modern history at all is to court controversy, flouting as it does the central, grounding assumption beneath contemporary transphobia: that transition is a novelty, that trans life must be defined by its newness and experimental nature. The assumption that trans life is a specifically modern phenomenon, in sharp contrast to the apparently timeless stability of cisgender modes of identity and embodiment, has been foundational to both the lethal politics of trans-antagonism in the present moment and also to early modern gender and sexuality studies. Until very recently indeed, the field has flatly disavowed the possibility that trans history might reach back to early modernity, instead bracketing historical gender variance within the cisnormative model of "transvestism."[9] In place of this limiting approach, I argue that trans embodiment in the Renaissance was not chiefly understood as a question of clothing or a fantasy explored through the fictions of the stage. Instead, this book insists that transition *happened*, both socially and surgically, and that the significance of such alterations was glossed through the categories provided by theology.

Pursuing the logics at work in Holinshed's account of the Oxford council, which turns on the crucifixion of a false Christ discovered to be "both man and woman," opens onto the central gambit of this book: that, in an era before medicine declared eminent domain on the practice and discourse of transition, theology offered a conceptual vocabulary for thinking about trans embodiment. In this respect, *Glorious Bodies* reorients early modern gender studies away from performance and the protocols of identification, turning instead to premodern religious writing as a key way to access a trans history that stretches back to the Renaissance. Pairing early modern literature with a wide range of primary sources including midrash, canon law, sermons, Biblical commentaries, saint's lives, prodigy books, Inquisitorial records, and anti-conversion polemics, this book sketches a theology of transition in the sixteenth and seventeenth centuries. From the gestational Adam of Genesis, created "male and female," to transmasculine saints undergoing martyrological mastectomies and the apocalyptic eradication of gender in the resurrection of the flesh, early modern religious writing offers a rich vein of scripts, images, and reference points for thinking about the malleability of gender. Many of the theological narratives circulating through early modern texts imagined transitional gender as holy, even paradisial; in their plenitude, such genders cleave most closely to the image of a God who surely lacks nothing.

And yet, if Holinshed aligns his "Hermophrodite" with crucifixion and, in consequence, both Jesus and the martyrs of the early church, the Oxford council also calls into question the degree to which these sacred transfigurations edged into heretical territory. Like early modern religious writing more broadly, Holinshed tethers the crucified hermaphrodite's gender variance not only to the holy sexes of the first man and the son of God, but also to an unruly host of apostates, heretics, prodigies, witches, self-mutilators, eunuchs, and Jews. It is, in other words, difficult to fix the precise relation between religion and the transness crystallized in the "Hermophrodite" hanging from the cross, whose passion rehearses the beating heart of the Christian tradition while also marking its racial and doctrinal limit. *Glorious Bodies* hinges on this central interpretive crux, according to which transitional genders pose a crisis for the category of religion. At the same time, the difficulty of situating transness as either within Christian theology or outside it suggests that early modern trans history is bound up in the transformations that remapped religious difference as racial difference. In conversation with the urgent work of scholars of premodern critical race theory, this book builds an account of early modern transness that is not just a matter of gender, but of racialized gender, closely keyed to the historical development of white supremacy, anti-Semitism, Islamophobia, imperialism, and settler colonialism. Without minimizing the ways that early modern Christianity was implicated in these racist logics, this book nevertheless argues that secularism intensifies rather than resolves both racism and transphobia, reinscribing a normative cis white Protestantism while excising religion's affirmative trans capacities. *Glorious Bodies* resurrects premodern trans theology, then, to offer a counter-narrative to the secular state, currently attempting to criminalize transness out of existence, and also to the right-wing Christian consensus according to which transition is a kind of heresy.

## The First Crux: Holinshed's Hermaphrodite

To develop the central crux of this argument, according to which trans possibility is at once a signifier of sacrality and profane, idolatrous, and heretical, I will return to Holinshed and disentangle the many forms of transition embedded in the narrative of the Oxford Synod. To begin with, we might note that it isn't so strange to find a hermaphrodite at a crucifixion. As feminist and queer historians have long argued, Christological discourses often awarded Jesus a gender that transcended sexual differentiation, a physiology vested with a complicated arrangement of genitalia, and a body capable of both erection and lactation.[10] This medieval tradition, exemplified in mysticism and anchoritic literature, continued into early modernity, gracing poetry written across confessional divisions. In "Lucus 34," George Herbert imagines the apostles bickering over "access to the breast," with John crying out for the sacred teat: "Ah now, glutton, let me suck too! / You won't really hoard the whole / Breast for yourself! . . . I claim the milk / Mingled with the blood."[11] In the more restrained "Longing," Herbert inserts Jesus at the apex position of a lactational chain:

> From thee all pity flows.
> Mothers are kind, because thou art,
> And dost dispose
> To them a part:
> Their infants, them; and they suck thee
> More free.[12]

Throughout the poem, Herbert addresses Christ directly, employing a masculine title ("Lord Jesu," "Lord of my soul," "Lord hear"), but only to double down on his savior's maternal function. The loose analogy of the first line, that Jesus's pity flows like mother's milk, tightens into a causal connection in the stanza's second line, which insists that "Mothers are kind, *because* thou art." Here, the flow of milk from the mother's breast is not merely an image, but a function of Christ's hydraulic drip of "pity," poured out for believers on the cross in a holy let-down of nourishing blood. The "kindness" of the Lord licenses the use of merely human breasts, "disposing" to the lesser mothers "a part" capable of nourishment which, in Herbert's nested logic, they go on to dispose to their infants. This kindness of mothers makes them of a kind with the "Lord Jesu," who becomes an ur-Mother, the origin of all "flows," so that the child that suckles her mother's breast "sucks thee." Not only bleeding and feeding, the wound does double duty. Touched by the tip of the spear, the sacred flesh curls back into a bleeding vulvic orifice available for cultic veneration, irreverent fingering, and gestation. This final incision carves out a kind of holy neo-vagina through which Jesus gave birth to the church, who, personified as Ecclesia, was sometimes understood by way of Song of Songs as the Bride of Christ. Delivering a child who is also his wife aligns the crucified Jesus with another sacred androgyne: Adam, gravid with a child who is at once his spouse and himself.[13] Incarnational theology, in other words, was a theory of gender variance, and it was the penetrating techniques of crucifixion that opened up the divine body in such a way as to press it beyond binary sexuation altogether. As scholars including Leah DeVun, Jonah Coman, Sophie Sexon, and Ellis Light have argued, trans possibility was nestled into the pulsing heart of Christian theology, exposed at the dramatic height of the Passion.[14]

What Christ's complex embodiment means for incarnational gender, as well as the erotic responses it provokes, has proven to be a fraught subject for feminist and queer critics to navigate. Take, for instance, reactions to Herbert's "Bag," which envisions the crucified Jesus as a pouch into which believers can tuck any messages they might want to dispatch to God: "If ye have any thing to send or write, / (I have no bag, but here is room) . . . Look, you may put it very near my heart."[15] The precise gendered significance of this little "room," so very close to Christ's heart, is a matter of some debate. Michael Schoenfeldt unpacks the purse as "a kind of vaginal orifice," following the lead of Caroline Walker Bynum, according to whom the capacity to breastfeed and give birth rendered Christ distinctly "female," since, as she insists, "in medieval experience as in modern, it was women's bodies, not men's, that fed with fluid from the breast."[16] In Richard Rambuss's pointed rebuttal, the hollow becomes "a kind of scrotum."[17] Although these positions arrive at apparently incompatible conclusions regarding the impasse of Jesus's "bag," both interpretive moves are meant to stabilize Christ's sex and, in consequence, the types of desire his little sack solicits. The framework here is immutably binary: either Christ is equipped with a "kind of vagina," gives birth, and breastfeeds, in which case the holy body is female, or the scrotum flags an indelible "primary maleness" that ought not to be resignified.[18] Bristling at the instinct to "peremptorily reencode every representation of the penetrable male body as feminized *because* penetrated," Rambuss exhaustedly asks, "Are male bodies without their own orifices?" Certainly not. But what is elided here is the possibility that a definitive accounting of male bodies' orifices would have to include vaginas, and such bodies as these are not incompatible with the circuits of male homoeroticism that Rambuss so incisively locates in devotional poetics. An invaginated man at the center of a brutal, homoerotic scene of "all-male" violence, but also a pregnant mother with a swollen penis, the crucified Christ serves as a rich repository for both transmasculine and transfeminine possibilities.[19] That these trans potentials emerge as part of a scene of eroticized violence—as part of an execution—ominously looks forward to the transphobic futures of state violence. Long-haired and androgynous, genitals obscured, member swollen, punched full of wounds, lactating blood, rich in orifices, Jesus was never more transitional than at the moment of crucifixion.

For Holinshed to find a "Hermophrodite, both man and woman" at a crucifixion, then, was not entirely out of step with incarnational theology. And yet, if the Christ's sacred wounds and their stimulating gendered possibilities were suitable objects for devotional contemplation, stigmatics presented a rather more complicated case. In one sense, the spontaneous appearance of Christ's wounds on—for the most part—*women's* bodies promised to bring just a taste of divine gender transitivity into the world. Having witnessed the perpetually bleeding sores of sixteenth-century stigmatic Lucia Brocadelli, Cardinal Ippolito d'Este remarked that, in her, "Jesus Christ Himself was transformed into a virgin" (*Ipsum Christum Ihesum in virgine quadam transformatum*).[20] For the cardinal, Brocadelli's "remarkable wounds and stigmata" marked the descent of a Christ grammatically gendered as masculine (*ipsum . . . transformatum*) into the form of a mortal girl, a virgin like *the* Virgin, the better to "arouse in the minds of the faithful the love, devotion, and worship of God Almighty" (*quo fidelium mentes in Dei omnipotenti maximique amorem, devocionem cultumque excitari deberent*).[21] While the cardinal imagines a Christ who transitions into a feminine shape, the stigmatic who assimilated her putatively male savior also edged into gender variance. When the stigmatic Catherine of Siena's biographer Raymond of Capua expressed doubts about certain "extraordinary" revelations she claimed to have received, he witnessed a miraculous transformation in which the saint's "face turned into the face of a strange man," an "oval, middle-aged face" sporting "a short beard the colour of corn."[22] For her part, Catherine also imagined this merging with her masculine savior as an erotic exchange of flesh, claiming to sport not only his wounds but also his foreskin, which, she writes in her letters, she received from him as a wedding ring to seal their mystical union.[23] Sheathed in Christ's penile flesh and punctured with his vulvic wounds, the stigmatic bodies of Catherine of Siena and Lucia Brocadelli gestured toward a Christlike transcendence of merely binary gender.

This trans interpretation was, of course, not the only available way to gloss the gendered embodiment of any given stigmatic, which was more likely to be understood as evidence of fraud, self-mutilation, delusion, or compacting with demons. Such was the case of Brocadelli's infamous contemporary Magdalena de la Cruz, a Franciscan abbess who, in 1546, confessed to the Inquisition that she had faked her stigmata under orders from a demon who "appeared to her in the figure of an angel of light." In this angelic drag, the demon pushed "large needles through her feet" and instructed the nun to "crucify herself" by means of "some nails in the wall" so that "she would be viewed as holy."[24] From this vantage, the false stigmatic's lacerated body is a lure, a mere pretense of holiness that bad actors can cynically exploit for vanity and personal gain. Moreover, Magdalena's perverse mortification of the flesh was understood by the Inquisitors and her disgruntled fellow nuns as the sign of a diabolical compact whose effects were racializing.[25] In a letter to the inquisitorial tribunal, one of Magdalena's accusers wrote that she witnessed the nun in her cell "at midnight" in the company of "a very ugly and very dreadful black man," presumably for the purposes of fornication.[26] Indeed, this particular fantasy circulated throughout her tribunal. Yet another letter of complaint rewrote the initial scene of diabolical stigmatization by claiming that, at age twelve, Magdalena was visited by a demon who promised her great honors, sealing the pact by presenting her with a naked black man and bidding her to enjoy "carnal pleasures" with him.[27] Whereas Lucia Brocadelli and Catherine of Siena's stigmatic wounds registered as signs of holiness that aligned the saint with the transitional body of Christ, the public humiliation of Magdalena de la Cruz brings gender variance into a conceptual network with a series of racializing bruises, blemishes, tattoos, scars, and blots.[28] If Magdalena's lacerations were artificially acquired and thus ostensibly temporary, the possibility that the injuries were the somatic signs of an illicit, mixed-race sexual encounter invokes the specter of hereditary difference. The operations that reshaped the flesh of the pseudo-saint marked her with the stain of miscegenation, as if a blackness understood as demonic could be imprinted on her white skin and spread through her offspring, an instance of what Miles Grier, in work on race and textual materiality, calls "the slave stigma" of the "ink mark of servility."[29] In the suppurating wounds of the stigmatic, gender variance bleeds into racial difference.

Suspicion trailed even those stigmatics eventually judged to be genuine. As Tamar Herzig argues, this skepticism increased in the sixteenth century, such that "the very signs that were supposed to authenticate holiness were often regarded as proofs of deliberate simulation," a trend that spoke to broader anxieties about "religious dissimulation."[30] Naturally, Protestant reformers generally regarded stigmatics with flat disdain, as exempla of nothing but how easily Catholics were duped by their overly literal and idolatrous attachment to material signs.[31] But Catholic inquests also began from the premise that it was significantly less likely that any given stigmatic incarnated a paradisial gender plenitude than that she bore the signs of demonic sex, in all available senses of the term. As canonically insubstantial beings, demons both "lacked gender" and possessed it in superabundance, fluttering between male and female forms as incubi and succubi in order to seduce and defile their human lovers.[32] This ability to divest themselves of sex at will in the pursuit of sexual gratification parodically reenacted a capacity enjoyed by the angels among whose number they had once been counted. If Milton's angels are famously blessed with the condition C. S. Lewis nervously named "something that might be called trans-sexuality," this juicy detail does not emerge in the course of Raphael's exposition on angelic materiality, during which he explains to a mesmerized Adam that angels can "limb themselves . . . as they please," adopting the "color, shape, or size . . . as likes them best."[33] Instead, this particular perk of angelic corporeality is disclosed through an elaboration of demonic androgyny:

> With these came they, who from the bord'ring flood
> Of old *Euphrates* to the Brook that parts
> *Egypt* from *Syrian* ground, had general Names
> Of *Baalim* and *Ashtaroth*, those male,
> These Feminine. For Spirits when they please
> Can either Sex assume, or both; so soft
> And uncompounded is their Essence pure,
> Not ti'd or manacl'd with joint or limb,
> Nor founded on the brittle strength of bones,
> Like cumbrous flesh; but in what shape they choose
> Dilated or condens't, bright or obscure,
> Can execute their aery purposes,
> And works of love or enmity fulfil.[34]

As Milton knew from John Selden's *De Diis Syriis*, the ancient fertility god Baal was multiply sexed, appearing sometimes in the feminine form of Ashtaroth, since "neither the sacred texts nor the ancient mysteries of those nations distinguish between the sexes of the idols."[35] What begins as an attempt to separate the "general" assortment of Syrian sex demons into a neat and unbridgeable binary, slotting them into categories split by the hard enjambment separating "male" and "feminine," founders on the conjunctive "For" that launches into a description of spiritual bodies' gender transitivity. As soon as the sexual differentiation of the demonic population into male Baalim and female Ashtaroth is proposed, the distinction dissolves into a rapturous reverie on their fluid sexuation, which is paradoxically both a manifestation of their fallen nature and an extension of their former angelic embodiment. As Julie Crawford aptly notes in her account of Milton's transmateriality, *Paradise Lost* "holds out an ideal that minimizes or even erases the sexual differences between bodies, engaging a history of thought in which the most elevated state of embodiment is characterized by the absence of binary sex."[36] At the same time, the context in which the sharpest formulation of that most elevated condition is articulated—the pit of hell—throws that gender-variant ideal into question.

There were no demons summoned before the Oxford council, but there was a witch. As agents of demonic influence on earth, witches too were ascribed indistinct, hybrid, and nonbinary genders. Banquo hails *Macbeth*'s witches, "so withered and wild in their attire" that they "look not like th'inhabitants o'th' earth," with a deeply awkward declaration that might easily pepper a contemporary transphobic diatribe: "You should be women, / And yet your beards forbid me to interpret / That you are so."[37] It is not merely that gender transitivity was a sign of consorting with demons, and that genital variation was read as the sign of a demonic pact: witchcraft was also framed as a root cause of gender variance.[38] Heinrich Institoris's witch-hunting manual, the *Malleus Maleficarum*, jokes uneasily about witches who steal men's penises or enchant them into believing that their "virile members" have vanished, so that the afflicted man and his examiners "can see and feel nothing except a smooth body, uninterrupted by any organ" (*Nihil valeat videre & sentire, nisi corpus planum, & nullo membro interruptum*).[39] Reginald Scot's *Discoverie of Witchcraft* mocks Jean Bodin's account of demonic "transubstantiation" for blurring together the equally absurd possibilities of lycanthropy and gender variance, according to which "it may be naturallie brought to passe, that a girle shall become a boie; and that anie female may be turned into the male."[40] In an important caveat, however, Bodin notes that "neither the Devil, nor his ministers the witches" have the power to "remove a single member from a man except the virile organs, which they do in Germany [!], causing the shameful parts to . . . withdraw into the abdomen."[41] It is as if witches were early vectors of what has come to be called the "trans contagion" or "transgender craze," agents of chaos vested with a diabolical power to inflict transness on their helpless victims. A touch of this demonic trans panic infuses Holinshed's account of the Oxford council, which floats the possibility that the self-crucifying hermaphrodite's injuries were the machinations of one of his Marys, an elderly woman who drove him to "such wicked follie and madnesse" with her "sorcerie." In this sense, the cut body of the stigmatic hermaphrodite posed a complicated epistemological problem for Christian theology, gesturing both toward a Christlike transcendence of binary sex and a gender straight from hell.

At the same time, the "naughtie felowe"'s complicated gender also pointed outside Christianity altogether, finding an analogue in the last figure Holinshed hauls into court: the deacon who circumcised himself "for the loue of a woman that was a Iew." At this point, we have reached the kernel of historical truth about the Oxford council. There was no witch; there was no hermaphrodite; Stephen Langton certainly never arranged any crucifixions. But there was a deacon who converted, allegedly for love. Four contemporaneous annalists recorded the fate of the apostate.[42] When accused before the ecclesiastical court, it seems that the convert did indeed renounce Christ, although perhaps not in the dramatic fashion alleged by Matthew of Paris, according to whom the court presented a crucifix to the apostate who, in an anticipation of Andres Serrano, "pissed all over the cross" (*minxit super crucem*).[43] What is certain is that the deacon was degraded by ecclesiastical authorities, handed over to the lay power in the person of Fulk de Brent and an angry mob, and immediately burnt at the stake. All the other characters and plot points, the fake Christs, the stigmatics, the self-mutilators, the witch and the snitch, the crucifixions both voluntary and involuntary, all of these were later accretions to this central story. In this respect, the doubly crucified, stigmatic hermaphrodite was a kind of dreamlike afterimage of the self-circumcising deacon.

What is at stake here is not just the conflation of circumcision with castration, the possibility that a Christian man, and an ordained one at that, might succumb to a love that would lead to him to make an effeminating genital cut that could render him, too, a "naughtie felowe, both man and woman." In bringing circumcision together with crucifixion, the chroniclers open onto another paranoid fantasy that bound Jewishness to gender variance: the blood libel, the charge that Jews were kidnapping and crucifying Christian children in order to collect their blood for ritual use. This delusion was conceptually linked to the chief ways that Jewish men were understood to be ambiguously sexed, as the Christian blood was supposedly employed to close the wound of circumcision and to prevent male menstruation. Thomas Calvert's 1648 commentary to the anti-Semitic pamphlet *The Blessed Jew of Marocco; Or, a Blackmoor Made White* explains that "child-Crucifying" was intended to prevent the "monthly Flux of Blood" that afflicted Jewish "men, as well as females" as an inherited punishment for killing Christ.[44] Moreover, from the thirteenth century onward, ritual murder cases involved the accusation that Jews were circumcising Christian children before murdering them.[45] The logic, such as it was, seems to have been that rectifying Jewish men's gender indeterminacy by stanching the flow of blood that stood as a humiliating marker of their religious (and perhaps also racial) difference required a form of predatory genital cutting. In the minds of the Christians who consumed, circulated, and elaborated the blood libel, reenacting the crucifixion was not only the symptom of a specifically Jewish form of transitional gender but a means of inflicting it on Christian children. This fantasy of a violated Christian boy, subjected to a stigmatizing and degendering assault at the hands of Jews, enters the story of the Oxford Synod in one of its earliest iterations. In his *Historia Anglorum* (1255), Matthew of Paris claimed to have heard from a firsthand witness that the deacon apostatized by announcing before the archbishop that "he had been present at a sacrifice performed by the Jews, at which they crucified a boy" (*confessus est se palam interfuisse cuidam sacrificio, quod Judaei fecerant de puero quodam crucifixo*).[46] When the chronicler returned to the story of the Oxford Synod in his *Chronica Majora* (1259), however, his account had already changed. The innocent, victimized Christian child had been replaced by a fraudulent, self-crucifying hermaphrodite that the Church must punish, not protect.[47]

The central purpose of the Oxford Synod was the eradication of heresy, hardening the borders that separate Christian from non-Christian. In addition to providing the legal groundwork for burning apostates, the council also promulgated a series of anti-Semitic measures that, among other things, prohibited the construction of new synagogues and the employment of Christian servants in Jewish households, as well as issuing a mandate requiring England's Jews to wear distinctive badges.[48] And yet, these legal and doctrinal efforts to police the boundaries of Christianity falter in the presence of the cut body of the hermaphrodite whose transitional gender encodes both a violated Christlike innocence and a perverse, heretical, and Judaizing mortification of the flesh. These complexities are only compounded when Holinshed proposes that Stephen Langton and his "secular" colleagues dragged the "false dissembler" to a grove and "nailed them to a crosse," a disciplinary correction that redoubles the initial blasphemy of crucifixion. For in becoming a crucifier himself, the archbishop is reinscribed into the Passion narrative in the unenviable position of Pontius Pilate; or perhaps he should be counted among the Jews thought to stage ritual crucifixions at Easter—which, incidentally, was just around the time of year that the council was held. Then again, ordering a crucifixion also aligned Langton with the Turks who were accused of martyring their Christian captives by nailing them to crosses in a grotesque parody of the Passion.[49] If this judgment was intended to stabilize the divisions between Christian and non-Christian, orthodoxy and heresy, male and female, it instead intensifies their indistinction.

It is not only the category of Christian that loses its specificity and coherence in the presence of the crucified hermaphrodite whose body encodes a host of trans possibilities that took various shapes, ranging from the invaginated Jesus whose wounds are available for fingering, kissing, and birthing to the unclassifiable genders of witches and demons to suspiciously Jewish and Muslim forms of genital cutting. In attempting to pass judgment over this transitional "Hermophrodite," the distinction between the domains of religion and secularity also founders. For it is not the archbishop who undertakes the grim business of capital punishment, whether such punishment is a matter of burning, beheading, hanging, immuring, or crucifying the offender. Rather, he passes the convict over to "those to whom the execution was assigned," which Holinshed clarifies was "the secular power." It is unclear how "secular" a "power" might be once it sets itself to, variously, crucifying a hermaphrodite and burning a heretic. Confronted with the transitional body of a "Hermophrodite," this secular authority reverts to its theological origins in order to enforce the ends of Christian orthodoxy. That is to say, in Holinshed's hands, the Oxford Synod becomes a matter of political theology, in two senses. First, it marks the uneasy transfer of ritual vocabularies and disciplinary practices from the Church to a secular authority charged with the punishment of heterodoxy. Secondly, in its adoption of anti-Semitic legislation and its legal enshrining of the "secular" power's authority to purge heresy through fire, the council opens onto the futures of political theology in its Schmittian sense, as a juridical framework for genocide, fascism, and the state of exception. The following section pursues how the thick weave of forms of gender variance bundled into the center of Holinshed's theo-political parable in the person of the crucified hermaphrodite opens onto a number of new avenues for scholarship on political theology, as well as in trans studies.

## The Second Crux: Trans × Theology

A revival of interest in the work of Carl Schmitt and Ernst Kantorowicz early in the first decade of the 2000s has generated a venerable body of critical inquiry into the genealogies of secularism, the persistence of sacramental politics, and the bonds that unite the prehistories of liberalism and fascism.[50] Gender has not been a central or even a secondary category of analysis for scholars examining early modern political theology, and even in the cases where it is explicitly addressed, such inquiries do not draw upon the methods or analytical frameworks of gender studies or queer theory. In general, this subfield has strongly preferred abstractions to embodiment and scaffolds its historical, literary, and theoretical claims on concepts like sovereignty, legitimacy, contract, rights, citizenship, and corporate personhood. Indeed, to the extent that a body enters the conversation at all, it tends to be the *corpus mysticum*.[51] An important exception to the field's lack of engagement with the body is Urvashi Chakravarty's insistence that early modern political theology turns on racialization, understood as "bloodlines, somatic difference, and finally chromatic distinction," a position with which the argument I am making here is closely aligned.[52] To date, the somatic markings of transition—the stigmata of the trans body—have not struck critics as having any obvious relation to the exchanges between religion and politics, either in their early modern iterations or in the context of the present.

Scholarly investment in the collapse of constitutionalism, the friend/enemy distinction, the decisionist power of executive authority, and the limits of secular liberalism responded naturally to the exigencies of the Bush-era War on Terror. The crises of the present, however, require refining our analytical tools for diagnosing the failures of the secular state to deliver on its promises of tolerance, rationality, and rights-based citizenship. Twenty years later, the saturation of the political sphere by religion has taken the form of the terrifying ascendency of a hard-right Christian nationalism cohering around white supremacy, anti-Semitism, Islamophobia, and transphobia. The resurgent fascism of the present moment has entered the public sphere cloaked in a pathological hatred of trans people. Manufacturing consensus for its racist, militarist, and natalist project has entailed disseminating a paranoid fantasy in which trans predators are preying upon the nation's vulnerable youth. The panic around this purported "trans contagion" seducing confused youth into a disfiguring and sterilizing transition may have been incubated in evangelical and Catholic contexts, as in the Nashville Statement's denunciation of "transgenderism" as "an essential departure from Christian faithfulness," or Pope Francis's perverse insistence that trans people are a threat to "creation" on the order of "nuclear bombs."[53] Nevertheless, it is the secular state that has set itself to criminalizing transness through the cascade of bills entertained by state legislatures seeking to eliminate transition through the apparatuses of incarceration and state violence.

What we are witnessing in real time is how the ostensible neutrality of the secular state breaks down when confronted with what has been chillingly euphemized as "the trans debate." Faced with the mere existence of trans life, the liberal state chooses to exercise its lethal disciplinary force on behalf of a narrow Christian particularism. That is to say, the political visibility of trans life has occasioned an instance of what Julia Lupton and Graham Hammill describe as the "scene of recurring conflict" that defines political theology, in which the apparently separate spheres of religious and political life collapse together.[54] It is this recursive logic that binds the crucified hermaphrodite to modern fascism, so intent on policing gendered embodiment as a means to ensure the reproductive futurity of the white race. For uncanny echoes of the scene at the Oxford Synod linger in the contemporary political landscape of transphobia. Just as in Holinshed's account of the Oxford Synod, today's anti-trans dogma invokes a vulnerable youth who submits to a degendering cut prompted by the demonic insinuations of gender-variant women, or perhaps is driven to self-mutilation through the machinations of a Jewish conspiracy.[55] At the same time, the stigmatized body is also evidence of a willful fraudulence that requires harrowing and perhaps extralegal forms of correction: both "man and woman," the self-cutting "Hermophrodite" is a roguish "dissembler," a vector of heresy and corruption. In Holinshed's surreal rehearsal of the events of the Oxford council no less than contemporary anti-trans polemics, the categories of victim and perpetrator, naïve child and manipulative adult, consensual incision and violent assault, bleed together in the pierced and transitional body. Then as now, the clarity provided by religious and racial categories falter in the presence of the trans body. In the bracing image of the "naughtie felowe, both man and woman" nailed to a cross, we encounter the primal scene for a political theology of transphobia. The transtemporal purchase of Holinshed's crucifixion fantasia implies that understanding the genealogies of secularism requires both a robust account of race, as Urvashi Chakravarty has so compellingly argued, and also an account of transness.[56]

The version of trans history that I am building here opens up future directions not only for the fields of early modern studies and political theology but for trans studies as well. The presence of the crucified hermaphrodite at the council that established the legal precedent for the secular state's authority to burn heretics suggests that it is time for trans studies to reevaluate its unspoken commitment to secularity. In this commitment, the field reflects assumptions shared in the culture at large. After all, it is generally taken for granted that transness is an essentially secular phenomenon, that trans bodies are the byproduct of advanced medical technologies administered by physicians—the presumption that we are the surgeon's creatures, not God's. There are perfectly reasonable explanations for this resistance to theology, not the least of which is the matter of contemporary Christianity's relentless, lethal antagonism toward trans life, as represented in ongoing campaigns by evangelical and right-wing Catholic lobbying organizations to criminalize transition.[57] For this reason and others, Max Strassfeld and Roberto Che Espinoza have recently argued, the field of trans studies has "participated in discursively marking transgender as secular" through "the manufacturing of religion and trans as mutually antagonistic terms."[58] Strassfeld forcefully argues elsewhere that the "constructed incongruity" between theology and transness plays out poorly for both trans people and religion itself, doubling down on conceptualizing religion as "anachronistic, hostile to women, and solely misogynistic, thus preserving secularism as the realm of neoliberal choice and 'progress.'"[59] To this argument, I would add that secularism has utterly failed to shield trans people from religiously motivated persecution, which has increasingly taken the form of state violence. Indeed, the liberal state has merely lent a sheen of secular neutrality to the reactionary Christian agenda it relentlessly advances.

This is not a book that holds out hope for a better secularism, one less susceptible to cooptation by fascism, trans-antagonism, and white supremacy. Rather than doubling down on the same liberal secularity that has facilitated the ascendency of right-wing Christian transphobia, I contend that there is some political use to dwelling on the trans dimensions of religion. As such, the line of argumentation developed throughout this book is in alignment with critics in trans studies who have drawn on theology as a resource for imagining projects of trans worldmaking, scholars including Max Strassfeld, Joy Ladin, Roberto Che Espinoza, S. J. Crasnow, and Max Thornton.[60] Against the assumption that transition poses a threat to traditional values, the readings of early modern religious writing gathered in this book indicate that transness is not a new development incubated in medical settings arriving to corrupt theology from the outside. Instead, the religious archives, texts, and literatures that are the subject of the chapters that follow engage with transition in complex and often affirmative ways. It is not a coincidence that much of the scholarship on transness in premodern fields centers on religious writing, as in the work of Micah Goodrich, Gabrielle Bychowski, Blake Gutt, Ellis Light, Scott Larson, Leah DeVun, and Roland Betancourt.[61] Theological conceptions of incarnation, spiritual bodies of the afterlife, angelic and Edenic embodiment, mystical ecstasies, the soul's genderlessness, and martyrological transformations offered a rich repository of images of trans possibility. As such, this book and the archives it addresses militate for a postsecular turn in trans studies. It may be worth attempting to leverage these forgotten, or perhaps suppressed, histories of religion against Christian organizations hell-bent on exterminating trans life and the secular state exercising lethal violence on their behalf.

Moreover, locating a trans imaginary in early modern theology dislodges the assumption that secularism is the condition of possibility for trans life in the present, a premise that generates a framework for extending trans history into the centuries before sexology developed a diagnostic vocabulary for understanding gender variance as a matter of identity. The field of trans studies has historically been grounded in the period from the late nineteenth century through the present, for reasons that surely include the almost absolute exclusion of trans scholars from disciplines focusing on premodern periods. Secondly, the medicalization of trans life in contemporary society is so thoroughgoing that it is almost impossible for cis people—even those with expertise in gender studies and queer theory—to imagine transness existing outside modern medical authority. More recent work in trans studies, however, has begun to militate against the field's modern orientation, rightly insisting that trans history must be understood as the history of racialized gender, an adjunct to the historical development of white supremacy, enslavement, imperialism, and settler colonialism.[62] As scholars of premodern critical race theory have definitively established, these processes shaped every dimension of cultural and literary production in the sixteenth and seventeenth centuries. Moreover, as Dennis Britton, Ian Smith, Kim Hall, and others have powerfully argued, religion was a crucial vector of the strategies of racialization in its early modern iterations.[63] Tracking the trans dimensions of early modern religious writing, then, opens onto what C. Riley Snorton identifies in *Black on Both Sides* as the "racial narrative" of the "condensation of transness into the category of transgender."[64] *Glorious Bodies* attends to the free-floating imaginary of transness as it appears in theological narratives, with an eye to the processes that consolidate it into racial formations that align cisness with whiteness.

A scholar working in trans studies, I suspect, will not have found my approach to the question of trans history so arcane. What I have proposed is an account of early modern trans history as intimately entwined with the process of racialization and the legal apparatuses of discipline and punishment. In tracking how transitional genders were ascribed to populations understood to be threats to the nation, I have simply taken up the questions that animate the best and most important work in the field. And yet, a scholar trained in early modern gender studies may have arrived at this point with a mounting sense of frustration. This argument hasn't gone at all in the directions it might have been expected to go. The language of "gender identity" has not entered the conversation even one time; no efforts were made to tease out signs of dysphoria from a historical figure; at no point did I build a case that the crucified hermaphrodite or anyone else *was really* trans, whatever that means, and of course such a project would be difficult since almost none of these people existed in the first place. Indeed, I have entirely eschewed a diagnostic approach to trans history. If you came to this book to discover which of Shakespeare's characters is trans, you will set it down in disappointment.[65] Moreover, early modernists have their own vocabularies for addressing gender variance that I have pointedly declined to employ. Where are the accounts of crossdressing, of Shakespeare's plucky, pants-wearing heroines? And can we even call them heroines since, you know, *you can't even say the word woman anymore*? The final section of the introduction considers my own refusal to engage in this sort of analysis, or to label it "trans studies," by way of historicizing early modernists' hostility toward trans thought.

## Fear of a Trans Renaissance

In April 2023, as part of their professional development programming for secondary school teachers, the Folger Shakespeare Library announced a lecture by an eminent scholar on the trendy topic of "Shakespeare's They / Thems." The announcement reads: "Middle and high school students are more comfortable with non-binary gender identity than most of their parents and even some of their teachers. Shakespeare, writing for a theater where all women's roles were played by young men, was also comfortable with the performativity of gender and non-binary characters. . . . [T]his illustrated talk . . . will explore ideas about transgender identity among Shakespeare and his contemporaries, with a discussion focusing on the cross-dressed female protagonists of *As You Like It* and *Twelfth Night*."[66]

In case you were wondering, "Shakespeare's They / Thems" turned out to be Rosalind and Viola. The Folger talk summons these "cross-dressed female protagonists" as evidence that Shakespeare was "comfortable" with "non-binary" and "transgender identity," a comfort that he apparently shares with today's "middle and high school students," but not their parents and only some of their teachers. My concern here is not with Shakespeare's comfort, but with the comfort of Shakespeareans: the pleasures they have taken in discussing gender-variant bodies, their ease with the fetishistic language of "crossdressing" and "transvestism," and their pronounced discomfort with trans scholarship and trans people. What does the Shakespearean know of trans life? What exactly might an early modernist have to share with teachers and parents, so worried about this "transgender craze" tearing through the student body?

The answer would seem to be: very little. Trans studies arrived late to our field, which noticed that trans people existed at roughly the same moment as the culture more broadly: call it, for the sake of convenience, 2019, in the wake of what *Time Magazine* branded "the transgender tipping point." And yet, early modernists' long-standing reluctance to draw upon the established field of trans studies requires explanation. After all, for the past four decades, early modern studies has produced a steady stream of scholarship on gender, drawing from and, in turn, expanding the frameworks of feminism, gay and lesbian studies, and queer theory. The vocabulary of transness, however, has been almost entirely excluded from this rich and venerable body of work, an omission that is surprising, not least because transition was hardly unthinkable in the Renaissance, and indeed, the capacity of sex to change entered into writing across a kaleidoscopic variety of genres, including literature. Undeniably, the cultural codes governing gender variance were not identical to our own, but even so, the simple fact of historical distance cannot explain the absolute exclusion of transness from literary-critical accounts of early modern gender. After all, homosexuality also postdates the Renaissance by hundreds of years. Like transsexuality, it is a pathologized identity category whose clinical "invention" dates to late nineteenth-century sexology and her sister disciplines of criminology, psychiatry, and psychoanalysis.[67] From a Foucauldian perspective, at least, the genealogical origins of homosexuality and transness are separated from the Renaissance by precisely the same time span. And yet, while this historical distance has apparently posed an insuperable object to imagining a trans Renaissance, it has not prevented early modernists from finding ways to include the sixteenth and seventeenth centuries within the histories of (homo)sexuality. Even scholarship that emphasizes the difference that obtains between the discursive formations of Renaissance sexuality and those of our own moment has not insisted on the periods' absolute, irreconcilable disconnection. Instead, this branch of the field has adopted what Ari Friedlander calls the "historicist settlement," best glossed by Valerie Traub's assertion in *The Renaissance of Lesbianism* that we must "assume neither that we will find in the past a mirror image of ourselves nor that the past is so utterly alien that we will find nothing useable in its fragmentary traces."[68] In this spirit, this body of work has created nuanced, fine-grained accounts of early modern gender and sexuality that locate the precursor forms of contemporary gay and lesbian subject positions in the tribade, the sodomite, the friend, the bed-sharer, the secretary, and the favorite.[69] The historical differences between the contemporary construction of sexuality and its early modern predecessors have been leveraged to open up narrow, limiting, or bigoted understandings of sexuality in the present. And yet, the same conceptual maneuvers that have produced such rich scholarship on early modern sexuality have not even been attempted with transness as the central term. Do trans people have no ancestors? Are we not currently confronting constricted, violent narratives about trans embodiment that might be usefully challenged by historicist accounts of premodern transition? Why has it been possible to envision a gay or a queer but never a trans Renaissance?

A blunt but honest answer might be that it is easier for early modernists to imagine people in the Renaissance having gay sex than transitioning. It may simply be the case that, for a field almost uniformly comprised of cisgender scholars, trans people and the medical interventions we employ simply *feel new*, whereas homosexual activity, if not identity, can safely be projected backward in time.[70] By indulging this reflex, early modernists participate in the construction of transness as a novelty, a product of futuristic technologies, a way of life inconceivable mere moments ago. And it is not merely trans people but the field of trans studies that feels trendy and new, even though by any measurable standard it is an established rather than a budding field, boasting as it does a thriving academic journal, degree-granting programs at research universities, and two volumes of readers with a thousand pages of scholarship. Despite this, as Regina Kunzel noted almost a decade ago, it is customary to hail trans studies as "emergent," noting that while the "scholarly trope of emergency conjures the cutting edge, it can also be an infantilizing temporality that communicates (and contributes to) perpetual marginalization."[71] Indeed, "emergent" does not only signal novelty; it also means *urgent*, a danger to safety and well-being that requires instant redress. Contemporary politics have treated trans life as "emergent" in all available senses, as new and untested and thus as a danger—in particular, an imminent threat to children and, by extension, the reproductive future of the nation. Startled by trans teens, phobic parents and Jungian psychologists concocted a sham diagnosis that turns on the apparent suddenness of the urge to transition, "Rapid Onset Gender Dysphoria," a malady that claims new victims with the swiftness of a "contagion" or "craze" or "terrible new plague."[72] Likewise, the legislative push to criminalize trans health care frequently turns on the claim that gender-affirming care is "experimental."[73] Trans life, apparently, comes out of nowhere and spreads with uncontrollable speed; confined to the present time, its temporality is one of emergence, rapidity, shock, and abruptness. When early modernists reject in advance the possibility of a trans history that stretches back to the Renaissance, implicitly because it feels ahistorical or presentist, they participate in the construction of transness as emergent.

And yet, what *feels* historical is not necessarily so in reality. For then as now, people transitioned. In the Renaissance, and indeed, long before then, they lived as multiple sexes, surgically modified their genitals, and inhabited the capacious zones stretching between male and female. Often we have records of trans lives because, in circumstances that resonate with our contemporary political landscape, these people were criminalized for their gender variance, captured by judicial systems that subjected them to invasive and violating genital examinations like those undergone by Marin le Marcis and Marie-Germain.[74] Moreover, premodern gender transitivity was not restricted to instances of natal anatomical ambiguity, as with the "hermaphrodites" recorded by Montaigne and Paré, or to what is now called social transition, as with Eleanor Rykener, a transfeminine sex worker, embroiderer, and tapster who was brought before London's mayor and aldermen for committing "unspeakable" and "libidinous" acts with one John Britby in a stall in Soper's Lane.[75] Surgical transition, too, was practiced in the period, as indeed it had been since antiquity.[76] At times, these procedures were "corrective," but the goal of such interventions was not always to produce normatively gendered bodies.[77] Castration was sometimes practiced for its own sake. Within the early modern English imaginary, eunuchs may have been affiliated with Ottoman and Italianate decadence, and gelding may have been associated with extrajudicial practices of retributive justice.[78] Nevertheless, instances of voluntary castration occurred in England, too, as in the case recorded by James Yonge, a naval surgeon and fellow of the Royal Society, who treated "a young Man about twenty years old, living with *Alderman W.* (whose Nephew he was) [who,] from some disappointment in Love, as was imagined, or rather as himself confessed, on a Religious account, to cure salacious heats, did castrate himself, by griping up the *Testicles*, with the whole *Scrotum* in one hand, and with a keen Knife in the other cutting them off close to the body; the sudden pain and effusion of bloud made him faint and fall back on the Bed, where he wat while he thus acted *Origen Secundus*."[79]

If the surgeon held any particular moral judgment on the matter, he kept it to himself. Yonge did not treat the incident as especially scandalous, nor did he spend much time troubling himself about the youth's motivations. Instead, he merely described the steps he took to patch the wound with turpentine oil and refresh the patient with "a glass of Sack," noting that "the Wound in a months time was almost cicatrized," at which point the Alderman's relation "followed his business."[80] The incident may have been outré, but it was not unprecedented. Indeed, Yonge himself named the precedent that would have felt most obvious to his readers when he called the youth a "second Origen," invoking the Church Father who, in his youth, castrated himself in what Eusebius described as a "too literal and extreme" interpretation of Matthew 19:12, which praises those who have "made themselves eunuchs for the kingdom of heaven."[81] Dismissing the psychological explanations proposed by others, who "imagined . . . some disappointment in Love" behind the urge to take up the razor, Yonge accepts the youth's own "confession," which inserts the act of reshaping the genitals into a religious lineage stretching back to the early church.

What these examples demonstrate is that transition was not merely figurative, metaphorical, or poetic, but a social and physiological reality. With or without surgical modification, moving between the sexes—or being stranded between them—was a possibility that, when actualized, sometimes carried serious legal and social penalties. Moreover, vocabularies existed for discussing these cases and their significance, ranging from the practical matter of treating hemorrhages contained in medical textbooks like Yonge's to the sensational accounts of Turkish eunuchs populating travel narratives, the legal records contained in Inquisitorial examinations, the prodigy books of Paré and Duval, and the devotional writing that is the subject of this book. Transition *happened*, sometimes surgically. It is therefore not unreasonable to ask why the conceptual strategies deployed for queer history have felt unavailable in these instances, particularly since, other than explicitly using the language of *transition*, no part of the stories I have just rehearsed is new. Marin le Marcis, Marie-Germain, and Eleanor Rykener, eunuchs and castrati—these figures are not marginal in early modern literary studies. Interpretive accounts of these cases have anchored magisterial, agenda-setting statements in historicism, cultural studies, and gender and sexuality studies. Since the 1980s these figures have been parsed in every conceivable way except for their relation to trans history. The paradigmatic instance of this conceptual move, with profound methodological consequences for the shape of early modern gender studies, can be found in Thomas Laqueur's discussion of the shepherd Germain in his seminal *Making Sex*:

> Girls could turn into boys, and men who associated too extensively with women could lose the hardness and definition of their more perfect bodies and regress into effeminacy. Culture, in short, suffused and changed the body that to the modern sensibility seems so closed, autarchic, and outside the realm of meaning. One might of course deny that such things happened or read them as entirely metaphorical or give individual, naturalistic explanations for otherwise bizarre occurrences: the girl chasing her swine who suddenly sprung an external penis and scrotum, reported by Montaigne and the sixteenth-century surgeon Ambroise Paré as an instance of sex change, was really suffering from

> androgen-dihydrotestosterone deficiency; she was really a boy all along who developed external male organs in puberty, though perhaps not as precipitously as these accounts would have it. This, however, is an unconscionably external, ahistorical, and impoverished approach to a vast and complex literature about the body and culture . . . In the world of one sex, it was precisely when talk seemed to be most directly about the biology of two sexes that it was most embedded in the politics of gender, in culture.[82]

Unconscionable, external, ahistorical, and impoverished. The terms Laqueur wheels out to fend off this dangerous mishandling of Germain's "sex change" are primed to generate mockery. *Of course* no one in the Renaissance knew about dihydrotestosterone or 5-alpha-reductase syndrome or androgen insensitivity. How absurd to think that endocrinology might have had any explanatory value for the scene related by Montaigne and Paré! Had Laqueur avoided chemical nomenclature, however, the actual target of his animus would be more readily apparent: the possibility that Germain was intersex, and thus potentially implicated in a trans history that Laqueur can only imagine as coextensive with modern medical authority. In collapsing transness, utterly and without remainder, with the pronouncements of endocrinologists, Laqueur defends Montaigne from a trans analytic that he can only imagine as narrowly diagnostic. Specifying a hormonal mechanism behind Germain's "sex change" by way of the "external" and "ahistorical" epistemology of modern medicine is the only conceivable outcome of such a reading. That the medical regime that governs transition in the present might itself be available for historicization, or that it might exist in some kind of continuity with the disciplinary regimes and genital examinations described by Duval, Paré, and Montaigne, are not possibilities that Laqueur bothers to entertain. Instead, the only kind of relation between a sixteenth-century transition and contemporary trans existence that he cares to imagine is one of naïve, narcissistic, ahistorical mirroring. Laqueur's disavowal thus accomplishes a neat trick, protecting the "vast and complex" discourses of premodern gender from a trans perspective that he, with no irony, makes the representative of a "closed" and "autarchic" account of embodiment. Like Origen, who "gelt himself" after "allegoriz[ing] plain Scriptures" which "ought to be understood mystically," the trans reader is constitutively given to a stubborn, even idolatrous literalism.[83] To acknowledge trans possibility is to be duped by a carnal attachment to the materiality of sex where, in truth, there is only the "mystical" figurations of gender. Indeed, Laqueur cautions, those passages where a text "seemed most directly" to address "biology" are a trap, and it is there that they speak most insistently of "gender," which the sophisticated reader will understand as metaphor, meaning, and discourse. A trans reading is not only mistaken; it is *immoral*, "unconscionable" in its presumptuous anachronism that would map the perpetually "emergent" category of transness onto a past that, we are told, could never have accommodated it. So it is that the foreclosure of trans possibility becomes the precondition for a learned, mature, and nuanced historicism capable of accessing the "vast and complex" riches of early modern gender.

Since trans possibility was safely cordoned off from the Renaissance, the field took up a different critical keyword to capture Renaissance gender variance while skirting the "external" and "ahistorical" intrusion of transition: "transvestism."[84] In centering crossdressing and the boy players staffing Shakespeare's "transvestite theater," the academic discourse on Renaissance gender and sexuality has turned on the friction imagined to exist between the surface-level disguise of appareling and the stable, knowable biological realities ascribed to the sexed body beneath. Gender might be indeterminate, subject to the infinite deferral and free play of signification, or it might name the site of historically specific cultural constructions, but in this model *sex* remains comfortably fixed. Tucked away under the costuming and cosmetics lies an anatomical truth so protrudent that it can be comfortably clocked at the remove of four centuries. It is thus taken for granted that the actors who played women's roles were "not biologically female," so what both historical audiences and contemporary critics encounter in our assessment of Renaissance theater could only be "the fact of the male body"[85] or the "reality of the young male player."[86] And so we are assured, time and again, that women were absent from the English theater, whose erotics depended upon the "exclusion of real female corporeality"[87] and "the denial to women of access to the histrionic exchanges in which they excelled and we took pleasure."[88] Likewise, in the course of her account of *The Roaring Girl*, Marjorie Garber assures us that "everyone onstage knows [Moll Cutpurse] is a woman—although everyone offstage, presumably, also knew she was played by a boy."[89] Gender may be hard to pin down, but sex is what everyone can be presumed to know, a "reality" or "fact" whose truth is immediately apparent across time and space.

Given the boundless attention the field has lavished on "the transvestite" as a silent object to be stripped and anatomized, perhaps I might be permitted this small space to return the favor, parsing out the erotic impulses that have driven early modernists to forty solid years of tedious and repetitive fantasizing about "the boy beneath the dress."[90] A touch of voyeurism, even fetishism, is detectable in projects that compulsively seek out "transvestites" only to disrobe them, a prurient interest that, on occasion, is avowed directly. Lisa Jardine explains the "critical stir" aroused by "cross-dressing on the Renaissance stage" by noting that "we all of us, I think, respond one way or another to the erotic potential in concealed sexual identity, the prospect of being lured into desiring the androgynous desirable object—the object whose sex is problematic, or insufficiently clearly defined by the customary signs of dress and demeanour."[91]

Even in naming the source of her enjoyment, Jardine struggles to take ownership of it. Desire hovers between the critic who seeks out the "erotic potential" buried in "concealed sexual identity"; the problematically sexed figure who has "lured" her into arousal, provoking her into "desiring" the "desirable object"; and the "we all of us" who, she speculates, surely share such predilections. The evasive language according to which she, like everyone else, reacts strongly to the mere thought of a gender-variant body signals the deep ambivalence of her critical pleasures, as does her caginess about what precisely she feels about the object of her attention, responding, as she does, "one way or another." It is unclear just how broad a collective is signaled by this "we all of us," whether it refers to early modernists or humanity, but either way it is not a collective capacious enough to house "problematically sexed objects" like *me*; and so, from my position firmly outside of this "we all," let me clarify the nature of the pleasures Jardine confesses to, which remain so obscure to her. What she describes is the chaser's enjoyment, an attraction tinged with repulsion and aggression; she will later characterize the "boy dis-covered as a girl" and the "boy who walks the street cross-dressed as that comely girl" as the stuff of "grotesque fiction."[92] The psychodrama that unfolds when the critic encounters the stimulating possibilities of "concealed sexual identity" is plotted as a process of undressing, peeling back the layers of clothing to disclose the "reality" of sex embedded in the body. That is, as Robert Clark and Claire Sponsler breezily assert, "transvestism is a representation which always carries with it the possibility of an unveiling," as if the only conceivable response to gender nonconformity is a striptease performed under the watchful eye of the scholar.[93] Such derision and fetishism, apparently, are the basis for a "suitably historicised reading of cross-dressing and gender confusion in Elizabethan and Jacobean drama."[94] Presented with a Renaissance "cross-dresser," the early modernist can only imagine her clothes dropping to the floor.

Trans studies has a name for this trope: "the reveal." This convention in mainstream media involves the sensationalized and often violent disclosure of a character's trans status to build narrative momentum, introduce a shocking plot twist, or relieve tension through publicly humiliating a trans woman. Unsurprisingly, scholarship on Renaissance "transvestism" privileges such moments of revelation as they arise in early modern drama, as in the conclusion to Jonson's *Epicoene*, when "the transvestite figure is finally revealed as the boy the actor who played him really was."[95] What I want to emphasize here, however, is that "the reveal" is not merely the privileged content of this body of scholarship, but its methodology. Indeed, even deconstructive and psychoanalytic work that explicitly leverages "the transvestite" as a destabilizing force to dismantle biological essentialism cannot quite free itself from the pull of "the body beneath,"[96] the "open secret" of the "presence of the man's (or boy's) body beneath the woman's clothes,"[97] or the "*frisson* [of] the secret-on-the-surface waiting to be detected."[98] In building their cases for a triumphant gender undecidability on the mechanisms of the reveal, such arguments double down on the very divisions between surface and depth, gender and sex, artifice and anatomy, that they explicitly seek to overturn. This, indeed, is the precise function of the reveal as a narrative device, which, as Danielle Seid cannily argues, "stages a denaturalization of widespread assumptions about gender and sex—namely that one's gender must match one's sexed body—but it typically does so in a manner that regulates and corrects gender noncompliance, narratively reinscribing a binary gender system as 'natural' and desirable."[99]

While "the reveal" might have felt like a historically appropriate way to talk about Renaissance "transvestism," this narrative device in question has histories of its own, the most obvious of which is its circulation in media properties in the 1980s and 1990s. Talk shows and films like *Dressed to Kill* (1980), *Sleepaway Camp* (1983), *Silence of the Lambs* (1991), and *The Crying Game* (1992) staged their trans characters' gender presentations as a disguise to facilitate violent, psychotic, or predatory impulses and then punished and humiliated them for their "deception."[100] This is the media environment in which the literary-critical craze for "transvestites" emerged, and which established the tropes that would be echoed in scholarship on Renaissance "crossdressing:" that the truth of sex resides in the genitals; that trans people are deceptive and predatory; and that the natural reaction to gender variance is a mixture of fascination, arousal, and disgust. Indeed, references to *The Crying Game* abound in this work. One essay on *Twelfth Night*'s "transvestism" goes so far as to assert that "connecting *The Crying Game* to *Twelfth Night* . . . hardly represents a challenge; the connection practically makes itself."[101]

In short, "transvestite" is not a neutral term. It did not arrive in early modern studies somehow unfettered by its own complicated genealogies, which derived not only from media history but also from twentieth-century medicine. In fact, far from bracketing trans identity or circumventing the invention of the category of transgender, the language of "transvestism" is sourced from directly from twentieth-century trans history. For the introduction of the term "transvestite" into medical discourse, we can thank Harry Benjamin, a man Ethel Person eulogized as a "creative maverick" who held the "deanship of transsexualism."[102] Once a friend and fellow traveler of Magnus Hirschfeld, Benjamin moved to the United States in 1913, where he peddled quack cures for tuberculosis before shifting his attention to performing rejuvenating vasectomies. In the 1950s, Benjamin became the de facto point person for trans people seeking surgical and hormonal care, particularly in the wake of the media sensation surrounding Christine Jorgensen, whose gender-affirming care he helped arrange. It was in this context of branding and self-promotion that Benjamin haphazardly and incoherently invented the diagnostic markers of "transvestism" in opposition to what he called "true transsexualism."[103] This distinction was taken up by the system of university-based gender identity clinics at UCLA, Stanford, and Johns Hopkins that tightly controlled access to trans medicine in the 1960s and 1970s. In this clinical context, crossdressing was addressed as a symptom requiring interpretation, the basis of a differential diagnosis that separated prospective patients into the discrete categories of transsexual and transvestite. According to these diagnostic protocols, the "true" transsexual expresses an unshakable cross-gender identification from early childhood. She focuses to the exclusion of all else on genital surgeries, intends to transition into a private life of normative heterosexuality, and appears sufficiently attractive to the cisgender experts in charge of her case.[104] The "transvestite," by contrast, is a degenerate possessed of any number of psychopathies and perversions, including fetishism, narcissism, exhibitionism, bondage, masochism, and a sexual excitement induced by wearing rubber garments.[105] In the eyes of healthcare providers, including those willing to offer gender-affirming care, both groups were disordered, even delusional. The difference was that the transsexuals were eligible for medical transition.

Confronted with a mass of patients seeking transition-related care, gender identity centers attempted to sift out the "real" transsexuals from the mass of perverts, paraphiliacs, fetishists, schizophrenics, and repressed homosexuals who ought to be rejected, involuntarily committed, or even lobotomized.[106] The border between the two groups, however, proved difficult to maintain. Every clinical encounter was shaped by a concern that a patient might misrepresent herself as normatively transsexual while hiding deviant motivations, particularly since cisgender clinicians uniformly regarded their trans clients as inherently deceptive and as unreliable narrators of their own inner experiences.[107] Sexologists established criteria for surgical eligibility and then were suspicious when patients told them what they wanted to hear. In the minds of the clinicians who pronounced themselves authorities over transness, the request for surgery created an epistemological problem: how could someone truly know that they wanted such an extreme and distasteful procedure, and how could the specialists who performed it be sure that the patient would never come to regret it and sue them? Thus, as Beans Velocci argues in a brilliant and enraging account of the correspondence between Elmer Belt and Harry Benjamin, transsexuals were understood as subjects constitutively "incapable of making their own bodily decisions" and "needing to be protected from themselves."[108] The solution to this problem involved a dilation of the diagnostic process as it was formalized in the university clinics through the onboarding of psychiatrists and psychologists with their batteries of personality tests; demanding that patients acquire multiple letters from mental health professionals attesting to the patient's soundness of mind, which often required many years of therapy; mandating humiliating and invasive physical examinations looking for any signs of "hermaphroditism"; and a "real-life test" that involved socially transitioning for a minimum of two years prior to receiving hormones or surgery, which of course was quite dangerous. These diagnostic criteria were enshrined into recognized standards of care with the establishment of a professional organization for clinicians working in trans health, the Harry Benjamin International Gender Dysphoria Association in 1979; and, in 1980, with the entry of "transsexualism" into the *Diagnostic and Statistical Manual.*

The effects of these elaborate requirements were threefold. First, they radically expanded medical authority over trans life, awarding treatment on the basis of compliance with the hostile and capricious demands of cis healthcare providers.[109] Secondly, as the diagnostic procedures became increasingly elaborate, they created more opportunities to reject prospective patients by classifying them as delusional transvestites rather than "genuine" transsexuals. The clinics, after all, explicitly aimed to restrict eligibility for elective surgery as far as possible, and in this aim, at least, they were successful: of the two thousand applications for surgery received by the Johns Hopkins clinic in its first two years of operation, the center approved only twenty-four procedures.[110] Finally, the diagnostic criteria produced the transsexual subject as an engine of discourse defined by her willingness to rehearse a self-narrative whose rigid coordinates had been plotted in advance by cis "experts" with narrow and self-serving ideas about what constituted an acceptable, normative presentation of transness. One consequence of the psychiatric construction of transsexuality was a restriction of trans speech to the genre of autobiography which, as Viviane Namaste argues, is "the only discourse in which transsexuals are permitted to speak."[111] Even as the ambit for acceptable trans speech narrowed, writing *about* transness exploded, generating an entire cottage industry of psychiatrists, sociologists, behavioral scientists, and physicians to compel and then dissect trans narrativization for any sign of transvestic impulses, teasing apart our life histories, sexual desires, and feelings about our bodies to separate the worthy patients from the fetishistic transvestites.

The rapid uptake of "transvestism" as a central organizing concern for early modern literary studies in the 1980s did not exist outside of this clinical history, as if this choice of subject were somehow uniquely free from the corrupting influence of modern identity categories. In rejecting the attested fact of transition in favor of fantasizing about the psyches and sartorial habits of Renaissance "transvestites," early modernists have not cleverly sidestepped the lure of an "impoverished" and "external" approach to Renaissance texts, an ahistoricism disavowed and projected onto the figure of the medically modified trans person who can only ever be an artifact of the present. Instead, the field simply adopted the models of gender identity developed by predatory, bigoted, and incompetent clinicians in the highly specific context of trans medicine as practiced in the 1960s and 70s and then treated those models as though they held explanatory value for sixteenth- and seventeenth-century literature.[112] This borrowing from twentieth-century sexology was then, with one important exception, rendered invisible. That exception is Marjorie Garber's *Vested Interests*, a volume whose influence on shaping the academic discourse on literature and "transvestites" would be impossible to overstate. For her account of the psychodynamics of transvestism and its relation to transsexuality, Garber relies heavily and utterly uncritically on the "research" of Robert Stoller, director of the UCLA Gender Identity Research Clinic, along with a smattering of John Money.[113] In addition to constructing a monstrously pathologizing account of transvestism and its relationship to transsexuality, under Stoller's leadership the UCLA clinic spent decades practicing brutal forms of conversion therapy on trans children, whom they diagnosed with disorders like "Sissy Boy Syndrome,"[114] in the hopes of staving off what Stoller named the "malignant condition" of "adult transsexualism."[115] Having identified her models, Garber proceeds to play at sexology herself, picking apart trans narratives packaged in case studies from the UCLA clinic alongside the autobiographies of Christine Jorgensen, Jan Morris, and Renée Richards.[116] At no point does she pause to consider how these kinds of trans memoirs were produced under pressure from the clinicians who awarded conformity to their preferred narratives with access to medical treatment.[117] Small wonder, given Garber's sources and methods, that her vicious, sneering contempt for trans people radiates off the page, as she witheringly mocks our surgically modified bodies ("essentialized, literalized, made into a grotesque cartoon"); our pleasure in them ("In spite of such unaesthetic results transsexual patients often go barechested, displaying what doctors call a 'poor reality' sense"); our family arrangements ("Their wives will address them as 'Donna' or 'Jeanne' or whatever, when they are wearing women's clothes"); our stupidly essentialist understanding of gender ("no one [except perhaps transvestites and transsexuals] interprets these signs literally or mimetically"); and our delusional, even "delirious" senses of self ("this is clearly not 'female subjectivity,' even though it goes by women's names. It is a man's idea of what 'a woman' is").[118]

I am now in a position to respond to the provocation that opened this section and offer an explanation for why it is that, from the 1980s until roughly 2019, early modern literary studies refused to engage with the conceptual possibility of transition despite its inexhaustible interest in gender variance, hermaphroditism, eunuchs, and boy players. The answer is that the generation of scholarship shaped by "gender studies queen" Marjorie Garber to pick apart modes of "transvestism" and "cross-dressing" has been operating within a mid-century model of trans identity and embodiment the entire time.[119] This commitment, ironically, has led to a second-order instance of anachronism. Unwilling to interrogate the historical origins of their own methodological models and contextual frames of reference, early modernists have continued to rely on increasingly dated diagnostic models of transvestism produced in the in the period from the late 1950s through the 1970s, long after Stoller's simple-minded psychoanalytic theories had become profoundly outmoded, after John Money had been utterly disgraced, and after other vocabularies for transness had entered mainstream usage. To be clear, the problem is not one of terminology. My complaint is not chiefly that "transvestite" was already a slur when it became fashionable in early modern studies, although that fact might have occasioned some reflection in the gender studies experts tossing it around; nor do I believe that a simple update in labels would resolve the matter, as if the terms "trans" or "transgender" had no complexities of their own.[120] The issue at stake is not one of language but of method. By drawing their account of transvestism from mid-century sexology, scholars built early modern gender and sexuality studies in the image of the gender identity clinic. In place of the psychiatrist, it is the literary critic who applies diagnostic protocols and judges how well her subject passes; who salaciously speculates on "the body beneath" their outward presentations; who evaluates their attractiveness and commitment to gender norms; who probes their psyches and dissects their speech for evidence of fetishism, repression, ideology, or homosexuality. The endlessly reiterated project of searching for and undressing early modern "transvestites" does not reflect a sober, serious investment in maintaining historical specificity. It is Renaissance studies as conversion therapy, a clinical practice successful beyond the wildest dreams of the sexologists, in that it has proven capable of generating an unending supply of deviants, transvestites, ideologues, and repressed homosexuals while reducing the number of trans people to an ideal zero.

At this point, it may be objected that I am being uncharitable. Surely this body of work is simply the product of a different time, and it is terribly unfair to hold it up to the impossibly exacting standards of actually existing trans people, as if none were available for comment until this very moment. To which I respond: we have not somehow escaped this "different time," either within the field or beyond it. It is necessary to clarify the transphobic paradigms of these foundational texts because they have effectively centered early modern gender studies around a version of "performance" that turns on a fundamentally transphobic distinction between surface and depth, costuming and "the body beneath." It has proven surprisingly difficult to break away from this orientation as, year after year, the field continues to churn out work on "cross-dressing" without interrogating the historical origins or conceptual limitations of this vocabulary. More importantly, the political movements, media landscapes, and theoretical frameworks that lent a trans-exclusionary shape to the initial wave of early modern feminist and queer studies are not artifacts of a remote past with no bearing on the present. The pathologization of trans people as predatory deceivers within the clinical context of psychiatry, the severing of trans people from the gay rights movement (and our subsequent value as a wedge issue), and the transphobic legacies of radical feminism have metastasized into the formidable assault on trans life that, today, we are attempting to weather.[121] In the hands of hard-right operatives, these anxieties, strategies, and alliances have been transformed into a political movement that is now openly calling for the "eradication of transgenderism."[122]

Acknowledging that early modern gender studies shares its intellectual origins with this movement is, perhaps, an uncomfortable proposition to confront, but such a reckoning is necessary precisely because of the political ascendency of transphobia. In this highly charged context, it is a matter of real urgency that early modern studies take care not to repeat its earlier missteps. At the bare minimum, this commitment would entail letting go of the language of transvestism and renouncing the fetishistic pleasures of "the reveal" as an interpretive strategy that milks the titillating strangeness of a gender-variant body to establish the edginess and acumen of the literary critic. Moreover, given the profoundly transphobic assumptions underwriting scholarship on Renaissance "transvestism," it would be a damaging error to repackage the body of work on "cross-dressing" as a canon of "early modern transgender plays." My stance here is firmly aligned with Sawyer Kemp's argument that critics should give up their fascination with "the magical transvestism of The Pants" and make some small effort to find trans possibility in "something other than clothing."[123] To announce that Shakespeare's bepantsed heroines are no longer mere transvestites but full-fledged trans men or, I suppose, "they / thems" is surely an appealing opportunity, asking as it does so very little of the critic, requiring none of the intellectual labor involved in familiarizing themselves with the field of trans studies or wrestling with the methodological questions that attend any efforts to find trans history. Indeed, it may be so comforting precisely because it leaves intact the diagnostic model of trans identity developed by cis physicians aiming to soothe cis anxieties about transition. Such an approach has not extracted early modern studies from the gender clinic but liberalized it just enough to allow a few token characters to scrape through the gatekeeping process.

Perhaps the more substantial request is that early modernists give up the pleasures of engaging in armchair sexology. The recent uptake of the critical vocabulary of trans studies within early modern studies makes the need for care and circumspection even more rather than less urgent. The temptation to reduce trans thought to raw material for the professional advancement of cis specialists remains fully intact. Witness a recent article in which Melissa Sanchez issues a stern corrective to the field of early modern trans studies for failing to acknowledge its "debts" to the scholars of early modern gender and sexuality studies who, she argues, were always doing trans studies in some vague capacity even prior to "the naming of a field."[124] Now that trans scholars have gone to the trouble of building a subfield that has acquired a small measure of attention and cachet, Sanchez retroactively awards its authorship to cis specialists. This claim is shocking not only in its cavalier disavowal of the explicitly trans-exclusionary nature of the field she defends, its unshakable attachment to transphobia as both a method and a professional norm, but in its mystifying charge that the handful of trans scholars only lately admitted to the profession are the true "gatekeepers."[125] In this hastily rewritten history of the field, it is the "most powerful members" of this shadowy trans cabal, apparently vested with influence over unnamed "presses" and "institutions," who are guilty of excluding hapless cis scholars whose only crime was, perhaps, fumbling their choice of terminology. And yet, as this introduction has demonstrated, early modernists no less than their sexologist forebears have long built their reputations by discoursing on transness, by naming, defining, dissecting, dismissing, and fetishizing it. In this framework, trans voices exist only as an "endless mill of speech" for the benefit of cis specialists. We are only ever to be the objects of analysis, never its subjects. Warning that "in adding our own voices, we may distort as much as we clarify," Sanchez attempts to discipline trans scholars for speaking out of turn, introducing cacophonous "distortions" to the clarity, precision, and restraint exercised by the genealogy of cis scholars she invokes. In claiming property rights over the field of early modern trans studies and belatedly ascribing its invention to a generation of cis critics who never once bothered to cite a trans scholar, much less position their texts and archives as contributing to some form of trans history, Sanchez brazenly carries on the transphobic legacy of a long line of sexologists, from Harry Benjamin to John Money, who mined trans thought to build their own brands and shore up their prestige.

To be clear, my point is not that early modernists must never claim any historical figure or fictional character as trans, nor that they should avoid engaging with trans scholarship altogether, overcorrections that would only satisfy the transphobic impulse to eliminate trans possibility from the past. What I am saying is that scholars attempting to locate premodern trans figures should exhibit a shred of self-awareness about the degree to which their accounts of transness have been shaped by predatory, self-aggrandizing cis "experts" or drawn from viciously fetishistic media tropes. Luckily, the theoretical frameworks responsible for the field's "transvestite" craze are not the only available models for thinking about trans history. Scholars who want to integrate a trans analytic into their accounts of early modern gender variance might instead take their lead from trans studies, which is not chiefly concerned with clothes or the protocols of identification, much less with the sexological project of evaluating who counts as a "real" transsexual according to whichever medical paradigms are ascendent in the current moment. Instead, trans scholars are historicizing the emergence of *cisness* as a medical, legal, and social category rather than treating it as a timeless given; they are discerning how transphobia has been mobilized by fascist movements, both historically and in the present; they are thinking about the consequences of the state's biopolitical management of gender; and they are constructing nuanced genealogies of the racialization of transness, the ways that trans history is intertwined with white supremacy, capitalism, imperialism, colonialism, anti-Semitism, and Islamophobia. These are historical processes that reach back to the sixteenth and seventeenth centuries. We as early modernists do not merely stand to gain from trans studies; we also have archives, texts, and histories that are relevant to these projects. I am not so sure, however, that *Twelfth Night* and *As You Like It* are among them. I am certain that they are not if all we are doing is simply renaming their "cross-dressing female protagonists" as "transgender." Instead of these glib attempts at rebranding an unsalvageable fetishism for "transvestism," early modernists might frame their inquiries into gender variance as an extension of the pressing, important work undertaken in trans studies rather than attempting to sort out who counts as trans as an end in itself.

My final plea is this: that the urgency of our current political climate might shape the work that we as early modernists do when we imagine trans history. I am writing this introduction in July 2023, and since the beginning of this calendar year, over five hundred anti-trans bills have entertained by state legislatures. These bills have already begun banning our access to public spaces like bathrooms and changing rooms; mandating genital examinations for teen athletes; forcibly detransitioning trans youth, separating them from their parents, and remanding them to conversion therapy; and threatening prisons sentences—up to life in prison—for doctors who provide gender-affirming care. The genocidal aims of this movement could not be more obvious. Take, for instance, an act proposed in Oklahoma that would criminalize transition for "children" up to the age of twenty-six, chillingly titled "The Millstone Act" in reference to Matthew 18:6, "whoever causes one of these little ones who believe in Me to sin, it is better for him that a heavy millstone be hung around his neck, and that he be drowned in the depths of the sea."[126] So many of these bills are being proposed, and at such a rate, that I cannot find an accurate count of them. I am telling you these things because I believe the seriousness of this political moment should infuse the work we undertake in this field. Trans life should not be an idle thought experiment, though scholars often treat it as such. The way we talk about the histories, theories, and possibilities of transness matters *right now*. In light of the exigencies of the present moment, it is urgent that early modernists stop recoiling from the possibility of a trans Renaissance, a fear that only contributes to the widely shared belief that trans life is without a history, an emergent threat that should be met with state violence. If ever there was a time for imagining trans history, for engaging in acts of rogue historicization, for rejecting the universalization of cisness, that time is now.

In keeping with this imperative, the chapters that follow begin with scenes from the present and imagine different conceptual pathways that might bind the Renaissance to the contemporary landscape of trans life. Each chapter opens with what appears to be a peculiarly modern instance of trans panic: Pope Francis's encyclical denouncing transition as a "threat to creation," the phobic fantasy that trans people are like teens who "identify as" animals, the rise of criminal mayhem laws to prohibit gender-affirming surgeries, and trans widows who imagine their partners' transitions as deaths they must nobly endure. In each instance, the logic of emergence is on full display. These cases formulate a threat assessment that assumes that trans life is experimental, untested, and new, a danger to the cis forms of embodiment understood to be natural and timeless. And yet, these rejections of transness open onto long-standing questions in theology, philosophy, and law. The affiliation of transition with death, the confusing sexuation of the "first man" as the image of God, the gendered taxonomies that separate human from animal, and the legal history of criminal mayhem have genealogies that reach back to early modernity and beyond. Situating these apparently modern forms of transphobia in their broader histories scuttles the comforting cis fantasy that transition is, in the pope's memorable turn of phrase, a "new sin."

In the first chapter, "A Woman's Prick: Trans Technogenesis in Sonnet 20," I offer a trans reading of Shakespeare's "master-mistress," belatedly "pricked out for women's pleasure," as an elaboration of early modern theological debates about gendered embodiment, technology, and human artifice in the book of Genesis. This chapter frames the exegetical history of the hermaphroditic Adam in patristic commentaries, midrash, astrological manuals, Neoplatonic dialogues, and lyric poetry as a setting for Shakespeare's exploration of how precisely one might craft a "woman's face." In these alternative readings of Genesis, the creation of the gendered body is an act of technical fabrication, or rather, an ongoing process of interventions, revisions, and modifications. I argue that the term Sonnet 20 takes up for this unfolding process of technical modification is "pricking." Whereas a uniform critical consensus has understood the "prick" as a penis, and thus a kind of genital reveal perched at the sonnet's end that definitively fixes the youth's gender as male, I attach "pricking" to the senses it had in the technical labor of handcraft, embroidery, and large-scale fresco painting. Reframed in this way, the creation of the "woman's face" is no longer the singular product of "Nature" or divine creation, but a scene of collaborative labor and feminized artisanship. In this respect, the sonnet anticipates work in trans studies that reclaims trans embodiment as prosthetic, handcrafted, and technically fabricated.

The second chapter, "Abortive Hedgehogs: Prodigies and Trans Animality in *The Duchess of Malfi*," continues to address the creaturely dimensions of trans life by attending to the play's stable of prodigious creatures, which includes graverobbing werewolves, hermaphroditic hyenas, and verniculated corpses. The text's gender politics and sexual pathologies have been exhaustively addressed within the frameworks of feminist and psychoanalytic criticism. However, such studies have not accounted for how the play links gender variance with animality, a pairing most evident in the text's fixation on prodigies. According to religio-medical tracts of the

Renaissance, prodigies were portentous signs of divine anger that included sweating statues, human-animal hybrids, racial anomalies, and monstrous births, especially the birth of hermaphrodites. The prodigious characters populating *The Duchess of Malfi* are rendered suspiciously gender variant on account of the curiosities of their birth or the excess of their sexual appetites—the Duchess and Ferdinand are fraternal twins, an ancient symbol of hermaphroditism, and gentle and feminine Antonio, who "cannot abide a woman," is rumored to be both Jewish and hermaphroditic. As rigid distinctions between gender roles become unmoored, the category of the human also frays, a process culminating in Ferdinand's descent into hysterical lycanthropy. With an eye to the creaturely transformations threaded through the text, "Abortive Hedgehogs" considers how the play's hermaphroditic imagination erodes the boundaries between human and nonhuman forms of life to explore what Mel Chen calls "the transness of animals."

The third chapter, "Egg Theory's Early Modern Style; Or, John Donne's Resurgent Flesh," locates an ancestral form of the strange fantasy that transition is a kind of death in the Christian doctrine of the resurrection of the body. From the patristics onward, resurrection theology occasionally floated the possibility that the "glorious body" of the afterlife would be a transitional body, whole and integrated, no longer subject to the degrading experience of sexual differentiation. This chapter tracks one curious afterlife of this trans resurrection in the morbid writings of John Donne. Across the wedding sermon for the nuptials of the Earl of Bridgewater's daughter, the secular poetry of *Songs and Sonets*, and the illness memoir *Devotions upon Emergent Occasions*, Donne returned to the possibility that death was a process of ungendering. This trans fantasy, I argue, was not merely a matter of the content of Donne's literary production, but also its style: in the dissociative lyrics that insert the speaker into any number of non-male personae and the metaphysical gestures that tease the possibility of transition only to retract, complicate, or occlude it, I find an early instance of what Grace Lavery calls "egg theory." An "egg," in online vernacular, is a latent trans person who is attempting to indefinitely defer transition. I argue that Donne's stylistic quirks, as well as his resurrection fetish, make him an egg theorist, or rather, an egg lyricist. I conclude the chapter by considering the racial dimensions of his apocalyptic community of the ungendered and the whiteness of egg poetics.

The final chapter, "Trans Mayhem in *Samson Agonistes*," begins with a legal history of criminal mayhem, a law that punishes injuries specifically intended to disable their victims and which, in the mid-twentieth century, was used to prevent doctors from performing trans surgeries. The legal history of criminal mayhem reaches back to early modern common law and a 1603 case recorded in Edward Coke's *Institutes* in which a "lustie rogue" named Wright "made himselfe impotent" by having a friend cut off his left hand in order to avoid working or conscription. I pair Wright's case with a text about forms of cutting that render their victims impotent and emasculated: Milton's closet play *Samson Agonistes,* a trans adaptation of the Book of Judges that mounts an inquiry into the political, theological, and sexual valences of debilitating injury. Gathering around Samson and assessing his maimed body, the play's characters ask the same questions as the jurists imagining a legal framework for the state's seizure of bodily capacities, the mandate to maintain a (re)productive body for the benefit of the nation. This chapter argues that within Milton's closet play lies a quiet celebration of trans mayhem, an account of wounding that embraces rather than recoils from vulnerability, one that rejects "usefulness" and "employment" as metrics for assigning value to bodies.

[ CHAPTER ONE ]

# A Woman's Prick

## Trans Technogenesis in Sonnet 20

In the interview that concludes *This Economy Kills: Pope Francis on Capitalism and Social Justice*, the pope fields a question on ecological disaster and man's responsibility toward the environment. In response, he offers a synopsis of various threats to creation, "the gift God has given to humanity," a list that includes global poverty, the "idolatry of wealth," and a "culture of waste" alongside climate change, euthanasia, and war.[1] Bundled into this catalogue of catastrophes are trans people, whom the pope denounces as "Herods" who "plot schemes of death and disfigure the face of man and woman, destroying creation," a danger comparable to nuclear bombs.[2] This was not the first time that Pope Francis publicized his charming opinions on transition. While addressing a group of Polish bishops, he condemned not only trans rights, but the very existence of trans people as an "exploitation of creation" and "the annihilation of man as the image of God."[3] At fault, he asserted, is an "ideology of gender" according to which "children—children!—are taught in school that everyone can choose his or her sex." His Holiness then darkly intimated that this insidious transgender pedagogy amounts to an "ideological colonization" not unlike those undertaken by "the Balilla and the Hitler Youth."[4] These comments may be surprising, coming as they do from Pope Francis, the *good* pope, endlessly praised by liberals for his generally progressive views on poverty and global capitalism, climate change, evolution, divorce, and gay rights. When asked about his attitude toward gay people, for instance, the pope shrugged off the question with a famously controversial response: "Who am I to judge?"[5] But whereas the homosexual is addressed in his capacity as "an individual person, in his wholeness and dignity," such grace is not to be extended to trans people, who represent a species-level threat.[6] Not your run-of-the-mill deviants, trans people are guilty of a "new sin against God the Creator" and embody an existential threat to life itself on the order of ecological catastrophe, genocide, and nuclear war.[7]

Solemnly invoking Genesis in support of policies that make trans life unlivable is a favored tactic of the religious right. In such circles, "creation" has become a byword for a divinely authorized design that enshrines binary sex as natural, moral, and inalterable. We are to understand that this well-ordered cosmos centered on the heterosexually paired cisgender couple is being menaced by the ideological system of "transgenderism." Pope Francis's assessment of the perils courted by a society that embraces its trans members is not different from these other reactionary positions in its stridency. What separates the pope's transphobia from his interlocutors, rather, is its theological sophistication and intellectual rigor. For the most part, conservative Christian organizations and thinkers are content to demonize trans people by limply gesturing at Genesis 1:27, which has God crafting the originary couple male and female, as if the meaning of that verse were self-evident.[8] The trans-antagonistic position espoused by Pope Francis, by contrast, flows from an elaborate conceptual system that threads together Biblical exegesis, social justice, and integral ecology. This particular account of Genesis is particularly insidious because it validates transphobia as part of a worldview that is, by and large, amenable to liberal thought. Like many other Christian exponents of transphobia, Pope Francis works on the assumption that trans embodiment is a recent phenomenon, a byproduct of cutting-edge medical technology that constitutes a uniquely modern threat to what is essentially settled theology. I contest this point of view by casting the trans-exclusive gospel of creation as an iteration of early modern theological debates about how the Book of Genesis handles gendered embodiment, technology, and human artifice. Rather than putting religion in its place by invoking a different master discourse (perhaps medical science or psychiatry), this critique mounts a theological challenge to the weaponization of Genesis as part of a project of religious transphobia. I propose Shakespeare's transfeminine revision of Genesis in Sonnet 20 as an alternative to the static, immobile creation trotted out in support of transphobia. As such, this chapter has two aims: first, to incorporate Genesis into trans history as a text that situates transition, rebirth, and prosthesis as part and parcel of creaturely life; and secondly, to explore the ongoing value of early modern religious writing for imagining trans lifeworlds today.

The ecological coordinates of Pope Francis's hostility to trans people emerged early in his papacy, a position crystallized in his first single-authored encyclical, *Laudato Si': On the Care for our Common Home.*[9] Borrowing its title from St. Francis of Assisi's *Canticle of the Creatures*, the encyclical outlines a theological platform for climate justice centered on the sacred intertwining of human life with the environs that support and sustain us. This "integral ecology," which draws heavily on Leonardo Boff's environmentalist strain of liberation theology, turns on the "conviction that the divine and the human meet in the slightest detail in the seamless garment of God's creation."[10] The suspicion that transition, or even androgyny, must catch and tear at this "seamless garment" finds a scriptural basis in Genesis 1:26 and 27: "Then God said, 'Let us make man in our own image according to our lickenes; and let them rule ouer the fish of the sea, and ouer the foule of the heauen, and ouer the beastes, & ouer all the earth, and ouer euerie thing that crepeth & moueth on the earth.' Thus God created the man in his image; in the image of God created he him: he created them male and female."[11]

A healthy social ecology and sense of environmental responsibility have their basis in the "great biblical narrative" in which God fashions man after His own image. These verses buttress the "infinite" and "inalienable dignity" afforded to each person who "is not just something, but someone," an agent endowed with "self-knowledge" and "self-possession" capable of "entering into communion with other persons."[12] The status of the human body as the *imago dei* guarantees the essential dignity granted to every person, the "fundamental, unearned, equally shared moral status" that forms the basis for rights.[13] Moreover, the creation of men and women in the likeness of God grounds the possibility of community and neighbor-love as an expression of divine love, while also establishing man's dominion over the created world, our "common home," as a kind of benevolent, paternalistic stewardship. Sexual dimorphism and complementary gender roles are foundational to this harmonious creation. "Valuing one's own body in its femininity or masculinity is . . . an essential element of any genuine human ecology," the encyclical reads, "whereas thinking that we enjoy absolute power over our own bodies turns, often subtly, into thinking that we enjoy absolute power over creation."[14] This line of thought was deepened and expanded in Francis's apostolic exhortation *Amoris Laetitia*, a celebration of marriage and family life that took aim at "gender ideology," assisted reproductive technology, and gay marriage as impediments to "caring for the environment as our common home."[15] More recently, the document "Male and Female He Created Them" castigates the "utopia of the 'neuter' [that] eliminates both human dignity in sexual distinctiveness and the personal nature of the generation of new life."[16] Here too, deviation from a cisgender norm is plaited together with a host of other degenerate practices that sever human life from the natural order of creation and divine providence. The "*educational crisis*" initiated by this insidious "gender theory" has seeded curricula with "ideas of 'intersex' or 'transgender'" that are covertly aligned with "similar theories" destined to "annihilate the concept of 'nature,' (that is, everything we have been given as a pre-existing foundation of our being and action in the world)."[17] By obliterating sexual difference, the trans body effaces the likeness of the Creator that inheres in the human form, the body which we must "accept . . . as God's gift" as a necessary precondition for "welcoming and accepting the entire world as a gift from the Father."[18] Like surrogacy and in vitro fertilization, hormone therapies and gender-affirming surgeries commodify the body and subject it to the clever but misguided techniques of physicians who abuse their creative powers to refashion the perfect work of God the Creator. From such a perspective, transitioning amounts to a hubristic assault on creation itself that undermines the material basis of community, personal dignity, and environmental harmony.

Pitting Genesis against trans embodiment in this way evinces a deep suspicion of artifice and artifactuality, the capacities of human ingenuity to generate a world of man-made creations that occlude, or even subvert, God's design. This fear of technical fabrication presses the pope's transphobia into long-standing philosophical debates concerning the nature and function of technics. Drawing on Aristotle, Bernard Stiegler glosses technicity as the "domain of skill" or craft that governs the transformation of "raw material" into fabricated products.[19] *Technē* comprises both skilled labor and actuated knowledge that modifies an environment by engaging with it: cooking is a technique, as is building a house, and so too are the routines of housekeeping. Rhetoric, speech, and poetry belong under the rubric of technical fabrication—*poiesis*, after all, means *making*, and like *technē* it entails a process of revealing, self-disclosure, and bringing-forth. From this perspective, technical practices mobilize the self-organizing energies of objects and environments in ways that may serve human desires but are not reducible to them. Instead, the bright-line distinction between the natural and the prosthetic blur in Stiegler's account, since human projects of thinking, making, and doing occur in concert with an object world that possesses its own creative energies. These lively powers, in turn, shape the human through a "double plasticity" that leads to the paradox of "the technical inventing the human, and the human inventing the technical."[20] Rather than forming sharply defined and hierarchically organized categories, humans and tools constantly modify each other as advances in technology redound on the human organism. This evolutionary spiral amounts to a "process of exteriorization" or a "pursuit of life by means other than life," a recursive coevolution of human and technical forms that Stiegler names *technogenesis*.[21]

By this logic, transitioning is a form of technical thinking. Not just produced through the skilled labor of a surgeon who assumes the position of God the Creator, transness is also the result of a wide diffusion of specialist knowledge. Given the hostility of the medical establishment to trans patients, transitioning has often been a DIY project that relies on skill sharing. Today, such enskillment is mediated through social networks and YouTube tutorials that offer guides for everything from vocal training to self-regulating pharmacological regimens, in the event that doctors prove hesitant, hostile, or incompetent.[22] The medical regimes, sartorial styles, dietary routines, and surgical interventions that facilitate transition render the trans body into a technical object. From the perspective of media theory, there is nothing especially radical or disparaging about this proposition, since the coevolution of humans and technics ensure that every human body is prosthetic from inception. It is this possibility of technogenesis that the pope rejects when he dismisses the "techniques and practices" of transition as a misguided product of human efforts to reverse engineer a world fashioned by God.[23] As creatures that are, in Susan Stryker's words, "technological constructions" pieced together from "flesh torn apart and sewn together again," trans bodies tangle the lines of mastery that flow from God to Adam and thence to his sons.[24] In this respect, transphobia is an expression of technophobia, a fear of how technology offers seductive tools that ultimately alienate us from our bodies, nature, and God. In order to preserve its coherence, then, the position articulated by the pope and his adherents must suppress two different problems: first, the long history of controversy attached to the ambiguous language that has God creating man "male and female"; and secondly, the philosophical disputes surrounding the capacities and dangers of human ingenuity. Both the theoretical and theological questions were at stake in early modern treatments of Genesis.

Despite the conviction with which right-wing reactionaries leverage the Biblical creation myth against trans populations, it is not so clear that Genesis reifies binary gender as native to the created body. Premodern theologians and philosophers read the language of Genesis 1:27, in which God creates man in his own image, as harboring a range of possible interpretations, not all of which fix binary gender as a natural, unadulterated state of being inscribed in creation itself. Witness the millennia-old debate about whether Genesis implies that Adam was a hermaphrodite.[25] The text of Genesis was sometimes understood to suggest that before Eve existed as a separate creature, woman was physically lodged within Adam's body. Rabbinic literature and the Gnostic gospels propose various arrangements for this body, which is variously called hermaphroditic, androgynous, or bisexual.[26] The Genesis and Leviticus Rabbahs suggest that Adam may have had two faces for his two genders; then, subsequently, perhaps God "sawed" the already two-faced Adam down to the trunk, equipping him with "two fronts" and "two backs," one male and one female.[27] Even the translation of "female" is not straightforward in the Genesis Rabbah, which translates the

Septuagint as stating that "a male with his female parts created he them" or even "a male with orifices He created him."[28]

As opposed to the fleshiness of the Midrashic accounts, a Platonizing impulse lies behind other Jewish and patristic works which assert that the "image of God" must reference an ideal, disembodied, and ungendered creation. These accounts splice Genesis with Plato's *Symposium*, enlisting Adam as the primal androgyne described by Aristophanes.[29] Philo of Alexandria, for instance, zeroed in on the shifting pronouns of Genesis 1:27 as evidence of an initial creation that was essentially spiritual, culminating in a being that was "incorporeal, neither male nor female, by nature incorruptible."[30] Only later did a secondary modification afford Adam a physical form, a gender, and a "helper" (that is, Eve).[31] Assigning Adam a body did not bring about the greater perfection of the prototype. Instead, gendered corporeality amounted to a traumatic deviation from an originary pattern that cleaved more closely to the likeness of God. The androgynous template Philo assigned to Adam appealed to later Egyptian Christian fathers, including Clement of Alexandria and Origen. Because God's likeness could not be adequately contained in the base matter of the body, Origen asserted, it must be "our inner man, invisible, incorporeal, incorruptible, and immortal which is made 'according to the image of God.'"[32] It is perhaps understandable that an androgynous template would have been so appealing to this particular church father, whose "youthful self-castration" remains something of a scandal in theological circles.[33] Other church fathers felt the loss of primal androgyny even more sharply. In *De hominis opificio*, "On the Fabrication of Man," Gregory of Nyssa imagines binary gender and sexual reproduction or "animal generation" as unfortunate effects of the Fall, a tragic movement away from the original unity that characterized bodily experience in paradise.[34] Moreover, the belief that the resurrection would restore us to the state of incorruptible, androgynous wholeness that characterized this initial creation appeared thereafter in the work of many patristics, including Basil of Caesarea, John Damascene, Gregory Nazanian, and Maximus the Confessor.[35]

The possibility that the human body, as wrought in the perfect image of God, might take an androgynous form vested with multiple sets of genitalia was, of course, never the dominant interpretation of Genesis. Despite the pedigree of its adherents, the Adam-androgyne was decried by no lesser an authority than Augustine, who confessed to a certain reluctance to even say "God made him male and female" for fear of suggesting "something monstrous . . . such as those they call hermaphrodites."[36] Later theologians fell in line behind Augustine's magisterial opinion, issuing huffy condemnations of the complexly gendered Adam. Scholastic commentaries on Genesis by

Peter the Chanter and Nicholas of Lyra, as well as the anonymous treatise *On the Human Body* firmly insisted that corporeal creation was marked by gender difference from the first.[37] The ill repute of the Adam-androgyne persisted through the Reformation and into the seventeenth century, generating denunciations that frequently took on a distinctly anti-Semitic character. Martin Luther's "Lectures on Genesis," for instance, condemns the "Talmudic tales" according to which "man was created bisexual and later on, by divine power, was, as it were, split or cut apart," along with all the "obscene details" such stories have accrued over time.[38] In a similar vein, Milton's *Tetrachordon* firmly rejects the possibility that "man at first had been created Hermaphrodite," despite the "accidental concurrence between Plato's wit" and "the Jews' fable."[39] Approaching the possibility from the vantage of Baconian empiricism, Thomas Browne's *Pseudodoxia Epidemica* rejects the primal androgyne as contrary to reason, refusing to "concede a monstrosity, or mutilate the integrity of Adam."[40] For Browne, the perfection of a body that could simultaneously experience all possible genders registers not as an enhancement but a diminishment, a grotesque mutilation of the normative human body. And so, despite Christianity's early adoption of the androgynous Adam, Renaissance scholars and theologians passionately repudiated the hermaphroditic model of creation that had been incubated in Jewish, Persian, Greek, and patristic belief systems.

And yet, even if the Adam-androgyne was roundly condemned, it was never fully stricken from the record, stubbornly persisting into early modernity quite in spite of its illustrious opposition.[41] Manuals of astral magic and alchemy adopted the hermaphrodite as an emblem of mystical transmutation.[42] The degendered soul envisioned by Origen circulated along with his *Homilies on Genesis*, edited by Jacques Merlin and later Erasmus, a text that went through nine printings in the sixteenth century.[43] The biform body of the first man entered the thought of Neoplatonists like Giovanni Pico della Mirandola and Leone Ebreo, who imagined the reintegration of ideal forms and drossy matter as a return to masculo-feminine perfection.[44] Often this ecstatic union was analogized to marital harmony or sexual embrace, as in Geoffrey Fenton's 1572 translation of Etienne Pasquier's *Monophile*, which praises the "woonderfull effectes" of a love that "distils two spirites into one bodye" as a method for "returning to the first *Androgina* of our father Adam."[45] The erotic dimensions of the hermaphroditic Genesis enlivened lyric poetry and drama, as in the work of Ben Jonson, whose *New Inn* has Lord Beaufort asserting that "man and woman / Were, in the first Creation, both one piece, / And being cleft asunder, ever since, / Loue was an appetite to be reioyn'd."[46] Despite the scorn and scandal, then, the queer genders implicit in Genesis could never quite be suppressed, remaining a rich conceptual reservoir for imagining expansive forms of embodiment. These theological debates surrounding the lineaments of Adam's gender and the desirability, or even sanctity, of a bigender body make it difficult to retrieve Genesis as a straightforward endorsement of binary sex. Adam's body, multiply gendered, hollowed out, womb-bearing, sawed in half, lacking nothing, seminal and inseminated, was never merely cisgender. Across a kaleidoscopic range of genres, early modern writers toyed with the complex, surprising, and queer configurations of gender and sexuality that animate the Biblical creation myth.

Moreover, in addition to disputes over the exact contours of the created body, the possibility that gender might be available for technical fabrication was also a source of religious controversy in the Renaissance. As Jennifer Waldron brilliantly argues in work on Protestant theology and media theory, reformers' iconoclastic suspicion of man-made images initiated debates over the dangers of human artifice, gender, and technology.[47] Waldron turns to Calvin's sharp distinction between the initial creation, which served as one of God's instruments for "reaching down and pulling humans up to him" and an object world manufactured from the "accretions of human culture" that not only "attenuated divine intentions but actively blocked them."[48] This religious critique of technics, Waldron argues, genders *technē* as feminine. Literature of the period associated femininity with artifice on the grounds that women were given to cosmetic practices that distort the "raw matter" of the body in its natural simplicity.[49] Worse yet, painting was not merely a surface-level intervention, a temporary adornment that could be removed to restore the subject to her unadulterated state. The shockingly toxic ingredients conscripted into early modern beauty routines could permanently alter the skin, hair, and neurological systems of those who used them. Bleaching the skin with a mixture made of quicksilver, lemon, and turpentine (to be worn for eight days) might indeed help a woman achieve that special glow, but, the recipe's author cautions, "you would think the said composition burned or flaied off the skinne of your face."[50] As Thomas Tuke warns in his *Discourse against Painting and Tincturing*, such practices appropriate the privileges of God the Creator and insinuate a split nature into the painted figure who, "though shee bee the *creature* of God, as she is a *woman*, yet is . . . her own *creatrisse*, as she is a *picture*."[51] There are religious ramifications to the technical practice of painting, which seem to transform the natural body into a particularly dangerous type of object. Tuke asks his browbeaten reader, "Dost thou love thyself artificiall, and like an Idoll?"[52] In loving herself "artificiall," the made-up woman is transformed into a graven image impiously adoring her own craftsmanship. By exercising creative power over the created body, the cosmetically enhanced subject commits a kind of sacrilege by transforming the human physique into an artifact, a technical object, rendered material.

This exegetical history of Genesis exposes the conceptual weakness behind the contemporary varietals of Christian transphobia espoused by papal encyclicals and evangelical statements. Such positions depend on a thin reading of Genesis according to which the creation of the gendered body was a single event that culminated in unambiguously sexed bodies built for heterosexual coupling. This interpretation is belied by the resilience of the Adam-androgyne, which speaks to the swarm of gendered possibilities nested within Genesis. To be constructed in the image of God does not necessarily mean being limited to a narrowly defined, patriarchal maleness. Instead, it might involve a capacious relationship to embodiment that entails simultaneously experiencing all conceivable genders and sexualities. Moreover, such accounts of Genesis suggest that the initial rollout of Adam did not go as planned. This creation was not a fixed point but an evolving process, an unfolding sequence of bodily configurations subject to revisions, modifications, augmentations, and retractions. These adjustments were not only top-down impositions mandated by an omniscient Creator-God. Instead, Genesis frames a scene in which human activity was implicated in the nascence of gendered embodiment: sinning, naming, entreating, desiring, sleeping, trusting, lying, rebelling, and appareling all contributed to the reformatting of corporeality, with important consequences for gender and sexuality. The fear that this creative restructuring of the body did not end with Genesis feeds into the technophobic suspicion of artifactuality that lies beneath the opposition to cosmetics and idolatry. As such, the Renaissance inherited a more elastic, expansive account of Genesis than the restrictive, cisnormative version promoted by right-wing reactionaries today. It was in this context that Shakespeare took up the cluster of issues at stake in the multiple varietals of creation: the transformative capacities of the gendered body; the obscure design for the human form; the *frisson* that attends body modification; the dangers of artifice, in all its senses; and the complicated ways we inhabit the "image" and "likeness" of God. While anti-cosmetic polemics attempted to shore up the distinction between the created body and its artificially manufactured double, Shakespeare's Sonnet 20 offers another way of thinking about gender, creation, and technicity. It is a poem, after all, about how precisely to make a face—a face so sublimely beautiful that it emanates an aura of irreality:

> A woman's face, with nature's own hand painted
> Hast thou, the master mistress of my passion—
> A woman's gentle heart, but not acquainted

With shifting change, as is false women's fashion;
An eye more bright than theirs, less false in rolling,
Gilding the object whereupon it gazeth;
A man in hue all hues in his controlling,
Which steals men's eyes and women's souls amazeth.
And for a woman wert thou first created,
Till nature as she wrought thee fell a-doting,
And by addition me of thee defeated,
By adding one thing to my purpose nothing.
  But since she pricked thee out for women's pleasure,
  Mine be thy love, and thy love's use their treasure.[53]

Sonnet 20 has a problem, and that problem is the face. Desiring the master-mistress entails confronting the issues that were always at stake in Genesis's account of embodiment: whether we can establish the original design for the gendered body, and whether the human capacity to modify our gendered habitus improves upon or damages that prototype. Resolving that confrontation between creation and creativity leads the poem through an assortment of scenes of material fabrication and manual labor, including the artist's workshop and the aristocratic woman's closet. Sonnet 20, I will argue, revisits Genesis 1:27 to offer a transfeminine version of the creation myth in which, as Stiegler proposes, the technically constructed body is not outside human experience but central to it.

Technicity is at stake from the very beginning of the poem. The initial suspicion about the potentially artificial features of the youth's beautiful appearance opens onto the poem's first site of artistic creation: the workshop of the master painter. The figure of Nature, who may be standing in for God, is mapped onto the figure of the artist, a coupling that was not unusual in the Renaissance. Giorgio Vasari, who invoked God and Nature interchangeably, was fond of casting *Deus artifex* (God the Artificer) as the first artist and man as the first artwork:

> God on High . . . descended with His intellect further down into the clarity of the atmosphere and the solidity of the earth, and, shaping man, discovered in the pleasing invention of things the first form of sculpture and painting. Who will deny that from man, as from a true model, statues and sculptures were then gradually carved out along with the difficulties of various poses and their surroundings? . . . Thus, the first model from which issued the first image of man was a mass of earth, and not without reason, for the Divine Architect of Time and Nature, being all perfect, wished to demonstrate in the imperfection of His materials the means

> to subtract from them or add to them, in the same way that good sculptors and painters are accustomed to doing when by adding or subtracting from their models, they bring their imperfect drafts to that state of refinement and perfection they seek.[54]

A sculptor, a painter, and an architect, God is a multimodal practitioner whose creation of the earth and of mankind forms the template for all artforms as the "pleasing invention of things." Playing fast and loose with Genesis, Vasari imagines a Creator-God bent over the earth, pressing his thumbs into clay, endlessly delighted by his own recreative capacities. This scenario invokes a primary technicity centered on God as the first Maker whose earliest sculpture, the human body, formed a "true model" for later artists, who gradually carved out statues with increasingly lifelike poses. This primary technicity, in turn, ensures that artistic endeavor serves as an extension of that initial creation, installing artists within a genealogy that links them to the Divine Craftsman. The unbroken bond between human artifice and divine workmanship manifests in the artist's *maniera*, a term derived from the Latin *manus*, or hand. Roughly glossed as "style," *maniera* also encompassed originality and authenticity; the facility and ease of *sprezzatura*; unfettered artistic license and freedom over the creative process; and finally, the ability to improve upon a model, often by cobbling together the most handsome parts of various bodies, piecing together "the most beautiful hands, heads, bodies, or legs" to generate "the most perfect figure."[55] In ascribing the master-mistress's beauty to the unimpeachable *maniera* of "Nature's own hand," Sonnet 20 valorizes the youth's form as the product of the kind of divine handiwork Vasari describes. The poem begins with a strong claim: no technical practices except those mobilized by Nature contributed to sculpting this exquisite body, explicitly rejecting any scenario in which human hands cleverly touched up the face in a way that marred the Maker's design. As such, the opening gambit accords this "woman's face" the dignity and authenticity befitting a masterpiece wrought by a painterly Nature.

Of course, the conceptual maneuvering necessary to position the master-mistress on the good and holy side of that divide requires almost gymnastic flexibility. In the same breath that declares the youth's beauty genuine and natural, the poem begins to inspect the "woman's face" like an art object whose authenticity has been thrown into question. Even ascribing the youth's creation to nature's "own hand" is equivocal and ambiguous, as it makes use of a formula that doubles the contractual stipulation in artistic commissions specifying that the work was to be rendered by "the master's own hand" rather than being farmed out to his apprentices.[56] As such, the very specification that is meant to bolster the composition's legitimacy simultaneously summons up the specter of plagiarism built into the workshop system. As Gregory Bredbeck notes, the acoustic pun in Nature's "own" hand, cognate with "one" hand, transforms the line into a "Janus-like statement," since "nature's *other* hand may soon grab a brush and paint again."[57] Indeed, the Sonnets more broadly militate against the assumption that nature's creative power is singular enough to be immediately recognizable as the real thing. Later in the sequence, nature's hand returns in a subversive reduplication of this image, when Sonnet 127 bemoans how "each hand hath put on nature's power, / Fairing the foul with art's false-borrowed face" and "slandr'ing creation" with a manufactured, rather than in-born, beauty (5–6, 12). Nature's hand can be appropriated to produce derivative, fabricated works that only appear to be the real thing. Despite the initial assertion that the youth's face was crafted through natural means, then, artifice is almost immediately proposed as an obstacle to be overcome, as expressed in the anti-cosmetic sentiment animating the sequence at large.[58] Although we are explicitly assured that the artful hand that built the face belongs to nature, "painting" is a term that squirms with paranoia by virtue of its proximity to cosmetics and hence to "seeming," "appearing" and "deceiving." The suspicion arises that the handcrafted face inhabits *maniera* in the bad sense, rendering the youth's body an unholy mixture of the most beautiful spare parts sourced from other bodies. With ambiguity typical of the sonnets, it is impossible to tell where artificiality begins and ends.

Seeking confirmation that the superficial impressions inspired by the youth's appearance are tethered to the material disposition of body and gender, the poem penetrates inward, matching the "woman's face" to a "woman's gentle heart." This gesture explicitly aligns external appearance with internal truth, the delicacy of the features with an emotional tenderness native to women. It may be that Shakespeare here anticipates a recognizably modern sense of subjectivity or interiority, what Katharine Eisaman Maus describes as a psychic realm which "passeth show" in two senses: first, that "it is beyond scrutiny, concealed where other people cannot perceive it," and secondly, that "it *surpasses* the visible—its meaning is unimpeachable."[59] Anne Ferry specifically attributes this conceptual development to the sonnets, which "concerned themselves with what a modern writer would call the *inner life*" precisely because "it was in love poetry that writers faced most directly the issues involved in representing what is in the heart."[60] If appearances are by nature deceptive and subject to misinterpretation, the depth model of selfhood may offer a more reliable access point to the youth's innate gender. In this fleeting hope that gender could be anchored in youth's inner world of experience and affect, the poem takes on a modernizing thrust that would become central to definitions of trans identity in nineteenth- and twentieth-century sexology.[61] From the perspective opened as the poem delves inward, the youth's true gender need not, and maybe cannot, be established through judging the shape of jaw, hairline, cheekbones, and brow against feminine norms. The work of categorization dispenses with external appearance, which is easily manipulable, as the poem seeks a solid ground for judgment in the affective, emotional, and psychic architecture of the "heart."

However promising, the forward momentum of this turn to interiority is halted and reversed almost immediately. The optimistic appeal to inwardness cannot survive the Sonnets' repeated refusals to affiliate the heart with emotional or even anatomical internality. After making its initial appearance in Sonnet 20, the heart returns in Sonnet 22 in the accusation that "all that beauty that doth cover thee / Is but the seemly raiment of my heart, / Which in thy breast dost live" and again in Sonnet 24, where "Mine eye hath played the painter and hath stelled / Thy beauty's form in table of my heart. / My body is the frame wherein 'tis held" (22.4–6, 24.1–3). The heart too is a surface, a page to be decorated, a canvas to be adorned, a homunculus to be costumed. There is no identity at work here, if by that we mean an interiority that is the unique property of an insular subject. The gravitational pull of the attractive face has expropriated and absorbed the lover's heart before subjecting it to further adulterations. The youth's beauty slithers inward, appareling the heart in a gaudy vestment. Sinking deeper, we are met not with a bedrock of inner truth but with the very façade we sought to elude. For a moment, it seems that the shifting sands of appearance can be cross-referenced with interior experience to locate the unadulterated truth of the self beneath the posturing and the paint. And yet, that possibility vanishes in the moment of its articulation. The "woman's heart" that stands as guarantor for the "woman's face" bears more than a passing resemblance to "woman's art," a punning substitution that restores the youth's imagined interiority to a duplicitous exteriority. With this homophone, the nobility of Nature's masterwork deteriorates into a feminized enskillment associated with craft and cosmesis. The heart, no less than the face, may be the product of a tampering, too-artful hand.

While the first quatrain attempts to bolster Nature's artifice as a life-affirming craft that binds the human body to the created order, the second quatrain aggravates the dilemmas flowing from technical fabrication by layering Nature's painting with the youth's gilding. In addition to well-documented economic anxieties about gold as a stable measure of value in the aftermath of catastrophic inflation and the influx of precious metals from the New World, the Renaissance also wrapped gold into controversies surrounding artistic technique. Combing through contracts stipulating painters' obligations in executing their commissions, Michael Baxandall found evidence that gilding was part of a broader reassessment of artistic value. Over the Quattrocento, requests for costly pigments like gold and ultramarine were steadily replaced by demands for skill. Essentially, this amounted to an insistence that instead of delegating all the labor to the workshop, the artist would personally handle the most significant parts of the painting—the figures and, in particular, their faces. In this way, Baxandall asserts, "the client will confer lustre on his picture not with gold but with mastery, the hand of the master himself."[62] From this perspective, gold leaf was a fraudulent shortcut to splendor, and its inclusion on a canvas signaled that the painter lacked the artistry necessary to produce a convincing illusion. Precious minerals like gold were an impediment to naturalism and the representation of unique and lifelike facial expressions. The ambivalent status of gilding speaks to an emergent split between the high art traced by the godlike hand of the master painter and the debased and derivative realm of craft. As a vector of gilding, then, the master-mistress would seem to fall away from the singular creative capacities of nature's own hand.

Moreover, by recruiting "gilding" into the dissection of the youth's authenticity, the poem nudges the act of artisanal creation toward the fraught world of religious iconography and the mortifying power of idols. Protestant suspicion of image-worship triggered waves of "chronoclasm" that targeted the lavishly gilded images, icons, and screenwork that beautified Catholic churches.[63] Calvin, for instance, associated these fine veneers with the sacrilegious "pomp" enriching Catholic churches, since "the temple of God cannot exist in its true triumph and glory" when it is "full of gilded trinkets."[64] At times, the sonnets seem to resist this iconoclastic impulse: Sonnet 33's invocation of the sun's "celestial" and "golden face . . . gilding pale streams," for instance, associates "gilding" with a natural, vivifying luminosity (33.3–4, 6). Elsewhere, however, such embellishment smacks of superficial beautification edging into deception, as in Sonnet 66, which castigates "gilded honor shamefully misplaced" (5), while at other points it takes on sinister connotations of mortification and decay, as in the "gilded monuments" and "gilded tombs" of Sonnets 55 and 101. Like a questionable icon, the master-mistress may well possess a face that has been "gilded" through painting, plucking, and contouring, technical practices that bury the natural body beneath an idolatrous substitute that offends heaven by, in Thomas Tuke's words, "dawbing the living face with dead colours."[65] The gilded face, like the gilded tomb, signals an inanimate, deadening materiality that the sonnets oppose to the breathy life afforded by poetry, the "pen" that can inspire eternal life "where breath most breathes," with whispers of the beloved's beauty flowing erotically from mouth to mouth (81.14). Like the bejeweled "stocks and stones" of idolatrous image-worship, the techniques that shaped the artificed face expand, rather than collapse, the distance between man and God.

The irreligiosity inhering within these cosmetic practices only deepens when the youth is pronounced a "man in hue all hues in his controlling." With this twist, the surface-level ornamentation implied by gilding takes on a menacing depth, since "hue," as in color, is printed "hew," as in cut. The meticulous brushwork behind the trompe l'oeil of the handcrafted femme face degenerates into a more agitated stroke. The light touch of tincturing escalates into digging, gouging, and carving. There is a transtemporal resonance to the line: to feminize the face through cutting, not merely contouring, anticipates the surgical interventions that modify and, to some commentators, *define* trans bodies.[66] There is perhaps not such a great historical distance between early modern face-painting and facial feminization surgery as we might think. Face-flaying was very much on the menu in the sixteenth century, although the procedure was not performed with knives but rather with chemicals like mercury sublimate. As we will see in the next chapter, which lingers over *The Duchess of Malfi*'s "abortive hedgehog," Bosola's dismissive name for a woman with a chemically abraded face, such cuts do not merely efface the work of "nature's hand," wresting the youth out of the gender assigned by God. Instead, they eject the hewn body from the natural order altogether, consigning it to prodigious monstrosity.

This ambivalence is heightened by the suspicion that the youth's technical practices are contagious, reproducing according to their own rules. A seductive force that radiates outward from the youth's face, whose eye darts about, "gilding the object whereupon it gazeth." The expert hand that crafts a femme face requires a technical mastery of pigment, such that the youth's unique abilities amass "all hues in his controlling." These skills, in turn, extend to a power over other complexions, as this false face makes other faces flush with desire. In this respect, the feminine artifice that crafted a supplemental face transmutes the youth's admirers into superficial and emasculated figures, mere "objects" that are "gilded" and "gelded" through their lust. This forced feminization might run deeper than the involuntary reflex of the blush, however. The quatrain suggests that "gilding" and "hewing" are the modes through which the prosthetic face reproduces itself via a complex matrix of identification and desire. That is, by inspiring a potent mix of attraction and perplexity in women's "amazed souls," the feminine illusion could engender further instances of cosmetic enhancement. In this reading, the artificial face is a template that could be taken up and copied by anyone who glances at it. Sonnet 3 accuses the youth of being "thy mother's glass," an image that Helen Vendler calls "replication-in-a-mirror" fundamentally at odds with "replication-by-breeding."[67] Here, fully in possession of a "woman's face," the youth becomes the mother of her own house, replicating not only *in* a mirror but *by mirroring*. In this scene of technical cocreation, the emergence and evolution of human bodies is midwifed by technological supplementation. The face requires painting to align itself with an idealized femininity; reciprocally, the prosthetic face grafts itself onto other faces. In this way, the technical extension co-opts human bodies to reproduce itself through a potentially endless "process of exteriorization." As such, the master-mistress of Sonnet 20 perversely literalizes the imperious demand of Sonnet 3, in which the youth is ordered to "Look in thy glass and tell the face thou viewest, / Now is the time that face should form another" (3.1–2). Aaron Kunin reads this suggestion as part of the procreation sonnets' "quasi-human sex education," a bizarre moment in which the poem relocates the youth's sex organs to his face "as though a single face could reproduce by parthenogenesis, like an amoeba dividing into two copies of itself."[68] The replication of the prosthetic face offers a queer twist to the imperative of Genesis 1:28, in which the recently sexed Adam and Eve are told to "be fruitful, and multiply, and replenish the earth, and subdue it." The advent of cosmetic technicity threatens to distort this natural order, replacing God's hierarchical, heteronormative, and anthropocentric creation with a species of technical reproduction that does not need binary gender to multiply or to replenish and subdue the earth.

To take up the vocabulary offered by media theory, the octave espouses an essential technophobia. The youth's body is not only suspect because it might be manufactured by her own hand and thus exist at a remove from the designs of God the Artificer. More concerning still, the feminine *technē* crystallized in the curious face of the master-mistress is a vector of contagion that infects and restructures all the bodies and "souls" in the youth's line of sight. The sestet purports to stabilize the youth's gender by turning away from surface-level phenomena altogether, giving up on the fruitless project of gleaning through potentially fabricated exteriors like the pretty face, demure disposition, feminine gestures, and come-hither glances. Instead, the final lines work to uncover the body in its initial, unadulterated state by revisiting the scene of the youth's genesis, when Nature "by addition me of thee defeated, / By adding one thing to my purpose nothing" after she "pricked thee out for women's pleasure." Critics looking for firm evidence for or against the sonnets' homoeroticism point to the prick as definitive proof, one way or the other. Joseph Pequigney, for instance, turns to the speaker's fascination with "the 'thing' that was 'prick'd out,'" to suggest that "such attention in itself might well argue something other than lack of interest in this organ."[69] Alan Sinfield suggests that "the Poet" expresses a sudden fixation on this "male sex organ" not because he is fending off homoerotic desire writ large, but as part of a spat over sexual versatility: "the Boy" must have scandalously offered to penetrate the Poet in an "off-stage action" that the readers should intuit.[70] Richard Halpern understands the sonnet as a sodomitical exposé that he not unproblematically aligns with *The Crying Game*.[71] Stephen Booth, by contrast, erects the prick as an insurmountable obstacle to sexual desire since "nature's addition is useless for the speaker's male purpose."[72] According to critical consensus, then, the sestet unwraps a fleshy appendage that fixes the meaning of the beloved's body with an indisputable finality. Faces can be painted, waists cinched, and brows plucked, but genitals remain fixed and immutable. In this sense, the prick of the final couplet purports to rescue us from the ambiguity, deception, and instability of the technical practices embedded in gilding and hewing. The existence of a penis determines the master-mistress's gender which, in turn, clarifies the kind of desire that the youth inspires in the 'Poet' as either homoerotic or platonic. From this perspective, lifting the skirt for a salacious peek offers concrete evidence for a "real," God-given gender that is only imperfectly disguised beneath the "artificiall" mask produced through technical innovations.

This reading, however, might concede too much to the prick. After all, the sonnet does not actually present us with the prick but rather with *pricking*, an activity that opens onto additional scenes of technical assembly. If the sonnet begins by hailing Nature as a master artist, catching her in the act of pricking loops back to situate two scenes of collective labor and material fabrication that the remainder of this chapter will explore: the aristocratic closet where women engaged in the prick-work of embroidery and the *bottega* or workshop where the Renaissance artist and his apprentices collaboratively crafted masterworks. In the context of the *bottega*, pricking would have signaled a variety of creative enterprise characteristic to fresco painting, a step in the *spolvero* technique of pouncing and tracing.[73] The first stage of constructing a fresco entailed the production of a cartoon, a drawing that sketched out the major figures in a composition. Once completed, the cartoon would be cut into smaller pieces, roughly the size of a single *giornata*, a section of the painting that could be completed with one day's labor. Each morning, that day's fragment of the cartoon would be tacked onto the wall, overlaid on the *intonaco*, the final and finest layer of plaster. Subsequently, the drawing was transferred to the wall by punching holes through the paper with a stylus, which might also be employed to carve fine incisions along the lines of the drawing. Once "pricked," the design was dusted with chalk or graphite powder. This procedure would leave an outline over which the artist and assistants could apply subsequent layers of paint, a suspension of pigment in lime slake. The following day, the process would repeat. Aligning the new *giornata* with the completed portions and modulating the design to account for any idiosyncrasies in the prepared wall was a fiddly and time-consuming affair. In order to coordinate and suture the sections without distorting the overall design, the artist and assistants would gouge reference marks into the plaster, joining the prickmarks and nail holes with a host of horizon lines and orthogonals, arrows and dots, circles and crosses.[74] While such marks were intended to be covered over by the finished painting, some remain perceptible in completed works while others linger beneath the surface, discernible only through raking light, X-radiography, and infrared photography. The finished fresco, then, may appear to be cohesive design perfectly conceived in the mind of a godlike maker, but such completeness is illusory: technical photography reveals that beneath the elegant surface lies a patchwork assemblage of preliminary sketches, plaster sections, and improvised gashes that tell the story of the painting's material genesis. In this sense, pricking does not speak to a singular moment of artistic creation. Rather, the technique invoked by the sonnet's couplet testifies to a protracted and collaborative scene of composition that necessarily entailed adjustments, fine-tunings, and improvised quick fixes.

Moreover, the technical procedure of pricking tended to fracture the unity of the creator-genius. The lengthy process involved in creating a fresco, from drafting and transferring to painting, entailed a collective effort requiring multiple hands working independently. With the advent of the *spolvero* method in the mid-fifteenth century, the design work no longer needed to happen rapidly on-site. Instead, the composition could be sketched out at a comfortable pace in the collaborative environment of the workshop. Indeed, as Marcia Hall notes, by allowing for greater "refinement in the differentiation of tasks," the technical procedure of cartooning expanded the size of *botteghe* and greatly increased their organizational complexity.[75] Artistic creation was no longer the exclusive purview of the master artist charged with painting the major figures, along with an assortment of heads and the hands. The fresco also depended on the labor and contributions of the *cartolai* who laid out, flattened, and squared the sheets of the cartoon; the *garzoni* who glued the sheets together, ground the pigments, and occasionally modeled; the *muratori* who prepared the wall; and the *collaboratori* who painted the background and minor figures and less erotically charged body parts. The addition of pricking to the fresco process meant that more voices, not fewer, were involved in the design and execution of a painting. Furthermore, cartooning allowed for developments in sales and marketing. As a method of design transfer, the technology of pricking meant that those same assistants could handily produce copies and variants as a side hustle, selling ready-made designs for a lower price than a commission. Thus, as Carmen Bambach argues, the pricked cartoon gestured toward a replicative technology employed not by accomplished artists but by "drones incapable of '*inventione*.'"[76] Adding further complications, as a counterfeiting technique the *spolvero* method confused the evidence of sole authorship, frustrating efforts to isolate and identify the hand of the master. Even a signed painting took on different and obscure meanings, not necessarily signifying that the work had been completed by the artist alone. Indeed, it might mean precisely the opposite: Tintoretto, for instance, appears to have only signed works produced by his *bottega*. In such a case, the signature means only that the master "assumed responsibility" for the craftsmanship and quality of the art object.[77] Given the fact of multiple authorship and workshop production, Bruce Cole claims that the fresco was the "quintessential product of the collaborative system that is Renaissance art."[78] This practice somewhat abated the aura of the finished product compared with "the golden age of the fresco" when "inspiration and genius crackled as the artist stood facing the blank wall."[79] Pouncing greatly simplified the artistic endeavor by parsing it out into delimited tasks that could be completed by apprentices, but that simplification came at the cost of a certain "crackling" virtuosity. That is to say, the cartoon was a technical development that pressed the business of artistic creation away from the unparalleled male genius and toward a flexible, adaptive practice of shared labor parceled out among skilled workers. As such, when Shakespeare sets Nature to pricking, he disrupts the poem's initial efforts to establish the youth's face as the product of the artist's "own hand," thus elevating it as the singular invention of a divinely inspired artistry.

In this sense, the cartooned body upends the assumptions underwriting the anti-cosmetic impulse that dominates the octave, in which the speaker tries to ferret out the gap between the youth's superficial femininity and the pricked-out body it disguises. In the Renaissance workshop, there was not a clean, binary distinction between surface and interior: painting with a cartoon was a process of accumulation in which multiple layers of pigment, paper, plaster, oils, quicklime, and chalk interact in a blend of physical media. Hardly the decisive moment, pricking is merely one step in a durational process that would necessarily involve adjustments and modifications to accommodate any number of unforeseen circumstances, ranging from environmental factors to directives from meddling patrons or the cost of materials. Likening the creation of man to an apprentice's hand gouging out a sketch, then, disrupts the teleological thrust of sexual development as a process that culminates in distinctively male genitalia with the arrival of the prick. Indeed, if Nature is "pouncing" the youth, it is unclear that her "pricking" leads to an unambiguous genital configuration, an extrusion rather than an indentation. In fact, the pricked cartoon is fully consumed by the process of transfer: the sheet, placed on wet plaster and then repeatedly pierced, was torn to fragments as the dotted lines were impressed into the wet, receptive surface. Instead of manufacturing a definitive "something," pricking a drawing offers nothing more than an outline, an empty space awaiting the gradual accretion of layer upon layer of material. In this scenario, Nature's pricking is both additive and subtractive: this prick is a puncture wound, only a prelude to the slow building up of the image. Like the perforated cartoon or the pierced sampler, the youth's pricked body is not its definitive form, but only an intermediate figure, a figure of mediation. Here, Nature is no longer the face-painter of the first lines who traffics in deceptive adornments and gold-encrusted icons. Rather, under the skillful hand of Nature, surface itself begins to take on some depth, pressing the two-dimensional work of painting into the third dimension. In this creation story, the master-mistress—prick included—is surface all the way down, a creature of pure, layered exteriority.

If pricking was associated with the production of showpieces for public spaces, it was also a domestic affair undertaken in the aristocratic closet, where women of a certain rank would engage in the prick-work of embroidery. As opposed to the aesthetic heights and enduring grandeur of monumental art, such pricking generated delicate and homely ephemera like samplers, pillowcases, book covers, ruffs, habiliments, periwigs, spangled headgear, chin-cloths, hoods, and napkins. Where the art world was dominated by a swaggering machismo, the domain of fiber arts was firmly associated with femininity and women's labor. Indeed, as Ann Jones and Peter Stallybrass note, for upper-class households of early modern England, "to speak of 'work' in relation to a woman of high rank was to mean needlework."[80] As feminist critics have long argued, for the leisured class, stitchery was an exercise in the womanly virtues of docility, service, obedience, and self-governance.[81] For genteel women, the purpose of embroidery was detached from merely utilitarian value. Rather, such work was designed for the moral conditioning of young women, above all by serving as an antidote to indolence. *The Needles Excellency* (1630), John Taylor's popular book of embroidery patterns, praised stitchery as a "mortall enemy to idlenesse," a grave sin that could compromise not only a woman's feminine demureness and sexual purity, but also her whiteness.[82] Juan Luis Vives's conduct manual *The Instruction of a Christian Woman* denounces those "idel" Christian women whose otiose lifestyles liken them to the "women of Perse land, drowned in volupteis and pleasures, syttyng amonge the company of gelded men."[83] Needlework establishes the embroiderer not only as a woman of leisure, whose pastimes serve no practical purpose, but also as a dutiful Christian woman whose continence and discipline make a sharp contrast to the imagined lasciviousness and gender fluidity of "Perse land." In other words, the woman's prick or, as Taylor puts it, the only "Pike" appropriate for "Woman-kinde," is not only a signifier of class, but also a marker of racialized gender, an accoutrement of femininity that shores up the whiteness of the pricking woman.

Nevertheless, the prick of the needle could not neatly separate elite women from their racialized counterparts, the "geldings" given to lives of depravity, because the material culture of fiber arts affiliated luxury textiles with a troubling foreignness.[84] Levantine and Turkish trade in the 1560s and 1570s brought Byzantine and Chinese silks, Turkish carpets, Persian tapestries, and Indian calicoes to England.[85] Both the materials and the techniques needed to manufacture high-end fabrics were drawn from outside the borders of England and Christendom. Hakluyt, for instance, requested that Englishmen in Turkey and Constantinople bring back both herbs for dyeing as well as "native dyers of wool and silk."[86] Moreover, stitchery itself did not fall exclusively into the domain of women of leisure whose sewing amounted to a frivolous pastime. Early modern textiles required a massive outpouring of the dangerous and grueling labor of sewing, laundering, starching, spinning, spangling, feathering, pleating, pinning, gathering, brocading, and knitting. Such drudgery was assigned to lower-class women whose work fueled informal economies of unlicensed and unguilded labor. Regarding the starched ruff, that famous marker of elite status, Natasha Korda notes that the collar's "exquisite delicacy, pristine whiteness, and fragile shape distance the body of the wearer . . . from the messy world of manual work" while requiring an endless, ongoing process of labor that was outsourced to working women, especially migrant "alien" women.[87] Firmly separated from the aesthetic heights of fine art, textile manufacture was, above all, a matter of labor, both the invisible toil of working women and the inconsequential labor of genteel ladies. From this perspective, when the sestet casts Nature as a prick-wielding woman, it reimagines creation as craft, not art. Making gender is not just work, but *women's* work. Here, gendered embodiment is not the end product of a single act of divine creation but the product of a humble and homespun artisanship that can be undertaken by anyone who sets out to spangle, mend, or embellish. With this possibility in mind, the couplet does not necessarily reference a stable, anatomical reality to contrast with the manufactured face. Rather, pricking makes visible the obscured labor that goes into outfitting, shaping, and contouring the gendered body, which is not given fully formed from on high but handcrafted at home.

Moreover, given its reliance on copying and imitation, the fiber arts are fundamentally incompatible with the concepts of originality, single authorship, and divine inspiration. Just as a finished fresco required the work of many hands, the material culture of textile manufacture depended upon collaboration, timed workflows, task management, and knowledge sharing. The material culture of the fabric arts involved communal labor that ranged from the intimate circles formed by a high-class woman and her ladies in waiting to the all-female workshops of silk spinners.[88] Moreover, like fresco production, textile manufacture also depended upon design transfer, and in this setting too, the *spolvero* technique paid dividends. Embroidery manuals like Giovanni Antonio Tagliente's *Essempio di Recammi* (1527) and Alessandro Paganino's *Book of Needlework* (1527) detail how pouncing could be employed to imprint a pattern onto cloth by punching holes through the ready-made design with a pin.[89] Pouncing sheets drawn from loosely bound pattern books allowed amateur needleworkers to replicate intricate geometrical shapes like knots, interlaces, and arabesques. Printed collections of ornamented patterns began to be published in the 1520s, a host of little pocket-sized volumes aimed at an audience of female amateurs and craftsmen. These ready-made designs were not original masterpieces with identifiable creators. The patterns themselves were "ruthlessly pirated" and plagiarized from other embroidery manuals and print sources.[90] Given its affiliation with replication and ornamentation, needlework would appear to belong firmly to the realm of craft, not qualifying as a properly artistic endeavor requiring unique genius and unparalleled imagination. And yet, creative decision-making was part and parcel of hand-stitching as well. Many pattern books included blank pages for the amateur to sketch out her own designs. *The Needles Excellency* asserts that in stitchery, "here Practice and Invention may be free" and, in a memorable analogy, compares an embroidering maid bouncing between patterns and embellishing her needlepoint to a "Squirrell [who] jumps from tree to tree."[91] Pricking did not entail mindless, mechanical repetition, but spoke to a lively mind capable of improvisation. Instead, as Janet Byrne notes, the sixteenth-century owners of embroidery manuals "tore out pages, pasted or nailed them to workroom walls, fingered, folded, cut, scribbled on them, chalked and pricked them for transfer."[92] Turning the abstract pattern into a material object meant destroying, not respecting, the initial design. In order to breathe life into the sketch, it might be marked up, passed around the room, bent out of shape, punched full of holes, and cut into shreds. In other words, the patterns were not ideal forms that needed to be executed precisely as delivered. Instead, the designs offered a bare-bones template that could be fleshed out in whatever ways suited the craftswoman's fancy.

If pricking does indeed reference the textile arts, then the sestet does not amount to an unveiling that reveals the scandalous flesh tucked beneath layers of powder and lace. Instead, the "cutwork" of stitchery is of a piece with the youth's hueing and hewing. Unwrapping the youth yields only another layer of fabric, as a "doting" Nature stitches together the youth's body like a sampler or drop cloth. In this respect, the sonnet's revised creation of Adam accords with an argument advanced by Jeanne Vaccaro in her work on the trans aesthetics and fiber arts, that stitchery works against the model of surface and depth according to which a "natural" body awaits discovery beneath a manufactured exterior.[93] Here, the gendered body is fabric all the way down, a contrivance wrought through a distinctly feminized form of labor. In the place of the definitively male God the Creator who shapes man as His living image, this playfully amended version of Genesis offers us a feminine Nature the Needleworker, a decision with significant consequences for the gender dynamics at work in the poem. If, as anti-cosmetic polemics maintained, the *Deus artifex* personally crafted the human form as a unique masterpiece, then the body feels precious, even fragile, and tampering with its composition can only mar the Maker's design. Here, however, the prick-bearing body does not occupy the place of honor as the singular image of God the Creator, with bodily contours fixed for all time according to divine fiat. Instead, the master-mistress is merely a cambric cradled in Nature's lap, a derivative form copied out of a pattern book and then pricked out, one stitch at a time, by Nature's thrusting and penetrative needle. Out of the museum and into the home: Sonnet 20 wrests the gendered body from the rarefied world of art and places it firmly in the realm of craft, skilled labor, and the micro-political routines of domestic life that comprise *technē*. Treating the body as a kind of craft project restores it to our hands; the fleshy materiality of the body is no longer off-limits behind panes of glass but something to be fingered, looped, stretched, and ripped. The paradigm of pricking, then, renders gender into an open-ended process of slipped edges and dropped stitches, raveling and unraveling, working and reworking, copying and embellishing, pattern-making and improvising. That is to say, when gender is handmade, it is transitional. From this perspective, pricking does not offer an antidote to the artificially constructed face, nor does it stabilize the youth's gender. On the contrary, the pricked body is itself a pure fabrication, a technical creation that has been transitional and contingent from the moment of its inception.

Just like the rest of the youth's body, that prick is both real and manufactured. It cannot be clearly distinguished from other material signifiers of gender, like the false beards, codpieces, and handkerchiefs that Will Fisher situates as central elements of gendered identity in early modern culture.[94] Unlike the iconoclastic thrust of anti-cosmetic polemic, the sonnet's revision of Genesis refuses to naturalize the prick as a signifier of maleness that could be easily opposed to the fabricated face. For this reason, affirming or refuting homosexual overtones in the sonnets through prick-centric arguments projects a degree of stability and legibility onto the gendered body that the poem itself consistently rejects. Like the Adam hermaphrodite, the master-mistress passes through various states of gendered embodiment that engage with sexuality in complex ways. First fashioned as a woman and for a woman, the youth is both the product and the instrument of lesbian desire, since, as Valerie Traub notes, Nature has "homoerotically fallen in love with her female creation."[95] As Simone Chess argues, the varieties of pleasure experienced and inspired by the youth can encompass not only homoerotic and Sapphic desires, but also "queer-gender attraction" since the poem "eroticizes and admires male effeminacy and androgyny."[96] I want to extend this line of argumentation into the space cleared by trans studies, which has firmly detached gendered significance from any given body part. So too for Sonnet 20—whatever this "something" is that Nature plucked out of the youth's body, the speaker is perfectly happy to acknowledge it a "nothing" or vulva. The poem suggests that the addition of a prick expands the menu of erotic possibilities available to the youth's lovers, but it does not necessarily channel that desire into a cisnormative frame. Moreover, as the final couplet notes, the prick was put in place "for women's pleasure," a phrase that we might read in both the subjective and objective sense of the genitive: the prick not only gives pleasure to women, it also offers its host-body the kind of pleasure that is experienced by women. In this respect, the poem leaves open the possibility that the master-mistress remains the woman she was first created quite in spite of her genital configuration. Already outfitted with a woman's face and woman's heart, by the end of the poem the youth also has a woman's prick.

And so, if the poem begins with an entrenched suspicion of artificial bodies, it ends with an embrace of technicity as an essential feature of creation in the first instance. Indeed, the Nature that fashioned the master-mistress exists at a remove from God already, since she is herself a personification of the created world. As Jane Bennett argues, this kind of anthropomorphism often indicates a recognition of "the material agency of nonhuman or not-quite-human things" and therefore works against the anthropocentrism that is "too often bound up with fantasies of a human uniqueness in the eyes of God."[97] The created world creating the human: this scene fleshes out the "double plasticity" that Stiegler attributes to technicity, or what Mark Hansen calls "the quasi-autonomy of the technical . . . the transductive coupling of the living and technics."[98] Prick or no prick, the created body is prosthetic from inception; there is no unadulterated body upon which transformations are externally, artificially enacted. The production of the gendered body is not something that happens in an instant, aligning its contours with a divine schematic that holds for all time. On the contrary, Shakespeare's twist on Genesis confounds the dictum in Jeremiah so often trotted out in support of transphobic policy, in which God proclaims "Before I formed thee in the wombe, I knewe thee, and before thou camest out of the wombe, I sanctified thee."[99] Rather than representing gender as fixed from birth, or conception, or the hazy pre-conception state alluded to in Jeremiah, creation is an act of technical fabrication or, to be more precise, an ongoing process of technical interventions and modifications. In other words, when Shakespeare sets Nature to pricking, he envisions creation as a form of technogenesis.

In this respect, Sonnet 20 anticipates work in trans studies that seeks to defang the charge of artificiality by reclaiming prosthesis, like Susan Stryker's "Words to Victor Frankenstein" or other developments in trans studies flowing from the posthuman turn. We might think of Rosi Braidotti, who splices trans identity with Donna Haraway's cyborg; or the work of micha cárdenas, who binds transgender subjectivity with the extended bodies of a digital and mediated world; or the affirmative biopolitics of Paul Preciado's *Testo Junkie*, which unspools the natural body in a world of transbiologicals.[100] While this subset of work solicits connections between trans bodies and new, edgy, digital forms of life, scholarship by Mel Chen, Eva Hayward, and Jeanne Vaccaro seizes upon transgender experience in its affinities with animal life, ecological systems, and fabricated materials.[101] According to these critical positions, far from removing trans subjects from the natural world, the prosthetic techniques that generate and regenerate trans bodies gesture toward another creation, a queer futurity in which, as Spinoza asserts in his *Ethics*, we do not know yet what a body can do.[102]

There may be something a touch too schematic about how this argument aligns Shakespeare with trans studies and posthumanism only to pit them against contemporary and early modern forms of technophobia. To draw too sharp a distinction between Shakespeare's technophilia and theology means ignoring how Sonnet 20 thinks with religion. A more nuanced account of the sonnets' flirtation with technogenesis requires bringing together trans studies and theology in the space cleared by Shakespeare's version of Genesis. By imagining gendered embodiment as a process, an unfolding emergence over time, Sonnet 20 explicitly bears on the human in its capacity as creature, a figure glossed by Julia Lupton as "a made or fashioned thing, given its existential urgency by the sense of continued or potential process, action or emergence in relation to a sublime maker."[103] The creature is a technical object, made or fashioned but also capable of self-fashioning. For this reason, Lupton affiliates creatureliness with the discourse of virtue, tracking the conditions that allow the potentials or latencies harbored within a creature to flower, and also with the Arendtian concept of natality, "the possibility of beginning something anew," the "sense of initiative" or "element of action" that is "inherent in all human activities."[104] Poised just on the other side of the procreation sonnets, which promote such a narrow account of how exactly "from fairest creatures we desire increase," the master-mistress offers a more expansive vision of what natality might encompass: not only the production of children, but other forms of rebirth, self-disclosure, and transition (1.1). From the vantage opened by Sonnet 20, then, the pope's view of creation appears as it really is: constricted and immobile, robbed of its vibrancy and vitality. Far from ushering in an "age of sin against God the Creator," trans people embrace the contingency and possibility that has always been embedded in the story of creation.[105] By celebrating the gendered body precisely insofar as it is a technical production, Shakespeare complicates the anthropocentric move that elevates man to the image of God, which is so often presented as a timeless and universal truth, not by dismissing religion as ideology but rather by fixing our attention on the entangled, chaotic, lively world in which human life is incubated. In the giddy, giggly pleasures of Sonnet 20, Shakespeare invokes a different creation, one governed by an infatuated Nature who crafts a world teeming with animate life in which all bodies are artificial and all genders are prosthetic.

[ CHAPTER TWO ]

# Abortive Hedgehogs

## Prodigies and Trans Animality in *The Duchess of Malfi*

In the online cesspools where anti-trans sentiment steeps, it is a commonplace that a "man identifying as a woman" is a case as absurd and delusional as someone identifying as a wolf or a badger. Loath as I am to enter those briny waters, an excerpt from Sheila Jeffrey's screed *Gender Hurts* will have to serve as a representative sample:

> The claims of transgender activists to "rights" for their gender identities are in imminent danger of being discredited by a proliferation of rather more unusual identity politics online, which are presently trying to build movements and rights-based political campaigns, [as in the] online communities of persons who consider themselves to have identities of other races, knowns as transethnics, or to be half human and half animal, therians, or fictional characters, fictives, or nonhuman, otherkin . . . Online social activists who have accepted that persons should have human rights based on their "identities," rather than on the basis that they are members of oppressed groups, can have difficulty knowing where to draw the line. The politics of these more unusual identities are based on transgenderism, but there is considerably more scepticism online about how much respect should be paid to them. Claims by men that they are really women meet with a more sympathetic response than claims by a white woman that she has always been a Korean cat.[1]

In the mind of the transphobe, everything depends upon the psychic mechanism of identification. The "truth" of transition—to the extent they will grant it any kind of truth—exists only in the fuzzy, unverifiable interior world of affect, in contrast to the apparently self-evident social and biological realities that separate men from women on the basis of bodily habitus, genitalia, chromosomes, or (what is most recently heralded as the undeniable marker of sex) the relative size and mobility of gametes. The conceptual move at work involves stripping trans experience of all context, divorcing it from the communities in which it takes shape, erasing the histories that fashioned it, dismissing the modes of oppression it encounters, and ignoring the medical and legal discourses that produced it. This accomplished, the trans-exclusionary feminist can point to "gender identity" as a category precisely analogous to any number of other identity formations, including what C. Ray Borck exhaustedly names the "sociologically nonexistent thing called *transrace*" or the online fantasy of animal identification.[2] Unlike the white woman who claims to be a Korean cat,[3] who is to be mocked and perhaps pitied, the trans woman's gender identity masks a monstrosity of the criminal sort, an interior world which allegedly incubates any number of perversities, fetishes, and predatory impulses. As it emerges in the tedious manifestos of the "gender critical," then, transness is doubly animalistic: first, in its psychotic parallel to cross-species identification, and secondly, in the bestial impulses it disguises. In this vein, Jeffreys and her ilk imagine a world terrorized by trans monsters who seduce impressionable teen girls and harvest their organs, or who violate women's spaces to commit sex crimes. Speaking in the House of Commons, Jeffreys announced that trans women "parasitically occupy the bodies of the oppressed."[4] This particular analogy, profoundly troubling to anyone familiar with the histories of fascism, resolves into a third mode of trans-animal commonality: their mutual exclusion from the category of the human.

Little wonder, then, that trans people have a complicated relationship to the category of monstrosity. From Susan Stryker's manifesto "My Words to Victor Frankenstein" to Hil Malatino's coalition of trans monsters, scholars working in trans studies have wrestled with, rejected, and reclaimed the charge of monstrosity that is so frequently levied at our bodies, denigrated as artificial, prosthetic, defective, mutilated, or inhuman.[5] This chapter adds to this line of work by unspooling the long histories of a fantastical figure haunting the fever dreams of transphobic activists: the animalistic trans predator. This reading comes by way of an analysis of a figure that Foucault situates as the precursor to the modern "monster" of criminology and abnormal psychology: the prodigy, a portentous body that blurred boundaries between male and female or affixed animal limbs to human trunks. Unlike the psychological animality that characterizes the criminal monster, whose beastly desires lurk in a shadowy inner world of identificatory fantasies, the transspecies nature of the early modern prodigy was resolutely material, embodied, and literal. Not a matter best suited to the secular investigations and treatment plans cooked up by the soft sciences, the prodigy was the object of religious inquiry, a being whose curious shape flowed from the infinitely transformative capacities of creaturely life. This chapter tracks the movement from the theological prodigy to the abnormal monster in John Webster's *The Duchess of Malfi* (1612), a play swarming with fattened blackbirds and irregular crabs, horse-leeches and tithe-pigs, tame elephants and the boneless lampreys that wriggle in a man's mouth. In binding gender to animality, Webster's revenge tragedy is a study in what Mel Chen calls animacy, the vital energies that inhere in nonhuman figures that form the setting and support system for human life.[6] It is the gambit of this chapter that the animal intimacies of *The Duchess of Malfi* rehabilitate the prodigy's extraordinary (albeit threatening) generativity to reconfigure the weave of relations between trans embodiment, sociality, and the category of the human.

Foucault dedicated his lectures from 1974–1975 to the subject of abnormality, a domain that "stitches together the judicial and the medical" within a system of power and knowledge that produces, arranges, and categorizes behaviors according to a typology of deviance.[7] The elaboration of the abnormal individual, replete with sexual pathologies and antisocial proclivities, occurred in the nineteenth century at the conjunction of the fields of criminology and psychiatry. The ancestral form of the abnormal subject, in Foucault's accounting, is the prodigy or monster, a figure originating in Roman law and relevant through the eighteenth century, when it is gradually replaced by the motiveless cruelty and instinctual perversion of the deviant. This vestigial figure is

> essentially a mixture. It is the mixture of two realms, the animal and the human: the man with the head of an ox, the man with a bird's feet—monsters. It is the blending, the mixture of two species: the pig with a sheep's head is a monster. It is the mixture of two sexes: the person who is both male and female is a monster. It is a mixture of life and death: the fetus born with a morphology that means it will not be able to live but that nonetheless survives for some minutes or days is a monster. Finally, it is a mixture of form: the person who has neither arms nor legs, like a snake, is a monster. Consequently, the monster is the transgression of natural limits, the transgression of classifications, of the table, and of the law as table: this is actually what is involved in monstrosity.[8]

The corporeal variations classified under the rubric of monstrosity include transspecies creatures cobbled together from human and animal parts, ambiguously gendered hermaphrodites, and disabled bodies.[9] Such creatures, Foucault asserts, posed what was essentially a juridical problem rather than an ethical or spiritual one. As a "disorder of nature," the monster was a "legal labyrinth" that generated endless controversy about, for instance, whether a hermaphrodite might marry, and if so, the suitable gender of their spouse. In the eighteenth century, however, the monster's physiological difference undergoes a conceptual shift, registering no longer as "juridico-natural but juridico-moral." The animal retreats inward, becoming nothing other than "a certain morbid dynamic of the instincts." The figures at the center of this conceptual transition from "the monster to the abnormal" were the hermaphrodite and the conjoined twin. The medical, legal, criminological, and psychiatric discourses around the bodies and psyches of these creatures transposed "the old category of the monster from the domain of somatic and natural disorder" to the "domain of monstrous criminality," a "monstrosity that does not produce effects in nature and the confusion of species, but in behavior" or "character." No longer a classificatory problem for lawyers, the prodigy gives way to the "moral monster": the child-killer, the cannibal, and the perpetrator of incest.[10]

While Foucault insists that, prior to the eighteenth century, prodigies were understood through the lens of jurisprudence, in fact the discourse of monstrosity was, above all, a matter for theological interpretation. As its etymology indicates, the *prodigy* or *monster* was the bearer of a message from God; such portentous bodies were understood to herald death and social dissolution, pointing to the sinful nature of the communities that incubated them. Even in works that more or less haphazardly applied the models of natural philosophy to explaining the appearance of, for instance, a piglet with eight legs, a dog's head, and ambiguous genitalia, such prodigious phenomena were assigned a religious significance.[11] Although there is little scriptural warrant for monsters, Christian theologians from the patristics onward detected the voice of a disapproving God in prodigies. Ambroise Paré, barber-surgeon to Charles IX and Henri III, opens his teratological treatise by formulaically announcing that "such creatures proceed from the judgment of God" to "warn us of the misfortunes with which we are threatened [or] of some great disorder."[12] These twisted and hybrid bodies were interpreted as somewhat vague signs of divine disapprobation, announcing God's judgment upon the sins of a community that was in imminent danger of catastrophic punishment.[13] As such, the literature of prodigies was saturated with apocalyptic imagery. Collections of such mirabilia amplified the ominous tone struck by these apparitions by cycling through scriptural passages warning of the end times. Popular verses were drawn from Book of Daniel and especially the apocryphal Book of Ezra, which invoked an era of crisis in which "Blood shal drip out of the wood, and the stone shal giue his voice . . . and the fyre shal oft breake forthe, & the wilde beasts shal change their places, and menstruous women shal beare monstres."[14] Sixteenth- and seventeenth-century publics had a ravening appetite for stories of such curiosities, tales of which were collected in volumes including Jacob Rueff's *The Expert Midwife* (1554, English trans. 1637), Lykosthenes's *The Doome Warning All Men to Iudgement* (1557, English trans. 1581), Pierre Boaistuau's *Certaine Secrete Wonders of Nature* (1560, English trans. 1569), and Ambroise Paré's *Des monstres et prodigies* (1573, English trans. 1634).[15] Although the majority of prodigy writing was generated on the Continent, its wild popularity ensured that the literature circulated rapidly to England. Pierre Boaistuau, whose *Histoires tragiques* included the novella that Shakespeare would adapt into *Romeo and Juliet*, presented a lushly illuminated manuscript copy of his *Histoires prodigieuses* to Queen Elizabeth as a gift upon her accession in 1559, a year before it appeared in print.[16] In addition to appearing in scholarly treatises, prodigious mirabilia appeared in a kaleidoscopic variety of print media: gender-variant prodigies graced the pages of sermons, broadsheets, wonder books (*Wunderzeichenbücher*), black-letter ballads, chronicles, publicly posted drawings, private correspondence, diaries, polemical pamphlets, and the quasi-tabloid *canards*.[17]

The origins of the prodigy can be traced back to the Roman Republic, in which *prodigia* signaled a rupture in the *pax deorum* (the peace of the gods) requiring swift rectification through a collective, public performance of ritual atonement.[18] Clustered together under the rubric of prodigy were such diverse incidents as lightning strikes on sacred ground; sweating statues; speaking animals or the incursion of wild beasts into the city of Rome; rainfalls of blood, stone, or milk; and irregular births, particularly the birth of hermaphrodites.[19] Such portentous occurrences demanded a form of expiation, generally the lustration of the city walls, as well as the expulsion of the anomalous body from the community. In the case of hermaphrodites, this expulsion normally took the shape of death by exposure; the infant was locked in a chest and put out to sea.[20] Medieval and early modern writers added to the list of prodigious occurrences, displaying a strong preference for human-animal hybrids and hermaphrodites, which were normally depicted as conjoined twins affixed together at the back, sides, or groin and sporting various combinations of "natures" or genitals.[21] Such gender ambiguity was not restricted to purely human prodigies, however. Renaissance wonder books gleefully describe colts with human faces, men with the heads of parrots, and cows giving birth to "half-men" in bestial transformations that frequently terminate in anomalous genital configurations.[22] Some prodigy narratives associate animality and gender indeterminacy by way of analogy. The *Relación verdadera y caso prodigioso y raro* (1688), for instance, detects something animalistic in the shape of "a creature born both boy and girl, with two natures: that of the girl in its customary location, and that of the boy in the middle of the forehead," noting that the child reminded the author of nothing quite so much as "a sow who brought forth two piglets stuck together on the backs," and "when the lower one walked, the other moved its little feet in the air."[23] Other accounts insist on the literality of the trans-animal body, as in the case of the infamous "monster of Ravenna" (born 1512), allegedly the offspring of a nun impregnated by a friar, a creature that sported wings, a horn, and claws while also "participating in the natures of both male and female."[24] When the creature was brought to the attention of Pope Julius II, His Holiness condemned the prodigious child to death in the old Roman fashion, ordering the infant tossed in the sea.

The obscure gender of the prodigy pressed the creature across divisions not only of species but also of religion and race. Take, for instance, Martin Luther and Philipp Melanchthon's polemical pamphlet *Of Two Woonderful Popish Monsters* (1523), a widely disseminated tract that denounced papal corruption through an allegorical dissection of a "Popish Asse" allegedly dredged out of the Tiber river.[25] Like its companion the "Monk-Calf," the Pope-Ass was compiled from a complicated collection of limbs drawn from human and animal sources: a donkey's head sprouted from a human trunk laced with fish scales and appended with a griffin's leg, an elephant's foot, and a tail that partially obscured "the head of [an] olde man issuing out of his buttockes." In the heavy-handed explication of the theo-political significance of each limb, some question arises concerning the creature's gender. Although the pamphlet specifies that the subject is "the heade of this Asse, ioyned with a *mannes* bodye" and refers to the monster with masculine pronouns, the most jarring visual element of the accompanying woodcut, supplied by Lucas Cranach the Elder, is the creature's prominent breasts and swollen abdomen, as if the Pope-Ass were heavy with child. Luther and Melanchthon draw attention to the lewdness of "this Popish Asse who sheweth before all mens eyes openly, and without any shame his belly of a woeman, naked and bare." The gender deviance of this convenient allegorical prop binds Catholic excess to both animality as well as a disturbing foreignness: "vncouer[ing] fullye the feminine bellye of the Popishe Asse" likens the "execrable fithynesse" of the "greate manye prophane people amonge the Christians" to the uncleanliness and sin of "the Panyms and Turkes."[26] It is the curious gender of the donkey-pope, "*his* belly of a woeman," that feeds most directly into a network of affiliation with those other beings noted for their excess, lasciviousness, and effeminacy, the "paynims" and Turks who served a prodigy-adjacent function in Luther's writings, where they were designated as signs of God's displeasure with the Christian nations of Europe.[27] In associating prodigiousness with religious difference, Luther and Melanchthon were not unique. Prodigy collections threaded together their tales of androgynous and semi-animal "misbirths" with vicious speculative accounts of the corporeal strangeness of non-Christian bodies. Boaistuau's volume of the *Histoires prodigieuses*, for instance, tucks a chapter on Jews right between sections on "Flouds and wonderfull Inundations of Waters" and "a man [who] washed his face and handes in scalding Leade."[28]

The prodigy's somatic variation blurred together confessional divisions and racial difference, as in a story that circulated through multiple wonder books about how Hippocrates "saued a princesse accused of adulterie, for that she was deliuered of a childe blacke lyke an *Ethiopian*, hir husbande being of a faire and white complexion, which by the persuasion of *Hippocrates*, was absolued and pardoned, for that the child was like vnto a [portrait of a] *Moore*, accustomably tied at hir bed."[29] Both Boaistuau's and Paré's renditions of this story are illustrated with woodcuts that pair the black child with another monster created through "the ardent and obstinate imagination [of the] mother": a "maide, rough and couered with haire like a beare," which resulted from her pregnant mother "hauing too much regarde" to a picture of John the Baptist.[30] When the mother imprinted upon the picture of the John the Baptist cloaked in his camel-hair shirt, she shaped her fetal daughter in his image. Such creaturely transformations have a Biblical warrant in a scene from Genesis that overlays human sexuality onto animal generation. Paré suggests that these physical variations subsequent to the mother's encounter with visual stimuli are

> even verified by the authority of Moses (Chap. 30 [of Genesis]) when he shows how Jacob deceived his father-in-law Laban and enriched himself with his livestock by having rods barked and putting them in the watering trough, so that when the goats and ewes looked at these rods of various colors, they might form their young spotted in various colors: because the imagination has so much power over seed and reproduction that the stripe and character of them remain on the thing bred.[31]

The prodigies that result from visual impressions cross the divisions of gender, race, and species. The furry woman is masculine, in that her form echoes the hyper-butch ascetic John the Baptist, while her bearlike pelt of body hair renders her animalistic, of a kind with the other bestial hybrids catalogued in the wonder book, like the child with the face of a frog or the monster with the face of a man and the body of a goat. In blurring together the two cases under consideration, the woodcut's visual arrangement of bodies also calls into question the hirsute woman's whiteness, not only because the amount and distribution of body hair varies according to ethnicity, but also because of her proximity to the black child, who reaches out to hold her leg and looks up at her as though she were his mother.[32] Created a monster by her mother's impressionable gaze, she becomes potentially a progenitor of prodigies herself.

Although popular print culture often framed prodigies as signals of providential displeasure with political or social affairs, the problem with such bodies was not that they were unnatural. Indeed, from the perspective of an emerging natural philosophy, such creatures gestured toward the "inexhaustibly fecund and varied" capacities of the natural world.[33] As such, discourses of monstrosity positioned prodigies in a complex relationship to reproduction. On one side, these hybrid and hermaphroditic forms arise from an unmanageable, excessive generative force that refuses to remain within appointed bounds, as Livy put it when framed prodigious bodies as the byproducts of "nature wandering into procreative areas that belong to another."[34] At the same time, prodigies were also affiliated with sterility, stillbirth, and miscarriage, as Isidore of Seville claims in his *Etymologies* when he asserts that portentous monsters "do not live long—they die as soon as they are born."[35] These linkages are apparent in, for instance, a Jacobean pamphlet centered on the delivery of monstrous triplets in Flanders.[36] According to this "True Relation," the children were born misshapen, with the flesh of the girls molded into ruffs and petticoats. The boy emerged from the womb with a death's head on his hand and lived just long enough to exclaim that "Dearth and Plague should couer the whole World, and that they were sent to giue notice of it to all men" before "speech and life left him together." In one sense, the offspring are prodigious on account of their inviability. Dying almost as soon as they are delivered, the newborns are incapable of advancing the reproductive futurity of a family name. At the same time, the monstrous children are the product of an overabundance of generativity. In place of a single child, triplets emerge in too-fleshy bodies already capable of speech, as though the growth process had been disastrously accelerated. The fecundity they embody, however, is affiliated with death, epidemic, and famine. In other words, as Julie Crawford argues, a monstrous delivery of this sort was "simultaneously a birth and a death" that pointed to "a crisis's regenerative possibilities."[37] The pamphlet proposes a name for this unbridled vitality that merges with morbidity when it describes the children as "abortive," a term that, as it happens, is also central to the reproductive anxieties, transspecies transformations, and monstrous bestiary of *The Duchess of Malfi*.

We could do worse than diagnose the courtly environs of *The Duchess of Malfi* with an excess of wandering procreative impulses or a crisis of regenerative possibilities. After all, it is a play populated by any number of "political monsters," as Antonio puts it, ranging from the leeches and parasites cluttering up the court to a homicidal brother who succumbs to the melancholic affliction of lycanthropy, a wolf-man who moans to his doctor that he feels "hairy . . . on the inside."[38] The root cause of the transspecies monstrosities is diagnosed in the very first scene by Bosola, an assassin whose "corruption grew out of horse dung" (1.1.279–80). A frustrated scholar who turned to murder-for-hire when precarity forced him out of academia, Bosola serves as the play's resident theorist of transspecies intimacy. Having fallen prey to the machinations of Ferdinand and the Cardinal, Bosola complains bitterly that:

> [The Cardinal] and his brother are lie plum trees that grow crooked over standing pools; they are rich and o'erladen, stagnant with fruit, but none but crows, pies, and caterpillars feed on them. Could I be one of their flattering panders, I would hang on their ears like a horse-leech till I were full, and then drop off . . . There are rewards for hawks and dogs, when they have done us service; but for a soldier that hazards his limbs in battle, nothing but a kind of geometry is his last supportation. (1.1.48–60)

In this emblematic schema, the aquaculture of the court is not a wellspring of healthy flows, the fountain spraying "pure silver drops" that Antonio has just attributed to the well-managed French court he has recently visited.[39] Rather, the brothers preside over a standing pool, a closed system efflorescing into a grotesque ecology. Here, the lords are not cedars—the customary princely symbol of fixity and strength—but plum trees heavy with overripe fruit. Bosola unfurls a vision of vegetal life in which generation bleeds into decay, a stagnant fruiting that spawns clouds of insects and scavengers whose feeding is synonymous with decomposition. The only creatures able to thrive in such an environment are flatterers, legacy hunters, and dinner-chasers, a collection of parasitical courtiers who fatten themselves upon their noble masters. Participating in this abject ecosystem of influence renders human subjects animalistic, even vermicular monstrosities.

The initial elements of Bosola's rant cleaves to customary tropes that decry courtly corruption by likening flatterers to a host of insects and scavenging birds, including moths, drones, parasites, caterpillars, vultures, and worms. The second half of the complaint, however, dissects Bosola's animalization in language that moves beyond analogy. In order to be suited for the Cardinal's instrumental ends, Bosola has undergone a regime of taming and training that mirrors that experienced by creatures whose natural abilities in tracking, chasing, and killing were harnessed for human enrichment. Bosola was not born a killer. Years before, the Cardinal unearthed surprising capacities or "base qualities" in the reclusive scholar that suited him to the work of a spy and assassin (3.2.313). As soon as Bosola returns to court, the Cardinal continues the process of breaking Bosola in a way that sharpens his animalistic and instinctual qualities. The rhythms of preferment, reward, and distancing accustom Bosola to being handled and used, much in the way that a raptor must be "manned" to stand human touch. Bosola notes the parallels between his own treatment and falconry when he presents himself to Ferdinand saying, "I was lured to you" (1.1.224). In order to survive in the cruel environs of the court, Bosola must mortgage some of his humanity, becoming one of the "political monsters" that both he and Antonio decry (1.1.156). Complicating matters further, animal training was not a straightforwardly disciplinary or punitive activity. Edward Berry notes in his study of early modern husbandry that training animals to hunt requires not only correction but positive reinforcement, like the hart's neck that would be thrown to the hounds immediately after the kill to sharpen their desire to pursue game.[40] As Julia Lupton and Karen Raber have argued, taming subordinates an animal to the instrumental uses of a human agent, but it also creates a relationship of affection, communication, and support between hunter and hound.[41] For this reason, a touch of jealousy creeps into Bosola's invective when it lands on the special care tendered to the animals that populated aristocratic households. The lavish attention and commodious lodging enjoyed by a nobleman's hounds contrasts sharply with the abandonment experienced by "soldiers" like Bosola who stake their bodies and lives for their masters' benefit.

The complaint voiced by Bosola, then, does not center on his decline into animality, but on the shattered bonds of mutuality between himself and his handlers. Ferdinand and the Cardinal demand service while offering no guarantee of "supportation" beyond crutches that mark the "geometry" of debility.[42] Tallying the physiological costs of incarceration, poverty, and military service, Bosola notes how his position presses him toward social marginalization and disability. As such, quasi-animal Bosola's prodigious status exists on a spectrum with Paré's "man with no arms" who was nevertheless "strong and robust," able to perform "almost all the actions that another might do with his hands," such as "strike a hatchet against a piece of wood" right up to the point that he was convicted of petty crime and broken on the wheel.[43] Bosola has feelingly learned how little he matters, and he presents a precise reckoning to the Cardinal: "I fell into the galleys in your service, where, for two years together, I wore two towels instead of a shirt, with a knot on the shoulder, after the fashion of a Roman mantle" (1.1.34–36). In his itinerant maritime prison, Bosola exists in a state of extreme exposure, drifting to the margins of personhood. In the camp-like space of the galleys, Bosola is thrust into a state of social death in which he is exempted from the protections of the law but remains fully subject to its lethal disciplinary force.[44] Bosola's vicious misanthropy is the end effect of his own downward mobility, a precipitous descent that has pressed him to the very edges of the category of the human. Thus, the "hazards" endured by creatures like Bosola, driven by poverty into the service of abusive lords, insert them into uncomfortable relations of proximity, affinity, and competition with animal forms of life.

Small surprise, then, that Bosola understands so intuitively the linkages between animality and gender, a pairing that emerges when he embarks upon an ugly polemic against cosmetics, what he calls the "scurvy face-physic" that renders women's bodies monstrous (2.1.22). Beginning with misogynistic commonplaces, the outburst branches into strange reveries on the animal and excremental components of a woman's face:

> One would suspect [your closet] for a shop of witchcraft, to find in it the fat of serpents, spawn of snakes, Jews' spittle, and their young children's ordure—and all these for the face. I would sooner eat a dead pigeon, taken from the soles of the feet of one sick of the plague, than kiss one of you fasting. Here are two of you, whose sin of your youth is the very patrimony of the physician, makes him renew his foot-cloth with the spring and change his high-prized courtesan with the fall of the leaf. (2.1.35–43)

Scratch a woman's face and find an animal, or maybe a corpse. Gender norms of the period demanded that a woman's complexion meld the lily and the rose in a face featuring ruby lips, ivory teeth, and blue veins. Calibrating the body with such shifting, even contradictory feminine ideals required skin care regimens that drew on a kaleidoscopic variety of inhuman substances. Cosmetic practices of the period were rich in animal byproducts, including a range of greases, oils, and resins as well as less savory substances. The husbandry manuals of Hannah Woolley, Konrad Gesner, Girolamo Ruscelli, and others recommend that women stock their closets with mummy, hens and pigeons, egg whites, deer marrow, salamander blood, ox gall, ambergris, lead, mercury, civet, and urine.[45] Powdering, perfuming, and dyeing spread a thin membrane of inhuman matter over the human face. A material network binds the heightened femininity of the painted body to a teeming, howling bevy of animalia. For Bosola, this slimy paste evokes other creaturely couplings, like the carrion pressed against feet riddled with open, oozing plague sores; or the seedy exchanges threading together quack physicians, syphilitic patients, prostitutes, and the finely woven trappings discreetly covering the business end of the doctor's horse. In this sense, the animal excretions smeared on the prettified face weave a woman's body into a patchwork of affiliations with other forms of life excluded from personhood and full participation in the category of the human: the infant, as yet unable to control its bowels; the vermin, parasites, and sex workers marked as vectors of contagion and venereal disease; and Jews, whose spitting on Jesus marked the moment of their expulsion from the body of Christ.[46] This willful repudiation of Christianity, in turn, was understood to eject Jews—and Jewish men in particular—from both normative gender and the category of the human, as witnessed in the circulation of fantasies that Jewish men menstruated as a penalty for their alleged guilt in the death of Christ. The vicious anti-Semitism of the medieval and early modern Christian imaginary subsequently aligned Jewish gender variance with sexual indeterminacy of the hyena.[47] The inclusion of "Jew's spittle" thus links the gendered transformations and animal intimacies of the feminized face to the emergent logic of white supremacy that would be expressed in blood purity laws.[48] The technical interventions that bring the body into alignment with the norms of femininity thus blur boundaries between life and death, human and animal, adult and child, Christian and non-Christian, national and foreign.

As such, for Bosola, traversing the human-animal divide renders the possessor of a painted face into a particular kind of monster. This rendering becomes explicit when he invokes a French woman who, after a bout of smallpox, "flayed the skin off her face to make it more level," quipping that "whereas before she looked like a nutmeg-grater, after she resembled an abortive hedgehog" (2.1.26–29). The treatment in question was punishing, as it would have entailed rubbing her pockmarked complexion with a caustic substance like mercury sublimate.[49] Although this peculiar face is framed as a parable spun out to scold painted women, the story it tells is more nuanced. As the saying goes, a chance to cut is a chance to cure: perhaps she wants to smooth over social encounters that, since illness ravaged her complexion, have tended to veer into uncomfortable terrain; or perhaps she feels that her face has become uninhabitable, an ongoing source of grievance and alienation. For Bosola, self-flaying assimilates the woman not to a state of general animality; rather, she becomes a prodigy, like the Flemish triplets whose flesh was molded into elaborate finery. "Abortives" referred to monstrous births, as in *King John*, when Cardinal Pandulph imagines an ecosystem perturbed by "meteors, prodigies and signs, / Abortives, presages and tongues of heaven."[50] From Bosola's poisoned perspective, the transformations wrought by surgical or cosmetic intervention register as miscarriage, abortion, or premature delivery. Birth and death coincide in the peeled face, just as in the anomalous and "obortiue" triplets of the

Flemish "True Relation." The flayed face is animal, but also fetal. A kind of living morbidity, it hovers in a gestational limbo. The capacity of human artifice to remake the body itself sets off a crisis of "regenerative possibilities" wandering out of compass to the extent that they compromise the category of the human itself.[51]

What separates Bosola's screed from the tiresome mass of anti-cosmetic polemics is that he understands prodigious life as an inescapable element of the human condition, a reframing that emerges in his rant as the momentum of his own revulsion lifts him out of prose and into poetry:

> What thing is in this outward form of man
> To be beloved? We account it ominous
> If nature do produce a colt, or lamb,
> A fawn, or goat, in any limb resembling
> A man; and fly from't as a prodigy.
> Man stands amazed to see his deformity
> In any other creature but himself.
> But in our own flesh, though we bear diseases
> Which have their true names only ta'en from beasts,
> As the most ulcerous wolf, and swinish measle;
> Though we are eaten up of lice and worms,
> And though continually we bear about us
> A rotten and dead body, we delight
> To hide it in rich tissue. All our fear,
> Nay, all our terror, is lest our physician
> Should put us in the ground, to be made sweet. (2.1.41–56)

If Bosola initially recoils from the midwife's attempts to hide the "deep ruts and foul sloughs" of her face through cosmetics, here he confesses to an almost nauseating reaction to the unadulterated face, finding in it nothing "to be beloved" (2.1.25). Unlike Hamlet, who neatly distinguishes between the natural and, by extension, shapely body created by God and the deceptive mask produced by painting when he spits at Ophelia that "God hath given you one face, and you make yourselves another," when Bosola peels back the paste he confronts not only a monster, but a prodigy (3.1.142–43). Peeking into the closet launches him into a world in which the edges of "man" are not only soft and penetrable, but a fertile breeding ground for bacterial, viral, and insectile forms of life. These diseases possess their own vital energies that remap the human body into animal shapes, like the "ulcerous wolf" of lupus sores and the "swinish" rashes of measles. If our tissues are indeed "rotten," in that they host lice and worms, Bosola misspeaks when he ventures that the body that "we continually bear about us" is "dead." Rather, as his own examples prove, human flesh is too much alive, a vibrant matter intimately entwined with nonhuman actants that will ultimately consume the body, returning us to the complex soil systems from which we were fashioned when we are interred in the ground "to be made sweet."[52] The "wandering procreation" that Livy associated with prodigious life is on full display here, as the normative ideals governing reproduction, kinship, and the separation of kinds are thrown into confusion. In a sharp pivot from his condemnation of the painted face, caked with animal matter, here the thin layer of "rich tissue" mercifully separates us from knowledge of our own monstrous animality. This lively morbidity feeds normative bodies into a network of relationality with prodigies, from the abortive hedgehog at her mirror and the political monsters populating the court to Paré's hermaphroditic colt-men. In its refusal to remain bound in fixed categories, either those traced by gender or the human and nonhuman divide, Bosola's continually decaying, perpetually breeding prodigy gestures toward and undermines divisions between any number of categories: humans and animals, male and female bodies, or animate and inanimate matter.

Bosola's rapturous reflection on death and decay floats another possible name for prodigious life, a designation that binds the play's transspecies transitions to questions rich in philosophical and theological significance. That term is "creature," a figure that pulls the play's cross-species dalliances toward the scene of primal creation in Genesis, a text that advances multiple and contradictory messages about the exceptionality of human life. In one sense, as the living image of God and the unique repository of a divinely mandated stewardship over the earth, man is the king of creatures. At the same time, humans too are created beings, fashioned by a divine craftsmanship, generated as part of the same sequence that gave rise to all other forms of life. In this respect, as Laurie Shannon notes, the Book of Genesis presses humans and animals into relations of mutuality and interdependence, since both are "living artefacts of Creation" who experience a "shared status that is at once contingent and stakeholding."[53] Such interspecies communions were certainly political, as Shannon beautifully argues, but they might also entail more earthy, fleshy forms of mixing. In his commentary on Genesis, medieval exegete Rashi extends a profoundly controversial reading of Adam's naming of the animals, which he understands this way: Genesis 2:19–23 "teaches that Adam mated with every species of domesticated animal and wild animal, but his appetite was not assuaged by them."[54] It was only after this series of imperfectly satisfying dalliances that Eve was drawn out of Adam and given him as a helpmeet. In this sense, Adam's own wandering procreative impulse marched him through a host of wild and woolly animal encounters on his way to reproductive heterosexuality and binary gender. The long history of these alternative interpretations of Genesis undermines the premise that the text envisions creation as culminating in clear, hierarchical distinctions between genders and species. Indeed, Genesis frames creation not so much as a single event but as an ongoing process. As Julia Lupton notes, the future active participial root of *creatura* opens onto "the possibility of further metamorphosis," lending the created being a divinely authorized capacity for reinvention, discovery, and self-fashioning.[55] Like the Adam-androgyne and technically-enhanced youth of Sonnet 20, the prodigy possesses a creaturely capacity for unruly transformation, as the possessor of a procreative impulse fully capable of reconfiguring relations of intimacy across divisions of species and gender. That is to say, the prodigious life marked by human-animal hybrids, improper mixing, sexual impurity, gender fluidity, and unpredictable transformations is a feature of creation, not a bug.

As the beneficiary and steward of creation, man may be presumed to sit atop the hierarchy of created beings, but for Bosola those lines of mastery have become tangled and confused. The intelligencer whose "corruption grew out of horse dung" is too enmeshed in the sordid pitfalls of creaturely life to imagine himself an elevated *imago dei* charged with parsing out human from animal and prince from parasite (1.1.279–80). That dubious honor belongs to Ferdinand, who cannot abide signs of life in women generally. When Castruchio mentions that his wife Julia suspects that "too much laughing" makes her "too full of the wrinkle," Ferdinand recommends having a "mathematical instrument made for her face that she might not laugh out of compass" (1.1.129–32). Ferdinand's hyperbolic hostility to Julia's giggles is not merely evidence of social maladjustment, but a biopolitical problem arising from the blurred distinctions between human and animal forms of life. For Aristotle, laughter is proper to human experience alone, since "none of the other [animals] laugh."[56] At the same time, there is something of the animal about a laughing body, a certain regression when speech gives way to howls, cackles, shrieks, snorts, and titters. The *Schoole of Good Manners* (1595) warns against those who "laugh so unreasonably, that therewith they set out their teeth like grinning dogs."[57] It is difficult to say whether Ferdinand objects to laughter because it is a reminder of Julia's humanity that actively frustrates her ornamental function by "filling her full of the wrinkle," or whether he recoils from the vulgar, animal energy expressed in the bark of laughter. Faced with the open mouth, the flash of teeth, he takes recourse in a fantasy of control premised upon the tools of science and husbandry. This "compass" is both a measuring device and a machine of torture that will brutally restrain any vital impulses that press a woman's body beyond fixed boundaries. The apparatus Ferdinand desires is reminiscent of another instrument that stopped the mouths of disorderly wives by mangling their tongues: the "scold's bridle," a tool that trains and restrains unruly women as though they were horses.[58] Ferdinand arrogates to himself a sovereign power to control the lively energies of others while acknowledging no external restraint on his own. In a self-satisfied moment, he ventures to Bosola that "He who can compass me and know my drifts / May say he hath put a girdle 'bout the world / And sounded all her quicksands" (3.2.84–85).

Despite Ferdinand's efforts to expunge animal elements from his environs, no character in *The Duchess of Malfi* manages to escape creaturely prodigiousness—including the Duchess herself, a woman who insists on handling courtship, marriage, and pregnancy on her own terms, drifting outside the normal structures charged with managing reproduction. From Ferdinand's perspective, the dangerous, uncontrollable recreative force wielded by his sister erodes her humanity, leaving her an "irregular crab, / Which, though't goes backward, thinks that it goes right / Because it goes its own way" (1.1.310–12). The beast lives within: Ferdinand warns the Duchess that women "luxurious" enough to remarry are afflicted with a "liver more spotted / Than Laban's sheep" (1.1.289–91). The Duchess's impressionable desires, which lead her to follow her wandering eyes to a new marriage bed, are, in Ferdinand's calculation, no different than the breeding program Jacob employed with Laban's flock, a scriptural reference that affiliates the Duchess with Paré's furry woman and the black child, also products of fetal imprinting like Laban's lambs. Indeed, the Duchess's sexual license pulls her out of the realm of the human and into the monstrous domains of prodigious life. Once the Duchess's secret family is discovered, Ferdinand announces to the Cardinal that "This night I have digged up a mandrake . . . and I am grown mad with it," identifying "this prodigy" as "a sister damned" (2.5.1–3). Struggling to find images appropriate to the betrayal he feels, Ferdinand invokes the mandrake, a plant whose humanoid shape intimated strange varietals of sexual entanglement between human bodies and vegetative life. Generated by the urine or semen of a hanged man dripping onto the soil, harvested safely only by a hand slaked in menstrual blood, the ambiguously gendered mandrake crystallized ideas about transhuman sexuality and reproduction.[59] Like the trans*plant* poetics Vin Nardizzi finds in the vegetable blazon of Pyramus's face, the mandrake scrambles together human bodies, flora, and fauna, even rerouting the steady progress of seasonality by imagining that dying precedes concupiscence and conception.[60] The mandrake's fanciful origin story purges the human mind from the scene of parturition. Here, the body acts on its own, and reproduction occurs as the purely unintentional aftereffect of a postmortem erection. Although the scattered seed cannot lead to human offspring, it is not barren but terrifyingly vegetative, capable of breeding humanoid monsters. The vital impetus that spawns the fleshy root is simultaneously sterile and overly fruitful, traversing the boundaries of life and death. In this sense, then, the mandrake possesses an "abortive" generativity that is akin to the Duchess's procreative powers, her ease in falling pregnant with children who fall outside the bounds appointed by her misogynistic brother.

There is indeed something prodigious about the reproductive pathways followed by the Duchess, who brings forth offspring that might well be called abortive, in that, with a single exception, they are destined to die in their infancy. Turning to the wonder books' favored explanatory mechanism for monstrous misbirths, Antonio immediately "sets a figure for [his son's] nativity" (2.2.77). The horoscope brings bad news: "*The Lord of the first house, being combust in the ascendant, signifies short life; and Mars being in a human sign, joined to the tail of the Dragon, in the eighth house, doth threaten a violent death*" (2.3.60–63). The malignant stars take a quasi-bestial shape, Mars "in a human sign" appended with the dragon's tail, a configuration that, in astrological manuals of the Renaissance, was understood to presage a brief life hastening to any number of brutal ends. Augier Ferrier's *Learned Astronomical Discourse* (1593) remarks that such a star chart would destine the child to "be hanged and strangled, or smothered, or otherwise killed in his bedde," or perhaps succumb to "poisons, venims, and violent medicines."[61] If the illicit union between the Duchess and her steward engenders inviable children, destined to die early and violent deaths, the young widow is also extravagantly, abundantly fruitful. While she gives birth to the eldest of her children with Antonio in act 2, by the beginning of act 3 another pair of children have materialized. Delio makes a joke of it: when the happy father remarks that, since his friend's last visit, the Duchess has "had two children more, a boy and a girl," Delio remarks that "Methinks 'twas yesterday . . . verily I should dream / It were within this half hour" (3.1.7–11). The condensed time of the theater collapses the pregnancies together, staging a single delivery for three children. She is, as Antonio quips, "an excellent / Feeder of pedigrees." A little giggle between the boys—casting his wife as a first-rate "feeder" presses the language of aristocratic descent into the terrain of animal husbandry, the feeding and breeding of stock. The Duchess's great fertility and the sudden appearance of multiple children after a single birth puts her on a spectrum with the mother at the center of a case recounted by Paré, in which an Italian woman named Dorothea "gave birth to twenty children in two confinements." The surgeon explains that such extraordinary fertility stems from a "superfluity of matter" in the womb, which is, he notes, also the cause of hermaphrodites, who "also come from a superabundance of matter."[62] Delighting in a reproductive capacity that is excessive, unmanageable by the patriarchal structures in place to control it, feeds the Duchess into forms of kinship with too-pregnant prodigies, abortive monsters, and misbegotten hermaphrodites.

Just as the barber-surgeon Paré clusters together prodigious fertility and gender ambiguity, so too does Ferdinand, who finds another animal emblem of errant procreativity appropriate to the situation at hand: "Methinks I see her laughing— / Excellent hyena!" (2.5.38–44). Marshaling her sexual energies according to her own whims and marrying outside her social class have, in Ferdinand's mind, loosened the Duchess's participation in the category of the human and pressed her into relations of affinity with a creature notable for its curious relation to gender. The "fanciful zoology" inherited from classical sources accorded the hyena a penchant for sexual versatility that apparently flowed from the creature's ability to change its gender annually.[63] Popular belief in the hyena's capacity to inhabit different genders, or perhaps its simultaneous possession of both male and female genitalia, circulated through a variety of sources, including Aristotle, Pliny, Ovid, the *Physiologus*, and the apocryphal Epistle of Barnabas.[64] The loose relationship to gender made this particular animal an icon for a variety of sexual sins including sodomy, adultery, and hermaphroditism. Partaking in this canine nature thus leads the Duchess to keep curious company, uniting her under the sign of the hyena with Julia, the adulteress who cuckolds and unmans her husband "Castruchio" with the Cardinal. It also links her with Ganymede/Rosalind from *As You Like It*, who warns Orlando that he might discover that his new lover might "laugh like a hyen" when he slips into bed. As Mario DiGangi notes in his work on the homoerotics of service, this creaturely coupling opens the marriage boudoir to a number of trans and queer configurations, including the possibility of inviting a different kind of "ganymede," a "page or household servant," into bed with them.[65] This, indeed, is precisely what Ferdinand imagines is happening, as he slips into intrusive thoughts of his sister performing the "shameful act" with a collection of "strong-thighed bargemen," or "one o'th'woodyard who can quoit the heft," or perhaps some "lovely squire" who "carries coals up to her privy lodgings" (2.5.42–45).[66] The figure of the hyena threads the Duchess's apparently normative practices of "animal generation" into a fabric of relationality with prodigious forms of life that include the semi-human sodomite and the bestial hermaphrodite.

It is tempting to dismiss Ferdinand's imputation of a prodigious, even bestial non-normativity to his sister; it is he, after all, who imagines the bargeman's strong legs and the delicious squire ascending the staircase.[67]

And yet, there is something queer about the Duchess, who does, after all, display a preference for intimacy with those in her service. This preference is certainly on view with her choice of spouse, a "slave that only smelled of ink and counters," whom she "claims" for herself, while Antonio plays the bride-to-be who protests his "virtue" and expresses his reluctance to marry and have children (3.3.72, 1.1.428, 446). A slightly bemused Antonio, aware of the inversion of gender roles at play in his rapid courtship, remarks only that "These words should have been mine, / And all the parts you have spoke" (1.1.459–60). The desire for cross-class kinship leads the Duchess not only into the arms of her blushing steward, however, but also to the close companionship of her friend, accomplice, and bedmate Cariola. In brilliant work on "bedroom intimacies" and the "pleasures and the uses of same-sex intimacy," Julie Crawford outlines the often erotic networks of affinity that characterized early modern domestic arrangements.[68] In this vein, Crawford notes that the Duchess spends most of her nights not with her husband, but with Cariola, who insists she will never marry, and who playfully tells Antonio that she "lies with [the Duchess] often" and "knows she'll much disquiet" him, since his wife makes for the "sprawlingest bedfellow" (3.2.11–14). Cariola shares her mistress's bed, keeps her bosom counsel, and undertakes the labor of nurturing her children. In other words, the secret family that the Duchess engineered for herself is not comprised of a heterosexual couple, but a triad that distributes relations of care, comfort, and intimacy.

Once her remarriage and second family has been discovered, or the mandrake-like prodigy pulled out of the earth and displayed, the Duchess becomes a problem inviting divergent solutions from her brothers. From the Cardinal's perspective, his sister's unmanageable procreative impulses amount to a legal issue. A man with secret lovers of his own, the Cardinal is manifestly untroubled by any ethical or religious qualms that might follow from the Duchess's choice of spouse, and unlike Ferdinand, he never succumbs to obsessive fixations on her sexuality.[69] In all likelihood, the grounds of the Cardinal's opposition to his sister's remarriage are purely fiscal. While Ferdinand claims that it was he himself who "had a hope, / Had she continued widow, to have gained / An infinite mass of treasure by her death, / And that is the main cause," his weak protestation of greed is hardly convincing (4.2.267–70). After all, the majority of his stage time leading up to the murder has been dedicated to explicating and indulging his pathologies, which have been searchingly explored in the criticism. While this vision of "infinite riches" probably does not reflect Ferdinand's true motive, it is possible to detect the Cardinal's sober practicality in his brother's late-arriving excuse. Confronted with a sister who has interrupted his ability to manipulate the legal norms of inheritance to his own benefit, the Cardinal seeks juridical remedies.[70] These measures are delivered in a dumb show that pantomimes

> *the* Cardinal's *instalment in the habit of a soldier, performed in delivering up his cross, hat, robes, and ring at the shrine, and investing him with sword, helmet, shield, and spurs. Then* Antonio, *the* Duchess, *and their* Children, *having presented themselves at the shrine, are (by a form of banishment in dumb show expressed towards them by the* Cardinal *and the state of Ancona) banished, during all which ceremony, this ditty is sung to very solemn music by churchmen.* (3.4, sd)

The dumb show captures two legal transitions that are explicitly paralleled. The first of these alterations secularizes the Cardinal in a ceremony that divests him of the "reverend garments" and religious paraphernalia that signify his removal from the worldly affairs of politics and war (3.3.3). As Andy Kesson notes, this ritual, given only in a long stage direction, snuffs out the character's "definitive social identity," leaving him "a Cardinal who is no longer a Cardinal."[71] Simultaneously, the ceremony creates a Duchess who is no longer a Duchess. While the rite undergone by the Cardinal unburdens him from the legal obligations that demand his separation from the secular world, the Duchess and her family are pressed outside of the law altogether. There is no legal warrant for any of the depredations that follow rapidly from their banishment, as the Marquis of Pescara clarifies when he transfers Antonio's land to Julia, at the suit of the Cardinal: "It was Antonio's land, not forfeited / By course of law, but ravished from his throat / By the Cardinal's entreaty . . . I am glad / This land, ta'en from the owner by such wrong, / Returns again unto so foul an use / As salary for his lust" (5.1.41–52). As any number of characters state clearly and repeatedly, neither the Duchess nor Antonio has committed any crime, and so what befalls their estates is not the outcome of a regular judicial process. Instead, the Duchess and her dependents are thrust outside of the law altogether. Forced into a state of extralegal precarity, the little family is stripped of the protections that would secure their persons and property. This process, too, animalizes the Duchess and her offspring: gazing upon the strangled corpses of his niece and nephew, Ferdinand remarks only that "the death / Of young wolves is never to be pitied" (4.2.243–44). In this respect, the Cardinal handles his sister's wandering procreative impulses in much the same way that the Romans dealt with their hermaphroditic prodigies, or how Pope Julius II washed his hands of the Monster of Ravenna: exempted from the law, rendered vulnerable to violent death, she is set adrift.

For Ferdinand, by contrast, the Duchess's prodigious energies do not constitute a legal problem, but rather a medical one. Ferdinand locates monstrosity not in the sprawling networks of creaturely life that characterize Bosola's reveries, but rather in the realms of psychology and biology. Dismissing the customary explanatory mechanisms for prodigious phenomena, Ferdinand insists that the "witchcraft" in question is a propensity for deviance and disobedience that "lies in her rank blood" or lingers in the recesses of her "will" (3.1.73, 78). The Duchess quite rightly describes her confinement and the grotesque spectacles she must endure as "tyranny" and compares her treatment to the disciplinary techniques of torture, comparing herself to "a wretch that's broke upon the wheel" who must live only "To be executed again" (4.1.78–80). Nevertheless, Ferdinand styles himself not as an executioner, but as a "physician" driven to "cruel" extremes by the "intemperate agues" that, convincingly or otherwise, he imagines himself repairing (4.1.137). His baroque schemes may well register as "psychological torture," and yet the engineer of these spectacles perversely insists that he intends to "apply desperate physic" and work toward her "cure" (2.5.23, 4.2.42).[72] He implements a regime of hospitalization, or rather, he empties out the "common hospital" and recreates it within the confines of the prison where the Duchess is detained (4.1.122). According to Ferdinand's diagnosis, the most suitable place for the Duchess is not the scaffold, but the sanatorium, where she will take her place in a taxonomy of madmen that includes

> a mad lawyer, and a secular priest,
> A doctor that hath forfeited his wits
> By jealousy; an astrologian,
> That in his works said such a day o'th'month
> Should be the day of doom, and, failing of't,
> Ran mad; an English tailor, crazed i'th'brain
> With the study of new fashion; a gentleman-usher
> Quite beside himself with care to keep in mind
> The number of his lady's salutations
> Or "How do you" she employed him in each morning;
> A farmer, too, an excellent knave in grain,
> Mad 'cause he was hindered transportation. (4.2.45–55)

The collection of patients in the makeshift hospital Ferdinand arranges for his sister are not obviously prodigies in the old-fashioned sense. Their bodies pass unmentioned; there is no indication of corporal variation that would require decoding, as in the "woeman's belly" of Melanchthon's Pope-Ass or the griffin's claw possessed by the Monster of Ravenna. In this respect, as Brett Hirsch asserts, the play addresses the madness experienced by these unfortunates according to the "medical, naturalized terms" of illness, not the superstitious models of witchcraft, demonology, and astrology. The residents of the "common hospital," then, are not monsters or wonders; instead, they suffer from perfectly understandable experiences of "emotional and occupational stress."[73] From this perspective, *The Duchess of Malfi* presses its prodigious world into what Sonya Loftis identifies as a "proto-medical model" of mental illness, disability, and abnormality.[74]

And yet, something of the prodigy lingers in the "masques" of the "mad folk" among whom the Duchess will spend her final hours (4.1.120, 124). Although Ferdinand employs them only as sound machines, generators of a "hideous noise" that will torment and disorient his captive sister, their monstrous role as portents who deliver stern warnings of divine disapproval in the immorality and excess of their social world emerges in the snippets of discourse they pronounce on the stage (4.2.1). The first of the crew expresses surprise that "Doomsday [has] not come yet," promising to "draw it nearer" by making "a glass that shall set all the world on fire" (4.2.72–73). Others denounce lechery, singling out those who counterfeit religiosity only to "have [their] hands in a wench's placket," or greed and litigiousness, condemning a "law [that] will eat to the bone" (4.2.92–93, 99). The wonder books' fixation on racial and religious mixing also erupts in the cacophonous masque, as the "Third Madman" (presumably the "secular priest") laments that "Greek has turned Turk; we are only to be saved by the Helvetian translation" (4.2.89–90). Moreover, while the chorus of madmen are not compounded from the human-animal hybrids of the type favored by the pamphlet literature of monstrosity, they are nevertheless rendered bestial, as is best captured in the song they perform to "a dismal kind of music" to plague the Duchess:

> Oh, let us howl some heavy note,
>     Some deadly dogged howl,
> Sounding as from the threat'ning throat
>     Of beasts and fatal fowl,
> As ravens, screech-owls, bulls, and bears!
>     We'll bill and bawl our parts,
> Till irksome noise have cloyed your ears
>     And corrosived your hearts.
> At last, whenas our choir wants breath
>     Our bodies being blest,
> We'll sing like swans, to welcome death
>     And die in love and rest. (4.2.60–71)

The monsters' *monstrum*, their ominous proclamation, emerges from and then retreats to a sound bath of animal noise. Billing and bawling, screeching and howling, the speech of the "wild consort" does not rise to the level of human discourse but hovers somewhere between recognizable complaint and pure noise; such plaintive sounds may as well have emerged from the "threatening throats" of wild animals. This particular brand of beastliness cannot be sourced to witchcraft, nor does it offer evidence of a conception subsequent to engaging in sex with demons or livestock. Instead, the play asserts that the animality of the madmen resides in their minds. They are feral only in the violence of their fantasies and the uncontrolled danger posed by their sexual drives, as in the secular priest who announces he will "lie with every woman in my parish the tenth night" and "tithe them over like haycocks" (4.2.79–80). No longer a byproduct of the infinitely recreative powers of the natural world, the animal natures of the "mad folk" are a matter of psychosexual pathology that justifies their exclusion from the category of the human.

Likewise, the "physic" Ferdinand prescribes his sister takes aim at her personhood and humanity by intervening in her physiological processes and undermining her mental stability. The plan, such as it is, begins by exacerbating the Duchess's anguish in order to "bring her to despair" by goading her with a dismembered hand allegedly belonging to Antonio, and presenting her with a waxwork diorama of her murdered family (4.1.113). Not unlike modern forms of aversive conditioning, which stimulate pain and disgust in connection with images of the antisocial behavior that psychiatrists seek to eliminate, the wax figures are intended to generate a shock response, so that "hereafter" she "may wisely cease to grieve / For that which cannot be recovered" (4.1.58–59).[75] This accomplished, he transforms the space of her confinement in such a way that she will be forced to remain in a state of vigilant and perturbed wakefulness:

> I will send her masques of common courtesans,
> Have her meat served up by bawds and ruffians,
> And, 'cause she'll needs be mad, I am resolved
> To remove forth the common hospital
> All the mad folk, and place them near her lodging;
> There let them practice together, sing, and dance,
> And act their gambols to the full o'th'moon.
> If she can sleep the better for it—let her. (4.1.119–27)

In blocking his sister's access to sleep, this scheme amounts to something more than cruelty for cruelty's sake: denying rest is instead, as Julia Lupton and Benjamin Parris have argued, a biopolitical strategy.[76] In Parris's Foucauldian account, exerting control over a subject's access to or experience of dormancy constitutes a "form of physiological and affective constraint by which the living human body is involuntarily seized and stripped of the faculties that situate it in the world."[77] The slumbering body inhabits the domain of biological life (*zoē*) rather than political life (*bios*), disengaging itself from the world, retreating from sociality, and yielding up conscious awareness. Nevertheless, in attending to the physiological needs of the body, the somatic rhythms of rest provide necessary support for the emergence of the legal, political, and ethical endeavors of the *bios politikos*. As such, Ferdinand's assault on the prepolitical sphere of dormancy "denies the forms of recognition that confirm the personhood of the creature" (Lupton 101). That is to say, "the Duchess" as an office, institution, and sovereign cannot exist if the biological creature invested with that title is driven into extreme distress and executive dysfunction. Excluded from personhood and political life, the Duchess cohabitates with a bestiary of dehumanized creatures, from the sex workers and rogues who "serve her meat" to the madmen whose noise erodes her ability to sleep, speak, and think. In this respect, Ferdinand takes up the legal machinations employed by the Cardinal and relocates them to the realm of medicine, the space of hospitalization and incarceration he constructs to confine and "cure" his sister.

The gruesome spectacles, the denial of sleep, the constant roar of noise, the close confinement, and the madmen's antimasque are not only intended to press the Duchess outside of the regime of personhood, but also to degrade her humanity and reduce her to a bestial condition. Bosola relates the nature of this treatment plan:

> A great physician, when the Pope was sick
> Of a deep melancholy, presented him
> With several sorts of madmen, which wild object,
> Being full of change and sport, forced him to laugh
> And so th'impostume broke; the selfsame cure
> The Duke intends on you. (4.2.38–43)

As his sister's procreative energies wander out of compass, the laughter that haunts Ferdinand returns. Unlike his earlier flights of fancy, which involved disturbing fantasies of controlling, dominating, and silencing the laughing Julia, his brother's "creature," with his psychopathy in full flower Ferdinand wants to force his sister to show her teeth, to embody the hyena that he is convinced she harbors within. If his stratagem fails to induce insanity, it succeeds in bringing forth the Duchess's prodigious nature, launching her into a litany of curses ominous enough to shock the misanthropic Bosola.

SERVANT: [I am] one that wishes you long life.
DUCHESS: I would thou wert hanged for the horrible curse
Thou hast given me! I shall shortly grow one
Of the miracles of pity. I'll go pray—no,
I'll go curse.
BOSOLA: Oh, fie!
DUCHESS: I could curse the stars—
BOSOLA: Oh, fearful!
DUCHESS: And those three smiling seasons of the year
Into a Russian winter—nay the world
To its first chaos.
BOSOLA: Look you, the stars shine still.
DUCHESS: Oh, but you must
Remember, my curse hath a great way to go.
Plagues, that make lanes through largest families,
Consume them!
BOSOLA: Fie, lady!
DUCHESS: Let them, like tyrants,
Never be remembered but for the ill they have done!
Let all the zealous prayers of mortified
Churchmen forget them!
BOSOLA: Oh, uncharitable!
DUCHESS: Let heaven, a little while, cease crowning martyrs,
To punish them!
Go, howl them this, and say I long to bleed. (4.1.90–106)

Finally at her breaking point, the Duchess swears off life itself. With the apparent death of her children and husband, as well as the loss of her title and position, the ties that tether her to the world have been fully severed. She "longs to bleed" and rebuffs Bosola's offer to save her life, on the grounds that "I have not leisure to tend to so small a business" (4.1.84). If the extremity of her final hours has loosened the Duchess's attachment to life, her energies have not slackened. Instead, when Bosola and then the unnamed servant encourage her to endure in anticipation of a "long life," the intolerable possibility of survival lends the Duchess a new dynamism, amplifying rather than diminishing her vigor. Brushing off the repeated demands that she live, the Duchess commits herself unreservedly to death and decay, channeling all her vital energies into the poetic task of unmaking the world.

Calling down plagues that eat through "the greatest families" and ecological catastrophes that disrupt the steady cycles of the seasons, the curse gives voice to a vibrant, vital morbidity pitched against the family unit, the salvific power of religion, and the renewal of the created world. Like the monstrous Flemish triplets who announced upon their birth that "Dearth and Plague should couer the whole World," or the hermaphroditic Monster of Ravenna, the Duchess concludes her storyline as a vessel for the animate, abortive energies of monstrosity, a creature "transshaped" into an engine for prodigious announcements that resound even after her death (3.2.30).

With the vicious murder of his sister executed, Ferdinand fully succumbs to his bestial impulses in the most dramatic instance of transspecies mutation in the play, falling into a frenzied state of "lycanthropia" (5.2.6). Ferdinand's physician describes the "very pestilent disease" afflicting the prince in these terms:

> In those that are possessed with't there overflows
> Such melancholy humor they imagine
> Themselves to be transformed into wolves,
> Steal forth to churchyards in the dead of night,
> And dig dead bodies up—as two nights since
> One met the Duke 'bout midnight in a lane
> Behind Saint Mark's Church, with the leg of a man
> Upon his shoulder; and he howled fearfully,
> Said he was a wolf—only the difference
> Was, a wolf's skin was hairy on the outside,
> His on the inside—bade them take their swords,
> Rip up his flesh, and try. (5.2.5–19)

In explaining away Ferdinand's wolfish antics, the play settles conclusively for the modernizing impulses that structured the mad folk's antimasque in act 4. That is to say, the animal transformation he undergoes is not a matter of the material networks of creaturely life that Bosola identifies in the abortive hedgehog's painted face, nor could he be classified as a hybrid body that could be the object of prognostication. Instead, this lycanthropic episode relocates animality from body to mind, centering on the internal world of black bile, affect, instinct, and hysteria.[78] At once dissociating and feeling out a new psychic identification, Ferdinand muses that "the wolf shall find her grave and scrape it up— / Not to devour the corpse" as a demonic sorcerer might, but rather "to discover / The horrid murder" (4.2.293–95). This hallucinatory wolf-nature, visible only to Ferdinand, merely externalizes his pathologies through a number of concerning behaviors, like graverobbing with overtones of necrophilia and cannibalism. In adopting a psychological model of lycanthropy, critics have largely agreed with the doctor who insists that the transformation is a matter of imagination, unpacking the various interior truths or social realities reflected in his animal identification: his incestuous drives, perhaps, or his complicity in the Duchess's murder, or maybe his Catholicism.[79] Not a prodigy but a psychotic, Ferdinand is "hairy on the inside"; his wolfishness is symbolic or symptomatic rather than innate or demonic.

Reclassifying Ferdinand's lycanthropy as a species of melancholy rather than a divinely crafted wonder plucks him out of the prodigy books' assortment of bestial and hermaphroditic amalgams whose gender variance can be sourced to their plural "natures," in all senses of the word. Nevertheless, a certain gender instability follows from Ferdinand's mental wolfishness. In part, this is because melancholy itself was a gendered phenomenon divided, as Drew Daniel notes, between a "discursive, Aristotelian, 'light,' genial, and masculine" form and the "somatic, Galenic, 'heavy,' morbid, and feminine" version that more accurately describes Ferdinand's diagnosis.[80] As Lynn Enterline argues on Lacanian grounds, Ferdinand's lycanthropic melancholia "profoundly unsettles a recognizable difference between male and female subjects" just as it "unsettles a recognizable difference between humans and animals."[81] These canine delusions feminize Ferdinand, not because his gender is compounded from animal matter, as is the case for the abortive hedgehog or the painted woman Bosola denounced, but because of his relationship to his tempestuous, unmanageable drives. The conceptual range of the effeminacy in question here was not exhausted in the modern sense of a kind of fey womanishness. Drawing on classical precedents, early modern writers understood the effeminate man as especially voluptuous and irrational, someone who is subjected to his passions rather than in control of them.[82] As Rebecca Bushnell demonstrates, from Plato's *Republic* forward, this logic bound the image of the ravening wolf to the figure of the tyrant, a creature also utterly in servitude to his ungovernable appetites and effeminate tendencies.[83] Ferdinand's tyranny is the subject of much commentary within the play and the criticism: Cariola denounces her mistress's "tyrant brother" who indulges in a "tyranny" so extreme it "was never practiced till this hour," while the Duchess submits to his torments only because she is "chained to endure [his] tyranny" (4.2.2–4, 56–57).[84] While Jennifer de Reuck dismisses David Dawson's "effeminate interpretation" of the role in Dominic Dromgoole's 2014 Blackfriars production of *The Duchess* as a choice that "drained Ferdinand of menace and tragedy and rendered the play's denouement incoherent," she misses the logic that would have rendered Ferdinand's brutish tyranny threateningly femme to an early modern audience.[85] At the convergent edge of psychopathy, effeminacy, and tyranny, the lycanthropic Ferdinand is not a prodigy. Rather, in his gender deviance and animal identification, both of which signal his deep-seated predatory instincts, the duke is *abnormal*, the ancestral form of both criminology's "moral monster" and the "woman who identified as a Korean cat."

The psychologizing transspecies encounters of the play's final movement sanitize the prodigious ecology that has dominated the play's first four acts by rendering it merely figurative, if richly symbolic and ripe for close reading. Likewise, transforming Ferdinand into an avatar of abnormality recasts the Duchess a paragon of normality, extracting her from the creaturely entanglements that have accrued to her character in the aftermath of her secret marriage. We might dismiss these aspersions of monstrosity alongside the normally unflappable Cardinal who, listening to Ferdinand rant about mandrakes and hyenas, rejects such invective as evidence of a monstrous nature that he understands as both delusion and disability, dismissing his brother's charges as "intemperate noise" that "Fitly resembles deaf men's shrill discourse, / Who talk aloud, thinking all other men / To have their imperfection" (2.5.51–54). Indeed, nothing could be easier than handwaving the accusations of animality directed at the Duchess and her extravagant procreative energies as the projections of a manifestly unwell brother, the debased criminal mind of Bosola, or the morally depraved social environs of the Italian court. Her sexuality may have been "transgressive"[86] or "subversive,"[87] but it was not deviant or commercial; her facility in ruling and wooing her husband may be masculine, but she could not be described as butch or mannish; surely she is not one of those "great women of pleasure" like Julia, even if her quick courtship of Antonio eerily parallels Julia's gunpoint seduction of Bosola; her bedsharing arrangement with Cariola suggests nothing unseemly, just that they are very close friends; her fertility exists within expected bounds, unlike Paré's monstrous women "who carry several children during one pregnancy"; her hospitalization was not the product of any defect of her own mind, but was imposed by her brother's cruelty, unlike the "wild consort" of bestial "mad folk" who deserve their confinement; her poverty is ennobling, unlike Bosola's, which is degrading; her "white hand" surely owes nothing to powder, unlike the painted woman Bosola harasses.

By and large, these are the conclusions reached by the play's critics, who see in the tragic heroine a figure of what Mary Beth Rose calls the Protestant "heroics of marriage," a discourse that idealizes private life and marital intimacy.[88] Once her vital energies and sexual drives have been fully domesticated, the Duchess's gender can be purged of the prodigious blot staining her with a hyena-like androgyny through an interpretation that restores her to a normative or perhaps even exemplary womanhood: Judith Haber pronounces her to be in possession of "a subjectivity that is specifically female," following Webster's efforts to "reimagine speech, sexuality, and space—most particularly, the space of the female body—in 'feminine' terms."[89] Troublingly, this concentrated core of femaleness is most clearly manifested in her susceptibility to violence. Again and again, critics find in the Duchess a "heroic yet vulnerable femininity,"[90] or a waxlike "softness that renders her vulnerable to Ferdinand's attack [but] also allows her to love and live," suggesting that her capacity to endure violence speaks to both "her humanity" as well as "her gender."[91] Unlike her brother, the gender failure whose abject effeminacy leaves him more animal than human, the Duchess appears as the very height of gender normativity, unblemished humanity, and uncompromised innocence. In short, the account of gender and animality established by the play's final turn eerily anticipates contemporary trans panic: the Duchess's humane, genteel, and above all blameless female self emerges in sharp contrast to the wolflike predator whose intrusion into the women's space of his sister's chamber amounts to an "uninvited penetration" that follows "the logic of rape" and ends in a frenzy of bestial violence.[92] Such a creature is best left to the devices of the "barber-surgeons" like the physician of act 5, who announces that, if "They'll give me leave," he will "buffet [Ferdinand's] madness / Out of him" (5.1.27–28).

The argumentative scaffolding of this avowedly feminist defense of the Duchess's integrity and normativity, which insists that the Duchess's pleasures cannot detract from her perfect humanity, comes at a certain cost. Such a reading doubles Antonio's initial assessment of the Duchess as a paragon among women, when he recommends that "all sweet ladies [may] break their flatt'ring glasses / And dress themselves in her," or even Bosola's encomium asserting that, should she desire "soldiers," her story will "make the very Turks and Moors / Turn Christians, and serve [her]" (1.1.197–98, 3.2.277–78). What the boys notice is that rhapsodizing the Duchess as a gender exemplar exerts a norming effect that operates not only on the other "sweet ladies" of the court who fail to meet her irreproachable standards, but also on the racial populations whose sodomitical deviance and religious difference can be corrected through the power of her example.[93] That is to say, the conceptual turn that makes both gender and animality a matter of interior feeling, sexual drives, and criminal impulses mounts a defense of the Duchess by perching her at the summit of what Mel Chen calls an "animacy hierarchy," a schema that "conceptually arranges human life, disabled life, animal life, plant life, and forms of nonliving material in orders of value and priority."[94] Elevating the Duchess and Antonio as exemplary representatives of reproductive heteronormativity not only polices the unruly drives of women like Julia, who strategically employ their charms to secure money and property, but also subordinates and redirects the unruly, even animalistic vitality of the "Turks and Moors," turning them into orderly ranks of Christian soldiers for the instrumental use of the archetypical white couple. In this respect, the redistribution of animality that accrues to the "wild consort" of madmen, the perverted effeminacy embodied by Ferdinand, and the Ottoman and Moorish soldiers belongs not only to the history of gender, but racialized gender.

It is not necessary, however, to defend the Duchess by uncoupling her gender from its animal dimensions. There is nothing inherently defamatory in the proposition that there is indeed something of the prodigy about the Duchess, in that she fully embraces the potentials and possibilities of creaturely life. The vital capacities she wields wrap her into surprising networks of affinity and communion with other prodigious figures within and beyond the play: the kept woman and the hanged man; the mad residents of the "common hospital"; the wounded soldier and the prisoner in the galleys; the hermaphrodite and the women who share beds; the sex worker, her physician, and his horse; and the Turks and the Moors. Moreover, rehabilitating the Duchess's prodigious dimensions links her gendered embodiment with that experienced by the women with flayed and painted faces. From a creaturely perspective, the regenerative impulses behind the Duchess's sexuality, marriage, and multiple pregnancies are not different in kind than those that motivate the cosmetically enhanced woman.

The abortive hedgehog was supposed to be a joke, a limit case for women who manufacture an artificial femininity that God never granted them. Such women, Bosola tells us, damage and compromise their humanity, falling into an animal existence and then, if they persist, into something even further removed from God's design. And yet, from the creaturely perspective opened by Genesis and by Bosola's own meditation, the woman with the flayed face takes on a different significance. Going under the knife does not press her outside of creation, marking a falling-away from a divine schematic for the human form that is fixed and inalterable. Rather, the peeled face is the expression of a creaturely capacity for transition that extends to manifold forms of trans cutting. For the abortive hedgehog, but also for the Duchess, entering into gender entails a becoming-animal that expresses the "wandering procreative impulses" that Livy detected in the prodigy, or the "radical uncertainty" and "generative affectivity" that Mel Chen attributes to the queerness of animacy. For Chen, these transspecies couplings exemplify the process by which "humans achieve their final form" by "interacting with," rather than excluding, their "animal countervalences."[95] And yet, from the creaturely vistas opened by *The Duchess of Malfi*, this pronouncement might be too rigid. The prodigy has no "final form" to achieve, no single way of inhabiting her body or humanity. Becoming-woman entails an ongoing process of interventions and modifications that mix the human body with animal matter and inhuman substances. In this sense, the play offers up models of transspecies intimacy that, as Harlan Weaver asserts, "demonstrate how the illicit tendrils of trans formations weave new webs that join multiple and diverse bodies and beings, making them kin in spite of kind."[96] The wild vitality native to creaturely life presses us all into new and unpredictable forms of entanglement across species and gender; we are only "made sweet" through transspecies communion.

[ CHAPTER THREE ]

# Egg Theory's Early Modern Style

## Or, John Donne's Resurgent Flesh

To be transgender is to have a certain intimacy with death. This closeness to the edge is not only a consequence of existing in a political landscape precision-made for directing precarity, vulnerability, and violence toward trans people.[1] There is also a conceptual proximity between transness and dying. According to a widespread belief, transition marks the passing away of a prior self, a loss that demands acts of public mourning, little bathetic displays that might be performed in the office, or indulged on social media, or aimed directly at the person with the gall to transition. Daniel Lavery remarks that there is "something willfully perverse about bereavement in the face of new life," the non-transitioner's reflex to "enter into mourning, to reenact the rituals of death, [and] to borrow its vernacular" when confronted with a transition experienced by the person undertaking it as vivifying and enlivening.[2] In its extreme forms, the loose analogy between transness and death tightens into an absurd and sinister literalism, as in the case of the activist group composed of self-identified "Trans Widows," cis women who imagine themselves as the grieving survivors of their spouses' transitions. "For two years I watched my husband die," Christine Benvenuto declares in her memoir, issuing a death announcement for her very much alive and thriving trans ex-wife. "Serving witness to the dismantling of the face I loved, there was no step that didn't sear. No stage was passed without mourning."[3] From this funereal perspective, trans people have the bad taste to survive our own deaths. Not content to vanish quietly, we stubbornly carry on with the routines of life, shambling along like reanimated corpses, mere "mummy possess'd." Like their conceptual kin, the parents afflicted by their children's "Rapid Onset Gender Dysphoria,"[4] the "Trans Widows" imagine the transitioning body as undergoing decomposition, succumbing to a disease that eats away at "healthy tissue."[5] Unlike the clean severance promised by a natural death—a fate routinely invoked as preferable to being burdened with trans kin—transition pitches the body into a living morbidity that turns a beloved child or spouse into an agent of corruption, a vector of death that radiates an enervating, exhausting, debilitating effect on the besieged family unit.

Although its detractors frame the "social contagion"[6] of transition as a problem for secular-liberal governance, this chapter lingers with the residually religious dimensions of this fantasy, locating an ancestral form of the conceptual proximity between gender transition and death in the Christian doctrine of the resurrection of the body. According to this belief, at the end of time the dead would be raised not as disembodied spirits, but as flesh and blood, in the very body they occupied in their time on earth, but improved, even perfected. From Paul forward, Christian theologians have imagined that just on the other side of the apocalypse, the frail, mortal bodies of the saved will be transfigured into an unblemished and transcendently beautiful shape. What happens to gender in this regenerated body proved, perhaps surprisingly, to be a matter of some debate: perhaps it would be abolished altogether, or there would be some manner of mass transition event, or maybe binary gender would be reinforced with all the complicated and indeterminate bodies sorted out once and for all. In attempting to describe the radical physiological transformation awaiting us at the end times, premodern theologians confronted, often awkwardly or indignantly, the central questions at stake in controversies about trans medicine in the present: what does it mean when gender is "imperfect," and how might it be made whole? What is a body for, and what kinds of transformations might it undergo? Which physiological variations bar a subject from entering into community? To which normative processes must "defective" bodies submit in order to be deemed worthy of (eternal) life?

This chapter exhumes the trans possibilities and secular afterlives of resurrection theology by way of the necrotic imagination of John Donne, the "flesh-creeper, the sorcerer of emotional orgy," who returned to the matter of resurgent flesh across a kaleidoscopic range of genres including paradoxes, secular poetry, holy sonnets, illness memoir, epistolary correspondence, sermons, and even portraiture.[7] Critics have framed Donne's "resolute and constitutional morbidity" as part of any number of social and political discourses and therefore as relevant to topics as various as secularization, suicide, materialist philosophy, humoral theory, and temporality.[8] This chapter, by contrast, builds its argument on an element of Donne's writing that has been minimized, politely ignored, or taken as symptomatic for almost anything else: that, for Donne, death initiates a terrifying and confusing but also pleasurable and desirable process of ungendering. Whereas exponents of corporal resurrection overwhelmingly, if not unanimously, understood the glorious body to be firmly planted in its assigned gender, for Donne the cadaver's disintegration never quite terminates in a resurrection that restabilizes it by "curing" all its defects and restoring its gender to a normative shape. In this respect, I argue that resurrection theology afforded Donne a conceptual vocabulary for a very specific mode of simultaneously entertaining and disavowing trans possibility, what Grace Lavery calls "egg theory."

An egg, in the terminally online vernacular of a certain subset of trans culture, is a latent trans person, someone hiding behind a hard shell that, with some luck, will eventually crack so the chick can poke her head out. The egg's theory, Lavery notes, "is chiefly that they (he, she, ze, etc.) cannot transition," or that transitioning must be resisted, indefinitely deferred, or substituted with the many compensatory pleasures of foreclosed desire.[9] Here, I detect Donne's own deeply peculiar egginess not only in his poetry's content, the intrusive thoughts a glorious, agender resurrection perched just on the other side of an equally exciting process of decomposition. Egg theory also shapes its form (the lyric escapades that decorporealize the speaker into any number of non-male personae, ranging from a noxious cloud to a name scratched into a windowpane to Sappho) and style (the irritating metaphysical gestures that tease trans possibility only to retract, disavow, occlude, or endlessly complicate it). This trans Donne becomes visible by relinquishing an assumption that has been foundational to both the (anti-)feminist Donne and the gay Donne of recent criticism, namely that Donne's gender politics and queer potential are explicable only in relation to the poet's assigned sex, understood to be a stable and transhistorical given quite in spite of Donne's explicit fantasizing about that gender's dissolution.[10] If trans studies offers insights capable of reframing Donne's position in early modern studies, his corpus also breaks down into fruitful soil for trans theorizing in a number of registers: the eggy deferral demanded by eschatology speaks to ongoing conversations about trans temporality, while the ecstatic visions of a decaying, transitioning corpse that becomes "interinanimated" with other bodies seems evocatively close to the assemblages at the center of work on trans materiality.[11] While acknowledging the trans possibility embedded in the vermiculated corpses, atomized bodies, and genderless splendor of Donne's resurgent flesh, this chapter also considers his—and the egg's—essential whiteness, unearthing the submerged connection between Donne's egg theology and the racial politics of Christian universalism. To this end, this chapter drifts on the trans undercurrents of Donne's resurrection theology through the sermon preached at the wedding of the Earl of Bridgewater's daughter to Edward

Herbert's wastrel son, the thorny abstractions of the *Songs and Sonets*, and the ravages of illness catalogued in Donne's sickness memoir *Devotions upon Emergent Occasions*.

While the possibility of a physical resurrection had been raised in diverse and complex forms in early rabbinical literature, within Christian theology the key scriptural warrant for the resurrection of the flesh can be found in 1 Corinthians, chapter 15, which concludes with Paul slyly offering to "shewe you a secret thing," that on the final day, "in the twinkling of an eye," the "trumpet shal blowe, and the dead shal be raised up incorruptible, and we shalbe changed" (1 Cor. 15:51–52).[12] The language is provocative and obscure in equal measure: the more deeply Paul probes this "secret thing," the more the entire conceptual apparatus threatens to collapse into paradox, with a "spiritual bodie" or a "corruptible" form that not only can but "must put on incorruption" (1 Cor. 15:44, 53). Because the epistles are so coy about the specific kind of body we will inhabit in the afterlife, it was left to exegetes to fill in the blanks, a project that immediately generated a host of interpretive problems that ranged from philosophically sophisticated to risible. What weight, height, and age would the risen body have? How attractive will the saved be, and will they have scars or beards? Will aborted fetuses rise, and if so, in what form? What would happen in the case of cannibalism, when the meat of one body has been consumed and "converted into [another's] flesh,"[13] or in the aftermath of chain consumption, when, as Hamlet posits, "A man may fish with the worm that hath eat of a king, and eat of the fish that hath fed of that worm" so that "a king may go a progress through the guts of a beggar?"[14] If indeed every atom belonging to every believer would be located by God and patched together, would this maximally intact body reintegrate "excremental" matter, like hair clippings, cut fingernails, and baby teeth?

While the responses to these provocations varied wildly, each answer attempted to adjudicate which body parts were "essential" to human identity, like faces, and which were superfluous or ornamental, like chest hair. That is, as Will Fisher notes in work on the "ambiguous corporeality" of beards, these controversies reflected the complexities of determining where the body proper begins and ends.[15] Perhaps surprisingly, genitalia struck a number of early Christian theologians as a borderline case. Given that sexual reproduction or "animal generation" would presumably have no place in the afterlife any more than other unseemly bodily processes like eating, urinating, and defecating, some ambiguities remained concerning the status of the raised genitals. Adherents to the theory of primal androgyny sometimes entertained the possibility that death would restore us to the sublime sexlessness of our initial creation. Perhaps our glorified bodies will be like angels,

Gregory of Nyssa thought, beautiful and terrible once they shed their mortal bodies like a "dead and ugly garment made of the skins of [brutes]," happily freed from those organs that "pertain to marriage."[16] Origen, whose eagerness for a foretaste of the afterlife prompted him to undergo castration and join the ranks of those who have made themselves eunuchs "for the kingdome of heauen" in accordance with Matthew 19:12, believed that the dead would abandon physical markers of gender entirely, rising as smooth and featureless spheres.[17] Or possibly, as Clement of Alexandria speculated, the resurrection would accomplish a mass transition, with "woman translated into man" in order to render the entire population of heaven "equally unwomanish and masculine and perfect," although what this translation would mean for the anatomical configuration of the blessed, he left to the imagination.[18] Such theological positions embrace the trans potential of the afterlife when they assert that bodies are capable of changes that will liberate them from normative gender, radically alter their experience of embodiment, or do away with sexuation entirely. Indeed, these texts go even further, announcing that such transitions are holy and that sloughing off gender brings the human body closer to the image of divinity in which we were created, a wholeness that was sacrificed with the fall. It is a rationale that, as Leah DeVun argues, erects "nonbinary sexes as the anchors of eschatological time: its origin and its final reconciliatory end."[19]

Of course, at no point in church history was the celebration of apocalyptic transition the party line. In general, Christian thought followed Tertullian, Augustine, and Thomas Aquinas in emphasizing that the dead would rise in their assigned genders with genitals intact and unambiguous, like God intended. The consensus position was that gender indeterminacy was fundamentally incompatible with the most essential features of corporeal experience after the resurrection: the body's miraculous restoration to perfect health, physical integrity, and surpassing beauty. What was inadmissible in the ranks of the blessed was weakness or any kind of physical impairment. In general, theologians understood genital variation as one subset of the "defects" that would be resolved by the process of glorification, which would produce bodies sporting perfect physical integrity and consummate health.[20] Augustine, for instance, insisted that the glorious body would be voided of everything that might result in "ugliness" or "unsightly excess," with the "omnipotent Artist" smoothing over any "botch" or "blemish" or "excrescences" in His damaged creation, such that there would be "no defect left in any risen body."[21] In this reinvigorated form, any amputated or missing limbs would be supplied, and there would be a general norming of bodies in terms of height and weight, bulking up or whittling down "those who, on earth, are too thin or too fat."[22] Similarly, a hermaphroditic body would be split into two people or reshaped entirely to rise in the form "which nature would have given him had she not been diverted from her goal," in the words of the Dominican theologian Hugh of Saint-Cher.[23] This emphasis on the physical and spiritual repair addressed gender indeterminacy as just another defect to be rectified by the hand of God, an unfortunate (if not strictly unnatural) happenstance of the mortal world, something easily remedied by a resurrection taking the form of a divine corrective surgery.[24]

It should come as no surprise that this luminous, radiant being with its perfect health, irrepressible vitality, and clear sexual dimorphism was also racialized. For some theologians, the regenerative process of glorification would modify not just the genitalia, fat distribution, and muscle mass of resurrected flesh, but also its skin tone. Augustine's encomium to the pallid beauty of the glorious dead, all of whom would be graced with a "pleasing complexion" glowing with a majestic "brightness" that "will shine like the sun"[25] was taken up by medieval theologians like Bernard of Clairvaux and Otto of Freising, who specified that the resurrection would extend whiteness to those of "disagreeable" color, specifically the "Ethiopians," a position attested through early modernity and into the eighteenth century, where it became a question debated in abolitionist circles.[26] That is to say, resurrection theology was not only about ranking and evaluating individual bodies; it was a body of thought that was eminently political, policing the borders of an idealized community purged of any members who were non-white, disabled, or gender nonconforming.

Controversy over the resurrection fizzled out by the sixteenth century, with the hotly contested quibbles over the fate of fingernails, nipples, and tonsured hair resolving into a dignified Augustinian consensus that held across confessional divisions.[27] The general feeling seemed to be that when it came to the resurrection, it was best not to ask too many questions. As Erin Lambert remarks, even though theologians were constantly accusing their opponents of heresy for their positions on prayers for the dead, purgatory, funerary rites, and psychopannychism (the belief that the soul sleeps in its grave until the final judgment), only "in rare cases did they accuse one another of promoting false doctrines on the resurrection."[28] All the more surprising, then, that in the seventeenth century, John Donne, the dean of St. Paul's, would dedicate so much energy to dissecting what amounted in this milieu to a non-issue: the uncomfortable anatomical particulars of the eschatological body. Donne's morbid imagination has, of course, been subjected to repeated dissection: John Carey speculates that in Donne's love poetry, "death intrudes to an extent which, with any other poet, would seem debilitating," suspecting that the goal was to "treat death as a form of life, or to vivify it," giving the reader the sense that death is "more dynamic" and "more flamboyant" than life.[29] Sounding a similar note, Stanley Fish insists that Donne is "sick and his poetry is sick," taking the extraordinary liberty of diagnosing his thought as "bulimic."[30] Donne was not particularly interested in the healthy, living body; rather, the decomposing corpse or the resurrected flesh was the body that mattered.

Noting the general atmosphere of Protestant "discomfort" with resurrected flesh, Ramie Targoff offers that "it is tempting to conclude that he resembles neither an early modern Protestant nor an early modern Catholic so much as a medieval church father."[31] The temporal drag of Donne's resurrection fetish, however, is counterbalanced by the future orientation of the subject itself, which pitches the Dean out of the Reformed present into a headlong rush toward the apocalypse. In secular and devotional literature alike, Donne's preferred temporal mode is anticipation.[32] This is someone who is "naked first," who has disrobed before you have undressed or entered the room, even before you have agreed to have sex in the first place, someone who, in Aaron Kunin's words, is "waiting for you before you get there."[33] The forward momentum of Donne's thought is not, however, the bog-standard eagerness of the epithalamium, with its impatience for consummation. The pace of desire outstrips the short-term satisfaction of sexual release, barreling past the climax, past the sacrament of marriage, past the lovers' natural deaths until it enters the indeterminate time span between burial and judgment day, a conceptual zone where Donne can linger over the obscure changes that await the body as it returns to the earth. By morning the mistress has already withered to "mummy"; the spurned lover and aloof woman will share a grave; before the wedding is even conducted, the virgin in the bridal chamber rests in her bed like a corpse whose "bodies print / Like to a grave, the yielding downe doth dint" (*Loves Alchymie* 24, *Epithalamion made at Lincolnes Inne*, 4–5). What consistently fascinated Donne was how a body, to all appearances beautiful and healthy in the present moment, was already undergoing a rapid and unstoppable deterioration:

> Who would not be affected to see a clear and sweet river in the morning, grow a kennel of muddy land-water by noon, and condemned to the saltness of the sea by night? And how lame a picture, how faint a representation is that, of the precipitation of man's body to dissolution? Now all the parts built up, and knit by a lovely soul, now but a statue of clay, and now these limbs melted off, as if that clay were but snow; and now the whole house is but a handful of sand, so much dust, and but a peck of rubbish, so much bone.[34]

The slow time of decomposition accelerates, as the anaphoric *now* that notices the body's liveliness in the present moment overlaps with the imminent *now* of its unraveling. The "lovely soul" that knits the body together is already evaporating, fleeing the scene and abandoning the "built up" edifice to dissolution. It is as if the present moment were continually punctured by decay, every instant opening onto an unfathomably distant future in which the body has already returned to dust and the mountains have returned to the sea. Short-circuiting the schedules that govern our daily experience, the rhythms of growth, rest, labor, courtship, and reproduction that make a life, this vision of historical time is nothing but the progress of death: "That which we call life is but *hebdomada mortium*, a week of death, seven days, seven periods of our life spent in dying, a dying seven times over; and there is an end" (*Death's Duel* 171). The asynchronous pulse of Donne's thought, now channeling fourth-century patristics, now perched at the end of history, refuses to accommodate itself to the normative temporality that governs labor, reproduction, and family life.

Indeed, Donne's obsession with the rotting body and its glorious repair crops up in the queerest places, like the 1627 wedding of the Earl of Bridgewater's daughter, Lady Mary, to Richard Herbert, a happy occasion which the distinguished Dean perhaps slightly spoiled by preaching a marriage sermon on Matthew 22:30: "For, in the resurrection, they neither mary nor are given in mariage, but are as the angels of God in heaven."[35] After some throat-clearing that dutifully catalogues what is expected of the officiant for an aristocratic wedding, the sermon takes a hard left, pivoting into an abstruse and alienating contemplation of the corpse's decay and recomposition in the resurrection:

> Where be all the splinters of that Bone, which a shot hath shivered and scattered in the Ayre? Where be all the Atoms of that flesh, which a *Corrasive* hath eat away, or a *Consumption* hath breath'd, and exhal'd away from our arms, and other Limbs? In what wrinkle, in what furrow, in what bowel of the earth, ly all the graines of the ashes of a body burnt a thousand years since? In what corner, in what ventricle of the sea, lies all the jelly of a Body drowned in the *generall flood*? What cohaerence, what sympathy, what dependence maintains any relation, any correspondence, between that arm that was lost in Europe, and that legge that was lost in Afrique or Asia, scores of yeers between? One humour of our dead body produces worms, and those worms suck and exhaust all other humour, and then all dies, and all dries, and molders into dust, and that dust is blowen into the River, and that puddled water tumbled into the sea,

> and that ebs and flows in infinite revolutions, and still, still God knows in what *Cabinet* every *seed-Pearle* lies, in what part of the world every graine of every mans dust lies; and *sibilat populum suum* (as his Prophet speaks in another case) he whispers, he hisses, he beckens for the bodies of his Saints, and in the twinckling of an eye, that body that was scattered over all the elements, is sate down at the right hand of God, in a glorious resurrection. A Dropsie hath extended me to an enormous corpulency, and unwieldiness; a Consumption hath attenuated me to a feeble macilency and leannesse, and God raises me a body, such as it should have been, if these infirmities had not interven'd and deformed it . . . I shall have mine old eies, and eares, and tongue, and knees, and receive such glory in my body my selfe, as that, in that body, so glorifyed by God, I also shall glorify him.

Blithely skipping over the customary praise of the families joined by the match and the joyous expectation of children, the sermon opens up a temporal anomaly, clipping past the life that Lady Mary and Richard Herbert will share into a vividly rendered scenario about what will await them after a number of possible deaths and mutilations, all horrible: flesh dissolved in acid, limbs amputated, bones shivered by bullets, breath exhausted by respiratory failure. The sick body swells in the pseudo-pregnancy of dropsy as if it were gravid not with children, but with disease itself.[36] In place of offspring, husband and wife alike will engender only vermin that "suck and exhaust" their hosts, so that their bodies will be "destroyed contemptibly, by those whom [they] breed, and feed, by worms" (3.3, 92). Unlike the sacrament being celebrated, which makes the couple a single flesh, the processes Donne describes join the lovers not to one another, but to maggots and soil, to the "puddled water" that dribbles slowly into the sea. No longer recognizable as individuals, utterly unmoored from the family line and properties their marriage was designed to preserve, the atomized newlyweds become part of the "all" that "dies [and] dries," the nameless and numberless bodies that "molder" together over the course of "infinite revolutions."

This gruesome fantasy, of course, covers only the first half of the verse the sermon promises to elucidate; after the body horror of decomposition, the moldering corpses must spring to life again, restored by the hand of a loving God. And yet, it is not so clear what kind of body waits on the other side of this miraculous glorification. Donne refers us to Matthew, which specifies that the dead will rise "*as the Angels of God in heaven*," an analogy that works as a bit of a trans tease. As Donne well knew, angels had a complicated relationship to gender. From the early church onward, angels were imagined sometimes as sexless, sometimes as multiply sexed, a tradition that survived into early modern theology and literature.[37] Milton's angels, for instance,

> When they please,
> Can either sex assume, or both; so soft
> And uncompounded is their essence pure,
> Not tied or manacled with joint or limb,
> Nor founded on the brittle strength of bones,
> Like cumbrous flesh; but in what shape they choose
> Dilated or condensed, bright or obscure,
> Can execute their aerie purposes,
> And works of love or enmity fulfill. (*Paradise Lost* 1.423–31)

These spirits are vibrant and vital, flitting between genders as they mold their "soft" and "uncompounded" matter to whatever form they please as they chase pleasure across the cosmos. On these grounds, Julie Crawford hails Milton's Raphael as "the ur-bird of nonbinariness and radical transformation and rebirth," a transubstantial being in the mode of Karen Barad's transmateriality and Stacy Alaimo's transcorporeality.[38] This tradition informs Donne's own poetry as well. "The Relique" promises that the lovers' bodies will reduce together to a "bracelet of bright haire about the bone," a transcendent state in which "Difference of sex no more wee knew / Then our Guardian Angells doe" (5, 25–26). Given that Donne invokes this tradition while celebrating the sacramental union of two souls, a playful hint of the erotic fluidity of angelic life would not have been entirely out of place. In fact, it might have lightened the mood after a sermon that marched the wedding party through visions of their impending descent into worm meat. Instead, at the last minute Donne sidesteps both the asexual soul-merging of the Origenist tradition and the gender maximalism of Milton's angels, offering instead a kind of corporeal minimalism: our resurrected bodies will be like the angels who "are Creatures, that have not so much of a Body as *flesh* is, as *froth* is, as a *vapor* is, as a *sigh* is" (106). If decomposition "melts" the "limbs" as if this "clay were but snow," then the resurrection does not reverse that liquefaction by restoring the body to a solid state. Instead, glorification amplifies and accelerates the process, pressing the body into an even more extreme phase shift that will puff it into aerosol, a barely substantial whisper of vapor. It is as if Donne's vision of paradise involves having the smallest possible amount of body.

And yet, the sermon does not entirely foreclose the prospect of postmortem gender fluidity and wild angelic sexcapades. Typically, and infuriatingly, Donne dangles the infinite possibilities of the *vita angelica* only to refuse to confirm or deny anything about the final shape that will be taken by the angel-adjacent bodies produced by the resurrection: "Now when we would tell you, what those *Angels* of God in heaven, to which we are compared, are, we can come no nearer telling you that, then by telling you, we cannot tell" (8.3, 105). As it happens, centuries of exegesis had assigned a wide range of positive qualities to angelic life and sociality which, presumably, will also characterize resurrected flesh. Donne teasingly raises a dozen or so of these properties only to negate them, one by one, as in "we know that they are *Spirits* in *Nature*, but what the nature of a spirit is, we know not" (8.3, 105). Ultimately, Donne decides, the angels are

> *aenigmata Divina*, The Riddles of Heaven, and the perplexities of speculation. But this is but till the Resurrection; Then we shall be like them, and know them by that assimilation. We end this branch with this consideration, If by being *like* the Angels, we shall *know* the Angels, we are more then *like* our selves, we are our selves, why doe we not know our selves? (8.3, 106)

It is not so clear to Donne that we will understand the precise constitution of resurrected flesh even when we are inhabiting it. This final "assimilation" to angelic materiality must radically transform the mortal body and its cognitive capacities, and yet paradoxically this process also makes us "more like our selves." In which case, Donne wonders, why do we not know ourselves now? With this last "consideration," the sermon grinds to a halt, having gone nowhere and proven nothing. Angelic life devolves into a figure for dissociation, the impossibility of self-knowledge, and a vanishingly minimal experience of embodiment. Despite possessing an unlimited energy for communicating in gruesome detail the "corruption" that the body will undergo, Donne is flatly uninterested in the actual shape of the glorious body, teasingly withholding any concrete belief about what will exactly happen when, on the final day, God hisses us into "so very a body, so perfectly a body [as] shall we have there" (8.3, 98).

In broad strokes, then, Donne concurs with the mainstream opinion that the resurrection will repair the corpse's particulation and putrefaction, smoothing over the frailties and deficiencies that accrue to the body over its life span. At the final hour, the sermon allows, our scattered "seed-pearls" will be extracted from the bowels of the earth and ventricles of the sea by an omniscient God who will restore our bodies down to the atomic level. And yet, even this miraculous process that will "recompact that body, and then re-inanimate that man" does not solidly plant the restored flesh in a normative shape by eliminating physical impairments and overriding the queer possibilities breeding in the necrotic flesh that so captures Donne's attention (7:115). Instead, marriage itself shall disappear:

> They shall not mary, because they shall have none of the uses of mariage; not as mariage is *physicke* against inordinate affections; for, every soule shall be a Consort in itselfe, and never out of tune: not as mariage is ordained for *mutuall helpe* of one another; for God himself shall be intirely in every soul; And what can that soul lack, that hath all God? Not as mariage is a second and a *suppletory* eternity, in the continuation and propagation of Children; for they shall have the first *Eternity*, individuall eternity in themselves . . . they need not supply any defect, by a propagation of children. (99)

While earlier theologians had catalogued the precise physical deficiencies that would be scuttled in the afterlife, a list that included both fatness and thinness, shortness and gigantism, amputated limbs and congenital variation, John Donne found exactly one "defect" to be "supplied": the fragile mortality that requires the "propagation of children." Absent this need, conjugality itself will cease to exist, since "Christ [will] exclude that, of which there is clearely no use in heaven, Mariage" (8.3, 99). A poor stopgap for the fulfillment that will come with immortality and the perfect union with Christ, marriage is nothing but a limp defense against "inordinate affections," a means to the secondary and derivative "eternity" of reproduction and species life. Even so, Donne allows, if marriage is not ideal, it is at any rate mandatory. We are "bound by the generall law to mary," however unsatisfactory it might prove. Thus, instead of praising marriage and family life, the sermon discourses at surprising length on the "sects of Heretiks" that "opposed Mariage," the Adamites, Tatians, Encratites, and Pelagians; then the semi-Pelagians, semi-Tatians, and semi-Adamites (8.3, 101). If the body's "corruption" in the grave is queer, its resurrected flesh is queer as well, although in a different key. It may not be possible to know much about raised flesh, but what seems clear to Donne is that there will be no procreation, no monogamy, and no couple form.[39]

Curious matter for a marriage sermon, which, for all intents and purposes, appears to be transitioning into a funeral sermon. Over the course of the hour during which Donne held the wedding party hostage, the body of the speech decomposes into wormy syllogisms, unspools into strings of increasingly abstruse citation, and builds momentum only to run into dead ends. Donne preached three wedding sermons, and while all of them expressed "ambivalence about marriage" and "marriage to women" in particular, neither of the other two reached the same heights of perversity and morbidity.[40] One suspects this was a purposeful choice. The nuptials Donne celebrates with sucking worms, bloated corpses, and vaporous angels were held for the shatteringly wealthy Egertons, a family intimately woven into the fabric of Donne's own familial misfortunes. The Earl of Bridgewater, father of the bride, was none other than John Egerton, son of the late Thomas Egerton, the Lord Keeper of the Seal, in whose service a young Donne utterly scuttled any possibility of a secular career by eloping with the Egertons' niece, a little stunt that landed the bridegroom, the minister, and the best man in Fleet Prison and subjected Donne and his rapidly expanding family to decades of grinding poverty.[41] Perhaps it was a mistake on the part of the Lord Keeper's son, twenty-five years later, to summon the dean of St. Paul's to officiate the auspicious occasion of his only daughter's marriage. In place of the bovine pleasantries that sometimes characterized Protestant wedding sermons of the period, which were meant to reinforce a normative view of domestic life and companionate marriage, in particular the wife's subordination to a husband and the joyful production of children, Donne chose violence.[42] Refusing to praise benevolent paternalism and reproductive futurity, Donne instead rushes ahead into the queer temporality of the resurrection, a time when marrying will be useless; when bearing children would be pointless; and when bride and groom will be merged not with one another, but with Christ. What the "Epithalamion made at Lincolnes Inne" explores by way of an uncomfortable analogy—that marriage is *like* death, the officiant is *like* the sacrificial priest—the wedding sermon takes as a matter of fact: the young lovers *will* die, and this eventuality provides the occasion to speculate about whether marriage means anything at all. Donne's answer appears to be: maybe, but probably not.

What the Bridgewater wedding sermon clarifies is that Donne's attraction to the resurrection had everything to do with its queer potential. If Protestant homiletics elevated family life into an engine of social control and microcosm of political order, Donne's eschatological perspective desacralizes the patterns of monogamy, heterosexual coupling, and lineal descent at the heart of post-Reformation domesticity.[43] What these sermons do not address, however, despite their endless fixation on corpses and rising from the grave, is how the glorification of the dead transfigures gender, which is all the more curious given this issue's centrality within the theological tradition that Donne's devotional literature explicitly cites again and again. If Donne's theological writings coyly downplayed the trans potentials embedded in the glorious body, these possibilities erupt chaotically in the secular poetry of the *Songs and Sonets*. No less plagued by intrusive thoughts of death than the sermons, Donne's lyric imagines a postmortem experience of decay, particulation, and reconfiguration as a transition that loosens gender's death grip on body and soul alike. And yet, if in one sense death makes transition inevitable and universal, the lyrics build in plausible deniability, retracting the possibility in the very same breath. Both inevitable and impossible, the highest form of platonic unity but also a joke, a misunderstanding, a frivolous play on words, Donne's trans resurrection imagines an egg theology.

Take, for instance, the curious wake underway in "The Funerall," a poem that feeds Donne's ongoing obsession with the resurrection of the body and the familiar trans problem posed by the "challenge of collecting one's missing parts" to achieve a final, definitive form.[44] Here, the cadaver berates a crowd of confused mourners on its intense, unbreakable attachment to an ornament made from a woman's hair, an article that the corpse insists it must wear into the grave:

> Who ever comes to shroud me, do not harme
>     Nor question much
> That subtile wreath of haire, which crowns my arme;
> The mystery, the signe you must not touch,
>     For 'tis my outward Soule,
> Viceroy to that, which then to heaven being gone,
>     Will leave this to controule,
> And keepe these limbes, her Provinces, from dissolution.
>
> For if the sinewie thread my braine lets fall
>     Through every part,
> Can tye those parts, and make mee one of all;
> These haires which upward grew, and strength and art
>     Have from a better braine,
> Can better do'it; Except she meant that I
>     By this should know my pain,
> As prisoners then are manacled, when they'are condemn'd to die.
>
> What ere shee meant by'it, bury it with me,
>     For since I am
> Loves martyr, it might breed idolatrie,
> If into others hands these Reliques came;
>     As 'twas humility
> To afford to it all that a Soule can doe,
>     So, 'tis some bravery,
> That since you would save none of mee, I bury some of you.

In light of Donne's lifelong fascination with the resurrection, "The Funerall" reads as a jokey rewriting of 1 Corinthians 15, in which the talkative corpse takes up the Pauline promise to "shewe you a secret thing," but the thing in question is a weird hair bracelet. The ornamental "mystery" drags the entire corpus of scholarly quibbles over resurrected flesh into the poem behind it, composed as it is of the excremental matter of hair, long the focus of the most abstruse and easily mocked debates about glorification. In the space of three stanzas, the poem hits all the sticking points of resurrection theology's exegetical history, raising questions about which members of the body are so essential to the identity or "nature" of the deceased that they will be resurrected intact, and what happens when one creature consumes the bodily matter of another, as in the case of the stolen lock that will disintegrate along with the lover who absconded with it.

If this bizarre funeral gestures toward a "mystery" or "signe" that is fundamentally theological, given the conceptual vocabularies that Donne cites, modern readers tend to understand the little braid as raising a tangle of problems that are about identity as much as eschatology. For instance: what exactly is the connection between the dead body and this particular ornament? Are there identificatory mechanisms at work in the decision to be laid to rest bedecked in women's hair? Is this a sex thing? The scenario established by the "song" replicates the protocols of literary criticism: we, like the bereaved charged with handling, dressing, and eulogizing the body, take the poem and press it for meaning, shrouding its messiness and corruption in a narrative fabric that lends it a pleasing consistency. Like those grieving intimates who have come to take charge of the corpse, the reader confronts a confusing body and attempts to fix its meaning retroactively by smoothing over any indiscretions, contradictions, or ambiguities, all of which appear to be condensed down into a single "mystery" or "signe": the bracelet whose exact meaning seems hopelessly unclear. Here, however, the corpse talks back, stitching together its own self-account, speaking in the first person and attempting to describe the affects and relations among the "signe" and "my arme," "my braine," and "my . . . Soule" (3, 9, 5). And yet, even as the poem appears to comply with the demand for clarity, the actual disclosures heighten rather than dissipate the "mystery" behind the arrangement of "limbes" and "haire" (8, 3). This odd funeral scraps the neat summation of a eulogy, and instead the corpse itself lectures the silent mourners on the impossibility of making any meaning out of what they see: "do not harme / Nor question much / That subtile wreath of haire, which crowns my arme; / The mystery, the signe you must not touch" (1–4). Then, after directing us not to ask too many questions about the "mystery," the poem provides a number of possible explanations for it. They do not clarify matters.

The curious wording of this injunction lends a certain animacy to the braided keepsake, hence the urgency behind designating the hairwork as the sign *you must not touch*. It is almost as if the hair is not only sensible, shrinking away from an outstretched hand, but hypersensitive, both physically and emotionally; it can be harmed by careless fingering or disturbed by thoughtless questioning. That pain, in turn, may also be experienced by the corpse, which appears to exist in a complicated state of symbiosis with the severed hair. Not merely ornamental, the biomatter "mystery" is vested with the power to maintain the body's coherence, to "make mee one of all," a feat the bracelet manages more efficiently than does anything native to the speaker's own body (11). The filaments are favorably compared to the "sinewie thread my braine lets fall" that is charged with binding "every part" into a single whole (9–10). Indeed, deriving from an external source appears to be a competitive advantage: surely "these haires," vested with "strength and art" drawn from "a better braine, / Can better do'it" (12–14). As the body's own sinews lose their purchase, the fibrous skein of the amulet is recruited as a prosthetic nervous system under orders to "controule" and "keepe these limbes . . . from dissolution" (7–8). The hair that "grew upward" from the aloof beloved's head is not waste matter, atoms that, as Augustine predicted, would be reshuffled to smooth over any deficiencies in the resurrected body, replacing a missing tooth, padding the hips, or adding a few extra inches of height. Neither excrement nor ornament, the hair is infused with the virtues of woman's formidable "strength" and "art," and in its intimacy with her "braine" the lock appears to possess a map for organizing the entire organism. Once transferred to her spurned lover, the hair immediately resumes its basic function, maintaining the physiological integrity of its host-body. Here, it is not God who recompacts a scattered body poised on the cusp of decomposition, a process the corpse feels and narrates in real time. Rather, achieving physical union with some fragment of the unnamed "shee" is the engine of glorification that miraculously "whispers," "hisses," and "beckens" the body back together.

Although it is easy to dismiss the bracelet as surface-level accoutrement, a mere bauble that has no bearing on the essential nature of the chatty corpse it bedecks, "The Funerall" consistently refuses to parse the inner world of the soul or self from the merely external appareling of ornamentation. Interior and exterior twist together in the tangle of threads that knit together the unspooling body. Taking the cadaver at its word, the bracelet is neither decorative nor external; it is brain, nerves, soul, strength, and art. Even though the lock may have been procured from an external source, even though it may be "artificial" rather than natural to the body it bedecks, the lock is also a body part proper to the corpse it "crowns" (3). As Will Fisher powerfully argues with regard to codpieces, detachable beards, farthingales, and handkerchiefs, the hair bracelet serves as a detachable part that materializes gender by mediating, shaping, and bodying forth identity.[45] In the poem too, physiological transformation bleeds over into selfhood. The original soul has fled the scene, hastening "to heaven." Filling this void, the wreath serves as "Viceroy," an "outward Soul" that has parasitically invaded the body and will govern it in the absence of its previous occupant. As soon as the lock "crowns" this new body, she is immediately coronated its sovereign, a queen who regulates, "controules," and "keepe[s] these limbes" as "*her* Provinces." Megan Smith has argued that "The Funerall" is an exercise in kenotic self-emptying, a process that, I would argue, speaks not only to the theological arguments built by the poem but to its account of gender as well.[46] Soul and self are gone; the body is already disintegrating. In mind, body, and soul, nothing is left but "shee." In this respect, the physical union between the body and the hair bracelet redounds onto the speaker's core self, substituting a bad "braine" for a "better" one, the mind of a woman vested with the "strength" and "art" the body in shambles sorely desires.

There are the bones of a trans disclosure here, if you dissect the poem in just the right way. A first-person declaration points to a body, unmoored and partial, that is suffering a kind of dismemberment that feels like death. Relief, stability, and wholeness flow from accessorizing with women's hair. The ornament, then, is not a deceptive surface but an expression of an inner truth. And yet, extracting this trans narrative requires significant, maybe even excessive cutting. In the first place, it is unclear that all this prosthetic supplementation is strictly necessary. The bracelet's capacity to collect the body's disparate parts into a coherent core self is neither asserted nor denied outright, but hovers in a conditional, only a truth-claim "*if* the sinewie thread my braine lets fall . . . Can tye those parts." The phrasing might suggest that this ability should be obvious, but it also leaves space for doubt that the "braine" is up to the job. Everything that follows depends on accepting the slippery premise that the "braine" and its "sinewie threads" can effectively bind the limbs into a stable, self-identical whole, and it is not so clear that the poem itself adopts that position as straightforwardly true. The body is, after all, quite literally decomposing. Conversely, if the brain is incapable of governing the body, there may be no issue at all requiring the bracelet's purely hypothetical capacity to organize the limbs "better." No part of this logic is definitive. The confessional elements are framed syntactically and conceptually as a complicated, metaphysical thought experiment, and as soon as the line of argumentation begins to take shape the poem pivots midstanza to propose an alternative interpretation. The ornament unexpectedly becomes a sign of the impossibility of union, so that "By this [I] should know my pain, / As prisoners are manacled, when they'are condemn'd to die" (15–16). No longer an organic extension of the body equipped with vital capacities so powerful they overcome natural death, the bracelet suddenly becomes an inorganic obstacle to flourishing. Rather than saving the body from decay, the wreath now presses the body toward decomposition, fragmentation, and breakdown. Maybe the hair serves as a cruel reminder of what the body will never be. It is as if the poem is embedded with its own palinode.

Moreover, in gesturing toward the circumstances under which the hair was acquired and the cruel "shee" who gifted it, the poem moves toward an erotic explanation for the bracelet that adds fresh complications. With this twist, the overwrought, abstract speculations of the first stanzas are precipitously brought down to earth. Things take a crude turn. The bracelet comes to signal an unreciprocated attraction, and the death sentence becomes an overblown sexual frustration that turns the speaker into "Loves martyr" (19). Taking the hair to the grave might be nothing more than an expression of extreme pettiness: "since you would save none of mee, I bury some of you" (24). It is easy enough to leverage the sexual content of the poem's second half against the gendered dynamics that govern its first. The hair, after all, is not a wig or a weave; it crowns the wrist, not the head. The placement of the wreath is suspicious, always close to hand for stroking and fingering. Interpreting these pieces of a woman's body as a fetish object might allow us to override other possible explanations for the bracelet as evidence of a buried truth about gender. By the end of the poem, it seems that the mystery has been dispelled. Arcane theological conjectures and enigmatic phenomenological questions resolve into a straightforward exercise in misogyny and perversion.

And yet, the specter of sexual desire does not necessarily scuttle a trans reading. Work in trans studies has softened the walls that separate wanting to *be with* from wanting to *be*, as in Andrea Long Chu's work on sissy porn that theorizes desire and identification as comorbid symptoms.[47] In point of fact, refusing to recognize trans identification where it is tainted with the unbecoming insinuation of sexual pleasure is itself an artifact of a very particular mode of presentism: such a reading replicates the logic at work in the diagnostic criteria for gender identity disorder, which struggles to separate the "true transsexuals" from garden-variety homosexuals and sex freaks.[48] Indeed, importing this mode of trans-antagonistic presentism runs athwart Donne's own erotics, according to which the best possible outcome of sex is apparently the effacement of gender. Take, for instance, the provocation at the center of "The Extasie," in which a couple undergoes an out-of-body experience, launched by the force of their love into a state of perfect, disembodied mutuality. Speaking as a single soul, "one anothers best," they explain that

> This Extasie doth unperplex
> (We said) and tell us what we love,
> Wee see by this, it was not sexe,
> Wee see, we saw not what did move:
> But as all severall soules containe
> Mixture of things, they know not what,
> Love, these mixt soules doth mixe againe,
> And makes both one, each this and that. (3, 29–36)

As critics have noted, this blending of souls, mixed and remixed by love, takes the form of the hermaphrodite. Ruth Gilbert discovers in "The Extasie" a "hermaphroditic conjunction of forms" that is "evocative of the 'chemical wedding' found in alchemical symbolism," while A. R. Cirillo sources the sexless union of souls to texts including Marsilio Ficino and Leone Ebreo.[49] The theological coordinates beneath the idealized hermaphrodite, in both their alchemical and Neoplatonic varietals, associated the androgyne with the state of wholeness that characterized both the beginning and the end of time, the primal androgyne and resurrected flesh.[50] "The Extasie" likewise blurs together prelapsarian and eschatological embodiment by asserting that when love "entergrafts" the "two souls" into a hermaphroditic figure of changeless perfection, it "*interinanimates*" them, a perplexing term that could mean either "mutually breathes life into, or mutually removes the (ordinary) consciousness of, or both (since both do apply)" (9, 42).[51] Not yet given life, the souls have reverted to an almost fetal state as they rest in unbroken stillness on the "swell[ing]" and "Pregnant banke" of a river where the undifferentiated creature falls into an Edenic sleep on the cusp of its ensouling (an *in-animation*). And yet, if that inanimated slumber speaks to the paradisial bliss of Genesis enjoyed by the Adam hermaphrodite as they deliver their own wife, the hybrid figure also bends toward the inanimate afterlife. Donne, as ever, prefers death and glorification to birth and procreation. The merging bodies "like sepulchrall statues lay / All day, the same our postures were, / And wee said nothing, all the day" (18–20). It is as if the price of their union is the stillness not of the womb but of the grave.[52] One is tempted to suggest that, for Donne, death is not interesting because it is like sex; rather, sexuality exerts such a fascination because it is *like death*, a state in which the body will be freed from "sexe" and become ever more "mixt," both "this and that" (30, 36).

Of course, it is difficult to determine just how seriously to take Donne's praise of the amorous ecstasy that merges the lovers into a singular, asexual being. It is not entirely clear what kind of a "wee" the two become, or whether this elimination of gender difference is in fact as thoroughgoing as the speaker insists. The "new soule" remains plural, a "wee" rather than an "I," and when this hybrid creature makes its statement, it is not exactly the case that "both meant, both spake the same" (26). When the soul pronounces that "Wee see by this, it was not sexe, / wee see, we saw not what did move," they might describe a revelation, that the couple sees now, from the present of their ecstatic union, that they did not understand what actually moved (it was the soul all along, not the base matter of the body and its "sexe"); or it might mean that they do not now and did not in the past see what changed ("wee see [not], saw not"); and it also might mean that nothing moved, nothing changed, which would be in keeping with the claim that "th'Atomies of which we grow, / Are soules, whom no change can invade" (47–48). From the sublime heights of this out-of-body experience, the two finally "know / Of what we are compos'd, and made"; and yet, they also admit that "soules containe / Mixture of things, they know not what" (33–34, 45–46). Perhaps in seeing and not seeing, knowing and not knowing, in the convergence of present and past tense, the hyper-refined soul demonstrates its capacity to embrace every kind of experience, its unbroken and androgynous wholeness, a *complexio oppositorum* that approaches divinity. And yet, the listener capable of understanding "soules language" might also detect a quotient of friction in the soul's address (22). In their close but imperfect repetition, the couple's words are not exactly syncing up; perhaps the two are trying to talk over each other. It is as if the mention of "sexe" makes the creature glitch. Contradiction and dissonance flood the "unperplexing" announcement, re-perplexing it in ever more subtle metaphysical abstractions.

Certainly it is possible to read the final twist as a retroactive clarification that all the abstruse philosophizing was just an elaborate effort to manipulate "her" to "repaire" to "bodies" so that the speaker can release the little "Prince" out of his "prison," a reading that would understand the conclusion of "The Extasie" as cynical in precisely the same fashion as "The Funerall's" final stanza (60, 76, 68). Reading in this fashion, Janel Mueller argues that "The Extasie," like the rest of Donne's poetry, "deals with sexual difference by subsuming female otherness to male identity," thus making the poem an "object lesson" in "phallogocentrism" in that it "assimilates all being and all language to male dominance."[53] Mueller pays special attention to the souls that "negotiate" like "Armies," one of which must conquer and subjugate the other, as when the "abler soule" flows into the other and "Defects of lonelinesse controules," which from her feminist perspective signals a masculine invasion that occupies and silences the woman being seduced (17, 13, 43–44). And yet, this reading is begging the question; the argument follows only if we grant the premise that the speaker is male, which the poem gives us reason to doubt. Indeed, "The Extasie" seems to recapitulate the dynamics of "The Funerall" in which it is "shee" who is the "abler" of the pair, "shee" who creeps into the ungendered speaker's body in order to "controule . . . these limbes." For Mueller, as for Stanley Fish, Donne's essential, irredeemable maleness is evident in the rhetorical skill displayed by the poem's internal structure, the infuriating cleverness with which the speaker lures an unsuspecting woman to bed.[54] Far from following through on its lofty goal of demonstrating the perfect equality of lovers, then, the entire performance is staged for the amusement of the all-male coterie whose stand-in is the fictive auditor.[55] The knotty logical problems, the paradoxes, the Neoplatonism were mere pretexts for not only bedding the silenced woman, but seducing her for the purpose of impressing Donne's snickering, sexist friends.

It is not so obvious, however, that the relationship between the unnamed voyeur who quietly third-wheels the static, harmonious bliss of the "new soul" and the speaker is one of identity. This third party is described with the pronoun "he" and "him," marking him as one of the discerning but "Weake men" who "on love reveal'd may looke," in contrast to the speaker, who pointedly goes ungendered (25, 70). This reticence makes the gender distribution at play in the "love [that] was not sexe" complicated and difficult to parse: there is a "her" and a "mee," and then a "he" who hovers nearby, a nonparticipant who nevertheless cannot look away from the ecstasy that fascinates and perplexes him. The ecstasy that rockets the lovers into a "sepulchrall" resurrection body floating beyond gender may not have abolished "sexe" entirely, but merely allocated it to the shadowy figure who overhears their "dialogue of one," a little cache of maleness stashed by the wayside (74). This representative of the class of "weake men" may not be the speaker's double, the secret truth beneath the veneer of ungendered equality on display, so much as a figure of dissociation. The ecstasy of the poem's title cuts two ways: its displacement (*ex-stasis*) encompasses the rapturous transport beyond sexuation and also the alienation that splinters the speaker into both a participant and a mere onlooker, just "refin'd" enough "by love" to be capable of deciphering in part the "soules language" but finally unable to fully inhabit the genderless unity on display. It is as if, even in imagining the rapturous ecstasy beyond "sexe," Donne remains at least partially outside it, off to the side looking in, disengaged from the (in)action.

In life as in poetry, Donne struggled to be fully present. "I am not alwayes I," the cleric pronounced in a dreary Lenten sermon preached to Charles I. "Passions and affections sometimes, sometimes bodily infirmities, and sometimes a vain desire of being eloquent in prayer, aliens me, withdraws me from my self, and then that prayer is not my prayer" (9.9, 219). Donne confesses to this divided self in another sermon, in the course of contemplating the resurrection as promised in Job 19:26, "And though, after my skin, wormes destroy this body, yet in my flesh shall I see God." Here, Donne admits that

> I am not all here, I am here now preaching upon this text, and I am at home in my Library considering whether *S. Gregory*, or *S. Hierome*, have said best of this text, before. I am here speaking to you, and yet I consider by the way, in the same instant, what it is likely you will say to one another, when I have done. . . . I cannot say, you cannot say so perfectly, so entirely now, as at the Resurrection, *Ego*, I am here; I, body and soul. (3.3, 110)

This division, distraction, and inattention spreads Donne out over multiple space-times, translocating the dean from the pulpit to the home library, from the present tense of pronouncing a sermon to the remote pasts of Saints Gregory and Jerome. This estrangement flows from a number of sources, some of which are intellectual, like insecurity, and some of which are decidedly physiological, like the submerged flows of humoral passions that intrude into the disembodied scene of prayer and the "bodily infirmities" that split Donne from "my self." What these "bodily infirmities" might be is a point that the sermon leaves vague, but the poetry makes explicit. "The Canonization," for instance, begins by cataloguing the shortcomings of the speaker's deteriorating body which is aging in a way that makes its gender more pronounced. Anticipating the beloved's disgust, the poem pre-emptively invites her to "chide my palsie, or my gout, / My five gray haires, or ruin'd fortune flout" (2–3). Lingering over a balding, drooping, swelling body, what Donne elsewhere calls "My ruinous Anatomie," opens a wound that is partially patched by fantasizing about its far-off but destined end, a glorious ungendering (*A Valediction: Of My Name in the Window*, 24):

> The Phoenix ridle hath more wit
> By us, we two being one, are it.
> So to one neutrall thing both sexes fit,
> Wee dye and rise the same, and prove
> Mysterious by this love. (23–27)

If Donne's devotional writing explicitly states, again and again, that the resurrection will overcome this "aliening" of the self, such that finally it will be possible to say "*Ego*, I am here; I, body and soul," the secular poetry clarifies that this eschatological repair means accessing a form of gendered embodiment that does not involve sexual differentiation, becoming a "neutrall thing," a "something else" beyond the "difference of sex," a state of serenity in which we can safely and permanently "forget the Hee and Shee" (*The Relique*, 25; *The Undertaking*, 20).

If this moment can only be imperfectly anticipated from the here and now, the closest approximation to having the right body—the body as it should have been—was not actually sex, but poetry, "build[ing] in sonnets pretty rooms" (32). As it happens, this drive to inhabit other modes of embodiment is at the heart of trans poetics. As Stephanie Burt writes,

> We need poetry when literal faces and bodies and circumstances are *not* as good as it gets: we might enjoy reading and writing poetry for many reasons, but we need it when we feel that we need figuration, need something unavailable in the literal world. That "something" might be . . . a new face, a new body; it might be a way to make the inward person audible (if not visible) to other people, if the outward person cannot match what's inside . . . By writing poetry, by working in disembodied language, I can get out of the physical body I happen to have, can depict and counter the insufficiencies of the merely physical world; I can create other bodies for myself in words, some called Stephanie (or Kitty Pryde, or Kermit the Frog, or a lightbulb, or a hermit crab), some just called "I."[56]

Less radical than transition, less risky than full disclosure, the lyric form offers a way of crafting other selves, slipping into other bodies. For Donne, poet of dissociation *par excellence*, those other bodies included a cadaver undergoing dissection, a poisonous fog, a pair of compasses, a cannonball, an idol excavated several thousand years in the future, gold foil hammered to "ayery thinnesse," a featureless sphere, a name scratched into a window, a ghost, and Sappho (*A Valediction: Forbidding Mourning*, 24). A preference for a particular kind of embodiment is detectable in this list. Donne is interested in a barely substantial form, one that hovers on the cusp of dissolution when the tight weave of the body relaxes into a liquescent, cloudlike diffusion. That vague fog of body may have various sorts of connections to femininity, some obvious, others loose and hypothetical: the corpse's ribs crack open to reveal the woman within, "your Picture in my heart"; when the light is just so, and the woman happens to glance at the window, her face will be captioned with "my name," and in that moment "you see me, and I am you" (*The Dampe*, 4; *A Valediction: Of My Name in the Window*, 1, 12). At least one of Donne's poetic personas, Sappho, is unmistakably a woman.

Generally, though, Donne's poetic personas are not women, nor are they obviously feminine: they are multiply gendered or agender, or they are inanimate objects without any clear relationship to gender at all. What these lyric bodies are not, however, is male.

This drive to craft alternate selves was not restricted to Donne's poetic productions. After all, this was someone who deliberately cultivated multiple personas, not least of which was the "Jack" Donne, a young rake on whom the excesses of "D. Donne," the "Dean" or "Doctor" could be blamed.[57] The out-of-body experiences that could be approached through lyric were also available in other modes of writing. In a letter to Henry Goodyer, for instance, Donne proposed that

> I make account that this writing of letters, when it is with any seriousness, is a kind of ecstasy and a departure and secession and suspension of the soul, which doth then communicate itself to two bodies. And, as I would every day provide for my soul's last convoy though I know not when I shall die (and perchance I shall never die), so for these ecstasies in letters, I oftentimes deliver myself over in writing when I know not when those letters shall be sent to you, and many times they never are, for I have a little satisfaction in seeing a letter written to you upon my table though I meet no opportunity of sending it.[58]

This epistolary ecstasy, not unlike the one imagined on the "pregnant banke," wrests Donne away from a "ruinous Anatomie." Even when the letters are never sent, when their receipt is simply imagined, the act of composition offers a way out of the body and toward an incorporeal existence of pure mind, a "departure" and "secession" and "suspension" that borders on "my soul's last convoy." Of course, sometimes these missives were sent, and, freed from the hard constraints of physical embodiment, these "ecstasies in letters" produced pleasures that were intensely queer, or gay in unexpected ways.[59] Take, by way of example, Donne's heated exchanges with Thomas Woodward, which included the verse letter that begins "Pregnant again with th'old twins Hope, and Feare" (1). Receiving a letter in response induces a labor that is also a resurrection: "And now thy Almes is given, thy letter'is read, / The body risen againe, the which was dead" (7–8). Woodward's own missive, "To Mr. J.D.," doubles down on the trope of pregnancy in imagining the connection shared by the pair:

> Thou sendst me prose and rimes, I send for those
> Lynes, which, being neither, seem or verse or prose . . .
> Have mercy on me & my sinfull Muse

W$^{c}$ rub'd & tickled w$^{th}$ thyne could not chuse
But spend some of her pithe & yeild to bee
One in y$^{t}$ chaste & mistique tribadree.
Bassaes adultery no fruit did leave,
Nor theirs w$^{c}$ their swolne thighs did nimbly weave,
And w$^{th}$ new armes & mouthes embrace and kis
Though they had issue was not like to this.
Thy muse, Oh strange & holy Lecheree
Beeing a Mayd still, gott this Song on mee.[60]

In this "mistique," "holy," and lecherous exchange, the spark between T. W. and J. D. flashes into a dizzying array of alternate selves: the host bodies issue twinned muses, whose tickling tribadic climax impregnates T. W. with an offspring-poem that leaves J. D. both "pregnant with hope" and resurgent flesh, in all available senses. Dianne Mitchell recognizes in the verse letters a "breathtaking array of proxies" that "epitomize the queer poetics of mediation," a graceful way of avoiding the problems that necessarily follow from the search for the "real" gender or sexuality beneath the Bassas, muses, and maids.[61] Janet Halley, on the other hand, recoils in disgust from the "disturbing and ambiguous image" of the Muses rubbing each other off and impregnating the letter-writers. She goes on to assert that when T. W. "imagines his and Donne's Muses uniting in a lesbian consummation," he "cannot resist assimilating that image to one of erection and ejaculation ('spend some of her pithe')."[62] Sounding a similar note, Valerie Traub remarks, with a touch of distaste, that "it is one of the ironies of *lesbian* history that the first recorded instance of a variant for tribade in English occurs . . . in a letter from one man to another, and that tribadism in this case figures a creative encounter between men."[63]

By this point, it should be clear that I do not think that Donne was a man—although, for what it's worth, I don't think that he was a woman, either. In compulsively brooding over a death that is also a transition, and just as compulsively repudiating the very possibility, Donne strikes me as Egg Theory's poet laureate. Eggs have theories too, Grace Lavery reminds us, and

> Chiefly, the egg's theory is that they (he, she, ze, etc.) cannot transition. Not, generally, *must* not . . . Egg theory is not generally ethical, but technical. One simply cannot. Which among us, given the chance, would not? But of course it is not so simple; indeed, the categories at issue are endlessly complicated . . . The second step of egg theory is its abstraction, via a curious and ambivalent universalism, into a set of general observations

> about a system in which the desire is found aerosolized into a fine spray. Here is egg theory at its purest, a medium of thought form and desire, a desire with no object and with, perhaps, not even a subject to speak of; here, at last, is the compensatory hallucination of a system of delight and foreclosure. We may have different names for this system—we may call it 'affect,' we may call it 'queer,' we may call it 'aesthetic'; there are plenty of other names—all that is required is its ontology be both virtual and plastic. And it must assure us that transition is both impossible and inevitable, without exposing the dialectical negative of that contradictory image to too much light.[64]

The system does indeed have many names, and the version Donne capitalizes on to "aerosolize" this desire into a "fine spray"—call it a "dampe," if you like—is resurrection theology. Channeling the nagging desire to transcend sexual differentiation into a hyperfocused special interest in the resurrection offered an elegant solution for a need that doggedly persisted despite its apparent futility. It was a fantasy in which the unthinkable transition was *already happening*, that even as the body declined into more and more abject forms of ruinous male decrepitude, it was actually moving toward its eschatological destiny, the moment when all the misaligned, out-of-joint, improperly assembled parts would be reconstituted into a smooth and genderless body. Even better for someone safely ensconced in the egg's uncrackably hard shell, this miraculous transfiguration did not require any effort or explicitly stated desire, or indeed action of any kind, on his part: transition was simply something that was happening *to* him, but also to everyone else who had ever existed. That is to say, the potential transness of Donne's poetry does not only reside in the constantly reiterated desire to be a "neutrall thing," or as sexless as our guardian angels, or just a smooth sphere; it is also nestled inside the retractions, the disavowals, the too-muchness, the bathos, the tonal ambivalence, the tortured logic, the layers upon layers of irony, the haze of dissociation, and the failure to do heterosexuality the right way. I find it hard to believe that all of this has been marshaled for the purpose of convincing an imaginary woman to have sex with him. It seems more likely that the entire poetic apparatus, its most irritating metaphysical elements in particular, are defenses against a wish that could not be renounced any more than it could be realized, a disavowed desire preemptively declared to be impossible, unthinkable, or a joke: the need to be not a man or a woman, but "a something else" (*The Relique* 18). This is the "subtile" knot at the heart of Donne's erotic theology, the bind that will only be "unperplexed" by death, the "signe you must not touch."

If Donne was an egg theorist—or perhaps an egg lyricist—it would go some way toward explaining why this poetry has engendered so many egg critics, readers who stare down a reiterated wish to "forget the Hee and Shee" and nevertheless insist that Donne was in possession of a "stable, transhistorical male identity";[65] or that Donne was "in every sense a man";[66] or that while "Donne's ardent longings remain erotic . . . they have nothing to do with *female* sexuality";[67] or that Donne was a typical "male author" who, "like God, stands erect before the blank page of a female passivity and covers that page with whatever meanings he chooses to inscribe."[68] The lesbian personae adopted in the verse letters and lyric sometimes strike critics as simply too confusing to interpret: they tell us "nothing at all about his sexuality,"[69] or they suspect that selecting Sappho as an avatar is the sign of a creepy male preoccupation with lesbian erotica shared by "many educated young men [who] must have had a more than casual interest in the relations of women with each other."[70] Sometimes the queer genders at play in Donne's poetry are dismissed out of hand or taken as a joke: they are "more playful than sincere,"[71] or perhaps just "a poetic analogue to the durable British satiric tradition of female impersonation" and "transvestite sexual satire."[72] In such readings, expressing a desire to be rid of gender can be a symptom or a sign; it can be a satire or a cover story; it can signal the ugliest possible mode of heterosexuality or the sexiest conceivable form of homoeroticism. The only thing that it can never be is an actual desire in its own right.

In this respect, the confusing, inconsistent relationship to gender animating Donne's work has produced a body of scholarship that recapitulates the queer theory/trans studies border wars that were the central subject of Lavery's inquiry. "Egg Theory's Early Style" was chiefly a dissection of a logic detectable in the work of Eve Sedgwick, Chris Reed, and Chris Castiglia, writers who carefully excise trans possibility from the field's favored queer objects, which can then appear subversive in contrast to trans subjects conceived as regressive, normative, misguided, or preachy. Sedgwick's "How to Bring Your Kids Up Gay," as Lavery incisively demonstrates, denounces the medical "pathologization" of the "proto-gay child" as gender nonconforming, setting up a zero-sum game according to which every affirmed trans child comes at the impossibly steep price of a gay child.[73] Here, effeminacy is taken as a shorthand for homosexuality, serving as an unmistakable symptom of a same-sex object choice that could only be straightened out by addressing it as an expression of dysphoria. Something similar happens when critics are confronted with the Donne's eggish waffling around gender, which prods them to address this body of work as something that must be rescued from gender nonconformity in order to establish its gay male credentials. In *Closet Devotions*, the preeminent articulation of the gay Donne, Richard Rambuss rightly pushes back against readings of the Holy Sonnets that insist that Donne's fixation on bottoming for by God is necessarily a feminizing impulse. Rambuss's reading of the "Batter My Heart" sonnet is, in my view, an absolutely correct and ever-timely reminder of the top's solemn wisdom, that every body has holes, and using them for pleasure has never been the sole province of heterosexual erotics. But in a cheeky pivot, Rambuss goes on to warn against performing a "sex-change" on Donne, which is, in his accounting, "the preferred operation in feminist and gender-oriented criticism" (51). In his mind, such a procedure would take what is essentially a metaphor too literally, tumbling down a slippery slope to a critical maneuver in which "gender subsumes sex" and "produces its own 'silent other,' its own act of effacement" (52). Here, treating the gender play everywhere evident in Donne's corpus as anything other than a sign of same-sex eroticism amounts to a program of literary-critical conversion therapy stealing away gay men and straightening them out by means of a little cut.

And yet, it is not so clear that this "sex change" is a purely external pressure applied by an anxious critic eager to "tame" the poem's "outrageousness" and subversive gay energies (52). The calls are coming from inside the house: it is Donne who rhapsodizes about the promised degendering of the afterlife and the possibility of "forgetting the Hee and Shee" in the self-shattering climax of sexual union. Donne's poetry does not present its critics with a binary choice between gender and sexuality, and there is no sense in which acknowledging the transgressive genders threaded throughout the *Songs and Sonets* can only "efface" sexuality. Trans desire does not render the poetry normative, and it does not "tame" anything: it makes the poetry more queer, *and also more gay*, if in surprising ways that remain uncomfortable to critics like Elizabeth Harvey, for whom assigned sex dictates the conceivable limits of eroticism. In this way, early modern egg criticism transforms Donne into the bad object of both feminism and queer theory, or makes him a problem child at risk for "seduction" by a literary-critical "transgender craze." It is not a coincidence, I think, that the same slate of incoherent, contradictory accusations levied against trans women accrue to Donne as well: he is "hypermasculine,"[74] a "bully,"[75] and a misogynist, but also effeminate and weak, almost an incel *avant la lettre*; he is "predatory"[76] and intrusive, forcing his way into women's spaces where he does not belong; he is a faker and a "transvestite," a fetishist and a pervert; like the autogynephile, he gets off on imagining himself as a woman. The only way to handle Donne is to double down on his essential, immutable maleness, which means the only options available are to rehabilitate him as a gay man or discipline him as a sexist.

It is time that we let go of the transphobic assumption that the genders of the long-dead authors we study are self-evident and stable, or that our certainty about their genders marks the inviolable limits of what we can say about their poetic and erotic experiments. In this chapter, that relinquishment has meant finding in Donne's queer eschatology a trans theology of resurrection. This insight has some value for our understanding of trans history; it suggests that, in an era before medicine achieved a monopoly on defining, managing, and governing gender, religion offered an important conceptual resource for imagining transition, for thinking about the body's extraordinary plasticity. Moreover, recapturing the queer genders that have always been embedded within resurrection theology contradicts the reactionary transphobia of the evangelical right, currently aiding and abetting the legal assault on trans rights by denouncing transition as incompatible with traditional Christian values. Here, the transitions experienced by the resurgent flesh of the resurrection are not only licit but sacred. For Donne, death does not confirm a body's natural, inalterable gender but will open every body to extreme, almost unthinkable transfigurations. What remains to be seen, however, is how the trans resurrection Donne draws out of the grave connects to our contemporary necropolitical landscape in which trans bodies are marked for death. Answering this question requires thinking about the glorification not only in terms of the individual's relationship to gendered embodiment, but the collective that will be shaped by the resurrection. After all, resurrection theology has always been about community; it involves assigning differential value to bodies and eliminating those that will have no place among the ranks of the elect. It seems clear enough that Donne's vision of the afterlife was not one that constitutionally excludes trans people or admits them at the price of forcible conversion to their assigned genders. But what kind of eschatological community did Donne's trans theology accommodate?

Here, the lyric poetry cannot provide any obvious answers, populated as it is by a contracting commons of two—who are actually one—with the occasional imagined rival added to the mix, a tiny assemblage perpetually on the verge of collapsing back down to a singularity. The closest Donne comes to making a clear statement about the eschatological community appears neither in the sermons, eager to speak about the grave but reluctant to speculate about the afterlife, nor in the poetry, but rather in Donne's illness memoirs, *Devotions upon Emergent Occasions* (1624). Written while the author was sick unto death with a fever, possibly typhus, the *Devotions* collect Donne's characteristically morbid meditations on the progress of the contagion, the expectation of imminent death, and the disorienting experience of recovery. Donne frames the advance and retreat of the disease in the theological vocabulary of death and resurrection. The title itself is, as Debora Shuger notes, a Latinate pun that refers not only to the "unexpected (emergent) occurrence (occasion) of the author's illness," but also "the rising/resurrection ("emergent" from *emergo*) of one who had died ("occasions" from *occasus*)."[77] In the early stages of the infection, that promise of resurgence refers exclusively to the individual patient who faces death alone, lamenting the "Miserable, and (though common to all) inhuman posture, where I must practise my lying in the grave by lying still, and not practice my resurrection by rising any more" (18). At the very nadir of the disease's progress, however, the isolation of deadly illness opens onto an experience of dying that is collective:

> The church is Catholic, universal, so are all her actions; all that she does belongs to all. When she baptizes a child, that action concerns me; for that child is thereby connected to that body which is my head too, and ingrafted into that body whereof I am a member. And when she buries a man, that action concerns me: all mankind is of one author, and is one volume; when one man dies, one chapter is not torn out of the book, but translated into a better language; and every chapter must be so translated; God employs several translators; some pieces are translated by age, some by sickness, some by war, some by justice; but God's hand is in every translation, and his hand shall bind up all our scattered leaves again for that library where every book shall lie open to one another. (107–8)

Unlike the devastating solitude of the sickbed, which Donne laments bitterly, death itself folds the subject into new modes of affinity, relationality, and connection with the community of the dead. The baptized child and the buried man are "ingrafted" into the same sacramental body politic, which Donne explicitly identifies as a "universal" and "Catholic" collective. The metaphor at work establishes the resurrection as a "translating" (rather than erasing, deleting, or culling) that both preserves and dissolves the individual bodies of the dead. This bookbinding conceit runs somewhat athwart to the unity at play in the body politic metaphor, since when God "shall bind up our scattered leaves again," he does not gather them into a single folio. Instead, the resurrection terminates in a library where "every book is open to every other," an image of ecstatic interpenetration in line with the *Songs and Sonets*' disembodied union, or with the frothlike, vaporous bodies of the *vita angelica* Donne fancies in the Earl of Bridgewater's wedding sermon. Paradise may not be Origen's smooth spheres, but there is an eggishness to fantasizing about heaven as a giant library in which our final, perfect bodies will not be patrons leisurely browsing the aisles but will take the interpenetrating form of books reading each other.

If Donne's corpus breaks with the mainstream tradition on resurrection in its minimization of sexual difference, the *Devotions* additionally refuse the position that the final ascent to glory will restore the dead not just to life but to health. Instead of imagining a heavenly community of perfect bodies, freed from all defects, Donne instead proposes a commons of the sick in which we are bound together by disease, infirmity, and vulnerability:

> Affliction is a treasure, and scarce any man hath enough of it. No man hath affliction enough that is not matured and ripened by it, and made fit for God by that affliction . . . Tribulation is treasure in the nature of it, but it is not current money in the use of it, except we get nearer and nearer our home, heaven, by it. Another man may be sick too, and sick to death, and this affliction may lie in his bowels, as gold in a mine, and be of no use to him; but this bell, that tells me of his affliction, digs out and applies that gold to me. (109)

Following hot on the heels of the anodyne vision of the eschatological commons as a library filled with animatronic volumes comes this deeply unsettling analogy, according to which the mystical body of the church is tethered together by the vector of "affliction." In place of the vital, vibrant bodies purged of illness that theologians from Augustine to Luther and Calvin promised were awaiting the faithful in the hereafter, Donne rhapsodizes a collective bound by a shared, embodied experience of illness, what Drew Daniel identifies in a dazzling essay on *Biathanatos* and the biopolitics of self-killing as Donne's "political necrology."[78] In this passage, the *munus* at the heart of the community, the gift whose exchange produces the collective, is not Christ's sacrificial death, but the "affliction" that "lies in the bowels" of "another man" and which is shared like "currency."

It is tempting to valorize Donne's trans necrology and naked disdain for reproductive futurity, to celebrate a vision of an eschatological commons bound together not by social hygiene, strength, and health, but by infirmity, weakness, and death. This is a temptation that, I think, we should resist. With this extractive figure, in which "affliction" is a treasure buried inside other bodies "like gold in a mine," which the church "digs out and applies to me," we hit the limits of how far this body of work can be rehabilitated for trans thought, a threshold marked by Donne's relationship to whiteness. The metaphor of "mining" is an overdetermined one, connected as it is to the sexual politics of colonization. Donne mobilizes these senses in, for instance, Elegy XIX, hailing the mistress as "My America! My new-found-land . . . My Myne of precious stones, My Emperie" (27–29). Here I want to tread carefully, heading off the line of argumentation laid out by Elizabeth Harvey, according to whom Donne's inhabiting of female personae is itself a form of colonial violence. In a discussion of "Sapho to Philaenis," Harvey asserts that

> what appears to be Donne's generous bestowing of language and independence on Sappho, in direct contrast to Ovid's violation of her, turns out to be an act of colonization, an act that is perhaps most clearly visible in the metaphor central to Elegy 19, where the mistress's body and the New World become versions of each other . . . In a similar way in "Sappho to Philaenis" . . . the otherness of woman (Sappho) [is] domesticated and reshaped into an image of the self, a process that is mediated both by ventriloquism and voyeurism.[79]

This particular category error, so familiar from transphobic activists who insist that transition is no different than blackface, allows Harvey to assert that Donne adopting the persona of Sappho is a form of colonial appropriation. It is not only the case that, as C. Ray Borck cautions, gender and race function so differently as "categories of analysis, systems of dominance and oppression, occasions for unequal distributions of power, locations of community and empowerment, and individual subjectivities" that "it is impossible to hold them in comparison" without "oversimplifications and erasures" significant enough to render the project valueless.[80] Treating any form of lyric personification that does not align with the poet's assigned gender as a version of colonial violence is also an erasure of the sexual politics of European imperialism, which brutally eliminated the many varieties of transness and gender variance encountered during the process of colonization.[81]

When it comes to the question of Donne's place in trans history, the metaphor of colonization is less useful than its material reality. That is to say, Donne didn't just spice up sex poems with references to the New World; he was someone who participated in the colonial project as actively, if not always successfully, as possible. After spectacularly self-destructing in the Egerton household, Donne toyed with the possibility of making a career with the Virginia Company and, in 1609, when the company was undergoing extensive corporate restructuring, Donne lobbied to be appointed their London secretary.[82] Even after the post went instead to William Strachey, Donne continued to take an interest in the company's colonial endeavors, and in 1622 Donne was named an honorary member and appointed to its governing board.[83] Later that year, in the wake of the corporation's failure to turn a profit and the decimation of the Jamestown settlement by the military ascendency of the Powhatan confederacy, a delegation from the company invited Donne to deliver their annual sermon, endowed in perpetuity by an anonymous donor. On November 13, Donne addressed a crowd of three to four hundred people (one of whom, incidentally, was Thomas Hobbes) on the righteousness of the company's activities.[84] In particular, the sermon agitated in favor of converting the indigenous inhabitants of the New World, whose minds, like their territories, were a *terra nullius*.[85] Moreover, Donne asserted that even though the company had failed to turn a profit, the settlements would still have a beneficial effect, since even if

> the Plantation shall not discharge the Charges, not defray it selfe yet; but yet already, now at first, it shall conduce to great uses; It shall redeeme many a wretch from the Jawes of death, from the hands of the Executioner, upon whom, perchaunce a small fault, or perchance a first fault, or perchance a fault heartily and sincerely repented, perchance no fault, but malice, had otherwise cast a present, and ignominious death. It shall sweep your streets, and wash your dores, from idle persons, and the children of idle persons, and imploy them: and truely, if the whole Countrey were but such a *Bridewell*, to force idle persons to work, it had a good use.

Rhapsodizing over a London purged of its degenerate element, Donne imagines that the Virginia Company's colonial projects will enforce a salutary program of social hygiene through a program of impressment, incarceration, and transatlantic transportation.[86] The "great uses" of this penal colony chiefly involve forced labor, not only of the city's "idle" poor—and their children—but also of the enslaved persons already trafficked by the company, whose governor had already brought "20. and odd" African captives to Virginia in 1620.[87] The sermon was a hit—the Virginia Company proposed that it be printed as part of a fundraising campaign, to which Donne eagerly assented. In the printed edition's dedicatory epistle, Donne identifies with the "the Honorable Company of the Virginian Plantation," on the grounds that "now I am an *Adventurer*; if not to *Virginia*, yet for *Virginia*."

Although the Virginia Company sermon was not explicitly about gender, its imaginary of policing, incarceration, transportation, and forced labor is necessary context for situating Donne within trans history. That is to say, Donne's erotic fantasies about the corpse that undergoes a radical, liberatory ungendering sits uncomfortably alongside this endorsement of the plantation economy that, as Hortense Spillers argues, was built on the "profitable 'atomizing' of the captive body" in a "materialized scene" of "female flesh, ungendered."[88] For Riley Snorton, this necropolitical reduction of bodies to fungible flesh was the condition of possibility for "understanding sex and gender as mutable and subject to rearrangement in the arenas of medicine and law," as in the horrific violations that J. Marion Sims, the "father of modern gynecology," visited upon enslaved women whom he forced to endure dozens of unanesthetized surgeries as he developed a technique to repair vesicovaginal fistulas.[89] With this context in mind, the morbid community that Donne imagines in which the church "digs out" the "gold" in another man's bowels and "applies [it] to me" resonates differently, as does the queer fantasy about being a cadaver, simultaneously dead but also curiously animated, that sloughs off gender and is broken down into scattered "seed-pearls." That is to say, the resurgent flesh spun out in Donne's poetry may indeed break with the eschatological communities whose borders were so strictly policed in mainstream resurrection theology, in particular by treating physical impairment as a desirable, even sacred condition rather than a defect to be repaired. And yet, even if Donne persistently imagined death as the abolition of gender, the radical potential of this trans theology is curtailed by its relationship to whiteness. Indeed, as Melissa Sanchez argues, the possibility that resurrected flesh will be forcibly converted to whiteness is embedded in Holy Sonnet IV, "Oh my blacke Soule!," which stages the "black soul" being "summoned / By sicknesse" to a "doome" of imprisonment, only to be liberated by being washed in "Christs blood, which hath this might / That being red, it dyes red soules to white" (1–2, 5, 13–14). Where Sanchez understands this sonnet as giving shape to "an early formation of racial whiteness and cis-masculinity as the implicit characteristics of a universal Christian subject," however, the reading developed over the course of this chapter comes to a different, and differently troubling, conclusion.[90] Here, the racial formation in question does not turn on the essential and implicit cisness of the Christian elect; rather, whiteness is the condition of possibility for Donne's trans theology.

The glorious body that Donne "prepares towards" is neither the ungendered flesh that is detained in a state of infinite, unending violation; nor is it the fugitive flesh that, in Marquis Bey's accounting, possesses an "inexhaustible agility that evades capture and in fact names the constant eradication of oppressive apparatuses" (*A Nocturnall upon S. Lucies Day*, 43).[91] What Donne offers in the place of trans fugitivity is *identity*, in which trans possibility exists only as a secret nestled deep inside an individual subject, a "signe" or "mystery" that both solicits and resists decipherment by a specialist—a literary critic, perhaps, or a psychiatrist, psychoanalyst, or sexologist.[92] In other words, by producing trans longing as a matter of identity, a truth suspended within a complex interior world, Donne's tortured egg poetics prefigure the psychiatric model of the implicitly white trans subject who must express her truth for expert dissection.[93] Such transness is not an action or a relation so much as an utterly apolitical affective state, nothing more than a nagging feeling in in the back of the mind, a set of embarrassing emotions and partial identifications that are valid even if—or maybe especially if—they are never actualized. Tucking trans desire away in the mind palace liberates the white egg subject to do the work of empire and racial capitalism, perhaps by serving on the board of the Virginia Company or promoting an expansion of policing and forced labor, activities that created the material conditions for the emergence of the absolutely literal "atomizing" and "ungendering" of captive bodies that forms the racial genealogy of transness.

In a sense, this chapter has performed a perversely Donnean trick, constructing an elaborate argument only to swerve at the last minute into a new perspective that apparently undermines and frustrates what came before. And yet, even with these caveats in mind, it seems to me that Donne still belongs to trans history, if not for the poetry's subversive possibilities, then for what they reveal about the buried connections between religion, racialization, and trans subjectivity. The theological maneuvering that situates gender fluidity as internal state, subject to permanent deferral, anticipates the medical model of transition not only in its strategies of "discovery," but also in producing the category of transgender as a racialized taxonomy. The trans temporality of Donne's resurgent flesh, which not only can but *must* transition in order to take its place within the nonreproductive eschatological community, is a seductive vision indeed. And yet, Donne's trans theology can only appear radical if its essential whiteness slips by unnoticed or is rendered invisible by critical techniques that insulate gender from race.

[ CHAPTER FOUR ]

# Trans Mayhem in *Samson Agonistes*

In 1949, a twenty-two-year-old trans woman, known in the archives under the pseudonym Lynn or Val Barry, hit an impasse in her search for a physician willing to perform what we now call "gender confirmation surgery."[1] Even then, seventy years ago, the operation she was after, vaginoplasty, was not exactly experimental: it had been performed on cisgender women for eighty years and trans women for twenty.[2] In fact, trans patients had been undergoing genital reconstruction since as early as 1906, when Karl Baer received certain surgical interventions at Magnus Hirschfeld's Institute for Sexual Inquiry in Berlin. The precise nature of his treatment, unfortunately, remains unknown, as the records were destroyed in a Nazi book-burning in 1933. By the late 1940s, then, there was some reason to think that medical providers would be receptive to Miss Barry's request. In fact, the previous year, a hospital in her home state of Wisconsin had almost agreed to complete what she called her surgical "conversion." Unfortunately, at the last minute, they reversed their decision and refused to operate, offering instead, as if by way of a consolation prize, to give her a lobotomy. She declined and, grasping the complexity of the medical systems she hoped to navigate, began to look for an advocate. She reached out, as so many others would, to Dr. Harry Benjamin, an endocrinologist who had rebranded himself as a trans specialist after a notorious career capitalizing on scam cures for tuberculosis and "rejuvenating" vasectomies. Upon receiving Miss Barry's inquiry, Benjamin redirected her search toward the more liberal medical landscape of San Francisco, where physicians at the Langley Porter Clinic had begun providing the very occasional trans patient with hormone therapy. However, some question remained concerning the legality of this particular procedure, and so, as a preliminary measure, Benjamin, along with his collaborators Karl Bowman and Alfred Kinsey, sent a letter of inquiry to the state attorney and future governor of California, Edmund G. Brown, who responded in his official capacity that any physician who performed such an operation would be liable for prosecution for criminal mayhem.

Although by now it is synonymous with a kind of riotous disorder, the word *mayhem* is in fact cognate with *maim*, and it describes a very specific type of mutilating injury. In its precise legal definition, mayhem entails the intentional disfiguring or disabling of an otherwise comely and vigorous body. Curiously, the object of the debilitating assault is not only, nor even chiefly, the victim whose eyes are gouged out or whose testicles are removed. Rather, in the aftermath of such an attack, it is society itself that suffers a loss of capacity and resilience. Take, for instance, the odd crime scene at issue in *The State of North Carolina v. Bass*, a case in which the defendant was paid $29 to inject a local anesthetic into a patient's fingers so that he could cut them off at home to collect insurance money.[3] In upholding the physician's conviction for mayhem, Justice Moore wrote that "our government is deeply concerned, financially and otherwise, for the health of its citizens and that they not become a public charge."[4] Debilitating injury robs the state of a productive body, reducing a "healthy" subject into a public burden who drains rather than enhances the viability of the nation. Maiming was not merely a question of labor power, however; it was also about sex. In that historical moment, the government was also deeply concerned with the reproductive health of its citizens, which the state sought to manage and even optimize according to models of social hygiene and racial fitness.[5] For this reason, mayhem shadowed health centers, prisons, and eugenics boards, a charge levied when the wrong kind of person was forcibly sterilized, someone too rich, too able-bodied, or too white.[6] Whether directed at fingers or testicles, the cuts that constitute mayhem threaten the well-being of the state, which depends upon its subjects' capacity for labor and for reproduction, their ability to replenish the social body through producing healthy, desirable offspring.[7] The criminal offense of mayhem marks the point at which someone, often a doctor, interferes with the reproductive futurity of the nation. Although rarely actualized through an indictment, let alone a trial, the threat of mayhem prosecutions serves as a useful index for the shifting form of American biopolitics in the twentieth century, cropping up in controversies about compulsory sterilization; elective vasectomies; abortion; contraception; and, beginning in 1949, trans health care.[8]

Even in the 1940s, however, something about mayhem felt vestigial. The charge struck legal scholars and medical ethicists as curiously out of time, a relic of English common law that no one quite understood how to handle. "Nobody knows whether the old common law offence of mayhem still exists," complained one barrister trying to parse the legal status of contraceptives and bare-knuckle prizefighting in 1956.[9] Such frustration is everywhere evident in Harry Benjamin's correspondence with attorneys and sexologists about Miss Barry's case, in which he throws his hands up in frustration at "this medieval state of affairs."[10] The physician writes that "it is difficult to reconcile my common sense with the fact that statutes based on requirements of English kings in the middle ages should still be valid."[11] Benjamin means to be dismissive, of course, handwaving these trumped-up "medieval" charges countermanding his expertise as irrelevant to what he understood as a matter of public health. This chapter, however, takes his provocation seriously, reassessing the apparent break between legal assaults on trans medicine in the twentieth century and the pastoral power of care codified in early modern laws against maiming.

Premodern literature, flush with wounding, constitutes an important conceptual reservoir for scholars tracking mayhem's origins and afterlives, as in Graham Hammill's work on consent in *Venus and Adonis*; Ari Friedlander's exploration of poverty, impotence, and biopolitics; and Micah Goodrich's extraordinary essay on "biosalvation" in *Piers Plowman*.[12] This chapter adds to this growing body of critical work by applying a trans analytic to the legal and literary history of mayhem through a reading of Milton's *Samson Agonistes*, a text that is uniquely primed to explore the conceptual manifold of trans mayhem. A story that circles around a community thrown into crisis by the holes gouged into a hypermasculine war hero, Milton's closet play frames maiming as a threat to military readiness and national security. The text's account of the perils of debility is also heavily gendered, since Samson's incapacitation is described as a feminizing, castration-adjacent procedure. As characters collect around Samson's exhausted body, they propose various conceptual frameworks to navigate the morass of legal, political, and ethical questions raised by mayhem. Is there a viable social claim on individual bodily capacities? Is gender a resource that can be harvested by the state? Are there limits to the demand that we work ourselves to death for our country or expose ourselves to mutilating injury in war? Who should be blamed and punished when the nation loses access to a given body's powers? What do we collectively owe to those whose bodies have been rendered "useless" in our service?

In many respects, *Samson Agonistes*'s characters float answers to these questions that prefigure the extractive logic employed by mid-century states' attorneys bent on snuffing out the very possibility of trans life. As they assess Samson's defective body, his countrymen take for granted their access to and ownership over his strength and reproductive choices; they deplore the feminizing cut he endured as a collective wound that has degraded and incapacitated them all; and they struggle mightily to find someone to punish for it. Such perspectives dominate the play, a text that is shot through with a fear of the emasculating maim that softens and enervates, a laceration that can strike a body at peak masculinity and leave it dependent, defenseless, and femme. However, in Milton's hands, Samson's experience also registers the harms that follow from the state's seizure of bodily capacities, the mandate to maintain a lusty and productive body for the benefit of the nation. This chapter argues that within Milton's closet play lies a quiet celebration of trans mayhem, an account of wounding that embraces rather than recoils from vulnerability, one that rejects "usefulness" and "employment" as metrics for assigning value to bodies. In the cut that renders Samson unfit for military duty, Milton floats the possibility that there is a pleasure in weakness that is transformative, liberating, and ethical.

Harry Benjamin was right in identifying mayhem as an artifact of premodern jurisprudence. The crime's essential features, its relation to debilitating injury and military service, were outlined in the most influential legal treatises of the thirteenth century, including Henry de Bracton's *De Legibus et Consuetudinibus Angliae*, as well as the anonymously authored commentaries *Fleta* and *Britton*.[13] Despite its medieval origins, however, mayhem's ongoing significance was assured by its early modern career, in particular its appearance in the works of the seventeenth-century jurist Edward Coke, whose importance within Anglo-American jurisprudence is almost impossible to overstate. In the first volume of his *Institutes*, Coke recounts a case he heard on his circuit in 1603, when a man named Wright, whom he describes as "a young strong and lustie rogue," determined to "make himselfe impotent, thereby to have the more colour to begge, or to be relieved without putting himselfe to any labour," and so "caused his companion to strike off his left hand."[14] Both were indicted for mayhem, which, Coke explains, "signifieth a corporall hurt, whereby [a man] loseth a member, by reason whereof he is less able to fight." Relevant injuries include "putting out his eye, beating out his foreteeth, breaking his skull, striking off his arme, hand, or finger, cutting off his legge or foot, or [anything] whereby he loseth the use of any of his said members."[15] The gravity of the crime follows from the precept that "the life and members of every subject are under the safeguard and protection of the king . . . to the end that they may serve the king and their countrie, when occasion shall be offered."[16] One cut in particular would seem to diminish the bodily vigor necessary for those who might be pressed into a fighting corps. Castration was consistently flagged as the most extreme form of the crime imaginable, and thus the law reserved the harshest penalties for those who removed testicles—either their own or another's. Bracton's description of mayhem denounces those who remove or damage the testicles (*virilia absciderit*), either "on account of debauchery or in order to sell [the victim]" (*cum libidinis causa vel commercii*),[17] while William Hawkins's *Pleas of the Crown* (1716) notes that, although "all *maim* is felony, it is said, that anciently castration was punished with death, and other maims with the loss of member for member."[18] Even so, despite the gravity with which the courts dealt with gelding, the gonads occupied a curious position in the physiological map of mayhem. Unlike the feet, teeth, fingers, and bones singled out as necessary for self-defense, the testicles are rarely involved directly in battle. In his fussy and roundabout way, William Blackstone offers something approaching an explanation when he includes in his anatomical chart of mayhem not just fingers and foreteeth but "those parts, the loss of which in all animals abates their courage."[19] Gender creeps into the legal account of mayhem because of its close connection to military service, which demanded a full complement of intact, and thus fully virilized, soldiers.

In sourcing "animal courage" to the genitals, Blackstone's does not stray far from early modern models of physiology. In a discussion of Venetian castrati in his *Anthropometamorphosis* (1653), John Bulwer expounds on the Galenic schema that casts the testes as "a Fountaine of heat and strength" that

> communicate a certaine aire to the whole Body, by whose mediation virility is reconciled, [and] the body acquires strength and firmenesse, [and] is made more lively . . . which parts being cut away, besides that, men are deprived of the Generative power, they want all these conveniences, [and] the colour and heat grow dead and withered, [and] they are a made beardlesse, and altogether effeminiate . . . The *Parthians* used this out of Luxury for the retarding of Age, and the prolongation of life, it having been observed, that castrated Animals in any kind, and *Spadoes* by Art, live longer than they that retaine their virilities, and by this Artifice they retaine a better habit of Body, upon which score those Canibals who live neare the Equator, who hunt after men to eate them, when they have taken any Males of the neighbouring Nations, they many times geld them, and so fat them up for slaughter as we do Capons.[20]

A soldier needed his stones. Bulwer identifies the testicles as the anatomical repository of the "heat" that infused the body to generate a "firmenesse" of physique coupled with a "certaine aire" of masculinity captured in an aggressive, warlike disposition. Gelding depleted the potential soldier's heat, rendering him weak, debilitated, and effeminate. Such a creature was of no use to the press gang, a "withered" husk of a man incapable of defending his nation during wartime. Indeed, genital modification thrusts the cut body outside of the fold of the nation altogether according to a racial logic that affiliates "spadoes by Art" with Parthians and equatorial cannibals. Bulwer recoils from "Eunuchisme," a benighted and suspiciously foreign method "of degrading men" not only "from their manhood," but also from their humanity, leaving them little better than capons, livestock, or prey animals (344–45). Even so, he begrudgingly acknowledges that castration comes with "conveniences" of its own: prolonged youth and rejuvenation, extended life span, a pleasing plumpness, a better "habit of body," and a small and sweet voice. Bulwer was not alone in noting the advantages of emasculation. Indeed, his paragraph closely paraphrases a passage on the apparent longevity of deer from Thomas Browne's *Pseudodoxia Epidemica* (1646), in which Browne remarks that "we sensibly observe an impotencie or totall privation [of testicles] prolongeth life, and they live longest in every kinde that exercise [sex] not at all. And this is true not onely in Eunuches by nature, but spadoes by Art; For castrated animals in every species are longer lived then they which retaine their virilities."[21] Whereas Coke denounced mayhem as "*homicidium inchoatum*," an abortive homicide that falls just short of snuffing out life altogether, Bulwer and Browne understand the allure of castration as a procedure that radically enhances a given body's vitality.[22] Voluntary gelding—which did indeed occur in sixteenth- and seventeenth-century England—amounted to a misappropriation of the body's "generative power," an essentially selfish hoarding of heat, life, and manhood that properly belonged to the crown.[23]

To return to a key term from Coke's judgment against Wright, Bulwer frames castration as a maim that interferes with its victim's "lustiness," a term that denoted a general sense of health or wellness, as when Shakespeare has Bullingbrook profess himself to be "Not sick" but "lusty, young, and cheerily drawing breath," or when Paulina reports that Hermione has given birth to "a goodly babe, / Lusty and like to live."[24] In a more general way, lustiness signaled the lively energies and unique abilities possessed by both human and nonhuman actors. Robust vegetable growth or especially fertile soil could be described as "lusty," which might also name the potency possessed by an "inanimate agency" like "fire, wine, poison, [or] a disease."[25] Coke's outrage at Wright's self-inflicted injury, surely a scheme to avoid holding down a steady job, stems from his perception of lustiness as a positive and quantifiable social good, something necessary for national security and economic stability. At the same time, Wright's "lustiness" was equipped with a sinister edge, an uncomfortable proximity to the appetites that emerged sharply when paired with his alleged roguishness. To draw upon Ari Friedlander's groundbreaking work on early modern rogues as a population requiring biopolitical management, Wright's case was not only about the idleness and criminality of the poor, but also about their "sexual delinquency" and "prodigious fertility," a profligacy that threatens the very survival of the body politic.[26] A "lustie rogue" abuses his natural capacities, levying his energies and craftiness for socially destructive ends like drinking, whoring, and begging. From this angle, the cut of the axe rendered Wright impotent in the doubled senses of the term, leaving him both incapable of manual labor and unable to bridle his lascivious urges.[27] A petty criminal and breeder of bastards fully dependent upon parish support to scratch out a meager living, such a rogue can only drain valuable resources from the communities in which he is parasitically embedded. After his voluntary amputation, then, Wright joined the mass of unproductive bodies denounced by the Calvinist preacher Thomas Taylor as the "idle, lustie, and wandring beggars, who ought not to eate."[28]

Laws against maiming may have been cloaked in the language of care and safeguarding—life and limb are in the hand of the king, and so forth—but in reality they were a vehicle for extraction. The grave penalties attached to wounding were never intended to preserve bodily autonomy but to protect government property: the labor power and reproductive capabilities of its citizenry. Note how mayhem merges or even confuses subject and sovereign at a physiological level, remapping the body according to its ability to inflict and sustain violence, or to fortify the nation by performing honest labor. As such, whether the cut is consensual or not is irrelevant because the individual's powers of self-defense are not fully his own. From the opening made by mayhem, sovereign power slithers into the body, lingering over areas rich in capacity, arrogating to its own use the teeth, digits, limbs, sinews, and sense and sex organs that constitute the country's muscle. At the same time, mayhem law turns on the tenderness of these appendages, their fragility in the face of digging thumbs and grinding boots and arrant axes. This vulnerability becomes an opportunity for the state to broaden what in an anticipatory way we might call its police powers by invoking the language of protection to exercise punitive force against its own citizenry. Common-law mayhem, as elaborated by early modern jurists, becomes a vehicle by which, in time, the state will assume what Jasbir Puar calls the "right to maim," the unilateral authority to inflict debility on "undesirable" populations at home and abroad, measures justified through the language of self-defense.[29]

As would later be said of sodomy, mayhem proved to be "an utterly confused category" that hopelessly blurs the distinctions between victim and perpetrator, morbidity and vitality, consensual surgery and involuntary injury, and individual liberty and sovereign prerogative.[30] Maiming simultaneously enhances and depletes its victim's lustiness, leaving him an unsuitable farmhand but an industrious beggar, thief, brawler, and philanderer. The jurists, for their part, were not particularly invested in identifying, much less resolving, any of these incongruities. Unspooling the contradictions that animate the confused category of mayhem entails pivoting from legal archives to a literary account of wounding that folds together debilitating injury and forced feminization: Milton's *Samson Agonistes.* Milton's closet play is uniquely primed to explore the conceptual manifold of trans mayhem, most obviously because it is about a disabled soldier whose injury simultaneously incapacitates and feminizes him. It is also a text that, like the law of maims itself, inquires after the origins and ends of bodily capacitation. Along with the assembled Israelites of the Chorus, the play's readers cluster around Samson's prone body to, in Harapha's chilling words, "survey . . . each limb," measuring and assessing his remaining strength.[31] Within Milton's corpus, "surveying" could mean a lively assessment of a body's abilities, as when Adam describes his initial experience of awakening: "Myself I then perused, and limb by limb / Surveyed, and sometimes went, and sometimes ran / With supple joints, as lively vigor led" (8.267–69). For Milton's first man, surveying amounts to a vibrant, vital process of discovery, an ecstatic exploration of his physical energies that leads to increasing freedom, self-direction, and relationality. Testing his abilities and flexing his supple joints sets him in motion, moving him around the newly created world and pressing him to find his place in it.[32] If Adam's experience on his first day of life is energizing and invigorating, the surveying that Samson undergoes over the course of his final day is enervating and objectifying. Rather than integrating his new members into a coherent whole, the evaluation to which the imprisoned Samson is subjected plucks him apart, limb by limb. Here, surveying cleaves more closely to its function within property law. In appraising Samson's condition, the host of characters who descend upon the imprisoned hero assert their claims over his strength, his sexual favors, his attention, and his energies. That is to say, *Samson Agonistes* circles around the fundamental questions raised by common-law mayhem: what is a body for? To whom do our abilities belong? What happens when a body cannot fulfill its appointed purpose?

One line of thought pursued by the play to answer these questions is profoundly natalist. From this point of view, the place of Samson's extraordinary energies within his nation's destiny was fixed not only from birth but from the moment of his conception, which the Book of Judges describes this way: "There once was a man of Zorah, of a Danite family, Manoah by name; his wife was barren and had had no children. An angel appeared to the woman and said to her, 'Behold, you are barren and childless, but you shall conceive and bear a son . . . He will be the one who will begin to save Israel from the hands of the Philistines'" (Judg. 13:2–5).

Samson's story has always turned on the question of reproductive sexuality. The promise of deliverance packaged in Samson's muscular frame was not just the sole purpose of his own birth; it was the very condition of his mother's fertility. As such, the denuded and enslaved hero begins his self-inventory by questioning the significance of his own birth. In his opening reflections, tracing the paths he has followed through capacitation and debility, Samson asks:

> O wherefore was my birth from Heaven foretold
> Twice by an angel, who at last in sight
> Of both my parents all in flames ascended
> From off the altar, where an off'ring burned,
> As in a fiery column charioting
> His godlike presence, and from some great act
> Or benefit revealed to Abraham's race?
> Why was my breeding ordered and prescribed
> As of a person separate to God
> Designed for great exploits . . .
> With this Heav'n-gifted strength? O glorious strength,
> Put to the labor of a beast, debased
> Lower than bondslave! Promise was that I
> Should Israel from Philistian yoke deliver. (23–39)

Heaven itself arranged Samson's birth announcement, deputizing angels equipped with explosions and columns of fire to stage something resembling a Biblical gender-reveal party announcing that Samson was to be assigned *hero* at birth. As with all other forms of birth assignment, this means that the child entered this world with a place already carved out for him. The angel explained that Samson would be ordained as a Nazirite, with the terms of his service stipulated well in advance of his appearance on the scene: his "vow of strictest purity" was made for him by his mother; his dietary restrictions were specified by an angelic messenger; and his bodily comportment, down to the length of his hair, was dictated by divine mandate. While Milton erases Samson's mother from her son's tragic narrative, he unfolds the natalist biopolitics attending Samson's birth into a full educational program.[33] From infancy onward, the chosen child's "breeding" was tightly "ordered and prescribed" to maximize and control his abilities as part of an education that subjected him to extraordinary social, familial, and religious pressures designed to shape him into the deliverer "promised" to his nation. This pedagogy took as its special object his vital energies, fine-tuning the biological rhythms of his growth, nourishment, and libido, including failed efforts to redirect his substantial sex drive toward the "daughters of [his] own Tribe" and "Nation" (876–77). When Manoa claims that the angel had "Ordained [Samson's] nurture holy, as of a plant" (362), he indicates that his paternal role entailed overseeing the proper ordering of Samson's vegetative energies, his virtues and capacities. To take up the language of Wright's case, then, Manoa's charge was to cultivate Samson's "lustiness," optimizing his son's powers while also containing them within acceptable boundaries.

To frame matters in Arendtian terms, Samson's birth is all nativity and no natality. For Hannah Arendt, the possibility of worldbuilding and creative action depends upon "the constant influx of newcomers who are born into the world as strangers," little bundles of potential that can be actualized in any number of unpredictable ways.[34] No one has ever arrived in the world less a stranger than Samson, a promised deliverer ordained by God, a messianic prototype whose story was written for him in advance. The fantasy of conquest announced at Samson's conception only impoverishes the political imagination and shuts down every avenue for envisioning collective well-being except war, settlement, and genocide. Devising other uses for his abilities, different pathways for his judgeship, or new forms of relationality with the people he was sent to slaughter does not fall within the compass of his charge. Paradoxically, then, the "consecrated gift of strength" that is Samson's birthright diminishes rather than enhances his experience of freedom, as he feelingly understands when he laments that he has always lived "in power of others, never in my own" (78). Insuperable powers do not translate to liberty and agency. So much is riding on Samson's explosive strength: should he somehow mishandle or diminish his "gift," say, through poor marriage choices or inadvisable gossiping, his entire nation will be condemned to "bondage" and "servitude" (269–70). From the perspective of his countrymen, their chosen deliverer is a poor steward of his lusty energies, his sexuality in particular. Samson's strength must be protected *from Samson*, the unpredictable, impulsive instrument of divine will. The hero's "lustiness" cries out for governance, management, and intervention, so that he might fulfill his divinely appointed task: to do his country some service, when occasion shall be offered.

That is to say, Samson's physical gifts were not given to him so that he could actualize himself or pursue his own ends. Rather, they mark a debt that that was in arrears before he was even born, a deficit that must be repaid through constant, unending labor on behalf of his country. It is rarely remarked that *Samson Agonistes* is a text that is relentlessly obsessed with work. The play is comprised of a cascade of speeches that lament the derailing of "the work to which I was divinely called"; "the work from Heav'n imposed"; "the work for which thou wast foretold," since "thou, [Samson, were] solemnly elected / With gifts and graces, eminently adorned / To some great work" (226, 565, 1661, 678–80). They wonder whether God will "use him further yet in some great service" or "To what can [he] be useful, wherein serve" or whether he must "sit idle with so great a gift / Useless about him" and "at home lie bed-rid . . . idle, / Inglorious, unemployed" (1499–1501, 564, 579–80). What interferes with this imperative for productivity is an assault that constitutes criminal mayhem to the letter: the Philistines set about "cutting off, disabling, [and] weakening"[35] Samson's muscular body by "putting out his eye" and "violently depriving [him] of the use of [his] members" in order to render him "less able to fight" and "defend himself."[36] This problem isn't just Samson's, of course, because his boundless reserves of "Heaven-gifted strength" are not truly his own but are earmarked for the Israelites. This arrangement has complicated repercussions for Samson's bodily integrity. When Manoa thinks about his son, he does not imagine a single, unified subject. Instead, Manoa sees a full complement of soldiers packed into one convenient container, as his gaze lingers over "his hair / Garrisoned round about him like a camp / Of faithful soldiery," while "on his shoulders wav[e] down those locks, / That of a nation armed the strength contained" (1496–98, 1493–94). Manoa's blazoning eye fully elides the interiority and psychological complexity everywhere on display in Samson's own reckoning with his experience. Instead, this Leviathan-like image of corporate personhood absorbs the entire Israelite nation into Samson's body, which stores their collective stockpiles of military strength. In Kevin Curran's analysis, this model of personhood does not entail consciousness, selfhood, or psychological depth. Rather, the Hobbesian person is a "relational" structure, an object through which various transactions are accomplished.[37] In this case, Samson is the product and instrument of a covenantal transaction between God and the Israelites, an object through which they are to achieve their domination over the Levant. That means, as the Chorus never tires of reminding him, that Samson's strength does not belong to him. He may have been born with it, it may be "lodged" within him, he may feel it "diffused . . . through all my sinews, joints and bones" (1141–42). It doesn't matter—Samson does not own but merely mortgages his extraordinary abilities, which arrive heavily entailed.

The all-consuming work imposed upon Samson, so important that it overrides any claim he might have to self-determination or bodily autonomy, is ethnic cleansing. Samson's great task is to clear a coastal strip of the Levant for settlement by the Tribe of Dan, a project that Milton explicitly frames in the language of racial conflict that pits "Abraham's race" or "the unforeskinned race" against their "inhuman foes" (29, 1100, 109). In treating the Philistines as a cipher for racial difference, Milton did not innovate: Christian theologians had associated the Philistines with a defiling foreign presence as early as the Septuagint and pre-Vulgate translations of the Bible, which rendered the Hebrew *p'lishtim* as *allophyloi* and *alienigenae*, "those of alien stock" or "the foreign-born."[38] Beginning as early as the Crusades, the vague ethnic difference of the Philistines began to narrow, as Christian propagandists increasingly cast Muslims as the "New Philistines," an equivalence brokered by the two groups' allegedly shared weakness for idolatry, luxury, despotism, and effeminacy.[39] The transformation of Philistines into Muslims routinely shaped visual representations of the Samson cycle in early modernity.[40] Paintings of Samson's shaving or his destruction of the temple of Dagon sometimes clothe his Philistine assailants in Persian and Ottoman garb, as in Gerrit van Honthorst's painting of Dalila sporting a turban as she starts to operate on Samson's unconscious, vulnerable body.[41] Mattias Stom sets a semi-nude Dalila on the left as a figure of Orientalized seduction, and in submitting to her Samson has exposed himself to the violence bearing down on him from the right side of the frame. In Jan Steen's *Simson en Delila* (1668), Samson reclines on a Persian rug next to the remains of a recent feast. He is already separated from his sword, which lies limply on the floor next to a feathered turban that he appears to have recently doffed. As he slumbers, Dalila passes locks of Samson's snipped hair back to a turbaned man who stands in a group that includes a Black Philistine. Giving in to the luxurious, gluttonous pleasures flagged as "eastern" prepare Samson for a cutting that traffics his vital energies to his people's enemies, here marked as both non-Christian and nonwhite. In the figure of the quasi-Muslim Philistine, confessional divisions bleed into racial difference, a taxonomical distinction between kinds that turns on the biomarker of circumcision.[42] Seeding *Samson Agonistes* with the potent admixture of anxieties condensed into the biblical Philistine, then, participates in what Walter Lim calls Milton's "political Orientalism," a "solipsistic ethnic vision" that maps "Israel's exceptionalism" as God's chosen people onto the English nation.[43] Casting Samson as the torchbearer of the "new Israel" of the English republic both whitens and Christianizes the hero with whom Milton identifies while racializing his "faithless" and "inhuman" enemies according to a dynamic that, as Benedict Robinson notes, speaks to "the etiology of race in republicanism."[44]

In the minds of medieval and early modern exegetes, the Philistines' essential foreignness was not fully captured by surface-level variances in complexion or the idiosyncrasies of their religious practice. Understanding the full extent of their embodied difference meant reaching below the belt to examine the arrangement and use of their genitalia. The nonbelievers' enigmatic and perverse corporeality emerges most sharply in the events narrated in 1 Samuel: 5–6, when the captive Ark of the Covenant shatters the sea-god's idol on the threshold of his own temple. The *Geneva Bible* (1560) translates the battle between the graven images and its scorched-earth fallout this way:

> The Philistims toke the Arke of God, and broght it into the house of Dagon, and set it by Dagon. And when they of Ashdod rose the next day in the morning . . . beholde, Dagon was falle[n] vpon his face on the grounde before the Arke of the Lord, and the head of Dagon and the two palmes of his hands *were* cut of vpon the thresholde: onely the stumpe of Dagon was left to him. Therefore the Priests of Dagon, and all that come into Dagons house treade not on the thresholde of Dagon in Ashdod, vnto this day. But the hand of the Lord was heavy vpo[n] Ashdod, and destroyed them . . . [and] was against the citie with a very great destruction, and he smote the men of the citie bothe small and great, & they had emerods in their secret partes.[45]

The first casualty of the theomachy is Dagon himself, dismembered and skinned until only a twisted stump remains to his followers. When their false god's abjection fails to chasten the Philistines, who respond by inventing an exciting new superstition that involves jumping over the temple's threshold, the Lord escalates the situation, dealing out a series of devastating punishments that begins with an infestation of mice, and then afflicts the Philistines with a confusing plague of "emerods." At this point in the narrative, the Philistines send the Ark from city to city, from Ashdod to Gath to Ekron, which merely spreads the plague, with the captive Ark as a vector of contagion. The Philistines then go to their "Priests & the sothsayers" and ask how to put an end to their suffering, and their priests tell them that they should "giue vnto [the Ark] a sinne offring: then shal ye be healed. [Make] fiue golden emerods and fiue golden mice . . . ye shal make the similitudes of your emerods, and the similitudes of your mice that destroy the la[n]d."

They had emerods in their secret parts. The punishment for idolatry, for pitting the Ark against the graven image of Dagon, is that the entire nation is stricken with what, in the English, was rendered as "emerods"—that is, hemorrhoids. These translations loosely follow Jerome's Latin, which does not give a specific name to the Philistines' embarrassing condition, which, he says, causes their "entrails to project and putrefy"; he says only that God "*percussit eos in secretiori parte natium*," he struck them in the very hidden, or maybe recessed, parts of the buttocks. Jerome later specifies which secret parts he meant when he indicates that the five sin offerings were fashioned as "*quinque aureos anos*," five golden anuses. If hemorrhoids offer a neat explanation for the humiliating affliction lodged in the recesses of the rump, neither the precise nature of the plague nor its location—anal or genital—have ever been entirely straightforward. The shape of the golden "emerods" fashioned in recompense for the Ark's theft struck some commentators as profoundly phallic, suggesting some sort of genital affliction ranging from impotence to castration. The symptoms of this plague have been variously glossed as tumors, ulcers, abscesses, plague boils, syphilis, prolapsed intestines, "an affliction of the Philistines' *membra virile*."[46] Other, more visceral explanations were also proposed. In the *Antiquities of the Jews*, Josephus claims that the Philistines experienced "a grievous malady . . . inflicting most rapid dissolution," such that "they brought up their entrails all consumed and in every way corrupted by the disease."[47] Some commentators tethered the plague of emerods to the infestation of mice that seems to have accompanied it, as in the bracing explanation offered by Rashi, who writes that the Philistines endured a "plague of the rectum," in which "mice would enter their recta, disembowel them, and crawl out."[48]

These complexities are only compounded by the Hebrew, which specifies that the Philistines were stricken with *ophalim* (עפלים), a term that seems to mean swelling. That sense would be straightforward enough, except for the fact the term *ophalim* was marked off for *qere-ketiv*, a ritual reading practice according to which the text was written one way and read aloud differently, as in the case of the tetragrammaton, which is traditionally pronounced as Adonai.[49] This special instance aside, such replacements were largely a matter of textual clarification or updating archaic linguistic forms. The Philistines' plagued genitals, however, were an unusual case, part of a very limited set of euphemistic substitutions made for the sake of propriety.[50] In 1 Samuel, the apparently indelicate term *ophalim* was to be read aloud as *techorim* (טחרים), which meant hemorrhoids or abscesses. Commentators are often puzzled by this substitution, since abscesses are not in any obvious way less disgusting than swellings. The effect here is not one of clarification, but rather of multiplication, an accretion of plaguey symptoms that proliferate in new and ever more confusing forms the closer you look. The Philistines had *ophalim* layered with *techorim*, or maybe they had *techorim* out loud and *ophalim* silently. As it happens, *ophalim* appear at only one other point in the Hebrew Bible, in the catalogue of curses in *Ki Tavo* outlining the punishments that would be visited upon the Israelites should they revert to idolatry. Among the "extraordinary plagues," the "strange and lasting plagues" that would discipline the straying people were the *mitzrayim ophalim* (מצרים עפלים), the Egyptian inflammation (Deut. 28: 59, 27). It is as if a temporal and spatial anomaly opens up in the groins afflicted with *ophalim / techorim*, a mark of backsliding, a sign inscribed in the flesh that signals a movement away from monotheism and back to the old gods, away from covenantal obligation and back to disobedience, away from the Promised Land and back to Egypt.

What is happening with the bodies of the Philistines? In Robert Mills's handling of the episode, the plague of emerods amounts to a divine judgment on the Philistines' sodomitical tendencies, a sin that solicits an illness that "eat[s] the sinner up from the inside" and makes visible their internal contamination.[51] The insult suffered by the Ark of the Covenant, its mere proximity to the polluted and promiscuous cult of Dagon, is repaid by a pandemic engineered for sexual humiliation, a disease that targets the groin, genitals, or rectum. And indeed, the affiliation between the Philistines and sexual deviance only strengthened over time, finding one afterlife in sexology. As it happens, the outbreak of emerods was a perennial favorite in the medical literature of the late nineteenth and early twentieth centuries, within the transcendently strange genre of retrospective diagnosis. In this body of critical writing, physicians and psychologists with apparently nothing better to do attempted to perform differential diagnoses on historical, mythological, and Biblical maladies. Any number of potential diseases were suggested for the Philistines' affliction: dysentery and bubonic plague rose to the top of the list, but other contenders were typhus, proctitis, bilharziasis caused by parasitic worms, or hemorrhoids caused by inflammation subsequent to anal sex. Indeed, as one physician working in this arena caustically explained, "emerods" were simply a convenient shorthand for tumors, shriveled testicles, and "the endless ills of the *pathici*."[52] As Mitchell Hart notes, the outbreak of emerods in particular and Philistine degeneracy more broadly cropped up in work by medical experts pursuing the "connection between prostitution, venereal disease, and social and political disorder."[53] These medical studies offered a secularized version of the premodern account, submitting that the maladies endured by the Philistines were their natural punishment for the biological sin of sodomy rather than the religious sin of idolatry. At the same time, recognizing that the emerods serve as a commentary on the Philistines' sexual practices should not occlude the fact that the disease also refashions their gender. In the queer body of the stricken idolator, interior and exterior bleed together into an anatomical configuration that blurs any obvious distinction between male and female. Their innards extrude and genitals wither, and all the while lesions multiply into yawning, vaginal fissures. Ultimately these contemptible creatures resort to the prosthesis of golden phalloi in a pathetic bid to be made whole again. The obscure gender of the Philistines, unmanned and infinitely permeable, handmade and defective, marks their exclusion from the covenant: the curses catalogued in *Ki Tavo* threatens the Israelites with enslavement and *ophalim*, "the Egyptian inflammation," should they break the commandments (Deut. 28:27). In this sense, the racialized dimensions of Philistine heresy emanated from their "secret partes"—swollen, corpuscular, and unrecognizable. The perplexing, even incendiary nature of the Philistines' gender is both a symptom of idolatry and a punishment for it, a mark of difference that invites further violence from those whose chosen status manifests in their physical integrity and legible genitalia.

In the temple at Ashdod, we get a taste of how the Lord exercises his disciplinary power. In a roundabout fashion, the emerod pandemic constitutes mayhem, and not only because it throws the Philistine social order into confusion and disarray. The swelling, burrowing affliction also handily accomplished what the law of maims attributes to castration: it targeted the genitals to debilitate and feminize its victims, leaving them vulnerable, impotent, and helpless. The pestilence attacked men at the height of their military strength, fresh from an apparently definitive victory over the Israelites, reversing their conquest and compelling them to return the Ark they were holding hostage as an emblem of their domination. If the infliction of emerods amounted to mayhem in a general sense, the assault on Dagon constitutes maiming according to the letter of the law. Indeed, this is precisely how Milton characterizes the chastening endured by "that twice-batter'd god of *Palestine*"[54] when he visits Dagon in hell, calling him "one

> Who mourned in earnest, when the captive ark
> Maimed his brute image, head and hands lopped off
> In his own temple, on the grunsel edge,
> Where he fell flat, and shamed his worshippers." (1.457–61)

"Maim" is not a word that Milton favored, and in applying it to the bruising suffered by Dagon's "image" he employs it in the technical sense used by the common law: the repeatedly "battered" body has not merely experienced an assault, but an amputation that immobilized and defanged him. For his hubris, Dagon's limbs were plucked off one by one until the "brute" icon was a mute and recumbent stump, unable to rise and defend himself against his divine assailant. Milton's attention lingers on the communal context of Dagon's wounding as its affective charge radiates outward to "shame" his worshippers who stand frozen at the threshold littered with the fragments of their shattered idol. In *Paradise Lost* no less than in Coke's *Institutes*, mayhem terminates in a collective injury that disarms and devastates the social body as a whole.

For Milton, then, Dagon's abjection offered a point of entry into the political questions raised by debilitating violence, which explains its presence in *Samson Agonistes*, a play set prior to the events of 1 Samuel. This premonition of the idol's fall, which Manoa "as a prophecy receive[s]," foreshadows Samson's own demolition of the Temple of Dagon and aligns Samson's self-immolating assault as both an echo and anticipation of the mayhem generated at Ashdod (473). As such, the curious, temporally disjointed appearance of Dagon's stump within the narrative of *Samson Agonistes* offers one framework for understanding the origins and ends of Samson's extraordinary abilities: he was born to maim. Samson grimly predicts a near future in which the "God of Abraham"

> Will not connive, or linger, thus provoked,
> But will arise and his great name assert:
> Dagon must stoop, and shall ere long receive,
> Such a discomfit, as shall quite despoil him
> Of all these boasted Trophies won on me,
> And with confusion blank his Worshippers. (465–71)

Here, in place of emerods and mice, the divine violence rained down upon the "idolatrous rout" takes the curious verbal shape of "blanking." To "blank" most directly means to amaze or terrify into a state of nonresponsive silence, as when Adam hears of the "fatal trespass done by Eve" and, "amazed, / Astonied stood and blank, while horror chill / Ran through his veins" (*Paradise Lost* 9.889–91). In a showstopping reading of this passage as a scene of "petrification" and idolatry, Sharon Achinstein argues that the blanked Adam undergoes a transformation that involves "a recalibration of the human into something other—something much, much weaker."[55] To experience blankness is to feel the suffusion of a paralytic fear that arrests action and clouds thought while sharpening sensation. Feeling "blank" also describes the somatic texture of weakness. As John Baret explains in his *Aluearie, or, Triple Dictionary*, "to be Blanke" most closely carries the sense of the Latin *labascere*, the inchoative form of *labo*, meaning to totter, waver, or yield.[56] They who are blank, Baret continues, are lazy, unwell, and faint (*segnes sunt, la[n]guidi, et remissi*); their spirits are broken (*animo concidere, frangi*). To gloss the term, Baret offers a line from Terence's *Eunuchus*: "These fellowes be blanke, or out of harte and courage." Inhabiting a state of blankness means to be defeated, both mentally and physically, to be unable to muster the energy to fight back. Inflicting blankness is a tactic in psychological warfare, as when Samson's assault on the Temple of Dagon mires Gaza "in confusion" when, with his final feat of strength, he "execute[s] / His errand on the wicked, who surprised / Lose their defense, distracted and amazed" (1593, 1284–86). Slackening and going limp, frozen in a shock response, the blank body hovers on the cusp of yielding. In other words, *Samson Agonistes* frames blankness as the catastrophic end product of mayhem, the corporeal experience of "losing one's defense."

Moreover, when Milton refashions Dagon's demise as a matter of "blanking," he infuses *Samson Agonistes* with the racial animus that had accrued to the scene through centuries of Christian exegesis. After all, "blank" is a skin word with a place in the early modern racial imaginary. As Urvashi Chakravarty argues in a transformative essay on *King Lear*, the term contains an "explicit allusion to whiteness, not only in its proximity to the Spanish 'blanco' but also in its invocation of the spectre of the blank page as 'a white paper,' as Thomas Blount renders the term in *Glossographia*."[57] In tracking the word's racial undertones, Chakravarty invokes the presumably ironic name of John Blanke, a Black Anglo-Spanish trumpeter in the court of Henry VIII. For Imtiaz Habib, imposing this name upon the musician "bleached out all signs of an African identity" through the "sedimentary acculturation of Anglo-European assimilation."[58] Attending to the complex resonances of the blank lends a queasy clarity to the "great exploits" for which Samson was "designed." Samson's task is to blank the land of darkness, restoring it to the pristine whiteness of the empty page by blanching out any inky remnant. The same logic that casts Philistines as pseudo-Muslims afflicted with deformed genitalia bleeds into *Samson Agonistes*'s account of capacitation, of what a body is for: the appointed ends of Samson's God-given lustiness are ethnic violence and territorial acquisition. The same biopolitical rationale that measures, quantifies, and maximizes Samson's "gifts" commandeers these powers to prosecute a campaign of racial terror.

The annexation he pursues is not achieved just through indiscriminate killing, although clearly a great deal of that was required. Rather, Samson's unique talent was his ability to maim, a capacity that Milton amplifies in his rendition of Samson's military victories. The Chorus recalls that "Irresistible Samson," whom

unarmed
No strength of man, or fiercest wild beast could withstand,
[Who] ran on embattled armies clad in iron,
And weaponless himself,
Made arms ridiculous, useless the forgery
Of brazen shield and spear, the hammered cuirass,
Chalybean tempered steel, and frock of mail
Adamantean proof;

> But safest he who stood aloof,
> When insupportably his foot advanced
> In scorn of their proud arms and warlike tools . . .
> Old warriors turned
> Their plated backs under his heel;
> Or grov'ling soiled their crested helmets in the dust.
> Then, with what trivial weapon came to hand,
> The jaw of a dead ass, his sword of bone,
> A thousand foreskins fell, the flower of Palestine. (142–44)

Here, in the most cherished memories of his countrymen, we discover how it is that Samson applied the "gifts and graces" with which he was "eminently adorned / to some great work," his "people's safety" (679–81). Unable to slaughter all of his opponents, he wounds them so deeply and so spectacularly that they lose the ability to defend themselves. Samson is what the police call a "compliance weapon," a device for making a belligerent opponent tractable and receptive to direction. "Safest he who stood aloof"; the jawbone is a pedagogical tool that delivers a stern lesson to soldiers and men of military age, instructing the Philistine populace that the condition of survival is absolute, unqualified submission.

What the Chorus describes is asymmetrical warfare that turns on the uneven distribution of manpower between the Philistines and the Israelites, a differential capacitation that emerges in the sharp contrast between Samson's extreme nudity and his opponents' lavishly described but ultimately useless armor. This is not the last time that the Israelites "disparage glorious arms / Which greatest heroes have in battle worn" as ineffectual and craven (1130–31). Indeed, the play is strangely, consistently dismissive of armor, as in Samson's challenge to the boastful Harapha to face him "single and unarmed":

> Put on all thy gorgeous arms, thy helmet
> And brigandine of brass, thy broad habergeon,
> Vantbrace and greaves, and gauntlet, add thy spear
> A weaver's beam, and seven-times-folded shield,
> I only with an oaken staff will meet thee,
> And raise such outcries on thy clattered iron
> Which long shall not withhold me from thy head
> That in a little time while breath remains thee
> Thou oft shalt wish thyself at Gath to boast
> Again in safety what thou wouldst have done
> To Samson, but shalt never see Gath more. (1111–29)

What Samson denigrates when he mocks Harapha's embellished, overly complicated armor is the Philistines' relationship to embodiment. Hiding behind prettified gear is not only worthy of scorn because such apparel is "proud," "gorgeous," and "ornamental" and thus betrays a decidedly effeminate fondness for artifice and surface-level accoutrement, even on the ultramasculine space of the battlefield. It also smacks of idolatry, a disordered and inappropriate relationship to the object world.[59] Just as the worshippers of Dagon stricken with *ophalim* manufactured golden emerods to supplement their anatomical deficiencies, so too do the Philistine warriors attempt to augment their naturally weak and woundable bodies with a metal exoskeleton. The man who "weaponless / Ran on embattled armies clad in iron" acts out of an unshakable faith and the sure knowledge of divine protection, while the "idolatrous rout" places their trust in the products of human technology: tempered steel, folded hide, and mail frocks.[60] As Richard Godden argues in work on *Gawain and the Green Knight*, the protective gear of chain mail and hammered steel serves as a prosthesis, a second skin that covers over the knight's susceptibility to harm even as it evokes a "fantasy of a body that is whole, unpenetrated, [and] complete."[61] Samson and his "trivial weapon" explode that fantasy of physical intactness, making the "forgery" of arms "useless," even "ridiculous." There is an unsettling moral distinction being drawn here between Samson's bare-chested brawn and the Philistines' cowardly retreat to the prosthetics of armor. Samson's divine election bequeathed him an unwoundable body that required no modification to fulfill its destined ends, while the sinful and aberrant Philistines possess what Jeremy Citrome memorably calls "bodies that splatter."[62] The Chorus seems to think that the perfect integrity of Samson's body confirms the righteousness of his cause. By contrast, the Philistines' recourse to the assistive technology of armor speaks to their spiritual inadequacy, their exclusion from the covenant, and their alien status in the lands they have inhabited for generations.

Just as, in a few years' time, God would punish the Philistines with a disease that afflicted their loins, so too does Samson's "irresistible" assault culminate in an attack on his enemies' genitals, scattering "a thousand foreskins" across the field of battle. It is possible, and certainly more tasteful, to imagine the foreskin collection recounted by the Chorus as an uncomfortably vivid synecdoche that, in Gordon Teskey's words, substitutes a "heap of the dead" with a "pile of foreskins."[63] And yet, a literal reading of the line fits smoothly into the text's broader inquiry into the political, religious, and sexual valences of debilitating injury. As Michael Lieb notes, there is some Biblical warrant for Milton's staging of this "surgery" that would account for his impulse to "transform the ritual of circumcision into an act of war."[64] There is no mention of a foreskin harvest in the Book of Judges, so Milton has conflated the episode with two other Biblical passages that blur together tribal hostilities and failed intermarriage. The first of these intertexts is a gruesome scene in 1 Samuel in which David presents two hundred Philistine foreskins to Saul as a bride-price for his daughter Michal, a cross-class union that would conclude in her abandonment.[65] Samson's transcendent performance in the theater of war also hearkens back to the rape of Dinah, Jacob's only daughter, an episode that so interested Milton that he drew up a sketch for a tragedy based on the event.[66] The story is this: after "defiling" Dinah,[67] Shechem, the son of a Canaanite prince, dispatches an overture of marriage to her father: "The soule of my sonne Shechem longeth for your daughter: giue her him to wife . . . And ye shal dwel with vs, and the land shal be before you: dwel, and do your busines in it, and haue your possessions therein" (Gen. 34: 8–10). Dinah's brothers respond that they will agree to the match on one condition: "if ye wil be as we are," that is, circumcised, "then wil we giue our daughters to you, and we wil take your daughters to vs, and wil dwel with you, and be one people" (Gen. 34: 15–16). All the men of Shechem consent to circumcision, and the Geneva Bible translates what happens next this way: "And on the third day [after circumcision] (when thei were sore) two of the sonnes of Iaakob, Simeon and Leui, Dinahs brethren toke ether of them his sworde & went into the citie boldely, and slewe euerie male. Thei slewe also Hamor and Shechem his sonne with the edge of the sworde, & toke Dinah out of Shechems house, and went their way. *Again* the *other* sonnes of Iaakob came vpon the dead, and spoiled the citie, because they had defiled their sister" (Gen. 34: 25–27).

Within the literary culture of the Reformation, this passage was received as a commentary on the impossibility of intimacy and sociality across lines of ethnic difference. The Geneva Bible's marginal notes align the resistance felt by the sons of Jacob to their sister's betrothal to an uncircumcised man to the "abomination [of] them that are baptized to ioine with infidels."[68] The fate of the Shechemites served as a stark reminder that those within the covenant and those outside it can never become "one people." In the hands of Jacob's sons, the rite of circumcision does not usher in conversion, integration, and commonality, but marks a prelude to slaughter, rape, and enslavement. Figurative or otherwise, the knife rite Samson performs on the field of battle likewise perverts the covenantal and communal ends of the ritual. As Julia Reinhard Lupton argues, "Under Samson's hands, the violent stroke of circumcision, its act of physical de-completion, overtakes its symbolically integrative function as a rite of conversion and naturalization."[69] The rough trimming applied by Samson simultaneously removes the physiological marker of difference that separates the Philistines from their Israelite neighbors while also doubling down on that distinction, reducing the "inhuman" Canaanites to the little piece of flesh that marks them as "idolatrous, uncircumcised, unclean" (1364).

Stripped of its social and ritual functions, the nonconsensual circumcision Samson inflicts on the Philistine soldiers only weakens and humiliates them, sapping their reserves of strength. In this too, Milton affiliates Samson's tactical strike with the incision applied to the Shechemites, whose cutting served a biological rather than religious purpose, as Calvin remarks in his *Commentarie on Genesis*:

> For [Jacob's sons] being rather beastlike then manlike angrie, sought to ouerrunne the whole citie: but being not able to bring their mischievous purpose to passe against so many people, they deuise a newe platte, that when they were made weake with woundes, they might soudenly come uppon them . . . For they care not for circumcision: but onely seeke howe to make the miserable men weake and unapte to resiste them in the slaughter.[70]

For Calvin, Jacob's sons cover their violent intentions under a vanishingly thin veneer of religious devotion, a pretended piety that serves a convenient pretext for a maiming that will leave the Shechemites "weake with woundes" and "unapte to resiste" the "beastlike" incursion that will consume their city and scatter their people. In layering Samson's feats of might with the slaughter of the Shechemites, Milton frames "the work from heaven imposed" as mayhem, a strategic assault that diminishes their "faithless enemies'" capacity to mount resistance to the ongoing process of settlement. For Samson no less than for Jacob's violent sons, circumcision is a weapon of war, a wounding that temporarily debilitates the enemy as the first stage of a strike that will annihilate their people. Gender dynamics are at play in the mayhem Samson wreaks, with his bone-sword cropping the uncut blossom of their youth. The enforced carving of the Canaanites redounds on their gender, as the fleshy, overly literal "cutting off" edges uncomfortably close to what Milton describes elsewhere as an "amercement of their whole virility."[71] The passage is nakedly, unnervingly erotic; Jonathan Goldberg calls the slaughter a "defloration."[72] The verdant imagery of the thousand falling foreskins recalls the traumatic weddings of the episode's source material: Milton sets Samson to gathering a bouquet of foreskins in a consummation that bequeaths Philistia to Israel. The "great exploits" portended at Samson's nativity involve his talent for wounding his enemies in a way that simultaneously unmans and debilitates them. In concert with Bracton, Coke, and

Blackstone, then, Milton localizes those lusty powers of self-defense in the genitals, the soft flesh of the groin where "the flower of Palestine" grows.

The assembled members of the Chorus can barely contain their bloodthirsty satisfaction at the carnage Samson wrought in their name, self-soothing with memories of how he coupled hardcore violence with sexual humiliation, grinning at the memory of the "bold Ascalonite" cut down to size and the "old warriors" who "turned their backs," "soiling" themselves as they "groveled" in the dust. It is not so clear, however, that Samson shares their enthusiasm for his former deeds. Such butchery may have been pleasurable to watch from the sidelines, but it makes for a deeply unappealing workload. When the Chorus eulogizes the feats accomplished by "that renowned Samson," they do not describe heroism in the Homeric mode, single combat between well-matched, beautiful men (125). Samson's opponents are wildly overpowered and anonymous. Killing them requires no particular skill. In visual representations of Samson in battle, his Philistine victims are almost indistinguishable from one another, as if the same face had been pasted onto dozens of lifeless bodies. Generic corpses pile up around Samson's outsized and nearly nude frame, as though an assembly line were spitting out endless copies of the same nameless soldier for him to bludgeon to death. What Samson does on the battlefield is labor: tedious and uncreative, dramatic only in its aggregative effects, impressive only in how long he can keep exhaustion at bay. Samson is not an Achilles but a drone pilot, a middleman who deploys the massive killing capacity of a greater power against enemies of the state.

In fact, Samson does not spend a single moment wallowing in nostalgia for his glory days. After all, his unusual abilities locked him into a lifetime of compulsory military service, the dehumanizing and morally degrading labor of slaughtering the very people he persists in marrying. Moreover, in language I am tempted to describe as dysphoric, he also complains that his strength felt "vast, unwieldy, [and] burdensome," as if the brawn he was born with made his body too large, too muscular, too clumsy to inhabit comfortably (54). Far from expressing regret about the maim that cost him his "glorious" gift, then, Samson asserts instead that "to me strength is my bane, / And proves the source of all my miseries, / So many, and so huge, that each apart / Would ask a life to wail" (63–66). It seems to me that Milton makes a point that has, by and large, been missed: Samson's limitless strength was not an enviable condition, but an unendurable affliction. In his burnout and exhaustion, Samson itemizes the costs that come with living in a body after the nation has declared eminent domain on it.

If Samson's undeniable lustiness is the source of his servitude, it also offers him a pathway out. Her name is Dalila. What transpires between the man charged with Israel's deliverance and his "Infidel" bride appears to Samson's friends and the play's critics as an unfathomable mystery. Stanley Fish, for one, calls Samson's divulgence of the secret source of his power an action "apparently without cause."[73] Surely Samson must have been operating under some delusion or compulsion, or perhaps he was the unwitting victim of feminine deception by Dalila, "the worst of all possible wives."[74] And yet, Samson will admit no such thing:

> Well I knew, nor was at all surprised
> But warned by oft experience: did not she
> Of Timna first betray me, and reveal
> The secret wrested from me in her highth
> Of nuptial love professed, carrying it straight
> To them who had corrupted her, my spies,
> And rivals? In this other was there found
> More faith? . . .
> Thrice she assayed with flattering prayers and sighs,
> And amorous reproaches to win from me
> My capital secret, in what part my strength
> Lay stored, in what part summed, that she might know:
> Thrice I deluded her, and turned to sport
> Her importunity, each time perceiving
> How openly, and with what impudence
> She purposed to betray me, and (which was worse
> Than undissembled hate) with what contempt
> She sought to make me traitor to myself.
> Yet the fourth time, when must'ring all her wiles,
> With blandished parleys, feminine assaults,
> Tongue-batteries, she surcease not day nor night
> To storm me over-watched, and wearied out.
> At times when men seek most repose and rest,
> I yielded, and unlocked her all my heart,
> Who with a grain of manhood well resolved
> Might easily have shook off all her snares:
> But foul effeminacy held me yoked
> Her bond-slave. O indignity, O blot
> To honor and religion! Servile mind
> Rewarded well with servile punishment! (381–413)

Although Samson adopts the position shared by his father, the Chorus, and Miltonists alike, that Dalila was the aggressor, his framing of the event blurs any easy distinction between victim and perpetrator. Samson could not be more clear: he did not just know that Dalila meant to deprive him of the secret source of his power, he knew *well*. After all, they had roleplayed the scenario three times in advance of the real event. Dalila had made no secret of her intentions, and she employed no craft or "skill." Instead, she asked directly where his strength was stored and then "impudently" attempted to carve it out of his body like a tumor. Everything in Samson's experience pointed toward the inevitable outcome of disclosure, beginning with his relationship with the endlessly maligned Woman of Timna, a marriage that barely outlasted the wedding party. In accounting for his revelation to Dalila, Samson invokes his first wife, who pressed him for sensitive information and then gossiped about his response, a betrayal that prompted the bridegroom to murder all her bridal attendants. As Samson readily admits, the risks of revealing his secret were apparent, even obvious. He could have resisted—or rather, anyone "with a grain of manhood" might have "easily" extricated himself from the situation and preserved himself intact.

There is also the little matter of pleasure. If Samson takes no joy in the hypermasculine pursuits of war, if "walking about admired of all and dreaded" left him uncomfortable and arrogant, then in his salacious recollections of married life we get a taste, for the first time, of what Samson actually enjoys: giving up power (530). What the invulnerable supersoldier really wants is to be bound, silenced, and dommed by a gorgeous, high-femme partner. In particular, he expresses a preference for scenes in which verbal domination bleeds into bondage and physical humiliation. The ritual always begins the same way: interminable, exhausting debate. Pleasure flows from frustrating Samson's usual rhetorical prowess, his maddening ability to find a too-clever answer for any question put to him.[75] The rapid-fire dialogue builds an erotic charge laced with aggression as Dalila subjects her partner to a sequence of "tongue-batteries," "feminine assaults," and "blandished parleys" that stop his mouth and press him into states of physical ecstasy and mental depletion. Idle, prone, and limp, Samson is not merely attended to, but "over-watched," the object of such vigorous exertions that he is "wearied out." Surrendering to sleep, he instructs Dalila to bind him with "seuen greene cordes that were neuer dryed," or with "newe ropes," or to plait "seuen lockes of mine head with the threades of the woufe" and "fasten it with a pinne" to the wall (Judg. 16: 7–14). Asleep and unconscious, bound in increasingly baroque arrangements, the "irresistible" Samson allows himself to experience vulnerability and dependence, becoming just as "weake" as "an other man" (Judg. 16:7). For once, the judge can give up control, a pillow princess reclining in submissive silence and physical immobility while someone else spends all their energies, attentions, and labors on him. "Softened with pleasure and voluptuous life," Samson timidly allows himself to enjoy the experience of being disarmed, weakened, and conquered (536). By the time Dalila is finished, Samson is emptied out, a hollow container with no capacity for thought or resistance, a "servile mind" well-deserving of a "servile punishment," a "reward" that consists of binding, submission, and finally erotic release.

The erotics of this power exchange touch on the sensitive matter of Samson's gender, draining his virility until not a single "grain of manhood" remains. Under Dalila's direction, the impenetrable Samson softens and slackens, "yielding" and "unlocking" not just a "secret," but also an "effeminacy" that he experiences as both an external "yoke" and an internal condition. The feminizing effects of the couple's sex life turn their "sport" into an erotic experiment that would feel perfectly at home within the contemporary pornographic subgenre of sissification. This particular kink involves forcibly feminizing a submissive partner (often but not always a cisgender man) who is dolled up in pink, instructed to apply makeup, pressed into compromising postures, aggressively topped, and "brainwashed" or "hypnotized" into letting their inner sissy emerge. Andrea Long Chu argues that forced feminization transforms the fetish from a defense against the loss of the phallus to a guarantee of castration.[76] This, indeed, is the precise outcome of the elaborately choreographed sexual encounters between Samson and Dalila. Trusting Delila costs him his "tender ball[s]"—that is, his eyes—when she "shore me / Like a tame wether," or castrated ram (94, 538). The attack that incapacitates Samson also operates on his gender, actualizing the "foul effeminacy" and "impotence of mind" to which he attributes his many shortcomings (52).

If we take Samson's own description of his experience seriously, then, at least one possible explanation for his disclosure arises: that he opted out, that he was glad to be rid of a strength he never asked for in the first place. In trusting Dalila, Samson made an affirmative choice for a weakness that is also, as his wife reminds him, an experience of femininity. Upon encountering his former bride for the first time since his assault, Samson is understandably eager to disavow his participation in the collaborative scene of his divestiture. The snarls of misogynistic commonplaces with which Samson hails Dalila group her with "every woman false like thee," conjuring up a universal conspiracy of women who "break all faith, all vows, deceive, [and] betray" their duped but ultimately blameless husbands (749–50). Confronted with the instrument of his abjection, Samson loses all capacity for nuance, retreating to well-worn sexist tropes to paint himself as a victim, an innocent "beguiled" by a cunning and crafty opponent (759). In her rebuttal, Dalila softens the walls that separate masculine "weakness" and feminine "craft," transforming the "weakness" that he invokes as evidence of his own naïveté into a mark of his complicity in his own disarming:

> First granting, as I do, it was a weakness
> In me, but incident to all our sex,
> Curiosity, inquisitive, importune
> Of secrets, then with like infirmity
> To publish them, both common female faults:
> Was it not weakness also to make known
> For importunity, that is for naught,
> Wherein consisted all thy strength and safety?
> To what I did thou show'dst me first the way.
> But I to enemies revealed, and should not.
> Ere I to thee, thou to thyself wast cruel.
> Let weakness then with weakness come to parle,
> So near related, or the same of kind. (773–85)

Samson does not disagree: "Bitter reproach, but true" (823). Refusing to separate the pair's intellect, psyches, and communicative styles according to the unbridgeable division marked by sex scuttles the rhetorical edifice of Samson's flimsy defense: she was guilty of nothing except understanding Samson's desires, which she put into effect only after he had "shown [her] first the way." There is a capaciousness to the model of womanhood at work when Dalila invokes the "common female faults" she shares with Samson, and when she confesses to the faults of "*our* sex" the phrase is roomy enough to house both herself and her former husband. What both members of the couple share is a weakness that is characteristic of feminine experience, an "infirmity" that leads one to inquire and the other to tell secrets, apparently just for the pleasure of sharing. On one point, everyone agrees: there was "naught" to be gained from revealing the source of that "wherein consisted all thy strength and safety" except for weakness and effeminacy. What is implied, both in Dalila's self-defense and Samson's reminiscences about their sex life, is that the actual outcome was the intended outcome: pleasure and relief follow from voluntarily submitting to a powerlessness that is "so near related" to womanhood that it is, perhaps, indistinguishable from it.

What I am proposing here is that Samson, lacking any meaningful bodily autonomy or compass for action, turned to his people's "faithless enemies" for the support he never received from his countrymen (380). In this, Milton's Samson and Dalila bear more than a passing resemblance to that "lustie rogue" Wright and his anonymous coconspirator, two pairs that collaborated on a procedure that rendered one partner useless for the war machine. That is, in liberating Samson from a strength and virility he maligns as "burdensome," the shaving is not an assault, but a scene of care, what Hil Malatino describes as an action that "facilitates . . . emergence into a radically recalibrated experience of both bodymind and the world it encounters."[77] To be sure, walking away from his powers rewired Samson's bodymind, but it might also have transformed the world he inhabits, inserting him into relations of affinity and interdependence with the people he was appointed to slaughter. From this perspective, Dalila does not violate Samson's trust when she shaves and incapacitates him. The true betrayal, the unforgiveable betrayal, is what comes after, when she exploits his "intensified vulnerability" to hand him over to be tortured, enslaved, and incarcerated.[78] In doing so, she snuffs out the queer possibility embedded in the mayhem she wreaks with (and upon) Samson, who can no longer imagine any use for his remaining energies other than the mass murder his countrymen so eagerly desire, a conclusion that both satisfies their bloodlust and relieves them of any responsibility of caring for their debilitated deliverer.

The scene of trans mayhem that plays out in Samson's bridal chamber is a matter not only of gender but of racialized gender. Samson's lust—unmanageable, out of control, impotent, nonreproductive—terminates in a wounding that emasculates and debilitates him, while also blurring the bright-line boundary that separates the Israelites from their racialized enemies. In illustrating Samson's violation as a matter of being "subdued" by the "barber's razor," Milton helpfully fills out Blackstone's definition of mayhem, giving a plain name to that "part, the loss of which in all animals abates their courage": it is the *hair* (1167). This substitution isn't as strange as it might seem at first blush. As Patricia Parker and Greta LaFleur have argued, the cultural milieu of the seventeenth century associated forcible shaving of the beard and head with the fate endured by English sailors who fell into the hands of Ottoman pirates.[79] To be subjected to the razor compromised what Will Fisher calls "the ideology of bearded masculinity," flagging both the prisoner's enslaved status as well as his availability for sodomitical use.[80] The shaved head also portended conversion to Islam or "turning Turk," thus serving as a physical marker of a difference that was both religious and racial. Barbering, then, tended to precede the slits of circumcision (necessary for conversion) and castration (which transformed white captives into valuable eunuchs). *Samson Agonistes* builds out the racialized narrative of trans history that associates whiteness with cisness by adding another term to the mix: disability. At this point, a caveat is in order: the claim here is not that Samson *is transgender*, if we take that to mean that he identifies as a woman. Rather, what *Samson Agonistes* clarifies is that criminal mayhem is legal device that folds together racialization, transition, and physical impairment into the figure of a defiling cut that constitutes a threat to the nation-state.

*Samson Agonistes* sources this fear of trans cutting to deeply disturbing attachments to the purity, integrity, and generative capacities of the Israelites. Samson's trimming does not simply sap the collective resilience necessary for his country's survival but reroutes his God-given vitality to the enemy nation through a program of convict labor. A disoriented Manoa asks his son whether he will voluntarily "serve the Philistines with that gift / Which was expressly given thee to annoy them" (577–78). He will, claiming that the Philistines receive "the advantage of my labours, / the work of many hands" from his "servile toil" at the mill, where his exertions feed and fortify, rather than annoy and diminish, his "country's enemies" (1259–60, 5, 238). The "advantage" absorbed by the Philistines works at a biological level, parasitically leeching Samson's virility to enhance their nutritive and maybe even reproductive strength. "Grinding" was a sex word, as Milton knew. *The Doctrine and Discipline of Divorce* describes bad sex in a loveless marriage as "grinding in the mill of an undelighted and servile copulation."[81] In affiliating Samson's labor with the wrong kind of sex, Milton builds out a reading of Judges that the Palestinian Talmud glosses this way: "Grinding always refers to [sexual] transgression," as when Job says, "'Let my wife grind after another.' This comes to teach us that every Philistine would bring his wife to [Samson] in the prison-house so that she might be impregnated by him."[82] Jeffrey Shoulson understands this as a "condemnation of Samson's sexual prowess as a contributing factor to the once and future oppression of the Israelites by a physically strengthened pagan world," a threat that comes by way of what he calls an "amusing" proposition that Samson would "populate the Philistine nation with numerous infant supermen." As is often the case in the Samson cycle, the surface-level humor of his story twists into something darker: here, enslavement becomes sexual exploitation feeding anxieties about the Israelites' ethnic purity.

Now that he has outlived his purpose, the matter of Samson's continued existence confronts his friends, family, and jailers with complicated questions about care, a subject central to work in disability studies and activism.[83] The accommodations afforded him during his imprisonment intentionally fall short of meeting his biological needs: Harapha cuttingly reminds his captive opponent that he "hast need of much washing to be touched" (1107). The combination of carceral neglect, physical restraint, and disability have left Samson unable to clean himself, exposing him to a form of dependence normally associated with early childhood and senescence. Jackie DiSalvo points to Samson's "blindness," his "hairlessness," and his "soiled weeds" as evidence of an "almost infantile contingency and vulnerability" in the aftermath of his assault.[84] In associating Samson's fouled clothes with a childlike incapacity to control his bodily functions, the play subscribes to the "expectation that all people beyond a certain age will perform their own bodily hygiene"—an expectation that Tobin Siebers associates with lethal forms of marginalization.[85] So too in *Samson Agonistes*: in Harapha's mind, the stench radiating from Samson's fouled clothes serves as a material signifier of his exclusion from personhood along with the "slaves and asses thy comrades" (1162).[86] In his current condition, Samson is utterly unsuitable as an opponent in honorable combat, making "no worthy match / For valour to assail, nor by the sword / Of noble Warriour, so to stain his honour" (1164–65). It is as if Samson's bodily defect is contagious, threatening to "stain" and diminish any "noble" in his proximity, while also inviting further depredations from his enemies who make it their "daily practice to afflict [him] more" (114).

In short, Samson is in desperate, urgent need of care. When the assorted members of Samson's community arrive on the scene, they encounter a man in extreme distress, someone mired in suicidal ideation as he struggles to navigate a debilitating injury, the sudden loss of his social-support network, and a prison sentence he is not meant to survive for long. While the "holy" nurturance afforded to the young Samson had been tailored to ready him for a life of military service, the support he requires in his current condition is radically different. Tending to him promises no "great act" or "benefit" to "Abraham's race" (28–29). As Jennifer Terry argues, the spectacle of a disabled soldier's "woundscape" becomes the locus for thorny conversations about obligation, a chance to assess what is owed to those who have sacrificed their bodily integrity on behalf of the nation.[87] Gathering around Samson's "carelessly diffused" and "languished" body to survey his injuries might have prompted the Chorus to reflect on the kinds of care, support, and companionship they could extend to their friend, who is at once a debilitated warrior; a husband who suffered an unimaginable betrayal by his partner; and a prisoner trying to survive an abusive, dehumanizing incarceration (118–19). Samson's kin and compatriots might have asked him directly what he needs and wants, or how he imagines moving forward to build a meaningful life on his own terms. Instead, they whisper together about how soon he can get back to work. It is not that the "friends and equals of his tribe" are entirely without empathy, just that productivity is the only metric they have for assigning value to bodies. Incidentally, this metric is also how Samson understands his own worth, as he confesses to Harapha: "I was to do my part from Heav'n assigned, / And had performed it, if my known offense / Had not disabled me" (1217–19).

Two possible caregiving arrangements are floated as stopgaps to meet Samson's immediate needs by securing his release from prison and housing him in more humane accommodations. One is offered by Manoa, who holds out hope that in time, his son will make a full recovery:

> It shall be my delight to tend his eyes,
> And view him sitting in the house, ennobled
> With all those high exploits by him achieved,
> And on his shoulders waving down those locks,
> That of a nation armed the strength contained:
> And I persuade me God had not permitted
> His strength again to grow up with his hair
> Garrisoned round about him like a camp
> Of faithful soldiery, were not his purpose
> To use him further yet in some great service,
> Not to sit idle with so great a gift
> Useless, and thence ridiculous about him.
> And since his strength with eyesight was not lost,
> God will restore him eyesight to his strength. (1490–1503)

Careful noting of Samson's bodily comportment, particularly the length of his hair, makes way for a fantasy that Samson's powers, including his eyesight, will be restored. In other words, Manoa places his faith in cure, an "ideology" that, Eli Clare reminds us, "rides on the back of *normal* and *natural*" in its quest to eradicate defective bodies and minds from the social landscape.[88] Twitches of such eliminationist rhetoric punctuate Manoa's fatherly offer of care, as his initial, heady assertion that he will "delight" to "tend" to Samson gives way to something more selfish. This wounded Samson does not have inherent value. Disgust seeps into Manoa's imagined homelife with a son whose "useless" and "ridiculous" body sits "idle," the sheen of ennoblement flowing from the increasingly distant memories of those "high exploits" achieved in his prime fading rapidly and failing to add up to something like dignity. For Manoa, care is only a pathway to cure, a temporary interlude that will restore him to full health, rehabilitating both his strength and his eyesight so that his body can once again inhabit a pristine, unviolated condition.

Where Manoa assumes that cure is inevitable, Dalila banks on its impossibility. If the patriarch wants to shove Samson back onto the battlefield at the earliest possible opportunity, Dalila hopes instead for a future in which her former husband remains permanently, irreversibly housebound:

Let me obtain forgiveness of thee, Samson,
Afford me place to show what recompense
Towards thee I intend for what I have misdone . . .
Though sight be lost,
Life yet hath many solaces, enjoyed
Where other senses want not their delights
At home in leisure and domestic ease,
Exempt from many a care and chance to which
Eyesight exposes daily men abroad.
I to the lords will intercede, not doubting
Their favorable ear, that I may fetch thee
From forth this loathsome prison-house to abide
With me, where my redoubled love and care
With nursing diligence, to me glad office,
May ever tend about thee to old age
With all things grateful cheered, and so supplied,
That what by me thou hast lost thou least shalt miss. (909–27)

On the surface, the care Dalila can provide to Samson seems more attuned to his actual needs and the realities of his condition. In the place of a rehabilitation that would make him fit for military service, Dalila's caregiving promises to ensconce her husband in "leisure" and "domestic ease," supplementing his infirmity with any number of "things grateful," a host of "delights" and "solaces" that she leaves to his imagination. And yet, she too has demands of Samson. The scene of "nursing diligence" she proposes is disturbingly erotic, edging into sexual opportunism. Dalila spins out a fantasy in which her haughty, headstrong husband is remanded to bed where she can enjoy him at her leisure, focusing her "redoubled love and care" upon a man whose access to housing depends on remaining in the good graces of his hostess. The pleasure quivering through Dalila's pitch fetishizes Samson's isolation, dependency, and incapacity. In this, Dalila's appetites are not unlike those embraced by the "devotees" who pursue romantic connection exclusively with amputees, and whose predatory desires turn on the possibility of exploitation.[89] Samson rightly senses the danger in such an arrangement, which would soon reduce him to "perfect thraldom" (946). After all, since she so readily betrayed him "in the flower of youth and strength . . . how wouldst thou use me now, blind, and thereby / Deceivable, in most things as a child / Helpless, thence easily contemned, and scorned, / And last neglected?" (938–44). Given her earlier betrayal, Samson has more than enough license for assuming that Dalila means to amplify and exacerbate his infirmity, toying with him until she loses interest and then shrugging off her responsibility and leaving him "neglected" and abandoned. What Dalila presents as an exciting opportunity to live a life of leisure as a kept man begins to sound rather like another job. For his tenuous access to care and lodging, Samson will be expected to perform sexual and emotional labor for the woman who, in recent memory, engineered a scene that subjected him to world-shattering abuse. The offer of security, shelter, and erotic pleasure require him to set aside that trauma, to put it out of his mind and "bear not too sensibly . . . what remains past cure" (912–13).

"What remains past cure" might be the central question of *Samson Agonistes*. What is left after a wounding that makes it impossible for a body to fulfill its appointed purpose? Where should punishment be assigned when a virile man whose energies are needed to defend the nation submits to an emasculating and debilitating incision? One line of thought pursued by the play depends on the seizure of bodily capacities that infuses the legal logic of criminal mayhem. From this perspective, just as Samson's strength belonged to his community, so too does his violation. It is Samson who has endured the cut, but the Chorus participates vicariously in his injury, hovering over his abused body and stewing in an unbearable emotional admixture compounded from shame, terror, anger, and impotence. Samson's bodily impairments generate a structure of feeling that justifies extraordinary retaliation against the outsiders who are assigned blame for the Israelites' collective discomfort. Thus, in the play's offstage conclusion, the genocidal demolition of the Temple of Dagon that extirpates "the choice nobility and flower" of "each Philistian city" repeats Samson's wounding at scale, raining down "blood, death, and deathful deeds" upon "the whole inhabitation" (1654–55, 1512–13). The communal sense of wholeness lost to Samson's wounds is restored through a program of incapacitation that bequeaths "years of mourning / And lamentation to the sons of Caphtor" (1712–13). Just as the maimed Dagon "mourned in earnest" after he lost his limbs in a catastrophic assault, so too will the Canaanites endure a durational, open-ended period of suffering, loss, and lamentation. In this respect, Samson's suicide attack on the temple in Gaza resembles the war in Afghanistan more than it resembles September 11.[90] This widespread maiming of the enemy people successfully restores a sense of robustness, manliness, and vitality to the Israelites who, like the phoenix, "From out her ashy womb now teemed, / Revived, reflourishes, then vigorous most, / When most unactive deemed" (1703–5). This ending neatly solves the Israelites' two problems: the Philistines and a debilitated, emasculated Samson. Once their hero has outlived his immediate usefulness, this best of all possible outcomes is for him to be destroyed in a way that materially damages the enemies of the state. Now that his community is no longer burdened with any responsibility for his care, Samson can be resurrected as a symbol, a "monument" environed by "laurel ever green, and branching palm, / With all his trophies hung, and acts enrolled / In copious legend, or sweet lyric song" (1734–37). In place of a living, breathing son with embarrassing bodily needs and complicated opinions, the Israelites will have something better: a graven image, a silent and bloodless statue that arrives heavily annotated according to the ideological platform of its maker. Henceforth, Manoa imagines, "Thither shall all the valiant youth resort" to "inflame their breasts" with the memory of Samson's "matchless valor," while the "virgins also" will "visit his tomb with flowers" to "bewail" his "lot unfortunate in nuptial choice" (1738–43). In death, Samson's complexity vanishes: no trace of the reservations about his military career or his tortuous relationship with effeminacy can be found in the "copious" legenda affixed to the monument. Instead, Samson can be reduced to a convenient pedagogical device for managing the lusty energies of his country's youth according to a strictly binary gender schema, prompting the boys to march off to war and the girls to spend their sexual favors on men of their own nation.

Taken at face value, this triumphal conclusion opens onto the grim biopolitical afterlives of mayhem, in which collective feelings of vulnerability legitimate perpetual war and the state's unlimited right to maim. From this vantage, when the common law awards the state guardianship over its subjects' physical powers, it gives shape to a mode of sovereignty that needs defending from bodies that are transitional or impaired. The maimed body, multiply cut, unsexed and debilitated, becomes a collective wound that must be eliminated so that the nation-state can thrive. In this, Milton offers an answer to Harry Benjamin's exasperated question about why the ancient rights of English kings should be invoked to embargo trans surgeries in the twentieth century: it is because modernity has not replaced the form of governance in which the subject's capacities exist for the instrumental use of the nation, but radically and catastrophically expanded it. If Samson's unusual abilities made him exceptional, Heaven's own "nursling" and "choice delight," the collective claim on his vital energies are no longer reserved for elected deliverers (633). Today it is the "essential worker" who is the "hero," who owes every ounce of strength she possesses to the nation, to the economy, to Amazon. Such labor is always exhausting and, for those who are most vulnerable and marginalized, it is often debilitating, with no expectation of care waiting on the other side.[91] This seizure of bodily capacities and the elimination of care is perfectly in line with legislatures blocking the right to bodily autonomy and medical treatment necessary for gender transition.

Such policies have lethal consequences, particularly for the most vulnerable trans people, those who are not protected by whiteness and capital.

From its seventeenth-century origins onward, common-law mayhem has offered the state a way of penalizing, outlawing, and disallowing both trans and disabled life. For this reason alone, mayhem offers a compelling reason to think intersectionally about trans and disabled forms of embodiment. We could stop here, but it may be that Milton opens up another avenue for thinking through what Cameron Awkward-Rich calls "trans/crip conjunctions" that works in a reparative rather than critical mode.[92] In short, it is not so clear that *Samson Agonistes* imagines that mass slaughter is the only available way to handle those bodies deemed "most unactive" or "ingloriously unemployed." The keyword here might be *use*. The entire action of the play, to the extent that anything happens at all, is comprised of frantic attempts to find some kind of occupation for the weakened, blinded, and unmanned Samson. His father wants to push him back to the front lines after a little R & R; Harapha wants him for a punching bag; Delila wants to keep him like a pet or a sex toy. Samson rejects all of these potential pathways back into community and relationality, including the possibility of ransom. In fact, Samson only ever states a single, unambiguous desire. It comes in the first line of the play:

> A little onward lend thy guiding hand
> To these dark steps, a little further on;
> For yonder bank hath choice of sun or shade,
> There I am wont to sit, when any chance
> Relieves me from my task of servile toil,
> Daily in the common prison else enjoined me,
> Where I a prisoner chained, scarce freely draw
> The air imprisoned also, close and damp,
> Unwholesome draft: but here I feel amends,
> The breath of heav'n fresh-blowing, pure and sweet,
> With day-spring born; here leave me to respire. (1–11)

What Samson wants, what he explicitly requests, is not another job, but space to breathe. Plagued by a "deadly swarm" of "restless thoughts," he hopes to yield his conscious awareness to the minimal, involuntary somatic rhythms that support life. As a tactic for surviving his social death or "half-life," the time of his greatest debilitation, Samson turns to what Jean-Thomas Tremblay calls "feminist breathing," a "set of respiratory practices" outlined in women-of-color feminism that "supply strategies for moving through depletion."[93] Samson's breath has been stolen twice, first by the brutal environs of incarceration, where even the air is imprisoned, and then a second time by the rotating cast of friends, relatives, enemy combatants, messengers, and an estranged wife, all of whom demand his attention and engagement. They want to rehearse his birth story, inventory his erotic inclinations, and go over his history of sex partners; they want elaborate explanations for various choices he's made; they want displays of self-loathing and abjection; one wants to wrestle, until suddenly he doesn't. Before Samson marches off to the Temple, the Chorus remarks that "This idol's day hath been to thee no day of rest, / Labouring thy mind / More than the working day thy hands" (1297–99). Indeed it has not been a day of rest—the relentless needling inquiries aimed at finding Samson some task that would relieve him from the shame of being a "burdenous drone . . . robustious to no purpose," foreclose the only positive desire he's expressed: a solitary moment with choice of sun or shade, a tranquil pause with leave to respire (567–69).

To whom has he voiced this request? Whose "guiding hand" is it that leads him to "yonder bank?" It may be God—it does sound like the Psalms—in which case Samson is terribly alone, abandoned and unmoored.[94] But perhaps he has an actual guide, an image drawn from Greek tragedy that folds together disability and transition. Entering led by the hand affiliates Samson most obviously with Oedipus, but also with Tiresias, whose blindness was inextricably linked to an experience of multiple genders. If there is an affirmative biopolitics of mayhem to be found in *Samson Agonistes*, it is here, in this quiet moment before the narrative momentum will push Samson toward his final, genocidal destination. The hero whose bodily integrity was so complete that he never needed any assistive device asks for and is given support freely, for he has nothing to offer, a hand that guides him to a space where there is no call for him to be useful or labor or serve, where there is nothing to do but breathe.

[ EPILOGUE ]

# The Final Crux

## A Nonsecular Transition

In January 2021, a bill was submitted to the North Dakota state assembly that aimed to criminalize transition, although the word "trans" failed to make a single appearance in the text. Instead, in a surpassingly odd turn of phrase, what North Dakota House Bill 1476 targeted was "nonsecular self-asserted sex-based identity narratives."[1] What was in many respects a bog-standard anti-trans bill, flush with provisions to ban trans teens from playing sports and remove "undue restrictions" on conversion therapy, attracted some attention because its arguments turned on a strange and novel claim about secularity. The claim, such as it was, amounted to accusing transness of being a deeply held internal belief, an "unproven faith-based identity [and an] implicitly religious moral stance that is not predicated on self-evident neutral truth and is a story." From this perspective, you "believe" yourself to be in the possession of a particular gender in the same way you might believe in, say, transubstantiation or the resurrection of the body. In light of the "nonsecularity" of trans life, the bill asserts, any government policy that "directly or symbolically respects" trans people by updating gender markers on birth certificates or prohibiting gym coaches from performing genital inspections on suspiciously butch teen soccer players infringes upon the separation of church and state. As adherents to a debased religion with a "tendency to erode community standards of decency" and "promote licentiousness," trans people are walking violations of the establishment clause. In the paranoid excesses of the North Dakota bill, the church of the nonsecular gathers a curious congregation of queer and trans malefactors: "sexual orientation" is handwaved as a "mythology, dogma, doctrine, ideology, or orthodoxy" based on "a series of unproven faith-based assumptions"; "nonsecular marriage" refers to "any form of so-called marriage which does not involve a man and a woman"; "drag queen story time" entails a "nonsecular event where men dress up as women"; and, in what is possibly the most absurd definition of the bunch, "sex reassignment surgery" designates a "nonsecular medical procedure." A liturgy of drag queen story time, sacramental sex changes, grand rites of gay marriage—compared to the bloodless tedium of the anti-trans bills churned out by state legislatures on a weekly basis, the pearl-clutching affectation of the North Dakota bill borders on camp.

What might it mean to insist that trans life is a "nonsecular" phenomenon? In part, the language of the North Dakota bill attempts to weaken the affiliation between transness and the eminently secular authority of medical science. Gender-affirming surgery and hormone therapy have been endorsed as effective, valid remedies for dysphoria by all of the most significant professional organizations for doctors, psychiatrists, and social workers. Sensing the rhetorical purchase vested in this medical consensus, efforts to uphold trans rights routinely pronounce the names of these groups in a solemn litany, a defensive prayer that invokes the protective powers of the American Medical Association and the Society for Adolescent Health and Medicine.[2] Petulantly insisting that transness is "faith-based, not proven" and a matter of "naked assertions" rather than "self-evident objective fact" is an attempt to diminish the effective force of these endorsements. After all, trans people may be easily dismissed and ignored, but the professional expertise of physicians carries significant weight in both political discourse and in legal argument. Undermining this medical consensus has been a central aim of transphobic movements, as a necessary precondition for the widespread demonization of trans people as deluded self-mutilators and predatory groomers who deserve the full force of state violence. Just as evangelical Christian lobbyists and politicians once demanded that public schools teach young-earth creationism, insinuating that there was robust scientific debate about the validity of evolution, so too are columnists in the *New York Times* and the *Atlantic* currently insisting against all evidence to the contrary that there is a "controversy" about trans care among physicians. In the twisted rationale of the North Dakota bill, the gambit is that transitional care only appears to be scientific when in fact it is a "nonsecular sham," a retrograde superstition attempting to pass as modern medicine. What the North Dakota bill attempts is a kind of reveal, snatching the wig off trans life itself to expose the debauched religiosity that lies beneath the veneer of secularity.

At first blush, the account of secularism mobilized by the North Dakota bill seems entirely amenable to the high-handed dictates of the self-identified "freethinkers" and "New Atheists" whose anti-trans polemics begin from precisely the same premises, that transness is an irrational belief system like a religion and thus has no place in public life.[3] In the North Dakota bill, too, secularism serves as a shorthand for the norms of rationality and reason necessary to maintain social order and uphold the "general decency, safety, health and welfare of the community." And yet, if transition is a "faith-based" praxis that marks an irrecuperable breach of the "natural, neutral, and noncontroversial" principles of secular rationality, this secularism is nevertheless one that easily accommodates hard-right Christian extremism. Indeed, no sooner has the bill denounced the "nonsecularity" of transness than it asserts its intention to defend "secular marriage"—that is, a "legal union" between "one person who was born a biological male and one person who was born a biological female" who "become spouses of the opposite sex," as opposed to "nonsecular marriage," which refers to "so-called marriages between more than two people, persons of the same sex, a person and an animal, or a person and an object." What is here classified as "secular marriage" is precisely what, in the years leading up to *Obergefell*, used to go by the name "Biblical marriage." This conceptual maneuver seems to be making the rounds, as witnessed by a West Virginia bill that attempts to criminalize "non-secular" abortions (a "religious" act in which the "mother terminates the unborn child on the altar of convenience").[4] If secularism is the sole repository of rationality and ethics, the argument runs, then secularism is simply another name for Christianity, understood to have unique possession of a "noncontroversial" and "transcultural morality." Indeed, the argument seems to be that secularism is *only* valid when it serves as a fig leaf for all the pet projects of the Christian right, and any resistance to the state's brutal enforcement of a Christian nationalist agenda must flow from the "licentious" pseudo-religion that the bill, in a particularly chaotic turn of phrase, names "secular humanism." In her thorough and devastating analysis of HB 1476, Jules Gill-Peterson argues that this logic in fact *requires* the government to discriminate against trans people precisely to defend its secular neutrality, a process she associates with the state's declaring itself cisgender.[5]

The North Dakota bill is stupid. It is a ridiculous document motivated by the most cynical and avaricious bigotry, the product of an intuition that in the current climate, political power is most easily achieved by demonizing vulnerable minorities. The humor of its absurd, even postmodern attempts to redefine its central terms is slightly soured by the knowledge that such efforts to expose trans people to relentless, shattering violence are popular policies with immense traction. As it happens, the proposal was something of a joke even to Republican lawmakers: introduced on January 18, the bill was referred to the judiciary committee and withdrawn from further consideration a mere three days later. Not, of course, because of any compunction about the brutal remedies it imagined to the great inconvenience of living in a world that includes trans people—North Dakota has since passed a slate of far more severe measures than those contained in HB1476, whose proposals, by contrast, now seem downright tepid.[6] The problem seems to have been pragmatic rather than ideological. Fussiness over what constitutes an appropriately secular gender is a legislative nonstarter. Lobbyists and pollsters have concluded that the electorate is far more easily whipped into a frothing rage by outraged calls to protect children from "gender ideology." The deranged fantasy of the confused child, somehow forced or suborned into a medical transition, generates a bloodlust in the cis public that translates readily into political capital, as a host of irrelevant governors with presidential aspirations jockey to position themselves as the most extreme transphobe. This paranoia that pays such dividends at the polls is perfectly crystallized in the image adorning the cover of Abigail Shrier's monstrous book: an innocent little white girl in saddle shoes, a gaping hole where her uterus should be.

The vulnerable child who must be prevented from transitioning at any cost appears to be a secular figure, and yet, under the slightest pressure, this notion too reveals itself as a religious formulation. Although advanced under apparently nonreligious pretenses like "protecting women's sports," much of this legislation is drafted by Christian lobbying organizations like the Alliance Defending Freedom and the Heritage Foundation.[7] When Oklahoma lawmakers criminalized transition for minors, a category they defined as including everyone under the age of twenty-six, they did so under a bill they initially entitled the "Millstone Act" in a chilling reference to Matthew 18:6: "Whoever causes one of these little ones who believe in Me to sin, it is better for him that a heavy millstone be hung around his neck, and that he be drowned in the depths of the sea."[8] The appeal to an apparently universal and nondenominational desire to safeguard children is, in fact, the strategic expression of a specifically Christian political project. "Tempting" a child to transition, whatever that means, is framed as a kind of heresy that lures the "little ones" away from Jesus. The issue here is not merely that the child being protected from transition is presumptively Christian, but also that the state has declared eminent domain on the reproductive capacities of a citizenry it holds in a condition of perpetual minority. Transitioning is a sin against the Christian state, which arrogates to itself the sole power to determine who will be fruitful and multiply. Handwringing about the potentially sterilizing effects of gender-affirming care is thus never far removed from the fourteen-word shorthand for the eugenic goals of white supremacy and Christian nationalism, "we must secure the existence of our people and a future for white children," a conceptual proximity horrifyingly materialized in the spectacles of TERF rallies that now regularly attract the participation of heavily armed, black-shirted Nazis.

Despite its ham-fisted bumbling with terminology, then, the North

Dakota bill that identifies transition as a specifically "nonsecular" form of deviance suggests something real and important about the workings of state-sponsored transphobia: that trans life rests at the crux of a contemporary form of political theology. It is as if the mere existence of trans people activates the theological remainder buried in the shell of the disenchanted modern state that can only address transness as a crisis, an existential threat that requires emergency measures to repress. Confronted with the specter of transition, the secular state reverts to its origins in Christian doctrine, and the theoretically independent domains of religion and politics crash together in a catastrophic tempest of state violence. In this sense, the anti-trans bills seek to exploit what Carl Schmitt diagnosed as a strategic weakness of liberalism. Following the seventeenth-century wars of religion, Schmitt argued, the state retreated from the "despair and nausea" of "fruitless theological strife" in the hopes that secularism would produce a neutral ground to achieve consensus.[9] This process of secular neutralization was ultimately self-defeating, Schmitt argued, because the liberal state's principled tolerance for conflicting viewpoints inevitably rendered it susceptible to cooptation by undemocratic actors. He would know. In his time as Göring's darling in the mid-1930s, Schmitt authored frothingly anti-Semitic tracts in support of the party's seizure of state power, gleefully serving as the preeminent "legal theorist of the Nazi *Machtergreifung*."[10] As it happens, the National Socialists also vilified transition to achieve their political goals, blaming transness on the Jewish science of sexology. Indeed, the first official target of Hitler's regime was Magnus Hirschfeld's *Institut für Sexualwissenschaft*, which oversaw some of the first recorded hormone treatments and gender-affirming surgeries.[11] On May 6, 1933, the student wing of the SA stormed the Institute and publicly burned its irreplaceable archive of early trans medicine as part of a purge designed to restore the nation to a condition of racial and religious purity. And just as the fascists of Schmitt's generation exploited an anti-Semitism laced with transphobia to accomplish their political ends, so too have the fascists of our own time solemnly invoked a paranoid fantasy of the defiling cut of transition that drifts into eerily familiar anti-Semitic delusions, like the "globalist" cabal of Jewish funders they imagine pouring money into trans medicine and activism. Once again, transphobia is proving to be a keen instrument for theocratic agents to enter the secular sphere of democratic debate and permanently close it.

It is tempting to confront the rising tide of Christian nationalism by doubling down on the essential secularity of trans life, hiding behind the expertise of doctors and psychiatrists, insisting at increasingly loud volumes that our desires are rational, our lifestyles are normative, our treatments supported by the best science. We might dig in our heels and insist that it is the transphobes who speak from a position of religious extremism, and of course that is true, even for those who mask their sneering, self-important hatred in the guise of principled centrism. Even so, the temptation of the secular is one that we should resist. This resistance is necessary not only because professional specialists in trans health are poor allies, and because sexological accounts of transness *also* insist on our irrationality and incapacity to make decisions for ourselves.[12] It is also because, as the history of modern fascism should make abundantly clear, it is not possible to disarm Christian nationalism through civil debate, as if finding sufficiently clever and reasonable arguments could ever satisfy the genocidal bloodlust of the parties who want to eradicate trans people. Engaging in this debate, as if it were ever conducted in good faith, is not just a waste of our time. It is actively dangerous, a way of lending political legitimacy to the most extreme and bloodthirsty modes of trans-antagonism. Indeed, the "trans debate"—call it a "question," if you like—is simply the means through which fascists enter the apparently neutral realm of the public sphere as an expedient to seizing state power, a collapse we are now witnessing in real time. The secular state will not save us.

What might happen, then, if we stopped putting our faith in a secularism that cannot protect us? Perhaps, in a perverse little reversal, we should lean into the charge levied by the North Dakota bill and the Christian lobbyists who quietly authored it: that trans life is a nonsecular phenomenon, that its meaning is not exhausted in the secular reason of medical science and the endless taxonomizing of the sexologists. For the existential stakes of transition touch on matters of theological and not merely sociological significance: our creaturely capacity for transformation and rebirth; the gendered body's status as the image of a divine Creator; the sources and limits of our political obligations; and our responsibilities of care, acknowledgment, and recognition toward one another. The early moderns intuitively understood this theological significance when they tethered questions about transition to doctrinal debates about circumcision, conversion, and the resurrection of the flesh; or confessional controversies that turned on hermaphroditic prodigies and spontaneously transitioning saints; or Biblical scenes like Samson's effeminating cut and the complicated pregnancy of the first man. Instead of surrendering the ground of theology to reactionary Christian activists, perhaps there is a viable trans politics to be found in occupying it, reclaiming the trans possibility that has lain dormant in religious writing—rarely emerging as a dominant interpretation of the text, but always there for those of us who needed to find it.

The point is not that trans activism must necessarily *be religious*, particularly if the religion in question is Christianity. For as this book has argued alongside many historians and theorists of secularism, Christian theology is implicated in the historical development of the secular state that evangelical lobbies are currently instrumentalizing in the service of white supremacy and transphobia. But there may be purchase to be found by inhabiting the place of the "nonsecular," disidentified from both religion and secularity. Refusing to allow right-wing Christians to declare their sole interpretive authority over religion—including what counts as a "real" religion—a nonsecular trans politics also offers an alternative to what, to date, has seemed to be the sole refuge for trans life: the liberal state that has extended the possibility of inclusion for trans subjects willing and able to disappear into heterosexuality, capitalist production, and labor in the service of American racial empire. For those of us sufficiently white, wealthy, and able-bodied, the possibility of incorporation into the machinery of a white supremacist and necropolitical nation has always been available. When the North Dakota bill declares that transness is fundamentally incompatible with the aims of a secular state that serves as a front for Christian fascism and extractive capitalism, then, it does not describe the reality of trans life. But it is, perhaps, a politics that we might aspire to.

I want to give the final word to the figure from Holinshed's *Chronicles* whose curious career opened my inquiry into trans theology: the "naughtie felowe" discovered to be a hermaphrodite, "both man and woman," crucified by the Archbishop of Canterbury for faking stigmata and pretending to be Jesus, a trans cipher still hanging on the cross outside of Oxford where we left them. When it came to this particular "dissembler" and their crime, the chroniclers could never get their story straight. The crucified hermaphrodite spawns a series of doubles in a hallucinatory sequence, each with their own claim to gender variance: the witches who "should be women," the false stigmatic in whom "Jesus Christ is transformed into a virgin girl," the youth suborned into self-cutting through demonic influence, and finally the deacon who circumcised himself "for the loue of a woman that was a Iew." This book has expanded this raucous cohort of "naughtie" deviants with a host of fellow-travelers with their own trans capacities: penis-snatching demons; the pregnant Adam who delivers his own wife; the invaginated Jesus whose wounds leave him capable of gestation; Melanchthon's hermaphroditic and heretical Pope-Ass; the stigmatic Catherine of Siena who sprouts a miraculous beard; the church father who performs their own orchiectomy in accordance with Matthew 19:12; the dean of St. Paul's who cannot stop writing about an apocalyptic transformation that would dissolve the body into something that cannot be captured by "the Hee and Shee"; and Milton's Samson, who lays his head in the lap of his Philistine bride, voluntarily seeking out an effeminating cut that would render him useless for the war machine. Like the hermaphrodite nailed to the cross, these figures simultaneously exist both inside and outside the theological traditions that generated them: impossible to accommodate within the bounds of orthodox interpretation and yet never fully stricken from the record. Rather than attempting to resolve this particular contradiction—call it a crux—perhaps it is time to lean into the irrational pleasures and sublime possibilities of a nonsecular transness.

# Acknowledgments

> Beholde, I shewe you a secret thing, We shal not all slepe, but we shal all be changed.
>
> 1 Cor. 51

The theological concept of glory is fundamentally about transition, our openness to the experience of being changed in ways that allow for rebirth, transformation, and self-disclosure. In that glorious spirit, it is with profound gratitude that I reflect on the many colleagues, friends, and institutions who have supported me through the many transitions that ushered this book into the world. It first became possible to imagine this book—and a version of early modern studies in which trans thought was taken seriously—in 2017, when I walked into a Shakespeare Association of America seminar organized by Simone Chess and Will Fisher, carrying with me a little paper on Sonnet 20 and *The Duchess of Malfi*. My intellectual path, my career, and my life have all been transformed by my encounter with them and by our many years of collaboration since that first seminar. I am grateful not only for their invitation to coedit a volume on early modern trans studies and for the care with which they shepherded it into being, but for the remarkable degree of trust they placed in a first-year junior professor to shape the initial encounter between early modern studies and trans studies. I am grateful to Will for his infinite capacity for kindness, for the thoughtfulness with which he read every page of this manuscript, and for his keen intuitions about how an untenured trans scholar should navigate complex situations. It is only because of the many kinds of support extended by Simone Chess, my chavruta partner, my closest collaborator, and my best friend for many years now, that I was able to write this book at all. And I can admit it now: you were right about [redacted]. Thank you for your care, for your friendship, and for your trust. There is no one I would rather build a little field with than you.

Although this book was not begun at the Irvine campus of the University of California, the transition that produced it did. There, I had the extraordinary luck to study with Julia Lupton, whose example of brilliance, creativity, and generosity guides me at every turn. It was with Julia that I first experienced the pleasures of cowriting and collaboration, and if there is anything new to be found in my writing, it can be traced back to her influence. For her guidance during my many years of casting about, I owe her a profound debt. I am deeply grateful for Ken Reinhard's friendship and for the circles of philosophy, theory, and music that he introduced me to in our many years of driving around Los Angeles. I will always be thankful for the hospitality I received in the Lupton-Reinhard household, which opened so many new worlds for me. At Irvine, I was also fortunate to have benefited from the support, guidance, and mentorship of Jane Newman, Victoria Silver, Etienne Balibar, Elizabeth Allen, Rebecca Davis, and Rei Terada.

Many institutions have supported the completion of this book, first and foremost Bryn Mawr College, where this book was finished. I am thankful for the collegiality and good company of my friends in the Department of Literatures in English: Jen Callaghan, Pardis Dabashi, Chloe Flower, Jennifer Harford Vargas, Gail Hemmeter, Vanessa Petroj, Bethany Schneider, and Kate Thomas. I am especially grateful to Jamie Taylor, whose mentorship and care have guided me every step of the way. I had the privilege of sharing portions of this work at venues including Columbia University, Hendrix College, the University of Chicago, the London Shakespeare Seminar, the University of Sussex, Princeton University, the University of Toronto, Macalaster College, the University of Iowa, and the University of Pennsylvania. My thanks to the audiences at these locales, whose sharp questions have improved this book in every way.

I have been fortunate to work with Alan Thomas and Randolph Petilos at the University of Chicago Press, as well as Lindsy Rice and Meredith Nini, who have stewarded this project with such tremendous care and insight. I am also grateful to Jessica Wilson for her sharp eye, good humor, and indulgence in editing this manuscript. Jacob Romm supplied a brilliant index. I also owe a real debt to the Press's two anonymous readers, whose labor made this book better at every turn.

A raucous assembly of friends, fellow travelers, and coconspirators have enlivened the writing of this book at every step. I am particularly indebted to Ari Friedlander, whose penetrating comments have saved me from myself over and over again. I am also grateful to Sawyer Kemp, who has consistently enabled my most chaotic impulses. The participants at the EmoTrans conference have shown me what the very best kind of scholarship looks like. For innumerable modes of support and friendship, I am grateful to Brandi Adams, Kadji Amin, Abdulhamit Arvas, Mira 'Assaf Kafantaris,

Caz Batten, Liza Blake, Pearl Brilmyer, James Bromley, Urvashi Chakravarty, Julie Crawford, Kevin Curran, Ambereen Dadabhoy, Drew Daniel, Leah DeVun, Mario DiGangi, Holly Dugan, Dennis Foster, Joseph Gamble, Penelope Geng, Jules Gill-Peterson, Micah Goodrich, Miles Grier, Blake Gutt, Stephen Guy-Bray, Timothy Harrison, Emma Heaney, Derrick Higginbotham, Nicholas Jones, Homay King, Margo Kolenda-Mason, Natasha Korda, Greta LaFleur, Danny Lavery, Grace Lavery, Russ Leo, Zachary Lesser, Ellen MacKay, Aylin Malcolm, Laurie Marhoefer, Harry McCarthy, C. C. McKee, Vincent Nardizzi, Noémie Ndiaye, Lauren Robertson, Don Rodrigues, Lindsey Row-Heyveld, Marjorie Rubright, Nina Schwartz, Riley Snorton, Stephen Spiess, John Staines, Mecca Sullivan, Valerie Traub, Filippo Trentin, Elly Truitt, Kris Trujillo, Christine Varnado, Beans Velocci, Priscilla Wald, Sarah Wall-Randell, Katherine Williams, Owen Williams, and Jordan Windholz. I am lucky for your friendship and thankful I live in a world enriched by your brilliance. Let's never stop throwing parties.

I want to acknowledge the community of grad students whose work I have been lucky enough to encounter, particularly through their brilliant contributions to EmoTrans, a group that includes Ryan Campagna, Rho Chung, Daniel D'Elia, Alexis Ferguson, Lily Freeman-Jones, Sandra Goldstein Lehnert, Kadin Henningsen, Cory Huston, Theo Northcraft, Nat Rivkin, Jacob Romm, and Madison Wolfert. Your work is urgent and important. Thank you for reminding me what matters.

The work of writing this book was undertaken in the context of many communities that have supported and sustained me. I want to express my gratefulness for the joyful community I have found at Kol Tzedek, and in particular for the guidance of R' Becky Silverstein and R' Mónica Gomery. I also want to extend my special gratitude to my family, who have supported the many transitions required to produce both this book and the scholar behind it. The resilience, intelligence, and integrity of my mother, Cathy Gordon, have been my great example for as long as I can remember. Every day, I am thankful for the companionship, insight, and humor of Chris and Brittany Gordon, and Cait and Lyndsay Church. My thanks also to Sam, for many years of care.

Writing is a collaborative act, and I am so grateful to everyone whose brilliant work made my own possible. Thank you, friends. This book is for you.

Portions of chapter 1 appeared in *Shakespeare/Sex*, edited by Jennifer Drouin (New York: Bloomsbury/Arden, 2020), the Arden Shakespeare, an imprint of Bloomsbury Publishing Plc. An earlier version of chapter 2 was published by the University of Pennsylvania Press in "Early Modern Trans Studies," a 2019 special issue of *Journal for Early Modern Cultural Studies* 19.4, edited by Simone Chess, Will Fisher, and Colby Gordon, Copyright © JEMCS, Inc. A small section of chapter 3 was published as "'The Sign You Must Not Touch': Trans Confession and Lyric Obscurity in John Donne," in *postmedieval* 11.2 (2020).

# Notes

### INTRODUCTION

1. Raphaell Holinshed, *Holinshed's Chronicles, England, Scotland, and Ireland*, vol. 2 (New York: Routledge, 1965), 351.

2. Holinshed, *Holinshed's Chronicles*, 351–52.

3. Henry de Bracton, "Cum autem clericus sic de crimine convictus degradetur, quae est magna capitis diminutio, nisi forte convictus fuerit de apostasia, quia tunc primo degradetur, et postea per manum laicalem comburatur, secundum quod accidit in concilio Oxon[iensis], celebrato a bonae memoriae S. Cantuariensis Archiepiscopo, de quodam diacono qui se apostatavit p[ro] quadam Judea, qui cum esset per Espiscopum degradat, statim fuit igni traditus per manum laicalem," in *De Legibus et Consuetudinibus Angliae* (London: Miles Flesher and Robert Young, 1640), 123–24 (lib. 3, tract. 2, ch. 9, fol. 124).

4. F. W. Maitland, "The Deacon and the Jewess; Or, Apostasy at Common Law," *Law Quarterly Review* 2, no. 2 (1886): 153–65, at 153.

5. "Introduction," *Political Theology and Early Modernity*, eds. Julia Reinhard Lupton and Graham Hammill (Chicago: University of Chicago Press, 2012), 2.

6. The classic text linking secularism and the Reformation is Max Weber's *The Protestant Ethic and the Spirit of Capitalism* (New York: Routledge, 1992). See also Charles Taylor, *A Secular Age* (Cambridge, MA: Harvard University Press, 2007).

7. On the histories of the figure of the "hermaphrodite" and their relation to trans history, see in particular Hil Malatino, *Queer Embodiment: Monstrosity, Medical Violence, and Intersex Experience* (Lincoln: University of Nebraska Press, 2019).

8. On the profound transmisogyny that has shaped cis responses to *Twelfth Night*, see Sarah Wall-Randell's showstopping essay on Mark Rylance, "The Proper False: *Twelfth Night* and 'Original Practices,' 2002–2022," in *Twelfth Night: The State of Play*, ed. Emma Smith (London: Arden, forthcoming 2024).

9. To date, the only book-length study to engage with trans studies in any capacity is Simone Chess's *Male-to-Female Crossdressing in Early Modern English Literature: Gender, Performance, and Queer Relations* (New York: Routledge, 2016). The critical vocabulary of trans studies entered early modern studies with the 2019 publication of a special issue on "Early Modern Trans Studies" in the *Journal for Early Modern Cultural Studies* 19, no. 4, edited by Simone Chess, Will Fisher, and me. Other recent work on the trans dimensions of early modern literature includes Sawyer Kemp, "'In That Dimension

Grossly Clad': Transgender Rhetoric, Representation, and Shakespeare," *Shakespeare Studies* 47 (2019): 120–27, and "Two Othellos: Transitioning Anti-Blackness: A Dialogue with Skyler Cooper," *Shakespeare Bulletin* 39, no. 4 (2021): 651–65; Ezra Horbury, "Early Modern Transgender Fairies," *Transgender Studies Quarterly* 8, no. 1 (February 2021): 75–95; Marjorie Rubright, "Becoming Scattered: The Case of Iphis's Trans*Version and the Archipelogic of John Florio's *Worlde of Wordes*," in *Ovidian Transversions: 'Iphis and Ianthe', 1300–1650*, eds. Valerie Traub, Patricia Badir, and Peggy McCracken (Edinburgh: Edinburgh University Press, 2019): 118–49; Colby Gordon, "A Woman's Prick: Trans Technogenesis in Sonnet 20," in *Shakespeare/Sex*, ed. Jennifer Drouin (New York: Bloomsbury Arden Shakespeare, 2020): 268–89; "'The Sign You Must Not Touch': Trans Confession and Lyric Obscurity in John Donne," *postmedieval* 11, no. 2 (2020): 195–203; and "Hew," forthcoming in *Logomotives: The Words That Changed Early Modern Culture*, eds. Marjorie Rubright and Stephen Spiess (Edinburgh: Edinburgh University Press, 2024).

10. Feminist scholarship aligning Christ, particularly the crucified varietal, with femininity and womanhood has a distinguished pedigree whose most influential articulation can be found in Caroline Walker Bynum's *Jesus as Mother: Studies in the Spirituality of the High Middle Ages* (Berkeley: University of California Press, 1982) and *Fragmentation and Redemption: Essays on Gender and the Human Body in Medieval Religion* (New York: Zone Books, 2012). See also Karma Lochrie, "Mystical Acts, Queer Tendencies," in *Constructing Medieval Sexuality*, eds. Karma Lochrie, Peggy McCracken, and James A. Schultz (Minneapolis: University of Minnesota Press, 1997), 180–200; Martha Easton, "The Wound of Christ, the Mouth of Hell: Appropriations and Inversions of Female Anatomy in the Later Middle Ages," in *Tributes to Jonathan J.G. Alexander: The Making and Meaning of Illuminated Medieval and Renaissance Manuscripts, Art and Architecture*, eds. Susan L'Engle and Gerald B. Guest (London: Harvey Miller, 2006), 395–414; Richard C. Trexler, "Gendering Jesus Crucified," in *Iconography at the Crossroads*, ed. Brendan Cassidy (Princeton, NJ: Index of Christian Art, 1993), 107–20; Michelle M. Sauer, "Queer Time and Lesbian Temporality in Medieval Women's Encounters with the Side Wound," in *Medieval Futurity: Essays for the Future of Queer Medieval Studies*, eds. Will Rogers and Christopher Michael Roman (Boston, MA: Walter de Gruyter, 2021), 199–220.

11. George Herbert, *The Latin Poems of George Herbert*, trans. Mark McCloskey and Paul R. Murphy (Athens: Ohio University Press, 1965), 119.

12. George Herbert, *George Herbert: The Complete English Poems*, ed. John Tobin (New York: Penguin, 1991), 140.

13. For more on the Adam hermaphrodite, see Leah DeVun, "The Perfect Sexes of Paradise" in *The Shape of Sex: Nonbinary Gender from Genesis to the Renaissance* (New York: Columbia University Press, 2021), 16–39. Edenic gender is also discussed in chapter 1 of this book.

14. Sophie Sexon, "Gender-Querying Christ's Wounds," in *Trans and Genderqueer Subjects in Medieval Hagiography*, eds. Blake Gutt and Alicia Spencer-Hall (Amsterdam: Amsterdam University Press, 2021), 133–54; and "Seeing Mobility in Static Images: Tools for Non-Binary Identification in Late Medieval Sources," in *Medieval Mobilities: Gendered Bodies, Spaces, and Movements*, eds. Basil Arnould Price, Jane Elizabeth Bonsall, and Meagan Khoury (New York: Palgrave Macmillan, 2023), 77–108; Jonah Coman, "Queering Christ: *Habitus* Theology as Trans-Embodied Incarnation in

Late Medieval Culture," PhD diss., Glasgow School of Art, 2019, https://radar.gsa.ac.uk/7437/1/2020_Coman_Jonah_PhD.pdf; Ellis Amity Light, "Fluxing Fellowship: Bodily Fluids and Forms of Community in Medieval Devotional Literature," PhD diss., Fordham University, 2023, https://media.proquest.com/media/hms/PFT/2/reNdR?_s=E%2Frpp1KwXx67qQxPkq%2B2GA%2BTR2g%3; and Leah DeVun, "The Jesus Hermaphrodite: Alchemy in the Late Middle Ages and Early Renaissance," in *Shape of Sex*, 163–200.

15. Herbert, *Complete English Poems*, 142.

16. Michael Schoenfeldt, *Prayer and Power: George Herbert and Renaissance Courtship* (Chicago: University of Chicago Press, 1991), 249; Caroline Walker Bynum, "The Body of Christ in the Later Middle Ages: A Reply to Leo Steinberg," *Renaissance Quarterly* 39, no. 3 (Autumn 1986): 399–439, at 424.

17. Richard Rambuss, *Closet Devotions* (Durham, NC: Duke University Press, 1998), 36.

18. Rambuss, *Closet Devotions*, 38.

19. Rambuss, *Closet Devotions*, 36.

20. The cardinal's letter was included in Heinrich Institoris's defense of Brocadelli, *Stigmifere virginis Lucie de Narnia*, transcribed in Tamar Herzig's *Christ Transformed into a Virgin Woman: Lucia Brocadelli, Heinrich Institoris, and the Defense of the Faith* (Rome: Edizioni di Storia e Letteratura, 2013), 299.

21. In Herzig, *Christ Transformed into a Virgin Woman*, 300.

22. Raymond of Capua, *The Life of St. Catherine of Siena*, trans. George Lamb (New York: 1960), 77.

23. Caroline Walker Bynum, *Holy Feast and Holy Fast: The Religious Significance of Food to Medieval Women* (Berkeley: University of California Press, 1987), 175, 376–77.

24. Lu Ann Homza, ed., *Spanish Inquisition, 1478–1614: An Anthology of Sources* (Indianapolis, IN: Hackett Publishing Co., 2006), 171–72.

25. For a magisterial account of the ongoing legacies, within modern jurisprudence, of the premodern association between demons and blackness, see Cecilio M. Cooper, "Fallen: Generation, Postlapsarian Verticality + the Black Chthonic," *Rhizomes: Cultural Studies in Emerging Knowledge* 38 (2022). See also Debra Higgs Strickland, "Demons, Darkness, and Ethiopians," in *Saracens, Demons, and Jews: Making Monsters in Medieval Art* (Princeton, NJ: Princeton University Press, 2003), 61–93.

26. Homza, ed., *Spanish Inquisition*, 169.

27. "Tenía familiar dende que fue de cinco años y cuando le via de esta edad pensaba que era angel hasta que de doce años que confeso ser demonio y hizo pacto y convenencia con él y él prometió de sustenarla por gran tiempo en grandes onrras, y este diablo trijole un negro desnudo combidandola a deleites carnales," in Jesús Imirizaldu, *Monjas y Beatas Embaucadores* (Madrid: Editora Nacional, 1977), 47.

28. For the racializing logics of these forms of stigmatization, see in particular Miles P. Grier on tattooing in "Inkface: The Slave Stigma in England's Early Imperial Imagination," in *Scripturalizing the Human: The Written as the Political*, ed. Vincent L. Wimbush (New York: Routledge, 2015), 193–220; Urvashi Chakravarty on the *macula servitutis* in *Fictions of Consent: Slavery, Servitude, and Free Service in Early Modern*

*England* (Philadelphia: University of Pennsylvania Press, 2022), 171–97; and Patricia Akhimie on the racial character of "stigmatized somatic marks" of bruises and birthmarks in Shakespeare's *Comedy of Errors*, "Bruised with Adversity: Reading Race in *The Comedy of Errors*," in *The Oxford Handbook of Shakespeare and Embodiment*, ed. Valerie Traub (New York: Oxford University Press, 2016), 186–96, at 191.

29. Grier, "Inkface," 195.

30. Tamar Herzig, "Genuine and Fraudulent Stigmatics in the Sixteenth Century," in *Dissimulation and Deceit in Early Modern Europe*, eds. Miriam Eliav-Feldon and Tamar Herzig (New York: Palgrave Macmillan, 2015), 142–64, at 142, 157.

31. Carolyn Muessig, "Stigmata in an Age of Religious Change," in *The Stigmata in Medieval and Early Modern Europe* (New York: Oxford University Press, 2020), 218–48.

32. Dyan Elliott, *Fallen Bodies: Pollution, Sexuality, and Demonology in the Middle Ages* (Philadelphia: University of Pennsylvania Press, 1999), 53. On demonic gender, see also DeVun, *Shape of Sex*, 87–97.

33. C. S. Lewis, *A Preface to Paradise Lost* (New York: Oxford University Press, 1961), 113; John Milton, *Paradise Lost*, in *The Complete Poetry and Essential Prose of John Milton*, eds. William Kerrigan, John Rumrich, and Stephen M. Fallon (New York: Modern Library, 2007), 6.351–53.

34. John Milton, *Paradise Lost*, in *John Milton: Complete Poems and Major Prose*, ed. Merritt Y. Hughes (Upper Saddle River, NJ: Prentice Hall, 1957), 419–31.

35. "*sexum Idolorum scriptura sacra, nec prisca mysteria gentium distinguunt*," John Selden, *De Diis Syriis*, quoted in Jason P. Rosenblatt and Winfried Schleiner, "John Selden's Letter to Ben Jonson on Cross-Dressing and Bisexual Gods," *English Literary Renaissance* 29, no. 1 (1999): 44–74, at 57.

36. Julie Crawford, "Transubstantial Bodies in *Paradise Lost* and *Order and Disorder*," *Journal for Early Modern Cultural Studies* 19, no. 4 (Fall 2019): 75–93, 81.

37. William Shakespeare, *Macbeth*, ed. Nicholas Brooke (New York: Oxford University Press, 1990), act 1, sc. 3, lines 40, 45–47.

38. In a forthcoming essay in *Early Modern Witch Plays: A Critical Reader*, ed. Eric Pudney (London: Arden, 2024), Molly Hand draws upon disability studies to analyze the physical examinations that victims of witchcraft scares were forced to undergo.

39. Heinrich Institoris, *Malleus Maleficarum* (Frankfurt am Main: apud Nicolaum Bassaeum, 1580), pt. 1, q. 9, p. 125. On Kramer's ambivalence about whether it was actually possible for witches to remove their victims' genitals or whether this was some sort of demonic delusion, see Walter Stephens, "Witches Who Steal Penises: Impotence and Illusion in *Malleus Maleficarum*," *Journal of Medieval and Early Modern Studies* 28, no. 3 (Fall 1998), 495–529.

40. Reginald Scot, *The Discoverie of Witchcraft* (New York: Dover, 1972), 51.

41. Jean Bodin, *On the Demon-Mania of Witches*, trans. Randy A. Scott (Toronto: Centre for Reformation and Renaissance Studies, 2001), 101.

42. Maitland summarizes the sources in "Deacon and the Jewess," 157–60.

43. Matthew of Paris, *Historia Anglorum*, vol. 2, ed. Frederic Madden (London: Longmans, Green, Reader, and Dyer, 1866), 254. Then again, maybe he did. Elliott Horowitz draws on Hebrew sources from Germany and France detailing how Jewish

martyrs had urinated on crosses to raise the possibility that "the deacon had learned how to die defiantly, the Jewish way." See "The Jews and the Cross in the Middle Ages: Towards a Reappraisal," in *Philosemitism, Antisemitism, and "The Jews": Perspectives from the Middle Ages to the Twentieth Century*, eds. Tony Kushner and Nadia Valman (Burlington, VT: Ashgate, 2004), 114–31, at 127.

44. Thomas Calvert, *The Blessed Jew of Marocco: Or, a Blackmoor Made White* (York: T. Broad, 1648), 19–20, 31. For other instances of this particular fantasy, see Irven M. Resnick, "Medieval Roots of the Myth of Jewish Male Menses," *Harvard Theological Review* 93, no. 3 (July 2000), 241–63.

45. Matthew of Paris writes that in 1235, "seven Jews were brought before the king" to face charges that they had "kidnapped and circumcised a certain boy in Norwich, keeping him out of the sight of Christians for the course of the year, and intending to crucify him on Easter" (*septem Judaei adducti [sunt] coram rege apud Westmonasterium, qui in Norwico puerum quendam, quem furto sublatum jam per annum a conspectus Christianorum absconderant, circumciderunt, volentes eundem crucifigere in sollempnitate Paschali*). See *Historia Anglorum*, vol. 2, 375.

46. Matthew of Paris, *Historia Anglorum*, vol. 2, 254.

47. "And in that year a certain man was arrested, having in his body and members, that is to say, in his side, hands, and feet, the five wounds of the Crucifixion; and he was presented to the aforesaid council along with an accomplice, a certain person of both sexes, that is to say, a hermaphrodite, who had been blinded by the same aforementioned delusion" (*Hoc etiam anno comprehensus fuit quidam . . . habens in corpore et membris, scilicet in latere, manibus, et pedibus, quinque vulnera Crucifixionis; et in dicto concilio simul cum eo [quidam] utriusque sexus, scilicet ermofroditus, eiusdem erroris quo prior fuit obcaecatus cum suo complice praesentatus*). Matthew of Paris, *Chronica Majora*, vol. 3, ed. Henry Richards Luard (London: Longman and Co., 1876), 71.

48. On this legislation, see Nicholas Vincent, "Two Papal Letters on the Wearing of the Jewish Badge, 1221 and 1229," *Jewish Historical Studies* 34 (1994–96), 209–24.

49. An engraving in Pierre Dan's *Histoire de Barbarie et ses Corsaires* (1649) features a panorama of turbaned "Turks" executing Christian slaves in a variety of harrowing fashions: the victims are shot with cannons, flayed, immured, dragged to death by horses, impaled, and crucified. Greta LaFleur situates this engraving as part of a cultural imaginary in Christian print culture of the era that bound Barbary captivity to sodomitical violence in *The Natural History of Sexuality in Early America* (Baltimore, MD: Johns Hopkins University Press, 2018), 63–67.

50. On political theology in early modern studies, see Julia Reinhard Lupton, *Citizen-Saints: Shakespeare and Political Theology* (Chicago: University of Chicago Press, 2005); Eric Santner, *The Royal Remains: The People's Two Bodies and the Endgames of Sovereignty* (Chicago: University of Chicago Press, 2011); Graham Hammill, *The Mosaic Constitution: Political Theology and Imagination from Machiavelli to Milton* (Chicago: University of Chicago Press, 2011); Slavoj Žižek, Eric Santner, and Kenneth Reinhard, eds., *The Neighbor: Three Inquiries in Political Theology* (Chicago: University of Chicago Press, 2005); Lupton and Hammill, eds., *Political Theology and Early Modernity*; Jacques Lezra, *Wild Materialism: The Ethic of Terror and the Modern Republic* (New York: Fordham University Press, 2010); Jennifer Rust, *The Body in Mystery: The Political Theology of the* Corpus Mysticum *in the Literature of Reformation England*

(Evanston, IL: Northwestern University Press, 2014); Henry S. Turner, *The Corporate Commonwealth: Pluralism and Political Fictions in England, 1516–1651* (Chicago: University of Chicago Press, 2016); Paul Cefalu, *English Renaissance Literature and Contemporary Theory: Sublime Objects of Theology* (New York: Palgrave Macmillan, 2007) and *The Johannine Renaissance in Early Modern English Literature and Theology* (New York: Oxford University Press, 2017); Debora K. Shuger, *Political Theologies in Shakespeare's England: The Sacred and the State in* Measure for Measure (New York: Palgrave, 2001); Ken Jackson and Arthur F. Marotti, "The Turn to Religion in Early Modern English Studies," *Criticism* 46, no. 1 (2004), 167–90; Gregory Kneidel, *Rethinking the Turn to Religion in Early Modern English Literature: The Poetics of All Believers* (New York: Palgrave Macmillan, 2008); Nichole E. Miller, *Violence and Grace: Exceptional Life between Shakespeare and Modernity* (Evanston, IL: Northwestern University Press, 2014); Eric Song, *Love against Substitution: Seventeenth-Century English Literature and the Meaning of Marriage* (Stanford, CA: Stanford University Press, 2022); and a number of essays in *Political Aesthetics in the Era of Shakespeare*, ed. Christopher Pye (Evanston, IL: Northwestern University Press, 2020). The strongest case against political theology as a historical claim and literary-critical method is found in Victoria Kahn's *The Future of Illusion: Political Theology and Early Modern Texts* (Chicago: University of Chicago Press, 2014).

51. As it happens, the king's two bodies is a theory with trans dimensions of its own, as Grace Lavery demonstrates in "The King's Two Anuses," in *Pleasure and Efficacy: Of Pen Names, Cover Versions, and Other Trans Techniques* (Princeton, NJ: Princeton University Press, 2023), 33–66.

52. Urvashi Chakravarty, "Race, Natality, and the Biopolitics of Early Modern Political Theology," *Journal for Early Modern Cultural Studies* 18, no. 2 (Spring 2018): 140–66, at 141.

53. Council on Biblical Manhood and Womanhood, "Nashville Statement," article 10, accessed December 15, 2022, https://cbmw.org/nashville-statement/. For more on Pope Francis's views on trans life, see chapter 1, "A Woman's Prick."

54. Lupton and Hammill, eds., *Political Theology and Early Modernity*, 2.

55. While it is not the aim of this book to historicize the transphobia at work in National Socialism, it has never been far from my mind during the process of writing this book, particularly in its final stages. Blaming transition (and youth transition in particular) on a cabal of pharmaceutical interests funded by George Soros has become a standard feature of mainstream transphobic rhetoric. For an endorsement of this position by an explicitly neo-Nazi publication, see the pseudonymously authored volume *The Transgender Industrial Complex* (Montgomery County, PA: Antelope Hill Press, 2020).

56. Chakravarty, "Race, Natality, and the Biopolitics of Early Modern Political Theology."

57. Christian lobbies promoting anti-trans legislation and drafting the language for bills include Focus on the Family, the Family Research Council, the UK-based Christian Institute, and the Alliance Defending Freedom. See Hannah Dick, "Advocating for the Right: Alliance Defending Freedom and the Rhetoric of Christian Persecution," *Feminist Legal Studies* 29 (2021): 375–97.

58. Max Strassfeld and Roberto Che Espinoza, "Introduction: Mapping Trans Studies in Religion," *Transgender Studies Quarterly* 6, no. 3 (2019): 283–84. They also note

the role of radical feminist theologians like Mary Daly in shaping transmisogynistic theory and politics and the racialized definition of religion as practiced "elsewhere and else-when," an irrational custom inadmissible within the secular sphere assumed to be the unique purview of the West (293).

59. Max Strassfeld, "Transing Religious Studies," *Journal of Feminist Studies in Religion* 34, no. 1 (2018): 37–53, at 39, 53.

60. Max Strassfeld, *Trans Talmud: Androgynes and Eunuchs in Rabbinic Literature* (Oakland: University of California Press, 2022); Joy Ladin, *The Soul of the Stranger: Reading God and Torah from a Transgender Perspective* (Waltham, MA: Brandeis Press, 2019); Roberto Che Espinoza, *Activist Theology* (Minneapolis, MN: Fortress Press, 2019); S. J. Crasnow, "On Transition: Normative Judaism and Trans Innovation," *Journal of Contemporary Religion* 32, no. 3 (2017): 403–15 and "'Becoming' Bodies: Affect Theory, Transgender Jews, and the Rejection of the Coherent Subject," *CrossCurrents* 71, no. 1 (2021): 49–62; and Max Thornton, "Trans/Criptions: Gender, Disability, and Liturgical Experience," *Transgender Studies Quarterly* 6, no. 3 (2019): 358–67.

61. Leah DeVun, *Shape of Sex*; Roland Betancourt, *Byzantine Intersectionality: Sexuality, Gender, and Race in the Middle Ages* (Princeton, NJ: Princeton University Press, 2020); Micah Goodrich, "*Ycrammed Ful of Cloutes and of Bones*: Chaucer's Queer Cavities," in *Medieval Futurity: Essays for the Future of a Queer Medieval Studies*, eds. Will Rogers and Christopher Michael Roman (Boston, MA: Walter de Gruyter, 2021), 153–79; and Gabrielle Bychowski, "Reconstructing the Pardoner: Transgender Skin Operations in Fragment VI," in *Writing on Skin in the Age of Chaucer*, eds. Nicole Nyffenegger and Katrin Rupp (Boston, MA: Walter de Gruyter, 2018), 221–50 and "On Genesis: Transgender and Sub-Creation," *Transgender Studies Quarterly* 6, no. 3 (2019), 442–47. See also the essays collected in Gutt and Spencer-Hall, eds., *Trans and Genderqueer Subjects in Medieval Hagiography*, in particular Blake Gutt's "Holy Queer and Holy Cure: Sanctity, Disability, and Transgender Embodiment in *Tristan de Nanteuil*," 223–44; Scott Larson, "'Indescribable Being': Theological Performances of Genderlessness in the Society of the Publick Universal Friend, 1776–1819," *Early American Studies* 12, no. 3 (Fall 2014): 576–600; Ellis Amity Light, "Trans Activisms and Interspecies Entanglement in the Middle English *Patience*," forthcoming in the "Trans Natures" special issue of *Medieval Ecocriticisms*, eds. Aylin Malcolm and Nat Rivkin (2024); and many of the essays in *Trans Historical: Gender Plurality before the Modern*, eds. Greta LaFleur, Masha Raskolnikov, and Anna Klosowska (Ithaca, NY: Cornell University Press, 2021).

62. On transness and race, see especially C. Riley Snorton, *Black on Both Sides: A Racial History of Trans Identity* (Minneapolis: University of Minnesota Press, 2017); Jules Gill-Peterson, *Histories of the Transgender Child* (Minneapolis: University of Minnesota Press, 2018); Cameron Awkward-Rich, *The Terrible We: Thinking with Trans Maladjustment* (Durham, NC: Duke University Press, 2022); Francisco J. Galarte, *Brown Trans Figurations: Rethinking Race, Gender, and Sexuality in Chicanx/Latinx Studies* (Austin: University of Texas Press, 2021); Aren Z. Aizura, *Mobile Subjects: Transnational Imaginaries of Gender Reassignment* (Durham, NC: Duke University Press, 2018); Marquis Bey, *Black Trans Feminism* (Durham, NC: Duke University Press, 2022); *Trap Door: Trans Cultural Production and the Politics of Visibility*, eds. Tourmaline, Eric A. Stanley, and Johanna Burton (Cambridge, MA: MIT Press, 2017); Kadji Amin, "Glands, Eugenics, and Rejuvenation in *Man into Woman*: A Biopolitical

Genealogy of Transsexuality," *Transgender Studies Quarterly* 5, no. 4 (2018): 589–605; and many of the essays in *Feminism against Cisness*, ed. Emma Heaney (Durham, NC: Duke University Press, 2024).

63. Dennis Austin Britton, *Becoming Christian: Race, Reformation, and Early Modern English Romance* (New York: Fordham University Press, 2014); Ian Smith, *Race and Rhetoric in the Renaissance: Barbarian Errors* (New York: Palgrave Macmillan, 2009); Kim F. Hall, *Things of Darkness: Economies of Race and Gender in Early Modern England* (Ithaca, NY: Cornell University Press, 2018). See also Patricia Akhimie, *Shakespeare and the Cultivation of Difference: Race and Conduct in the Early Modern World* (New York: Routledge, 2018); Noémie Ndiaye, *Scripts of Blackness: Early Modern Performance Culture and the Making of Race* (Philadelphia: University of Pennsylvania Press, 2022); Matthieu Chapman, *Anti-Black Racism in Early Modern English Drama: The Other "Other"* (New York: Routledge, 2017); and Janet Adelman, *Blood Relations: Christian and Jew in* Merchant of Venice (Chicago: University of Chicago Press, 2008).

64. Snorton, *Black on Both Sides*, 8.

65. Fine, here is a partial list of Shakespeare's trans characters: Richard II, Goneril, Hotspur but not Hal, Marina, absolutely Hamlet, *absolutely not Portia*, Touchstone, Cloten, Lady Macbeth; everyone except the parents in *Romeo and Juliet*; and Marc Antony in *Julius Caesar* but not *Antony and Cleopatra*. Also, *Twelfth Night* is not a trans play, but Orsino is absolutely a chaser.

66. Gail Kern Paster, "Shakespeare's They / Thems," Folger Shakespeare Library Professional Development, accessed March 20, 2023, https://web.archive.org/web/20230319134056/https://www.folger.edu/whats-on/shakespeares-they-thems-professional-development-teachers/.

67. For work locating the origins of trans identity in late nineteenth-century sexology, see Susan Stryker, *Transgender History: The Roots of Today's Revolution* (Berkeley, CA: Seal Press, 2017) and Jay Prosser, "Transsexuals and the Transsexologists: Inversion and the Emergence of Transsexual Subjectivity," in *Sexology in Culture: Labelling Bodies and Desires*, eds. Lucy Bland and Laura Doan (Chicago: University of Chicago Press, 1998), 116–32. For a nuanced and compelling update to this genealogical project, see Amin, "Glands, Eugenics, and Rejuvenation."

68. Ari Friedlander, "Introduction: Desiring History and Historicizing Desire," *Journal for Early Modern Cultural Studies* 16, no. 2 (Spring 2016): 1–20, at 3; Valerie Traub, *The Renaissance of Lesbianism in Early Modern England* (New York: Cambridge University Press, 2002), 32.

69. Traub, *Renaissance of Lesbianism*; Laurie Shannon, *Sovereign Amity: Figures of Friendship in Shakespearean Contexts* (Chicago: University of Chicago Press, 2002); Julie Crawford, "Women's Secretaries," in *Queer Renaissance Historiography*, eds. Vin Nardizzi, Stephen Guy-Bray, and Will Stockton (Burlington, VT: Ashgate, 2009), 111–34; Alan Bray, *The Friend* (Chicago: University of Chicago Press, 2003); Mario DiGangi, *Sexual Types: Embodiment, Agency, and Dramatic Character from Shakespeare to Shirley* (Philadelphia: University of Pennsylvania Press, 2011); and Richard Rambuss, *Spenser's Secret Career* (New York: Cambridge University Press, 1993).

70. While we may assume that stealth trans people have always existed in this (and every other) profession, the field has historically refused to hire anyone whose trans status was a matter of public knowledge. In *Shakespeare in the Trans Archives*, Simone

Chess discusses the case of the trans woman Laura McAllister, an editor on the staff of DRAG magazine in the early 1970s. A biography provided in one of the periodical's "Drag Spotlight" describes "Miss McAllister" as a "young college professor in a large midwestern university" who really "knows her 'stuff'" (New York: Routledge, forthcoming).

71. Regina Kunzel, "The Flourishing of Transgender Studies," *Transgender Studies Quarterly* 1, nos. 1–2 (May 2014): 285–97, at 285.

72. Two scholarly articles have been published on "Rapid Onset Gender Dysphoria" (ROGD), one by Lisa Littman that raised such substantial concerns that the journal apologized for the essay and issued corrections and another by Suzanna Diaz (a pseudonym) and J. Michael Bailey that was retracted. See Lisa Littman, "Parent Reports of Adolescents and Young People Perceived to Show Signs of a Rapid Onset of Gender Dysphoria," *PLOS ONE* 13, no. 8 (2018) and Suzanna Diaz and J. Michael Bailey, "Rapid Onset Gender Dysphoria: Parent Reports on 1655 Possible Cases," *Archives of Sexual Behavior* 52 (2023): 1031–43. Florence Ashley tracks the ugly career of ROGD as a "politicised pseudo-diagnostic category" developed as "a deliberate attempt to weaponize scientific-sounding language to dismiss mounting empirical evidence of the benefits of transition for youth" in "A Critical Commentary on 'Rapid-Onset Gender Dysphoria,'" *Sociological Review* 68, no. 4 (2020): 779–99, at 779. On this point, see also A. J. Restar, "Methodological Critique of Littman's (2018) Parental-Respondents Accounts of 'Rapid-Onset Gender Dysphoria,'" *Archives of Sexual Behavior* 49, no. 1 (2020): 61–66. For a deliciously cheeky reimagining of this trans social contagion panic, see Cassius Adair and Aren Aizura, "'The Transgender Craze Seducing Our [Sons]'; or, All the Trans Guys Are Just Dating Each Other," *Transgender Studies Quarterly* 9, no. 1 (2022): 44–64.

73. This concern headlines a series of anti-trans bills proposing grotesque punishments for transitioning, the "Save Adolescents from Experimentation (SAFE)" Acts of Ohio (HB 454), Louisiana (HB 570), Missouri (HB 2649).

74. Ambroise Paré explains that Germain's transition required the witnessing not only of his mother, who was "very astonished by this spectacle," but also that of "Physicians and Surgeons" who "found that she was a man, and no longer a girl," which they dutifully "reported to the bishop," under whose authority "an assembly" was called to bestow upon the shepherd "a man's name." (*On Monsters and Marvels*, trans. Janis L. Pallister [Chicago: University of Chicago Press, 1982], 32). The surgeon Jacques Duval describes how he "probed the private parts of the aforesaid Marin with his finger, and in doing so found his virile member" (*Traité des hermaphrodits* [Paris: Isidore Liseux, 1880], 372). On the interplay between medical authority and legal judgment in the cases of hermaphrodites, see Lorraine Daston and Katharine Park, "The Hermaphrodite and the Orders of Nature: Sexual Ambiguity in Early Modern France," *GLQ* 1 (1995): 419–38.

75. The record of Eleanor's interrogation is transcribed in David Lorenzo Boyd and Ruth Mazo Karras, "The Interrogation of a Male Transvestite Prostitute in Fourteenth-Century London," *GLQ* 1 (1995): 459–65. Gabrielle Bychowski offers a trans rereading of the court documents in "The Transgender Turn: Eleanor Rykener Speaks Back," in *Trans Historical*, eds. LaFleur, Raskolnikov, and Klosowska, 95–113.

76. See Shaun Tougher, *The Roman Castrati: Eunuchs in the Roman Empire* (New York: Bloomsbury, 2022). For Roman encounters with the *galli*, eunuch priestesses

of Cybele, see Lynn Roller, *In Search of God the Mother: The Cult of Anatolian Cybele* (Berkeley: University of California Press, 1999). Joseph A. Marchal draws on trans studies to offer a nuanced treatment of eunuchs and *galli* in Pauline context in *Appalling Bodies: Queer Figures before and after Paul's Letters* (New York: Oxford University Press, 2020).

77. Leah DeVun, "The Correction of Nature: Sex and the Science of Surgery," in *Shape of Sex*, 134–62.

78. Abdulhamit Arvas, "Early Modern Eunuchs and the Transing of Gender and Race," *Journal for Early Modern Cultural Studies* 19, no. 4 (Fall 2019): 116–36.

79. James Yonge, *Currus triumphalis, e terebintho* (London: Printed for J. Martyn, 1679), 76. Alanna Skuse discusses this incident and a number of other cases in "'One Stroak of His Razour': Tales of Self-Gelding in Early Modern England," *Social History of Medicine* 33, no. 2 (2020): 377–93. In their forthcoming "Trans Feminine Histories, Trans Feminist Historiographies," Greta LaFleur discusses eighteenth- and nineteenth-century accounts of voluntary castration, in *Feminism against Cisness*, ed. Heaney.

80. Yonge, *Currus triumphalis*, 78.

81. Eusebius, *Ecclesiastical History*, vol. 2, trans. Roy J. Deferrari (Washington, DC: Catholic University of America Press, 1955), 16.

82. Thomas Laqueur, *Making Sex: Body and Gender from the Greeks to Freud* (Cambridge, MA: Harvard University Press, 1990), 7–8.

83. John Smith, *The Mysterie of Rhetorique Unveil'd* (London: Printed by E. Cotes for George Eversden, 1665), 6. In *Trans Talmud*, Max Strassfeld incisively situates Laqueur's rejection of the "bad reading" of Germain as excessively focused on the material body alongside the allegations of perverse literalism that often featured in anti-Semitic polemics as well, since "Jews insist on literal circumcision instead of literal circumcision, and so on," determining to lean into the position of the "'bad' trans/Jewish reader" rather than retreating from it (19).

84. A massive body of scholarship on Renaissance "transvestism" exists. For a sampling, see Lisa Jardine, *Still Harping on Daughters: Women and Drama in the Age of Shakespeare* (Brighton: Harvester Press Ltd., 1983) and "Boy Actors, Female Roles, and Elizabethan Eroticism," in *Staging the Renaissance: Reinterpretations of Elizabethan and Jacobean Drama*, eds. David Scott Kastan and Peter Stallybrass (New York: Routledge, 1991), 57–67; Linda Woodbridge, *Women and the English Renaissance: Literature and the Nature of Womankind, 1540 to 1620* (Urbana: University of Illinois Press, 1984), 139–58; Kathleen McLuskie, "The Act, the Role, and the Actor: Boy Actresses on the Elizabethan Stage," *New Theatre Quarterly* 3, no. 10 (1987): 120–30; Stephen Greenblatt, "Fiction and Friction" in *Shakespearean Negotiations: The Circulation of Social Energy in Renaissance England* (Berkeley: University of California Press, 1988), 66–93; Valerie Traub, "Desire and the Difference It Makes," in *The Matter of Difference: Materialist Feminist Criticism of Shakespeare*, ed. Valerie Wayne (Ithaca, NY: Cornell University Press, 1991), 81–114; Jean Howard, *The Stage and Social Struggle in Early Modern England* (New York: Routledge, 1994), 94–104; Jonathan Dollimore, "Shakespeare Understudies: The Sodomite, the Prostitute, the Transvestite and their Critics," in *Political Shakespeare: Essays in Cultural Materialism*, eds. Jonathan Dollimore and Alan Sinfield (Ithaca, NY: Cornell University Press, 1994), 129–53; Laura Levine, *Men in Women's Clothing: Anti-Theatricality and Effeminization, 1579–1642* (New York: Cam-

bridge University Press, 1994); Michael Shapiro, *Gender in Play on the Shakespearean Stage: Boy Heroines and Female Pages* (Ann Arbor: University of Michigan Press, 1994); Stephen Orgel, *Impersonations: The Performance of Gender in Shakespeare's England* (New York: Cambridge University Press, 1996); David Cressy, "Gender Trouble and Cross-Dressing in Early Modern England," *Journal of British Studies* 35, no. 4 (1996): 438–65; Juliet Dusinberre, "Squeaking Cleopatras: Gender and Performance in *Antony and Cleopatra*," in *Shakespeare, Theory, and Performance*, ed. James C. Bulman (New York: Routledge, 1996), 46–67; Richard Burt, "When Our Lips Synch Together: The Transvestite Voice, the Virtuoso, Speed, and Pumped-Up Volume in Some Over-Heard Shakespeares," from *Unspeakable ShaXXXspeares: Queer Theory and American Kiddie Culture* (New York: St. Martin's Press, 1998), 159–202; Clare McManus, *Women on the Renaissance Stage: Anna of Denmark and Female Masquing in the Stuart Court (1590–1619)* (New York: Manchester University Press, 2002); Phyllis Rackin, "Boys Will Be Girls," in *Shakespeare and Women* (New York: Oxford University Press, 2005), 72–94; *Transvestism and the Onnagata Traditions in Shakespeare and Kabuki*, eds. Minoru Fujita and Michael Shapiro (Boston, MA: Brill, 2006); the essays collected in James C. Bulmer, *Shakespeare Re-Dressed: Cross-Gender Casting in Contemporary Performance* (Cranbury, NJ: Associated University Presses, 2008); Terri Power, *Shakespeare and Gender in Practice* (New York: Palgrave, 2016); Courtney Bailey Parker, *Spectrums of Shakespearean Crossdressing: The Art of Performing Women* (New York: Routledge, 2020); and Pamela Allen Brown, *The Diva's Gift to the Shakespearean Stage: Agency, Theatricality, and the Innamorata* (New York: Oxford, 2021).

85. Juliet Dusinberre, "Women and Boys Playing Shakespeare," in *A Feminist Companion to Shakespeare*, 2nd ed., ed. Dympna Callaghan (Malden, MA: John Wiley and Sons, 2016), 269–80, at 269.

86. Parker, *Spectrums of Shakespearean Crossdressing*.

87. Dympna Callaghan, *Shakespeare without Women: Representing Gender and Race on the Renaissance Stage* (New York: Routledge, 2000), 35.

88. Lorna Hutson, "On Not Being Deceived: Rhetoric and the Body in *Twelfth Night*," *Texas Studies in Literature and Language* 38, no. 2 (Summer 1996): 141.

89. Marjorie Garber, "Logic of the Transvestite: *The Roaring Girl* (1608)," in *Staging the Renaissance*, eds. Kastan and Stallybrass, 230. It is not so clear, however, what exactly "everyone offstage" could be presumed to know with Garber's easy certainty. After all, as Simone Chess has recently pointed out, the gender transgressions of "the very best" boy players, like Edward Kynaston and the "Lady Rich Robinson," were not restricted to the stage, and so it may well be that they "were never boys in the sense of being cis-male, and that they therefore never grew up into normative adult manhood." See "Queer Residue: Boy Actors' Adult Careers in Early Modern England," *Journal for Early Modern Cultural Studies* 19, no. 4 (2019): 242–64, at 247. The first half of the claim, that *The Roaring Girl*'s other characters know that Moll Cutpurse "is a girl," is also bewildering. As Marjorie Rubright demonstrates, *The Roaring Girl*'s "titular hero|ine" is an engine of "lexical superfluity" who "engenders such a multiplicity of proper names, profusion of pronouns, and abundance of adjectives that, like the term 'trans' itself, the roaring girl 'refuses to deliver certainty through the act of naming.'" See "Transgender Capacity in *The Roaring Girl*," *Journal for Early Modern Cultural Studies* 19, no. 4 (Fall 2019): 45–74, at 45–46.

90. Orgel, *Impersonations*, 31.

91. Lisa Jardine, *Reading Shakespeare Historically* (New York: Routledge, 1996), 66.

92. Jardine, *Reading Shakespeare Historically*, 67.

93. Robert Clark and Claire Sponsler, "Queer Play: The Cultural Work of Cross-dressing in Medieval Drama," *New Literary History* 28, no. 2 (Spring 1997): 321.

94. Jardine, *Reading Shakespeare Historically*, 67.

95. Phyllis Rackin, "Androgyny, Mimesis, and the Marriage of the Boy Heroine on the English Renaissance Stage," *PMLA* 102, no. 1 (1987): 36. Sandra Goldstein Lehnert offers a thoughtful reassessment of this episode as part of a trans "scene" marked by a "community relationship and potential ethics of care between Epicoene and the Collegiates" that "partially resists the re-disciplining of the unwigging" in their PhD dissertation "Self-Knowing Parts: Materialism and Trans History" (CUNY Graduate Center, anticipated 2026).

96. Peter Stallybrass, "Transvestism and the 'Body Beneath': Speculating on the Boy Actor," in *Erotic Politics: Desire on the Renaissance Stage*, ed. Susan Zimmerman (New York: Routledge, 1992), 64–83.

97. Greenblatt, *Shakespearean Negotiations*, 93.

98. Marjorie Garber, *Vested Interests: Cross-Dressing and Cultural Anxiety* (New York: Routledge, 1992), 87.

99. Danielle M. Seid, "The Reveal," *Transgender Studies Quarterly* 1, nos. 1–2 (May 2014): 176–77, at 177.

100. On this media history, see *Disclosure*, directed by Sam Feder (Los Gatos, CA: Netflix, 2020), streaming documentary; and Cáel M. Keegan, "On the Necessity of Bad Trans Objects," *Film Quarterly* 75, no. 3 (2022): 26–37.

101. Jonathan Crewe, "In the Field of Dreams: Transvestism in *Twelfth Night* and *The Crying Game*," *Representations* 50 (Spring 1995): 101–21, at 102.

102. Ethel Person, "Harry Benjamin: Creative Maverick," *Journal of Gay and Lesbian Mental Health* 12, no. 3 (2008): 262.

103. It was not Benjamin who coined the term "transvestite," but Magnus Hirschfeld. In his 1910 book *Transvestites: The Erotic Drive to Cross-Dress* (*Die Transvestiten: Eine Untersuchung über den erotischen Verkleidungstrieb*), Hirschfeld employed the term to describe subjects whose sartorial habits had an erotic dimension as well as people engaging in surgical, hormonal, and social transition (trans. Michael A. Lombardi-Nash [Buffalo, NY: Prometheus Books, 1991]). While tensions between the various constituencies housed together under the label "transvestite" were present from the beginning, the eventual differentiation between these identity categories was a product of mid-century sexology.

104. Georges Burou, one of the few surgeons in the world willing to perform vaginoplasty from the 1950s–70s, refused to operate on insufficiently feminine women, as he explained to a tabloid in 1974. "I only intervene if it's possible to be fooled by her and really take her for a woman, endowed with all the obvious feminine sexual characteristics. Maybe it's not fair, but I don't want to create monsters, like big, fat, hairy-chested truck drivers. In that case, I systematically refuse" (Virginie Merlin, "L'homme qui change le sexe," *Paris Match* 1300 [April 1974]: 39, translation mine).

105. The diagnostic markers of transsexuality and transvestism are outlined in Harry Benjamin, *The Transsexual Phenomenon* (New York: Ace Publishing, 1966), 20–21; Robert Stoller, *Sex and Gender: The Development of Masculinity and Femininity* (London: H. Karnac Ltd., 1968); and Norman M. Fisk, "Gender Dysphoria Syndrome," *Western Journal of Medicine* 120, no. 5 (May 1974): 387.

106. For an instance of involuntary commitment and the specter of lobotomization, see chapter 4 of this book.

107. Notable in this regard is the case of Agnes, a trans woman who persuaded Robert Stoller, Richard Green, and Harold Garfinkel of the UCLA Gender Identity Clinic to approve her for surgery by convincing them that she had a congenital intersex condition, only to reveal eight years later that she had been self-medicating with estrogen since adolescence. On Agnes, see Dean Spade, "Mutilating Gender," in *The Transgender Studies Reader*, vol. 1 (New York: Routledge, 2013), 315–32; Gill-Peterson, *Histories of the Transgender Child*, 137–38; and the film *Framing Agnes*, dirs. Chase Joynt and Kristen Schilt (New York: Kino Lorber, 2022).

108. Beans Velocci, "Standards of Care: Uncertainty and Risk in Harry Benjamin's Transsexual Classifications," *Transgender Studies Quarterly* 8, no. 4 (November 2021): 462.

109. These demands often combined absurdly arbitrary benchmarks with a vicious commitment to structural violence and racist gatekeeping. For instance, Miss Major Griffin-Gracy, who was turned away from Harry Benjamin's clinic, reports that Benjamin would not offer gender-affirming care to trans women over the height of 5'6" and that it was well-known that he only treated white patients. See "Miss Major Griffin-Gracy, interview by A.J. Lewis," *New York Public Library Community Oral History Project: NYC Trans Oral History Project*, December 16, 2017, https://nyctransoralhistory.org/interview/miss-major/. For a biopolitical reading of the history of cis clinicians exercising power over trans life, see stef m. shuster, *Trans Medicine: The Emergence and Practice of Treating Gender* (New York: New York University Press, 2021).

110. Melanie Fritz and Nat Mulkey, "The Rise and Fall of Gender Identity Clinics in the 1960s and 1970s," *Bulletin of the American College of Surgeons*, April 1, 2021.

111. Viviane Namaste, *Invisible Lives: The Erasure of Transsexual and Transgendered People* (Chicago: University of Chicago Press, 2000), 273.

112. For another account of the uptake of sexological sociology within queer theory, see Heather Love, *Underdogs: Social Deviance and Queer Theory* (Chicago: University of Chicago Press, 2021).

113. It is, perhaps, a little unfair to characterize Garber's reliance on Stoller, whom she quotes at length and describes as "one of the most widely respected interpreters of gender identity today" (in 1992!), as *entirely* uncritical—she feels he insufficiently pathologizes the erotic nature of "female transvestites'" interest in male clothing in a rush to declare them transsexual.

114. Richard Green, *The Sissy Boy Syndrome: The Development of Homosexuality* (New Haven, CT: Yale University Press, 1987).

115. Stoller, *Sex and Gender*, vol. 2, 140. On the UCLA clinic, see Florence Ashley, *Banning Transgender Conversion Practices: A Legal and Policy Analysis* (Chicago: University of Chicago Press, 2022). Stoller understood his treatments to be successful when the "boys [*sic*]" (that is, trans girls), whom he "encouraged and taught to be mascu-

line," began "fighting with female siblings" and engaging in "physical attacks [on their] mother" ("Boyhood Gender Aberrations: Treatment Issues," *Journal of the American Psychoanalytic Association* 26, no. 3 [1978], 541–58, at 552). My thanks to Christa Peterson for alerting me to this reference. So much for the principled feminism informing *Vested Interests*.

116. Christine Jorgensen, *Christine Jorgensen: A Personal Autobiography* (New York: Bantam Books, 1967); Jan Morris, *Conundrum* (London: Faber, 1974); and Renée Richards with John Ames, *Second Serve: The Renée Richards Story* (New York: Stein and Day, 1983).

117. For trans scholars who have considered such problems with sophistication and insight, see Spade, "Mutilating Gender"; shuster, *Trans Medicine*; Jay Prosser, *Second Skins: The Body Narratives of Transsexuality* (New York: Columbia University Press, 1998); and Gill-Peterson, *Histories of the Transgender Child*.

118. Garber, *Vested Interests*, 14, 96, 103, 120.

119. Paul Bennett, qtd. in Sherry Velasco, *The Lieutenant Nun: Transgenderism, Lesbian Desire, and Catalina de Erauso* (Austin: University of Texas Press, 2000), 8.

120. For warnings against the lingering appeal of the taxonomical impulse, see Kadji Amin, "We Are All Nonbinary: A Brief History of Accidents," *Representations* 158, no. 1 (2022): 106–19 and "Taxonomically Queer? Sexology and New Queer, Trans, and Asexual Identities," *GLQ* 29, no. 1 (2023): 91–107.

121. For the emergence of the term "transgender" and the political consequences of its division from the category of "homosexual," see David Valentine, *Imagining Transgender: An Ethnography of a Category* (Durham, NC: Duke University Press, 2007). On the transphobic legacies of radical feminism, see the articles collected in "Trans-Exclusionary Feminisms and the Global New Right," eds. Serena Bassi and Greta LaFleur, *Transgender Studies Quarterly* 9, no. 3 (2022) and Heaney, ed., *Feminism against Cisness*.

122. Peter Wade and Patrick Reis, "CPAC Speaker Calls for Eradication of 'Transgenderism,'" *Rolling Stone*, March 6, 2023.

123. Kemp, "In That Dimension Grossly Clad," 123–24.

124. Melissa Sanchez, "Colonial Cacophony and Early Modern Trans Studies: Spenser with Julia Serano," *Spenser Studies* 27 (2023): 317–44, at 340.

125. Sanchez, "Colonial Cacophony," 339. Early modern studies hired its first openly trans person into a tenure-line position in 2016.

126. Oklahoma SB 129 (2023). Other bills calling themselves "Millstone Acts" have been introduced in Texas (HB 4754 [2023]) and South Carolina (HB 3730 [2023]).

## CHAPTER ONE

1. Andrea Tornielli and Giacomo Galeazzi, *This Economy Kills: Pope Francis on Capitalism and Social Justice* (Collegeville, MN: Liturgical Press, 2015), 149, 152.

2. Tornielli and Galeazzi, *This Economy Kills*, 149.

3. Pope Francis, "Dialogo del Santo Padre con i Vescovi della Polonia," February 8, 2016, transcript available at http://press.vatican.va/content/salastampa/it/bollettino/pubblico/2016/08/02/0568/01265.html#en.

4. "In-Flight Press Conference of His Holiness Pope Francis from the Philippines to Rome," January 19, 2015, transcript available at https://w2.vatican.va/content/francesco/en/speeches/2015/january/documents/papa-francesco_20150119_srilanka-filippine-conferenza-stampa.html.

5. Pope Francis, *The Name of God is Mercy*, trans. Oonagh Stransky (New York: Random House, 2016), 61.

6. Pope Francis, *The Name of God is Mercy*, 62.

7. Tornielli and Galeazzi, *This Economy Kills*, 150.

8. For instance, article 3 of the Nashville Statement, issued by the evangelical Council on Biblical Manhood and Womanhood, asserts that "God created Adam and Eve, the first human beings, in his own image, equal before God as persons, and distinct as male and female" ("Nashville Statement: A Coalition for Biblical Sexuality," Council on Biblical Manhood and Womanhood, accessed November 25, 2019, https://cbmw.org/nashville-statement/).

9. Pope Francis, *Encyclical Letter Laudato Si' of the Holy Father Francis on Care for Our Common Home* (Rome: Libreria Editrice Vaticana, 2015).

10. Pope Francis, *Laudato Si'*, 1.9. The encyclical references Leonardo Boff, a secularized Franciscan who critiqued capitalist destruction of the Amazon in *Ecology and Poverty: Cry of the Earth, Cry of the Poor*, trans. Phillip Berryman (Maryknoll, NY: Orbis Books, 1997). Boff asserts that an "integral liberation" of humanity and the environment would entail "a new covenant between human beings and other beings, a new gentleness toward what is created, and the fashioning of an ethic and mystique of kinship with the entire cosmic community" (112). *Laudato Si'* may also be in conversation with the work of Thomas Berry, an ecotheologian and Catholic priest of the Passionist order, who calls for an "ecozoic" era that fosters "integral multi-species communities" (Thomas Berry and Brian Swimme, *The Universe Story: From the Primordial Flaring Forth to the Ecozoic Era—A Celebration of the Unfolding of the Cosmos* [San Francisco, CA: HarperSanFrancisco, 1992]), 4. For feminist critiques of the shortcomings of the encyclical with respect to its gender politics, see Rosemary P. Carbine, "Imagining and Incarnating an Integral Ecology: A Critical Ecofeminist Public Theology," 45–66, and Sharon A. Bong, "Not Only for the Sake of Man: Asian Feminist Theological Responses to *Laudato Si'*," 81–96, both in *Planetary Solidarity: Global Women's Voices on Christian Doctrine and Climate Justice*, eds. Grace Ji-Sun Kim and Hilda P. Koster (Minneapolis, MN: Fortress Press, 2017).

11. Genesis 1.26–27, *Geneva Bible: A Facsimile of the 1560 Edition*, ed. Lloyd E. Berry (Madison: University of Wisconsin Press, 1969).

12. Pope Francis, *Laudato Si'*, 2.65.

13. Remy Debes, ed., *Dignity: A History* (New York: Oxford University Press, 2017), 2.

14. Pope Francis, *Laudato Si'*, 3.155.

15. Pope Francis, *Amoris Laetitia: Post-Synodal Apostolic Exhortation on Love in the Family* (Vatican City: Libreria Editrice, 2016), 44, 208.

16. Pope Francis, *"Male and Female He Created Them": Towards a Path of Dialogue on the Question of Gender Theory in Education* (Vatican City: Congregation for Catholic Education, 2019), 12.

17. Pope Francis, *"Male and Female He Created Them,"* 14.

18. *Laudato Si'*, 3.155.

19. Bernard Stiegler, *Technics and Time: The Fault of Epimetheus*, vol. 1, trans. Richard Beardsworth and George Collins (Stanford, CA: Stanford University Press, 1998), 93. Other important work in media theory that has drawn on Stiegler's account of technogenesis includes Mark Hansen, "Media Theory," *Theory, Culture and Society* 23, nos. 2–3 (2006): 297–306; and N. Katherine Hayles, *How We Think: Digital Media and Technogenesis* (Chicago: University of Chicago Press, 2012).

20. Stiegler, *Technics and Time*, 142, 137.

21. Stiegler, *Technics and Time*, 17.

22. Laura Horak considers how the "trans mediascape" enables trans youth to "author and affirm their bodies and selves" while "generating far-flung communities of support," in "Trans on YouTube: Intimacy, Visibility, Temporality," *Transgender Studies Quarterly* 1, no. 4 (2014): 572–85. See also Tobias Raun, *Out Online: Trans Self-Representation and Community Building on YouTube* (New York: Routledge, 2016); and Oliver L. Haimson, Avery Dame-Griff, Elias Capello, and Zahari Richter, "Tumblr Was a Trans Technology: The Meaning, Importance, History, and Future of Trans Technologies," *Feminist Media Studies* 21, no. 3 (2021): 345–61. Cassius Adair is writing a brilliant counter-history of trans digital culture in his monograph-in-progress, *The Transgender Internet*.

23. Audience with participants in the 23rd General Assembly of the Members of the Pontifical Academy for Life, Vatican City, May 10, 2017.

24. Susan Stryker, "My Words to Victor Frankenstein above the Village of Chamounix: Performing Transgender Rage," *GLQ* 1, no. 3 (1994): 237–54, at 238.

25. For a detailed account of the theological debates over Adam's gender configuration, see Leah DeVun's *The Shape of Sex: Nonbinary Gender from Genesis to the Renaissance* (New York: Columbia University Press, 2020), 16–39. Other work on the Adam androgyne includes Ernst Benz, *Adam, Der Mythus vom Urmenschen* (Munchen-Planegg: Otto-Wilhelm-Barth Verlag, 1955); Benjamin H. Dunning, *Specters of Paul: Sexual Difference in Early Christian Thought* (Philadelphia: University of Pennsylvania Press, 2011); and Wayne Meeks, "The Image of the Androgyne: Some Uses of a Symbol in Earliest Christianity," *History of Religions* 13, no. 3 (February 1974): 165–208.

26. On rabbinic discourse on the primordial androgyne, see Daniel Boyarin, *Carnal Israel: Reading Sex in Talmudic Culture* (Berkeley: University of California Press, 1993), 35–46; and David Daube, *The New Testament and Rabbinic Judaism* (London: Athlone Press, 1956), 72–85. For Gnostic endorsements of an androgynous creation and the cults of celibacy it inspired, see Dennis MacDonald, *There Is No Male and Female: The Fate of a Dominical Saying in Paul* (Philadelphia, PA: Fortress Press, 1987) and "Corinthian Veils and Gnostic Androgynes," in *The Image of the Feminine in Gnosticism*, ed. Karen L. King (Harrisburg, PA: Trinity Press, 1988), 276–92.

27. Quoted in *Eve and Adam: Jewish, Christian, and Muslim Readings on Genesis and Gender*, eds. Kristen Kvam, Linda Schearing, and Valarie Ziegler (Bloomington: Indiana University Press, 1999), 77–78.

28. For these translations, see Daube, *New Testament*, 72; and Boyarin, *Carnal Israel*, 36.

29. Plato, *Symposium*, in *Lysis, Symposium, Gorgias*, trans. W. R. M. Lamb (Cambridge, MA: Harvard University Press, 1925), 188–94.

30. Philo, *De opificio mundi*, in *Philo*, vol. 1, eds. and trans. F. H. Colson and G. H. Whitaker (Cambridge, MA: Harvard University Press, 1929), para. 134.

31. "There are *two* races of men," Philo opines, "the one made after the (Divine) Image, and the one moulded out of the earth," and it is only "with the second man that a helper [Eve] is associated" (*Allegorical Interpretation of Genesis 2 and 3*, in *Philo*, vol. 1, trans. F. H. Colson and G. H. Whitaker [Cambridge, MA: Harvard University Press, 1929], 227).

32. Origen, *Homilies on Genesis and Exodus*, trans. Ronald E. Heine (Washington, DC: Catholic University of America Press, 1981), 63. Adding new complexities, Origen explains that "this inner man consists of spirit and soul," and "the spirit is said to be male" while "the soul can be called female" (23).

33. Walter Stevenson, "The Rise of Eunuchs in Greco-Roman Antiquity," *Journal of the History of Sexuality* 5, no. 4 (April 1995): 506. The incident is described in Eusebius, *Ecclesiastical History*, vol. 2, trans. Roy J. Deferrari (Washington, DC: Catholic University of America Press, 1955), 6.8.2. According to Eusebius, the cutting was prompted by an overly literal interpretation of Matthew 19:12 and the desire to align himself with those "who have made themselves eunuchs for the sake of the kingdom of heaven," a move that leads Peter Brown to call Origen "a walking lesson in the basic indeterminacy of the body." See Peter Brown, *The Body and Society: Men, Women, and Sexual Renunciation in Early Christianity* (New York: Columbia University Press, 1988), 169.

34. Gregory of Nyssa, *De hominis opificio*, in *A Select Library of Nicene and Post-Nicene Fathers of the Christian Church*, eds. Philip Schaff and Henry Wace, trans. William More and Henry Austin Wilson (New York: Christian Literature Company, 1892), 22.5. On Gregory of Nyssa and the ungendered creation, see Sarah Coakley, "The Eschatological Body: Gender, Transformation, and God," *Modern Theology* 16, no. 1 (January 2000): 61–73. For an overview of modern controversy about Gregory of Nyssa and the perfection of the ungendered body, see Morwenna Ludlow, *Gregory of Nyssa, Ancient and (Post)modern* (New York: Oxford University Press, 2007), 167–79.

35. For the influence of this set of ideas within Eastern Orthodoxy, see Damien Casey, "The Spiritual Valency of Gender in Byzantine Society," in *Questions of Gender in Byzantine Society*, eds. Bronwen Neil and Lynda Garland (New York: Routledge, 2016), 167–82. On the transitions that accompany resurrection, see chapter 3 of this book.

36. Augustine, *On the Trinity*, ed. Gareth B. Matthews, trans. Stephen McKenna (New York: Cambridge University Press, 2002), 88.

37. Maaike van der Lugt, "Sex Difference in Medieval Theology and Canon Law," *Medieval Feminist Forum* 46, no. 1 (2010): 101–21.

38. Jaroslav Pelikan, ed., *Luther's Works*, vol. 1 (St. Louis, MO: Concordia Publishing House, 1958), 70.

39. John Milton, *The Divorce Tracts of John Milton*, eds. Howard Scott and Sara J. van den Berg (Pittsburgh, PA: Duquesne University Press, 2010), 249.

40. Thomas Browne, *Pseudodoxia Epidemica*, ed. Robin Robbins, vol. 1 (New York: Oxford University Press, 1981), 7.2.

41. On Renaissance iterations of the hermaphroditic Adam, see Ruth Gilbert, *Early Modern Hermaphrodites: Sex and Other Stories* (New York: Palgrave, 2002), 14–19; Marian Rothstein, *The Androgyne in Early Modern France: Contextualizing the Power of Gender* (New York: Palgrave, 2015), 7–20; Philip C. Almond, *Adam and Eve in Seventeenth-Century Thought* (New York: Cambridge University Press, 1999).

42. On the alchemical hermaphrodite, see Leah DeVun, "The Jesus Hermaphrodite: Science and Sex Difference in Premodern Europe," *Journal of the History of Ideas* 69, no. 2 (April 2008): 193–218. On astrology and the androgyne, see Elliott M. Simon, "Pico, Paracelsus, and Dee: The Magical Measure of Human Perfectibility," in *Gender and Scientific Discourse in Early Modern Culture*, 2nd ed., ed. Kathleen P. Long (New York: Routledge, 2016), 13–41.

43. Rothstein, *Androgyne in Early Modern France*, 10.

44. Giovanni Pico della Mirandola considers the Platonic implications of Genesis 1:27 in *Heptaplus, or Discourse on the Seven Days of Creation*, trans. Jessie Brewer McGaw (New York: Philosophical Library, 1977), 2.6. Leone Ebreo, a Sephardic exile from Spain's purge in 1492 of its Jewish population whose family settled in Italy, sources Platonism to Mosaic roots in *Dialoghi d'amore* (1535), which invokes the primal androgyne of Genesis to envision the decidedly corporeal reintegration of knowledge and love. On the erotics of Ebreo's *Dialoghi*, see Naomi Yavneh, "The Spiritual Eroticism of Leone's Hermaphrodite," in *Playing with Gender: A Renaissance Pursuit*, eds. Jean Brink, Maryanne Horovitz, and Allison Courdet (Chicago: University of Illinois Press, 1991), 86. See also Rossella Pescatori, "The Myth of the Androgyne in Leone Ebreo's *Dialogues of Love*," *Comitatus* 38, no. 1 (2007): 115–28.

45. Geoffrey Fenton, *Monophylo* (London: printed by Henry Denham for William Seres, 1572), 35.

46. Ben Jonson, *The New Inne. Or, The Light Heart* (London: printed by Thomas Harper for Thomas Alchorne, 1631), 3.2.78–81. On Jonson's use of the Platonic androgyne, see Patrick Cheney, "Jonson's *The New Inn* and Plato's Myth of the Hermaphrodite," *Renaissance Drama* 14 (1983): 173–94.

47. Jennifer Waldron, "Of Stones and Stony Hearts: Desdemona, Hermione, and Post-Reformation Theatre," in *The Indistinct Human in Renaissance Literature*, eds. Jean E. Feerick and Vin Nardizzi (New York: Palgrave, 2012), 205–27 and "Dead Likenesses and Sex Machines: Shakespearean Media Theory," *Oxford Handbook of Shakespeare and Embodiment*, ed. Valerie Traub (New York: Oxford University Press, 2016), 611–27.

48. Waldron, "Dead Likenesses and Sex Machines," 616.

49. On anti-cosmetic sentiment in Renaissance literature, see Frances Dolan, "Taking the Pencil out of God's Hand: Art, Nature, and the Face-Painting Debate in Early Modern England," *PMLA* 108, no. 2 (March 1993): 224–39; Annette Drew-Bear, *Painted Faces on the Renaissance Stage: The Moral Significance of Face-Painting Conventions* (Lewisburg, PA: Bucknell University Press, 1994); Farah Karim-Cooper, *Cosmetics in Shakespearean and Renaissance Drama* (Edinburgh: Edinburgh University Press, 2006); Dympna Callaghan, *Shakespeare without Women: Representing Gender and Race on the Renaissance Stage* (New York: Routledge, 2000), 78–88.

50. From Girolamo Ruscelli, *The Secrets of Alexis: Containing Many Excellent Remedies against Divers Diseases* (London: Printed by William Stansby, 1615), quoted in Karim-Cooper, *Cosmetics in Shakespearean and Renaissance Drama*, 56.

51. Thomas Tuke, *Discourse against the Painting and Tincturing of Women* (London: By Thomas Creede and Bernard Alsop for Edward Marchant, 1616), 57. "It is an hainous crime," Tuke continues, "to think that man can paint thee better then God. It is a grievous thing that God should say of thee, I see not the image, I see not the countenance, which my selfe have formed" (C2).

52. Tuke, *Discourse*, 8.

53. Stephen Booth, ed., *Shakespeare's Sonnets* (New Haven, CT: Yale University Press, 1977). Sonnets hereafter cited in text.

54. Giorgio Vasari, *Lives of the Artists*, trans. Julia Conaway Bonadella (New York: Oxford University Press, 1991), 3.

55. Vasari, *Lives of the Artists*. 277.

56. On this practice, see Stephen Orgel, "The Renaissance Artist as Plagiarist," *ELH* 48, no. 3 (Autumn 1981): 476–95.

57. Gregory Bredbeck, *Sodomy and Interpretation: Marlowe to Milton* (Ithaca, NY: Cornell University Press, 1991), 178.

58. On this point, see especially Kim F. Hall, "'These Bastard Signs of Fair': Literary Whiteness in Shakespeare's Sonnets," in *Post-Colonial Shakespeares*, eds. Ania Loomba and Martin Orkin (New York: Routledge, 1998), 64–83 and *Things of Darkness: Economies of Race and Gender in Early Modern England* (Ithaca, NY: Cornell University Press, 2018), 85–91; and Elizabeth D. Harvey, "Flesh Colors and Shakespeare's Sonnets," in *A Companion to Shakespeare's Sonnets*, ed. Michael Schoenfeldt (Malden, MA: Blackwell Publishing, 2007), 314–28.

59. Katharine Eisaman Maus, *Inwardness and Theater in the English Renaissance* (Chicago: University of Chicago Press, 1995), 4.

60. Anne Ferry, *The "Inward" Language: Sonnets of Wyatt, Sidney, Shakespeare, Donne* (Chicago: University of Chicago Press, 1983), 14.

61. The epistemological claim that gender can be deduced from unprompted expressions about "feeling" have centered definitions of "real" trans experience from Karl Heinrich Ulrichs' assessment of the cross-identified "urning" as an "*anima muliebris virile corpore inclusa*" (a woman's soul trapped in a man's body) to the diagnostic criteria for gender dysphoria in the DSM-5. See Karl Heinrich Ulrichs, *Memnon: Die Geschlectsnature des mannliebenden Urnings* (Schleiz: C. Hübscher, 1868), xxi.

62. Michael Baxandall, *Painting and Experience in the Fifteenth Century: A Primer in the Social History of Pictorial Style*, 2nd ed. (New York: Oxford University Press, 1972), 23.

63. On Reformation chronoclasm, see Michel Pastoureau, "La Réforme et la coleur," *Bulletin de la Société de l'Histoire du Protestantisme Français* 138 (1992): 323–42.

64. Edouard Cunitz, Johann-Wilhelm Baun, and Eduard Reuss, eds., *Calvini Opera*, vol. 41 (Brunsvigae: C. A. Schwetschke, 1853), 562.

65. Tuke, *Discourse*, C2.

66. On the problems with reducing trans bodies to the surgeries they (may or may not) have undergone, see for instance Trystan Cotten, "Surgery," *Transgender Studies Quarterly* 1, nos. 1–2 (May 2014): 205–7, at 205.

67. Helen Vendler, *The Art of Shakespeare's Sonnets* (Cambridge, MA: Harvard University Press, 1997), 59.

68. Aaron Kunin, "Shakespeare's Preservation Fantasy," *PMLA* 124, no. 1 (January 2009), 97.

69. Joseph Pequigney, *Such Is My Love: A Study of Shakespeare's Sonnets* (Chicago: University of Chicago Press, 1985), 34.

70. Alan Sinfield, *Shakespeare, Authority, Sexuality: Unfinished Business in Cultural Materialism* (New York: Routledge, 2006), 169–70.

71. Richard Halpern, *Shakespeare's Perfume: Sodomy and Sublimity in the Sonnets, Wilde, Freud, and Lacan* (Philadelphia: University of Pennsylvania Press, 2002), 26.

72. Booth, *Shakespeare's Sonnets*, 165.

73. On this method and its technical evolution through the Renaissance, see Carmen C. Bambach, *Drawing and Painting in the Italian Renaissance Workshop: Theory and Practice, 1300–1600* (New York: Cambridge University Press, 1999).

74. Bambach, *Drawing and Painting*, 73–76.

75. Marcia B. Hall, *The Power of Color: Five Centuries of European Painting* (New Haven, CT: Yale University Press, 2019), 57.

76. Bambach, *Drawing and Painting*, 407 n.81.

77. Hans Tietze, "Master and Workshop in the Venetian Renaissance," *Parnassus* 11, no. 8 (December 1939), 34–45, at 35.

78. Bruce Cole, *The Renaissance Artist at Work: From Pisano to Titian* (New York: Harper and Row, 1983), 76.

79. Cole, *Renaissance Artist at Work*, 88.

80. Ann Rosalind Jones and Peter Stallybrass, *Renaissance Clothing and the Materials of Memory* (New York: Cambridge University Press, 2000), 134.

81. Roszika Parker, *The Subversive Stitch: Embroidery and the Making of the Feminine* (New York: Routledge, 1989); Lena Cowen Orlin, "Three Ways to Be Invisible in the Renaissance: Sex, Reputation, and Stitchery," in *Renaissance Culture and the Everyday*, eds. Patricia Fumerton and Simon Hunt (Philadelphia: University of Pennsylvania Press, 1999), 183–203.

82. John Taylor, *The Needles Excellency* (London: Printed for Iames Boler, 1631).

83. Quoted in Maura Tarnoff, "Sewing Authorship in John Skelton's 'Garlande or Chapelet of Laurell,'" *ELH* 75, no. 2 (Summer 2008): 421.

84. See Roze Hentschell, "Treasonous Textiles: Foreign Cloth and the Construction of Englishness," *Journal of Medieval and Early Modern Studies* 32, no. 3 (Fall 2002): 543–70.

85. Lien Bich Luu, *Immigrants and the Industries of London, 1500–1700* (New York: Routledge, 2005), 32.

86. Jones and Stallybrass, *Renaissance Clothing*, 52.

87. Natasha Korda, *Labors Lost: Women's Work and the Early Modern English Stage* (Philadelphia: University of Pennsylvania Press, 2011), 97.

88. Korda, *Labors Lost*, 42–43.

89. Carmen Bambach carefully tracks the cross-fertilization between artistic practice and the artisanal world of textile production in "Leonardo, Tagliente, and Dürer: 'La scienza del far di groppi,'" *Achademia Leonardi Vinci* 4 (1991): 72–95. See also Femke Speelberg, "Fashion and Virtue: Textile Patterns and the Print Revolution 1520–1620," *Metropolitan Museum of Art Bulletin* 73, no. 2 (Fall 2015): 1–48.

90. Michael Snodin and Maurice Howard, *Ornament: A Social History Since 1450* (New Haven, CT: Yale University Press, 1996), 27.

91. Taylor, *Needles Excellency*, 3.

92. Janet S. Byrne, "Patterns by Master F," *Metropolitan Museum Journal* 14 (1979): 103–38, at 103.

93. Jeanne Vaccaro, "Feelings and Fractals: Woolly Ecologies of Transgender Matter," *GLQ* 21, nos. 2–3 (2015): 273–93, at 281.

94. Will Fisher, *Materializing Gender in Early Modern English Literature and Culture* (New York: Cambridge University Press, 2007).

95. Valerie Traub, "Sex without Issue: Sodomy, Reproduction, and Signification in Shakespeare's Sonnets," in *Shakespeare's Sonnets: Critical Essays*, ed. James Schiffer (New York: Garland Publishing, 1999), 431–54, at 440.

96. Simone Chess, "Male Femininity and Male-to-Female Crossdressing in Shakespeare's Plays and Poems," in *Queer Shakespeare: Desire and Sexuality*, ed. Goran Stanivukovic (New York: Bloomsbury Arden Shakespeare, 2017), 230–31.

97. Jane Bennett, *Vibrant Matter: A Political Ecology of Things* (Durham, NC: Duke University Press, 2010), ix.

98. Hansen, "Media Theory," 302, 305.

99. Jer.1.5., Geneva Bible (1560).

100. Rosi Braidotti, *Metamorphoses: Towards a Materialist Theory of Becoming* (Malden, MA: Polity, 2002); Paul B. Preciado, *Testo Junkie: Sex, Drugs, and Biopolitics in the Pharmacopornographic Era*, trans. Bruce Benderson (New York: Feminist Press at CUNY, 2013); micha cárdenas, *Poetic Operations: Trans of Color Art in Digital Media* (Durham, NC: Duke University Press, 2022).

101. Jeanne Vaccaro, "Feelings and Fractals" and "Felt Matters," *Women and Performance* 20, no. 3 (2010): 253–66; Eva Hayward, "Lessons from a Starfish," in *Queering the Non-Human*, eds. Noreen Giffney and Myra J. Hird (Burlington, VT: Ashgate, 2008), 249–64; Eva Hayward and Jami Weinstein, "Tranimalities in the Age of Trans* Life," *Transgender Studies Quarterly* 2, no. 2 (May 2015): 195–208; Mel Chen, *Animacies: Biopolitics, Racial Mattering, and Queer Affect* (Durham, NC: Duke University Press, 2012), especially chapter 4, "Animals, Sex, and Transsubstantiation," provocatively casting trans bodies alongside the "new biologicals" of "transbiology" as a new form of transubstantiation (189). See also Nicole Seymour, *Strange Natures: Futurity, Empathy, and the Queer Ecological Imagination* (Chicago: University of Illinois Press, 2013); Bailey Kier, "Interdependent Ecological Transsex: Notes on Re/Production, 'Transgender' Fish, and the Management of Populations, Species, and Resources," *Women and Perfor-*

*mance* 20, no. 3 (2010): 299–319; and the essays collected in *Tranimacies: Intimate Links between Animal and Trans* Studies*, eds. Eliza Steinbock, Marianna Szczygielska, and Anthony Clair Wagner (New York: Routledge, 2021).

102. Benedict de Spinoza, *Ethics Proved in Geometrical Order*, ed. Matthew J. Kisner, trans. Michael Silverthorne and Matthew J. Kisner (New York: Cambridge University Press, 2018), part III, proposition II.

103. Julia Reinhard Lupton, *Thinking with Shakespeare: Essays on Politics and Life* (Chicago: University of Chicago Press, 2011), 14.

104. Hannah Arendt, *The Human Condition* (Chicago: University of Chicago Press, 1958), 9.

105. Pope Francis, "Dialogo."

## CHAPTER TWO

1. Sheila Jeffreys, *Gender Hurts: A Feminist Analysis of the Politics of Transgenderism* (New York: Routledge, 2014), 186.

2. C. Ray Borck, "Negligent Analogies," *Transgender Studies Quarterly* 4, nos. 3–4 (November 2017), 679–84, at 684.

3. In a twist that will surprise no one, the "woman identifying as a Korean cat" was a hoax, and indeed is clearly described as such in the *Gawker* article Jeffreys cites as her sole evidence of "rights-based political campaigns" on behalf of animal-identified teenagers. One wonders how such work managed to get published in the first place.

4. Kashmira Gander, "Academic Says Trans Women Are Parasites for 'Occupying the Bodies of the Oppressed,'" *Newsweek*, March 15, 2018.

5. For a sampling of work on trans monstrosity, see Susan Stryker, "My Words to Victor Frankenstein above the Village of Chamounix: Performing Transgender Rage," *GLQ* 1 (1994): 237–54; Hil Malatino, *Queer Embodiment: Monstrosity, Medical Violence, and Intersex Experience* (Lincoln: University of Nebraska Press, 2019); Harlan Weaver, "Monster Trans: Diffracting Affect, Reading Rage," *Somatechnics* 3, no. 2 (2013): 287–306; and Anson Koch-Rein, "Trans-lating the Monster: Transgender Affect and Frankenstein," *Lit: Literature Interpretation Theory* 30, no. 1 (2019): 44–61.

6. Mel Chen, *Animacies: Biopolitics, Racial Mattering, and Queer Affect* (Durham, NC: Duke University Press, 2012).

7. Michel Foucault, *Abnormal: Lectures at the College de France, 1974–1975*, trans. Graham Burchell (New York: Picador, 1999), 41.

8. Foucault, *Abnormal*, 63.

9. On the history of disability and monstrosity that mobilizes a trans studies framework, see Hil Malatino, *Queer Embodiment*. On premodern monstrosity and disability studies, see the essays collected in Richard H. Godden and Asa Simon Mittman, eds., *Monstrosity, Disability, and the Posthuman in the Medieval and Early Modern World* (Cham: Palgrave Macmillan, 2019).

10. Foucault, *Abnormal*, 64–65, 73, 131, 74, 81.

11. On the complicated pig, which is visually aligned with an illustration of "two very monstrous infants, in whom only one set of female sexual organs is manifested," see

Ambroise Paré, *On Monsters and Marvels*, trans. Janis L. Pallister (Chicago: University of Chicago Press, 1982), 22.

12. Paré, *On Monsters and Marvels*, 5–6.

13. Prodigies began to be interpreted as signs of divine displeasure in the early Christian world; on Augustine and Beauvais, see John Block Friedman, *The Monstrous Races in Medieval Art and Thought* (Cambridge, MA: Harvard University Press, 1981), 3. On popular print sources and prodigies in the seventeenth century, see Jerome Friedman, *The Battle of Frogs and Fairford's Flies: Miracles and the Pulp Press during the English Revolution* (Cambridge, MA: Harvard University Press, 1961).

14. *Geneva Bible: A Facsimile of the 1560 Edition*, ed. Lloyd E. Berry (Madison: University of Wisconsin Press, 1969), 2 Esdras 5: 5, 8. On the reception of this verse in the Reformation, see Alastair Hamilton, *The Apocryphal Apocalypse: The Reception of the Second Book of Esdras (4 Ezra) from the Renaissance to the Enlightenment* (New York: Oxford University Press, 1999).

15. Jakob Rüff, *The Expert Midwife, or, An Excellent and Most Necessary Treatise of the Generation and Birth of Man* (London: E. G[riffin] for S. B[urton], 1637); Konrad Lykosthenes, *The Doome Warning All Men to the Iudgemente wherein Are Contained for the Most Parte All the Straunge Prodigies Hapned in the Worlde* (London: Ralphe Nubery, 1581); Pierre Boaistuau, *Certaine Secrete Wonders of Nature Containing a Descriptio[n] of Sundry Strange Things, Seming Monstrous* (London: Henry Bynneman, 1569); Ambroise Paré, *The Workes of That Famous Chirurgion Ambrose Parey Translated out of Latine and Compared with the French*, trans. Thomas Johnson (London: Th. Cotes and R. Young, 1634).

16. Wellcome MS 136. For a printed edition based on this manuscript, see *Histoires prodigieuses: MS 136 Wellcome Library*, ed. Stephen Bamforth (Milano: Franco Maria Ricci, 2000).

17. On *canards* and hermaphrodites, see Kathleen Long, *Hermaphrodites in Renaissance Europe* (Burlington, VT: Ashgate, 2006), 39. On *Wunderzeichenbücher*, see Philip M. Soergel, *Miracles and the Protestant Imagination: The Evangelical Wonder Book in Reformation Germany* (New York: Oxford University Press, 2012).

18. On Roman prodigies, see Bruce MacBain, *Prodigy and Expiation: A Study in Religion and Politics in Republican Rome* (Bruxelles: Latomus, 1982); Susanne Rasmussen, *Public Portents in Republican Rome* (Rome: L'Erma di Bretschneider, 2003); and Anthony Corbeill, "Weeping Statues, Weeping Gods and Prodigies from Republican to Early-Christian Rome," in *Tears in the Graeco-Roman World*, ed. Thorsten Fögen (Berlin: Walter de Gruyter, 2009), 297–310.

19. For a complete list of Roman prodigies in extant sources, see Ludwig Wülker, *Die geschichtliche Entwicklung des Prodigienwesens* (Leipzig: Universität Leipzig, 1903).

20. Veit Rosenberger, *Gezähmte Götter: Das Prodigienwesen der römischen Republik* (Stuttgart: Franz Steiner Verlag, 1998), 132–34.

21. On early modern prodigies, see Julie Crawford, *Marvelous Protestantism: Monstrous Births in Post-Reformation England* (Baltimore, MD: Johns Hopkins University Press, 2005); William E. Burns, *An Age of Wonders: Prodigies, Politics and Providence in England, 1657–1727* (New York: Manchester University Press, 2002); Lorraine J. Daston and Katherine Park, *Wonders and Other Orders of Nature, 1150–1750* (New York: Zone

Books, 1998); Jean Céard, *La nature et les prodiges: l'insolite au 16e siècle, en France* (Geneva: Droz, 1977); and Anne Jacobson Schutte, "'Such Monstrous Births': A Neglected Aspect of the Antinomian Controversy," *Renaissance Quarterly* 38, no. 1 (Spring 1985): 85–106.

22. Paré, *On Monsters and Marvels*, 67.

23. "Relación verdadera y caso prodigioso y raro, que ha sucedido en esta Corte el día catorce de mayo de este año de 1688," in Henry Ettinghausen, *Noticias del siglo XVII: relaciones españolas de sucesos naturales y sobrenaturales* (Barcelona: Puvill Libros, 1995). Perhaps the pigs reminded the writer of the young hermaphrodite because of the long history of the Adam androgyne. The Jesuit Esteban de Terreros y Pando's 1787 Castilian dictionary makes use of identical phrasing in its definition for "Hermafrodita," noting that "algunos Judios soñaron, que Dios crió á Adán, y Eva Androjenos, y pegados por las espaldas, y que luego los dividió: todo esto es fabula, y sueño" (see *Diccionario Castellano*, vol. 2 [Madrid: Viuda de Ibarra, Hijos y Compañia, 1787], 276).

24. Paré, *On Monsters and Marvels*, 6. Ottavia Niccoli tracks the circulation of the imagery and narrative of the monster of Ravenna in *Prophecy and People in Renaissance Italy*, trans. Lydia G. Cochrane (Princeton, NJ: Princeton University Press, 1990), 35–51.

25. Philipp Melanchthon and Martin Luther, *Of Two Woonderful Popish Monsters to Wyt, of a Popish Asse Which Was Found at Rome in the Riuer of Tyber, and of a Monkish Calfe, Calued at Friberge in Misne*, trans. John Brooke (London: Thomas East, 1579).

26. Melanchthon and Luther, *Of Two Woonderful Popish Monsters*, 7, 3, 5.

27. In his "Explanation of the Ninety-Five Theses" (1518), Luther frames Ottoman military dominance as God's "lash" through which "he himself punishes us for our iniquities because we do not punish ourselves for them." Thus, Luther bundles "the Turks, Tartars, and other infidels" into a catalogue of prodigies including "plagues, wars, insurrections, earthquakes, [and] fires," in *Luther's Works*, vol. 31, trans. Harold J. Grimm and Helmut T. Lehmann (Philadelphia, PA: Muhlenberg Press and Fortress Press, 1957), 92.

28. Boaistuau, *Certaine Secrete Wonders*, 26–28. Curiously, the woodcut from this last chapter has circulated under the caption "the gypsy who washed his face and hands in molten lead," although the man is never designated as such in the text, apparently because of a misidentification of his headgear. On this misattribution, see Henry Thomas Crofton, "The Former Costume of the Gypsies," *Romani Studies* 2 (1908): 207–31, at 221.

29. Boaistuau, *Certaine Secrete Wonders*, 13–14.

30. Paré, *On Monsters and Marvels*, 38.

31. Paré, *On Monsters and Marvels*, 38.

32. On the politics of racialized gender that shaped medical definitions of hirsutism from the nineteenth century forward, see Kimberly A. Hamlin, "The 'Case of a Bearded Woman': Hypertrichosis and the Construction of Gender in the Age of Darwin," *American Quarterly* 63, no. 4 (2011): 955–81.

33. Burns, *Age of Wonders*, 5.

34. Quoted in Anthony Corbeill, *Sexing the World: Grammatical Gender and Biological Sex in Ancient Rome* (Princeton, NJ: Princeton University Press, 2015), 153.

35. Isidore of Seville, from "The Human Being and Portents" (*De homine et portentis*), book XI of *The Etymologies of Isidore of Seville*, trans. Stephen A. Barney, W. J. Lewis, J. A. Beach, and Oliver Berghof (New York: Cambridge University Press, 2009), 11.3.5.

36. *A True Relation of the Birth of Three Monsters in the City of Namen in Flanders* (London: Printed by Simon Stafford, for Richard Bunnian, 1608).

37. Crawford, *Marvelous Protestantism*, 14.

38. John Webster, *The Duchess of Malfi*, ed. Michael Neill (New York: Norton, 2015), 1.1.156, 5.2.17–18. Hereafter cited in text.

39. On the emblematic structure of act 1, see Catherine Belsey, "Emblem and Antithesis in *The Duchess of Malfi*," *Renaissance Drama* 11 (1980): 115–34.

40. Edward Berry, *Shakespeare and the Hunt: A Cultural and Social Study* (New York: Cambridge University Press, 2001), 116.

41. On the affirmative and negative biopolitics of taming, see Julia Reinhard Lupton, *Thinking with Shakespeare: Essays on Politics and Life* (Chicago: University of Chicago Press, 2013), especially chapter 1, "Animal Husbands in *The Taming of the Shrew*," 25–68. On horses and affect, see Karen Raber, *Animal Bodies, Renaissance Culture*, especially chapter 2, "Erotic Bodies: Loving Horses" (Philadelphia: University of Pennsylvania Press, 2013), 75–102.

42. On disability and its intersections with trans studies, see Cameron Awkward-Rich, *The Terrible We: Thinking with Trans Maladjustment* (Durham, NC: Duke University Press, 2022) and "Bodies with New Organs: Becoming Trans, Becoming Disabled," in Jasbir Puar, *The Right to Maim: Debility, Capacity, Disability* (Durham, NC: Duke University Press, 2017), 33–62.

43. Paré, *On Monsters and Marvels*, 36.

44. For an incisive update of Orlando Patterson's pioneering work on social death, see Lisa Marie Cacho, *Social Death: Racialized Rightlessness and the Criminalization of the Unprotected* (New York: New York University Press, 2012).

45. Kimberly Poitevin, "Inventing Whiteness: Cosmetics, Race, and Women in Early Modern England," *Journal for Early Modern Cultural Studies* 11, no. 1 (Spring/Summer 2011): 59–89, at 76. Farah Karim-Cooper describes the use of flayed crows as a whitening tincture in *Cosmetics in Shakespearean and Renaissance Drama* (Edinburgh: Edinburgh University Press, 2006), 104.

46. See Brett D. Hirsch, "The Taming of the Jew: Spit and the Civilizing Process in *The Merchant of Venice*," in *Staged Transgression in Shakespeare's England*, eds. Rory Loughnane and Edel Semple (New York: Palgrave Macmillan, 2013), 136–52. Matthew Biberman considers the gender dynamics of Donne's "Spit in My Face, Ye Jews," in *Masculinity, Anti-Semitism and Early Modern English Literature: From the Satanic to the Effeminate Jew* (New York: Routledge, 2004), 77–85.

47. On Jewish male menstruation, see Irven M. Resnick, "Medieval Roots of the Myth of Jewish Male Menses," *Harvard Theological Review* 93, no. 3 (July 2000): 241–63. For the association between the gender variance of Jewish men and hyenas, see Leah DeVun, "The Hyena's Unclean Sex: Beasts, Bestiaries, and Jewish Communities," in *The Shape of Sex: Nonbinary Gender from Genesis to the Renaissance* (New York: Columbia University Press, 2021), 70–101.

48. On the racializing effects of blood purity statutes, see Jerome Friedman, "Jewish Conversion, the Spanish Pure Blood Laws and Reformation: A Revisionist View of Racial and Religious Antisemitism," *Sixteenth Century Journal* 18, no. 1 (1987): 3–30. In the context of early modern England, see M. Lindsay Kaplan, "Jessica's Mother: Medieval Constructions of Jewish Race and Gender in 'The Merchant of Venice,'" *Shakespeare Quarterly* 58, no. 1 (2007): 1–30.

49. On skin-flaying in cosmetics, medicine, and witchcraft, see Karim-Cooper, *Cosmetics in Shakespearean and Renaissance Drama*, 105–7.

50. William Shakespeare, *King John*, in *The Riverside Shakespeare*, 2nd ed., ed. G. Blakemore Evans (Boston, MA: Houghton Mifflin, 1997), 3.4.157–58.

51. Crawford, *Marvelous Protestantism*, 14.

52. On the vital materiality of worms, see chapter 7, "Political Ecologies," in Jane Bennett, *Vibrant Matter: A Political Ecology of Things* (Durham, NC: Duke University Press, 2010), 94–109.

53. Laurie Shannon, *The Accommodated Animal: Cosmopolity in Shakespearean Locales* (Chicago: University of Chicago Press, 2013), 41.

54. On this passage, see Eric Lawee, "The Reception of Rashi's 'Commentary on the Torah' in Spain: The Case of Adam's Mating with the Animals," *Jewish Quarterly Review* 97, no. 1 (Winter 2007): 33–66.

55. Julia Reinhard Lupton, "Creature Caliban," *Shakespeare Quarterly* 51, no. 1 (April 2000): 1–23, at 1. For other theoretical accounts of the creature, see Giorgio Agamben, *The Open: Man and Animal*, trans. Kevin Attell (Stanford, CA: Stanford University Press, 2004); Eric Santner, *On Creaturely Life: Rilke, Benjamin, Sebald* (Chicago: University of Chicago Press, 2006); and Lupton, *Thinking with Shakespeare*.

56. Aristotle, *Parts of Animals*, trans. A. L. Peck (Cambridge, MA: Harvard University Press, 2014), 283.

57. Quoted in Erica Fudge, "Learning to Laugh: Children and Being Human in Early Modern Thought," *Textual Practice* 17, no. 2 (2003): 277–94, at 281. Elias Canetti remarks that "laughter has been objected to as vulgar, because, in laughing, the mouth is opened wide and the teeth are shown," which speaks to "a feeling of pleasure in prey or food" that "reminds us of an animal," in *Crowds and Power*, trans. Carol Stewart (New York: Farrar, Straus and Giroux, 1984), 223.

58. On the scold's bridle, see Joan Hartwig, "Horses and Women in 'The Taming of the Shrew,'" *Huntington Library Quarterly* 45, no. 4 (Autumn 1982): 285–94.

59. On the anatomical variety of mandrake genitals in early modern botanical illustrations, see Diane Wolfthal, "Beyond Human: Visualizing the Sexuality of Abraham Bosse's Mandrake," in *Renaissance Posthumanism*, eds. Joseph Campana and Scott Maisano (New York: Fordham University Press, 2016), 211–52. On mandrake legends, see Anne van Arsdall, Helmut W. Klug, and Paul Blanz, "The Mandrake Plant and Its Legend: A New Perspective," in *Old Names—New Growth: Proceedings of the 2nd ASPNS Conference*, eds. Peter Bierbauner and Helmut W. Klug (Frankfurt/Main: Lang, 2009), 285–346.

60. Vin Nardizzi, "Shakespeare's Trans*plant* Poetics: Vegetable Blazons and the Seasons of Pyramus's Face," *Journal for Early Modern Cultural Studies* 19, no. 4 (Fall 2019): 156–77.

61. Quoted in Johnstone Parr, "The Horoscope in Webster's *The Duchess of Malfi*," *PMLA* 60, no. 3 (September 1945): 762–63.

62. Paré, *On Monsters and Marvels*, 24, 26.

63. John Boswell, *Christianity, Social Tolerance, and Homosexuality: Gay People in Western Europe from the Beginning of the Christian Era to the Fourteenth Century* (Chicago: University of Chicago Press, 1980), 140.

64. Aristotle militated against these beliefs, but in *Generation of Animals* conceded that hyenas might have an additional orifice (translated by A. L. Peck [Cambridge, MA: Harvard University Press, 1942], 757a, 2–13). On religious accounts of the hyena's gender, see Mary Pendergraft, "'Thou Shalt Not Eat the Hyena:' A Note on 'Barnabas' Epistle 10.7," *Vigiliae Christianae* 46, no. 1 (March 1992): 75–79.

65. Mario DiGangi, *The Homoerotics of Early Modern Drama* (New York: Cambridge University Press, 1997), 57.

66. Stephen Guy-Bray notes that squires are "junior participants in what is frequently a particularly intense homosocial relationship" and that such relations were "one of the acceptable faces of homoeroticism" in the period. See *Loving in Verse: Poetic Influence as Erotic* (Toronto: University of Toronto Press, 2006), 36.

67. DiGangi notes the sexual connotations of service clinging to squires and ushers, who were meant to be seen and admired "from *behind*" (*Homoerotics of Early Modern Drama*, 201).

68. Julie Crawford, "The Case of Lady Anne Clifford; Or, Did Women Have a Mixed Monarchy?" *PMLA* 121, no. 5 (October 2006): 1682–89, at 1683; and "Women's Secretaries," in *Queer Renaissance Historiography: Backward Gaze*, eds. Vin Nardizzi, Stephen Guy-Bray, and Will Stockton (Burlington, VT: Ashgate, 2009), 119. Her work extending this argument to *The Duchess of Malfi* was presented at the Folger Symposium on "Intersecting the Sexual," November 2019.

69. On religious injunctions against widows remarrying, see Margaret Lael Mikesell, "Catholic and Protestant Widows in *The Duchess of Malfi*," *Renaissance and Reformation* 7, no. 4 (November 1983): 265–79.

70. On the problems of inheritance and patrilineality in the play, see Michelle M. Dowd, "Delinquent Pedigrees: Revision, Lineage, and Spatial Rhetoric in *The Duchess of Malfi*," *English Literary Renaissance* 39, no. 3 (2009): 499–526.

71. Andy Kesson, "Trying Television by Candlelight: Shakespeare's Globe's *The Duchess of Malfi* on BBC4," *Shakespeare Bulletin* 33, no. 4 (Winter 2015): 609–21, at 618.

72. Jennifer Lodine-Chaffey, "'Beyond Death': John Webster's *The Duchess of Malfi* and Posthumous Influence," *Ben Jonson Journal* 26, no. 1 (2019): 113–32, at 119.

73. Brett D. Hirsch, "Lycanthropy in Early Modern England: The Case of John Webster's *The Duchess of Malfi*," in *Diseases of the Imagination and Imaginary Disease in the Early Modern Period*, ed. Yasmin Haskell (Turnhout: Brepols Publishers, 2011), 317.

74. Sonya Freeman Loftis, "Lycanthropy and Lunacy: Cognitive Disability in *The Duchess of Malfi*," in *Monstrosity, Disability, and the Posthuman in the Medieval and Early Modern World*, eds. Richard H. Godden and Asa Simon Mittman (Cham: Palgrave Macmillan, 2019), 209–25, at 210.

75. On critical reactions to the wax figures, see Margaret E. Owens, "John Webster, Tussaud Laureate: The Waxworks in *The Duchess of Malfi*," *ELH* 79 (2012): 851–77.

76. Julia Reinhard Lupton, "*Macbeth* against Dwelling," in *Shakespeare Dwelling: Designs for the Theater of Life* (Chicago: University of Chicago Press, 2018), 85–116; and Benjamin Parris, "Seizures of Sleep in Early Modern Literature," *Studies in English Literature* 58, no. 1 (Winter 2018): 51–76.

77. Parris, "Seizures of Sleep," 51.

78. S. J. Wiseman, Erica Fudge, and Brett Hirsch make compelling cases that, particularly in England, early modern writers were largely skeptical of werewolves and proposed similar psychologizing explanations for such legends; see S. J. Wiseman, "Hairy on the Inside: Metamorphosis and Civility in English Werewolf Texts," in *Renaissance Beasts: Of Animals, Humans, and Other Wonderful Creatures*, ed. Erica Fudge (Urbana: University of Illinois Press, 2004), 50–69; Erica Fudge, *Perceiving Animals: Humans and Beasts in Early Modern English Culture* (New York: St. Martin's Press, 2000), 51–55; and Hirsch, "Lycanthropy in Early Modern England."

79. Frank Whigham attributes this "inner wilderness" to the "incest taboo" in "Sexual and Social Mobility in *The Duchess of Malfi*," *PMLA* 100, no. 2 (March 1985): 167–86, at 168. Brian Chalk argues that "Ferdinand's lycanthropy reflects a typical Protestant association of wolves with the Catholic Church and its spiritual depredations" in "Webster's 'Worthyest Monument': The Problem of Posterity in *The Duchess of Malfi*," *Studies in Philology* 108, no. 3 (Summer 2011): 379–402, at 398.

80. Drew Daniel, *The Melancholy Assemblage: Affect and Epistemology in the English Renaissance* (New York: Fordham University Press, 2013), 88.

81. Lynn Enterline, "'Hairy on the In-side': *The Duchess of Malfi* and the Body of Lycanthropy," *Yale Journal of Criticism* 7 (1994): 85–129, at 91.

82. On early modern effeminacy, see Amanda Bailey, *Flaunting: Style and the Subversive Male Body in Renaissance England* (Toronto: University of Toronto Press, 2007); and Ian Moulton, *Before Pornography: Erotic Writing in Early Modern England* (New York: Oxford University Press, 2000).

83. Rebecca Bushnell, *Tragedies of Tyrants: Political Thought and Theater in the English Renaissance* (Ithaca, NY: Cornell University Press, 1990). On the tyrant as werewolf, see also Nicole Jacques-Lefevre, "Such an Impure, Cruel, and Savage Beast . . . : Images of the Werewolf in Demonological Works," in *Werewolves, Witches, and Wandering Spirits: Traditional Belief and Folklore in Early Modern Europe*, ed. Kathryn A. Edwards (Kirksville, MO: Truman State University Press, 2002), 181–97.

84. On Bosola's tyrannical disposition as a symptom of madness, see Karin S. Coddon, "*The Duchess of Malfi*: Tyranny and Spectacle in Jacobean Drama," in *Madness in Drama*, ed. James Redwell (New York: Cambridge University Press, 1993): 1–17.

85. Jennifer De Reuck, "'Plagued in Art': The Fashioning of an Aesthetics of Sacrifice in *The Duchess of Malfi*," *Shakespeare in Southern Africa* 27 (2015): 25–32, at 30.

86. Aspasia Velissariou, "Neither a Devil nor a Man: D'Amville in Tourneur's *The Atheist's Tragedy*," *Early Modern Literary Studies* 20, no. 2 (2018): 1–20, at 2.

87. Theodora A. Jankowski, "Defining/Confining the Duchess: Negotiating the Female Body in John Webster's 'The Duchess of Malfi,'" *Studies in Philology* 87, no. 2 (Spring 1990): 221–45, at 233.

88. Mary Beth Rose, *The Expense of Spirit: Love and Sexuality in English Renaissance Drama* (Ithaca, NY: Cornell University Press, 1988): 173.

89. Judith Haber, "'My Body Bestow upon My Women': The Space of the Feminine in 'The Duchess of Malfi,'" *Renaissance Drama* 28 (1997): 133–59, at 135.

90. Roberta Barker, "The Duchess High and Low: A Performance History of *The Duchess of Malfi*," in *The Duchess of Malfi: A Critical Guide*, ed. Christina Luckyj (New York: Continuum Books, 2011), 42–65, at 56.

91. Lynn Maxwell, "Wax Magic and *The Duchess of Malfi*," *Journal for Early Modern Cultural Studies* 14, no. 3 (Summer 2014): 31–54, at 44.

92. Haber, "My Body Bestow upon My Women," 140.

93. On the racial fantasies that affiliated Turks with sodomy, see Greta LaFleur, *The Natural History of Sexuality in Early America* (Baltimore, MD: Johns Hopkins University Press, 2018); Nabil I. Matar, "Sodomy and Conquest," in *Turks, Moors, and Englishmen in the Age of Discovery* (New York: Columbia University Press, 1999), 109–28; and Patricia Parker, "Barbers and Barbary: Early Modern Cultural Semantics," *Renaissance Drama* 33 (2004): 201–44. For a landmark account of the racialization of Ottoman eunuchs in conversation with trans studies, see Abdulhamit Arvas, "Early Modern Eunuchs and the Transing of Gender and Race," *Journal for Early Modern Cultural Studies* 19, no. 4 (2019): 116–36.

94. Chen, *Animacies*, 13.

95. Chen, *Animacies*, 129.

96. Harlan Weaver, "Trans Species," *Transgender Studies Quarterly* 1, nos. 1–2 (2014): 253–54, at 254.

## CHAPTER THREE

1. On the political structures that create the conditions for premature death for trans people, especially trans people of color, see Dean Spade, *Normal Life: Administrative Violence, Critical Trans Politics, and the Limits of Law* (Durham, NC: Duke University Press, 2015); Eric Stanley, *Atmospheres of Violence: Structuring Antagonism and the Trans/Queer Ungovernable* (Durham, NC: Duke University Press, 2021); Jules Gill-Peterson, *Histories of the Transgender Child* (Minneapolis: University of Minnesota Press, 2018); Paisley Currah, *Sex Is as Sex Does: Governing Transgender Identity* (New York: New York University Press, 2022); Treva Ellison, Kai M. Green, Matt Richardson, and C. Riley Snorton, "We Got Issues: Toward a Black Trans*/Studies," *Transgender Studies Quarterly* 4, no. 2 (May 2017): 162–69; Che Gossett, "We Will Not Rest in Peace: AIDS Activism, Black Radicalism, Queer and/or Trans Resistance," in *Queer Necropolitics*, eds. Jin Haritaworn, Adi Kunstman, and Silvia Posocco (New York: Routledge, 2014): 31–50; and Cassius Adair, "Licensing Citizenship: Anti-Blackness, Identification Documents, and Transgender Studies," *American Quarterly* 71, no. 2 (June 201): 569–94.

2. Daniel M. Lavery, *Something That May Shock and Discredit You* (New York: Simon and Schuster, Inc., 2020), 170.

3. Christine Benvenuto, *Sex Changes: A Memoir of Marriage, Gender, and Moving On* (New York: St. Martin's Press, 2012), 3, 130–31.

4. "ROGD" parents also sometimes conceptualize transition as death, as in the family who wrote an obituary for their trans teen who "pronounced [himself] dead" after "rapidly succumbing" to "a contagious pandemic among gifted suburban females" and "confused teens with autism." For the full text, see "I Am Not There. I Did Not Die," post by user BreathOfTheGarlic to the r/GenderCynical subreddit on Reddit.com, September 2020, https://www.reddit.com/r/GenderCynical/comments/j237s8/i_am_not_there_i_did_not_die/.

5. This fixation on "healthy tissue" is ubiquitous among transphobic groups; Texas HB 68 (2021) would criminalize any doctor who "remov[ed] any otherwise healthy or non-diseased body part or tissue" (4). For more on the state's interest in "healthy tissues," see chapter 4, "Trans Mayhem in *Samson Agonistes*."

6. Lisa Marchiano, "Outbreak: On Transgender Teens and Psychic Epidemics," *Psychological Perspectives: A Quarterly Journal of Jungian Thought* 60, no. 3 (2017): 345–66.

7. T. S. Eliot, "Lancelot Andrewes," in *Selected Essays* (New York: Harcourt, Brace and World, Inc., 1964), 299–311, at 302.

8. Drew Daniel, *Joy of the Worm: Suicide and Pleasure in Early Modern English Literature* (Chicago: University of Chicago Press, 2022); Daniel Juan Gil, *Fate of the Flesh: Secularization and Resurrection in the Seventeenth Century* (New York: Fordham University Press, 2021); Jessie Hock, *The Erotics of Materialism: Lucretius and Early Modern Poetics* (Philadelphia: University of Pennsylvania Press, 2021); Gary Kuchar, "Embodiment and Representation in John Donne's *Devotions upon Emergent Occasions*," *Prose Studies* 24, no. 2 (2001): 15–40; and Timothy Harrison, "John Donne, the Instant of Change, and the Time of the Body," *ELH* 85, no. 4 (Winter 2018): 909–39.

9. Grace Lavery, "Egg Theory's Early Style," *Transgender Studies Quarterly* 7, no. 3 (August 2020): 383–98, at 384.

10. Feminist critiques of Donne are legion, and with good reason. See, among others, Theresa M. DiPasquale, *Refiguring the Sacred Feminine: The Poems of John Donne, Aemilia Lanyer, and John Milton* (Pittsburgh, PA: Duquesne University Press, 2008); Maureen Sabine, *Feminine Engendered Faith: The Poetry of John Donne and Richard Crashaw* (New York: Palgrave, 1992); Elizabeth M. A. Hodgson, *Gender and the Sacred Self in John Donne* (Newark: University of Delaware Press, 1999); Elizabeth D. Harvey, "Ventriloquizing Sappho, or the Lesbian Muse," in *Ventriloquized Voices: Feminist Theory and English Renaissance Texts* (New York: Routledge, 1992), 116–39; Heather Dubrow, *Echoes of Desire: English Petrarchism and Its Counterdiscourses* (Ithaca, NY: Cornell University Press, 2018); Janel Mueller, "Women among the Metaphysicals: A Case, Mostly, of Being Donne For," *Modern Philology* 87, no. 2 (November 1989): 142–58 and "'This Dialogue of One': A Feminist Reading of Donne's 'Exstasie,'" *ADE Bulletin* 81 (Fall 1985): 39–42; Janet E. Halley, "Textual Intercourse: Anne Donne, John Donne, and the Sexual Poetics of Textual Exchange," in *Seeking the Woman in Late Medieval and Renaissance Writings: Essays in Feminist Contextual Criticism*, eds. Sheila Fisher and Janet E. Halley (Knoxville: University of Tennessee Press, 1989), 187–206; and Achsah Guibbory, "'Oh, Let Mee Not Serve So': The Politics of Love in Donne's *Elegies*," *English Literary History* 57, no. 4 (1990): 811–33. The gay Donne owes its formulation to Richard Rambuss, *Closet Devotions* (Durham, NC: Duke University Press, 1998) and George Klawitter, *Andrew Marvell, Sexual Orientation, and Seventeenth-Century Poetry*

(Madison, WI: Fairleigh Dickinson University Press, 2017) and "Verse Letters to TW from John Donne," *Journal of Homosexuality* 23, nos. 1–2 (1992): 85–102.

11. On trans temporality, see Jay Prosser, "Mirror Images: Transsexuality and Autobiography" in *Second Skins: The Body Narratives of Transsexuality* (New York: Columbia University Press, 1998), 99–134; Leah DeVun and Zeb Tortorici, "Trans, Time, and History," *Transgender Studies Quarterly* 5, no. 4 (2018): 518–39; Hil Malatino, "Future Fatigue: Trans Intimacies and Trans Presents (or How to Survive the Interregnum)," *Transgender Studies Quarterly* 6, no. 4 (2019): 635–58; Jack Halberstam, *In a Queer Time and Place: Transgender Bodies, Subcultural Lives* (New York: New York University Press, 2005); and Jian Neo Chen and micha cárdenas, "Times to Come: Materializing Trans Times," *Transgender Studies Quarterly* 6, no. 4 (2019): 472–80. On new materialism and trans studies, see Mel Chen, *Animacies: Biopolitics, Racial Mattering, and Queer Affect* (Durham, NC: Duke University Press, 2012); Karen Barad, "Transmaterialities: Trans*/Matter/Realities and Queer Political Imaginings," *GLQ* 21, nos. 2–3 (June 2015): 387–422; Stephanie Shelton, "The Influences of Barad's 'Transmaterialities' on Queer Theories and Methods," *GLQ* 25, no. 1 (2019): 119–24; and Jordy Rosenberg, "The Molecularization of Sexuality: On Some Primitivisms of the Present," *Theory and Event* 17, no. 2 (2014).

12. All Biblical quotations from *Geneva Bible: A Facsimile of the 1560 Edition*, ed. Lloyd E. Berry (Madison: University of Wisconsin Press, 1969). For Jewish accounts of the resurrection, see C. D. Elledge, *Resurrection of the Dead in Early Judaism, 200 BCE-CE 200* (New York: Oxford University Press, 2017); and Claudia Setzer, *Resurrection of the Body in Early Judaism and Early Christianity: Doctrine, Community, and Self-Definition* (Leiden: Brill, 2004).

13. Augustine, quoted in Robert M. Grant, "The Resurrection of the Body," *Journal of Religion* 28, no. 2 (April 1948): 120–130, at 197.

14. William Shakespeare, *Hamlet*, ed. G. R. Hibbard (New York: Oxford University Press, 1987), 4.3.27–31.

15. Will Fisher, *Materializing Gender in Early Modern English Literature and Culture* (New York: Cambridge University Press, 2007), 123.

16. Gregory of Nyssa, "On the Soul and Resurrection," in *Saint Gregory of Nyssa: Ascetical Works*, trans. Virginia Woods Callahan (Washington, DC: Catholic University of America Press, 1967), 266, 264.

17. In his treatise *On Prayer*, Origen rejects the insistence that the dead will kneel before God by announcing that "we must not in any way understand the heavenly bodies to be so formed as to possess physical knees, since their bodies have been proved to be spherical by those who accurately treat of these things." See *Origen's Treatise on Prayer*, trans. Eric George Jay (London: SPCK, 1954), 31.3.

18. Quoted in Benjamin H. Dunning, *Specters of Paul: Sexual Difference in Early Christian Thought* (Philadelphia: University of Pennsylvania Press, 2011), 51.

19. Leah DeVun, *The Shape of Sex: Nonbinary Gender from Genesis to the Renaissance* (New York: Columbia University Press, 2021), 14.

20. Irina Metzler argues that "notions of corporal resurrection with perfect bodies carry important consequences" for the nexus between disability and personhood, since apparently physical impairments were not important enough to identity to warrant

preservation in the afterlife. See *Disability in Medieval Europe: Thinking about Physical Impairment during the High Middle Ages* (New York: Routledge, 2006), 63.

21. Augustine, *The City of God, Books XVII-XXII*, trans. Gerald G. Walsh, S. J., and Daniel J. Honan (Washington, DC: Catholic University of America Press, 1954), 22.19, 468.

22. Augustine, *City of God*, 22.15, 469.

23. Quoted in Maaike van der Lugt, "Sex Difference in Medieval Theology and Canon Law: A Tribute to Joan Cadden," *Medieval Feminist Forum* 46, no. 1 (2010): 101–21, at 118. For the version of this claim made by twelfth-century Cistercian Otto of Freising, see DeVun, *Shape of Sex*, 32–35; and Caroline Walker Bynum, *Resurrection of the Body in Western Christianity, 200–1336* (New York: Columbia University Press, 1995), 183.

24. The invasive, violent, and nonconsensual surgical interventions performed on intersex people—many of whom are children—have been the subject of significant work in trans writing and activism. See in particular Hil Malatino, *Queer Embodiment: Monstrosity, Medical Violence, and Intersex Experience* (University of Nebraska Press, 2019).

25. Augustine, *City of God*, 22.19, 469.

26. Bynum, *Resurrection of the Body*, 183; see also DeVun, *Shape of Sex*, 34. On the trope of the white soul in medieval theology, see Bruce Holsinger, "The Color of Salvation: Desire, Death, and the Second Crusade in Bernard of Clairvaux's *Sermons on the Song of Songs*," in *The Tongue of the Fathers: Gender and Ideology in Twelfth-Century Latin*, eds. David Townsend and Andrew Taylor (Philadelphia: University of Pennsylvania Press, 1998), 156–86. For early modern iterations in devotional literature and visual art, see Grace Harpster, "The Color of Salvation: The Materiality of Blackness in Alonso de Sandoval's *De insauranda Aethiopum salute*," in *Envisioning Others: Race, Color, and the Visual in Iberia and Latin America*, ed. Pamela A. Patton (Boston, MA: Brill, 2016), 104–10. For the eighteenth century, see Christopher Trigg, "The Racial Politics of Resurrection in the Eighteenth-Century Atlantic World," *Early American Literature* 55, no. 1 (2020): 47–84.

27. The Catholic church reaffirmed its commitment to the Apostle's creed, the eleventh article of which asserts belief in resurrection of the flesh (*carnis resurrectionem*), at the Council of Trent (1563). For the text, see *Decrees of the Ecumenical Council: Trent to Vatican II*, vol. 2, ed. Norman P. Tanner (London: Sheed and Ward, 1990), 662. The Church of England adopted the Apostle's Creed, the Nicene Creed, and Athanasius's Creed, all of which also explicitly affirm the resurrection of the body; see Charles Hardwick, *A History of the Articles of Religion* (London: George Bell, 1876), 301.

28. Erin Lambert, "The Reformation and the Resurrection of the Dead," *Sixteenth Century Journal* 47, no. 2 (Summer 2016): 352.

29. John Carey, *John Donne: Life, Mind, and Art* (London: Faber and Faber, 1981), 201–3.

30. Stanley Fish, "Masculine Persuasive Force: Donne and Verbal Power," *Soliciting Interpretation: Literary Theory and Seventeenth-Century English Poetry*, eds. Elizabeth D. Harvey and Katharine Eisaman Maus (Chicago: University of Chicago Press, 1990), 223. For other accounts of Donne's fixation on death, see Ramie Targoff, "Facing Death," in *The Cambridge Companion to John Donne*, ed. Achsah Guibbory (New York:

Cambridge University Press, 2006), 217–32 and *John Donne, Body and Soul* (Chicago: University of Chicago Press, 2008); Achsah Guibbory, "John Donne: The Idea of Decay," in *Returning to John Donne* (Burlington, VT: Ashgate, 2015), 19–48; Robert Watson, "Duelling Death in the Lyrics of Love: John Donne's Poetics of Immortality," in *The Rest is Silence: Death as Annihilation in the English Renaissance* (Berkeley: University of California Press, 1994), 156–252.

31. Targoff, *John Donne, Body and Soul*, 172. This temptation is not, to be clear, one that Targoff herself succumbs to, although this chapter does.

32. On Donne's experiments with temporality, see Harrison, "John Donne, the Instant of Change, and the Time of the Body"; Hilary Binda, "'My Name Engrav'd Herein': John Donne's Sacramental Temporality," *Exemplaria* 23, no. 4 (Winter 2011): 390–414; Theresa M. DiPasquale, "From Here to Aeviternity: Donne's Atemporal Clocks," *Modern Philology* 110, no. 2 (2012): 226–52.

33. Elegy 19, "Going to Bed," 47. All quotations from *Songs and Sonets* are taken from *The Poems of John Donne*, ed. H. J. C. Grierson (London: Oxford University Press, 1929). See also Aaron Kunin, *Love Three* (Seattle, WA: Wave Books, 2019), 241.

34. John Donne, *John Donne's* Devotions upon Emergent Occasions, *together with* Death's Duel (Ann Arbor: University of Michigan Press, 1959), 116. All quotations from *Devotions upon Emergent Occasions* and *Death's Duel* hereafter cited in text.

35. John Donne, *The Sermons of John Donne*, vol. 8, eds. Evelyn M. Simpson and George R. Potter (Berkeley: University of California Press, 1956), 95. Hereafter cited in text.

36. On this point, Donne's sermon resonates with the conclusion of Mary Frith's memoirs, which casts dropsy as a kind of impossible trans pregnancy: "As for my belly, from a withered, dried and wrinkled piece of skin, it was grown the tightest, roundest globe of flesh that ever any beauteous young lady strutted with, to the ostentation of her fertility and the generosity of her nature. I must tell you I could not but proud myself in it, and thought nature had reserved that kindness for me at the last, insomuch that I could have almost been impregnated (as Spanish jennets are said to be begotten by the wind) with my own fancy and imagination, my conceit proving the same with conception." See *The Life and Death of Mrs. Mary Frith*, ed. Randall S. Nakayama (New York: Garland Publishing, Inc., 1993), 93.

37. As Leah DeVun argues, "by the thirteenth century" it was a "common perception" that angels "fluctuated between the sexes, or they expressed an androgyny that altogether transcended binary sex" (*Shape of Sex*, 89). On the gender of angels, see Dyan Elliott, "Tertullian, the Angelic Life, and the Bride of Christ," in *Gender and Christianity in Medieval Europe*, eds. Lisa M. Bitel and Felice Lifshitz (Philadelphia: University of Pennsylvania Press, 2010), 16–33. On chastity, the *vita angelica* and the "eschatological transcendence of gender," see Sarah Salih, *Versions of Virginity in Late Medieval England* (Rochester, NY: D. S. Brewer, 2001), 115.

38. Julie Crawford, "Transubstantial Bodies in *Paradise Lost* and *Order and Disorder*," *Journal for Early Modern Cultural Studies* 19, no. 4 (Fall 2019): 75–93, at 80.

39. On queerness and the couple form, see S. Pearl Brilmyer, Filippo Trentin, and Zairong Xiang, "The Ontology of the Couple: Or, What Queer Theory Knows about Numbers," *GLQ* 25, no. 2 (2019): 223–55.

40. Hodgson, *Gender and the Sacred Self*, 89.

41. William Empson rather shirtily describes the events following Donne's nuptials this way: Donne "couldn't have been certain when he did this that it would break his career, because it wouldn't have done if the father hadn't behaved foolishly; the father first insisted on having Donne sacked and then found he had better try to have him reinstated, which Egerton refused on the very English ground that the fuss about the matter had been sufficiently ridiculous already." See "Donne the Space Man," in *William Empson: Essays on Renaissance Literature*, vol. 1, ed. John Haffenden (New York: Cambridge University Press, 1993), 84.

42. On this point, see Susan C. Karant-Nunn, "'Fragrant Wedding Roses': Lutheran Wedding Sermons and Gender Definition in Early Modern Germany," *German History* 17, no. 1 (1999): 25–40.

43. On Protestant celebration of the household, see Lawrence Stone, *The Family, Sex and Marriage in England, 1500–1800* (New York: Harper and Row, 1977); Wendy Wall, *Staging Domesticity: Household Work and English Identity in Early Modern Drama* (New York: Cambridge University Press, 2002); and Natasha Korda, *Shakespeare's Domestic Economies: Gender and Property in Early Modern England* (Philadelphia: University of Pennsylvania Press, 2002).

44. Targoff, *John Donne, Body and Soul*, 117. Essays on "The Funerall" and resurrection include Megan Kathleen Smith, "Reading It Wrong to Get It Right: Sacramental and Excremental Encounters in Early Modern Poems about Hair Jewelry," *Philological Quarterly* 94, no. 4 (2015): 353–75; Erik Gray, "Severed Hair from Donne to Pope," *Essays in Criticism* 47 (1997): 220–39; and Eileen Sperry, "Decay, Intimacy, and the Lyric Metaphor in Jon Donne," *Studies in English Literature* 59, no. 2 (2019): 45–66.

45. Fisher, *Materializing Gender*.

46. Smith, "Reading It Wrong to Get It Right," 356–57.

47. Andrea Long Chu, *Females: A Concern* (Brooklyn, NY: Verso, 2019), 70–79.

48. On this history, see the introduction to this book. Such tendencies persist in the absurd work of Ray Blanchard and J. Michael Bailey, who understand transsexuality as a matter of fetishistic "autogynephilia," the sexual attraction to the image of oneself as a woman.

49. A. R. Cirillo, "The Fair Hermaphrodite: Love-Union in the Poetry of Donne and Spenser," *Studies in English Literature* 9, no. 1 (Winter 1969): 81–95; Ruth Gilbert, *Early Modern Hermaphrodites: Sex and Other Stories* (New York: Palgrave MacMillan, 2002), 166.

50. For a trans reading of alchemy, see Micah Goodrich, "Trans Animacies and Premodern Alchemies," in *Medieval Mobilities: Gendered Bodies, Spaces, and Movements*, eds. Basil Arnould Price, Jane Elizabeth Bonsall, and Meagan Khoury (New York: Palgrave Macmillan, 2023), 199–223. On the *rebis* or alchemical hermaphrodite, see DeVun, *Shape of Sex*, 163–207. On Ebreo and the Adam hermaphrodite in "The Canonization," see Ronald Corthell, *Ideology and Desire in Renaissance Poetry: The Subject of Donne* (Detroit, MI: Wayne State University Press, 1997), 92–93. John Freccero glosses Donne's sexless "ecstasies" with reference to Ficino's account of the Resurrection in "Donne's 'Valediction: Forbidding Mourning,'" *ELH* 30, no. 4 (1963): 335–76, at 354.

51. Arthur L. Clements, *Poetry of Contemplation: John Donne, George Herbert, Henry Vaughan, and the Modern Period* (Albany: State University of New York Press, 1990), 39. On the many valences of Donne's "interinanimation," see also Michael Ursell, "Interinanimation and Lifelessness in John Donne's Book Studies," *Studies in English Literature* 56, no. 1 (Winter 2016): 71–92.

52. In a wonderfully clever reading of this poem, Matthias Bauer and Angelika Zirker pluck the prefix off "interinanimate" to find "inter" and "interim," terms that resonate with "the intermediate state of the souls after death, called *refrigerium interim* by Tertullian and others," a frozen state of incapacitation where "they are waiting for the resurrection of the body" ("Sites of Death as Sites of Interaction in Donne and Shakespeare," in *Shakespeare and Donne: Generic Hybrids and the Cultural Imaginary*, eds. Judith H. Anderson and Jennifer C. Vaught [New York: Fordham University Press, 2013], 24).

53. Mueller, "Dialogue of One," 39, 41.

54. Fish, "Masculine Persuasive Force."

55. The definitive account of the circulation of the *Songs and Sonets* within Donne's fraternal coterie remains Arthur Marotti, *John Donne, Coterie Poet* (Eugene, OR: Wipf and Stock Publishers, 1986).

56. Stephanie Burt, "The Body of the Poem: On Transgender Poetry," *Los Angeles Review of Books*, November 17, 2013.

57. In 1619, Donne presented a copy of *Biathanatos*, a treatise upon the "misinterpretable" subject of self-killing, to Robert Carr with a letter that instructed him to "communicate" that "it is a Book written by Jack Donne, and not by D. Donne" (quoted in Adam H. Kitzes, "Paradoxical Donne: *Biathanatos* and the Problems with Political Assimilation," *Prose Studies* 24, no. 3 [2001], 3).

58. John Donne, letter XXI, "To Sir Henry Goodyer," in *John Donne: Selected Letters*, ed. P. M. Oliver (New York: Routledge, 2002), 27.

59. On the homoeroticism of Donne's verse letters, see Klawitter, "Verse Letters to TW from John Donne."

60. John Donne, *John Donne: The Satires, Epigrams, and Verse Letters*, ed. Wesley Milgate (Oxford: Clarendon Press, 1967), 212.

61. Dianne Mitchell, "John Donne's Poetics of Mediation," *Journal for Early Modern Cultural Studies* 18, no. 4 (Fall 2018): 73–99, at 85.

62. Halley, "Textual Intercourse," 200. I will simply note at this point that clitorises do indeed become erect, and cis women also ejaculate (squirt).

63. Valerie Traub, *The Renaissance of Lesbianism in Early Modern England* (New York: Cambridge University Press, 2002), 24, emphasis hers.

64. Lavery, "Egg Theory's Early Style," 384–85.

65. Thomas Docherty, *John Donne, Undone* (New York: Routledge, 2014), 200.

66. Quoted in Helen Carr, "Donne's Masculine Persuasive Force," *Jacobean Poetry and Prose: Rhetoric, Representation and the Popular Imagination*, ed. Clive Bloom (London: Macmillan Press, 1988), 96–118, at 97.

67. Debora Shuger, *The Renaissance Bible: Scholarship, Sacrifice, and Subjectivity* (Berkeley: University of California Press, 1994), 168.

68. Fish, "Masculine Persuasive Force," 228.

69. Ben Saunders, *Desiring Donne: Poetry, Sexuality, Interpretation* (Cambridge, MA: Harvard University Press, 2006), 64.

70. Harriette Andreadis, *Sappho in Early Modern England: Female Same-Sex Literary Erotics, 1550–1714* (Chicago: University of Chicago Press, 2001), 46.

71. Klawitter, *Andrew Marvell, Sexual Orientation, and Seventeenth-Century Poetry*, 112.

72. Corthell, *Ideology and Desire in Renaissance Poetry*, 66.

73. Lavery, "Egg Theory's Early Style," 395.

74. Matthew Biberman, *Masculinity, Anti-Semitism and Early Modern English Literature: From the Satanic to the Effeminate Jew* (New York: Routledge, 2004), 84.

75. Fish, "Masculine Persuasive Force," 241.

76. R. V. Young, "Love, Poetry, and John Donne in the Love Poetry of John Donne," *Renascence* 52, no. 4 (2000), 250–73, at 252.

77. Debora Shuger, "The Title of Donne's *Devotions*," *English Language Notes* 22, no. 4 (1985): 39–40, at 39.

78. Drew Daniel, "A Political Necrology of God," *Journal for Early Modern Cultural Studies* 13, no. 3 (Summer 2013): 105–25. "Necrology" here is an alternative to the vital materialism of Jane Bennett that, in Daniel's accounting, is more suited to the "theological ontology of negativity and death at play within Donne's text," an insight as relevant to *Devotions* as *Biathanatos* (115).

79. Harvey, *Ventriloquized Voices*, 128–29.

80. C. Ray Borck outlines a careful refutation of the logic behind pitiful appeals to "transrace" as a transphobic trump card, as in the work of philosopher Rebecca Tuvel, in "Negligent Analogies," *Transgender Studies Quarterly* 4, nos. 3–4 (November 2017): 679–84.

81. See, for instance, Deborah Miranda, "Extermination of the Joyas: Gendercide in Spanish California," *GLQ* 16, no. 102 (2010): 253–84; and Shraddha Chatterjee, "Transgender Shifts: Notes on Resignification of Gender and Sexuality in India," *Transgender Studies Quarterly* 5, no. 3 (August 2018): 311–20.

82. In a letter to Dudley Carleton, John Chamberlain writes that "Newes here is none at all but that John Dun seekes to be preferred to be secretarie of Virginia" (*The Letters of John Chamberlain*, vol. 1. ed. Norman Egbert McClure [Philadelphia, PA: American Philosophical Society, 1939], 284).

83. R. C. Bald notes that this appointment was "purely an honour, since [Donne] had not invested any money in the venture" (*John Donne: A Life* [Oxford: Clarendon Press, 1970], 435).

84. Much of the critical conversation on this sermon has affirmed or questioned Donne's "temperate" approach to colonization, as if it could be contrasted to the explicitly genocidal drive of the Company's other supporters, including his friend Christopher Brooke, who wrote a horrifying poem on the matter (*A Poem on the Late Massacre in Virginia*). On this subject, see Tom Cain, "John Donne and the Ideology of Colonization," *English Literary Renaissance* 31, no. 3 (2001): 440–76 and M. Thomas Hester, "Donne's (Re)Annunciation of the Virgin(ia Colony) in 'Elegy XIX,'" *South Central*

*Review* 4, no. 2 (Summer 1987): 49–64. For a sharp elaboration of the racial politics at work in this sermon, see Ryan Campagna, "The Interanimation of Race in John Donne's Creature Colonialism," in "White World-Making in Early Modern England: Ideological and Phenomenological Constructions of Racial Whiteness from Shakespeare to Milton" (PhD diss., University of Chicago, anticipated 2024).

85. Patricia Springborg argues that Donne's sermon served as a template for Hobbes's accounts of no-man's land in *Leviathan* in the context of Anglo-Dutch rivalry in "Hobbes, Donne and the Virginia Company: *Terra Nullius* and 'The Bulimia of Dominium,'" *History of Political Thought* 36, no. 1 (Spring 2015): 113–64.

86. On the politics behind Donne's theological argument for the penal colony, see Thomas Festa, "The Metaphysics of Labor in John Donne's Sermon to the Virginia Company," *Studies in Philology* 106, no. 1 (2009): 76–99.

87. Susan Myra Kingsbury, ed., *The Records of the Virginia Company*, vol. 3 (Washington, DC: Government Printing Office, 1933), 243.

88. Hortense Spillers, "Mama's Baby, Papa's Maybe: An American Grammar Book," *diacritics* 17, no. 2 (1987): 65–81, at 68.

89. C. Riley Snorton, *Black on Both Sides: A Racial History of Trans Identity* (Minneapolis: University of Minnesota Press, 2017), 12.

90. Melissa Sanchez, "Transdevotion: Race, Gender, and Christian Universalism," *Journal for Early Modern Cultural Studies* 19, no. 4 (Fall 2019): 94–115, at 107.

91. Marquis Bey, "Black Fugitivity Un/Gendered," *Black Scholar* 49, no. 1 (2019): 55–62, at 56.

92. For Donne's poetic obscurity as resistant to the psychiatric management of trans subjectivity, written with an optimism I can no longer muster, see my essay "The Sign You Must Not Touch: Lyric Obscurity and Trans Confession," *postmedieval* 11, no. 2 (2020): 195–203.

93. On the medical model of transness as a feature of the "expressive" theory of consciousness, see Grace Lavery, "The King's Two Anuses: Trans Feminism and Free Speech," *differences* 30, no. 3 (2019): 119–51.

## CHAPTER FOUR

1. My deepest thanks to Beans Velocci for sharing their notes on Val from the Kinsey Institute's archives, which were closed because of the pandemic at the time of this chapter's composition.

2. The earliest records of attempts to construct vaginal canals in cisgender women born without them, a condition known today as vaginal atresia or agenesis, date back to the fifth century BCE, with Hippocrates's *On the Nature of Women*, which recommends that a passage be opened with a pessary saturated in resin, ground copper, and honey. On this prehistory of vaginoplasty, see Robert M. Goldwyn, "History of Attempts to Form a Vagina," *Plastic and Reconstructive Surgery* 59, no. 3 (March 1977): 319–29. The first known transgender woman to undergo the procedure was Dora Richter, who received a vaginoplasty in 1931.

3. *The State of North Carolina v. Bass*, 120 S.E.2d 580 (1961).

4. *State of North Carolina v. Bass*, 120 S.E.2d, 586.

5. These projects were also, of course, profoundly and violently ableist. On these histories, see Nancy Ordover, *American Eugenics: Race, Queer Anatomy, and the Science of Nationalism* (Minneapolis: University of Minnesota Press, 2003); Wendy Kline, *Building a Better Race: Gender, Sexuality, and Eugenics from the Turn of the Century to the Baby Boom* (Berkeley: University of California Press, 2001); Alexandra Minna Stern, *Eugenic Nation: Faults and Frontiers of Better Breeding in Modern America* (Berkeley: University of California Press, 2016); and Adam Cohen, *Imbeciles: The Supreme Court, American Eugenics, and the Sterilization of Carrie Buck* (New York: Penguin Press, 2016).

6. Wendy Kline discusses the case of Ann Cooper Hewitt, the heiress who (unsuccessfully) brought mayhem charges against her mother for sterilizing her as a way of preventing her from inheriting her father's fortune (*Building a Better Race*, 108–18).

7. On the convergences between eugenics and transphobia, see Jules Gill-Peterson, *Histories of the Transgender Child* (Minneapolis: University of Minnesota Press, 2018); Kadji Amin, "Glands, Eugenics, and Rejuvenation in *Man into Woman*: A Biopolitical Genealogy of Transsexuality," *Transgender Studies Quarterly* 5, no. 4 (2018): 589–605; and Ezra Horbury and Christine "Xine" Yao, "Empire and Eugenics: Trans Studies in the United Kingdom," *Transgender Studies Quarterly* 7, no. 3 (August 2020): 445–54.

8. On abortion and mayhem, see Justin Miller and Gordon Dean, "Liability of Physicians for Sterilization Operations," *American Bar Association Journal* 16, no. 3 (March 1930): 159; John Keown, *Abortion, Doctors and the Law: Some Aspects of the Legal Regulation of Abortion in England from 1803–1982* (New York: Cambridge University Press, 1988), 14–15.

9. Leonard le Marchant Minty, "Unlawful Wounding; Will Consent Make It Legal?" *Medico-Legal Journal* 24, no. 2 (1956): 54–62, at 58.

10. Harry Benjamin to Alfred Kinsey, October 4, 1950, series IIC, box 3, Harry Benjamin Collection, Kinsey Institute, Bloomington, IN (hereafter HBC).

11. Harry Benjamin to Edmund Brown, November 22, 1949, series IIC, box 3, HBC.

12. Graham Hammill, "Epilogue: The Solecism of Power," *Studies in English Literature, 1500–1900* 58, no. 1 (Winter 2018): 193–204; Ari Friedlander, *Impotence: Disability, Sex, and Labor in Early Modern England* (in progress); Micah Goodrich, "Maimed Limbs and Biosalvation: Rehabilitation Politics in *Piers Plowman*," in *Trans Historical: Gender Plurality before the Modern*, eds. Greta LaFleur, Masha Raskolnikov, and Anna Klosowska (Ithaca, NY: Cornell University Press, 2021).

13. Henry de Bracton, *Bracton on the Laws and Customs of England*, trans. Samuel E. Thorne (Cambridge, MA: Belknap Press, 1968), 409–10; *Fleta*, vol. 2, eds. and trans. G. O. Sayles and H. G. Richardson (London: B. Quaritch, 1955), 1.38; and *Britton*, vol. 1, trans. Francis Morgan Nichols (Cambridge: Clarendon Press, 1865), 123–24.

14. Edward Coke, *The First Part of the Institutes of the Laws of England; Or, a Commentary upon Littleton*, vol. 1 (London: Printed for J. and W. T. Clarke, 1832), 127b.

15. Edward Coke, *The First Part of the Institutes of the Laws of England; Or, a Commentary upon Littleton*, vol. 2 (London: Printed for E. and R. Brooke, Bell-Yard, 1794), 288a.

16. Coke, *Institutes*, vol. 1, 127a.

17. Henri de Bracton, *De Legibus et Consuetudinibus Angliae* (London: Miles Flesher and Robert Young, 1640), 408. Unlike later legal treatises, which were concerned exclusively with men's capacity to fight, Bracton also indicates that "anyone who forcibly interferes with a woman's internal organs in order to produce abortion" is liable for mayhem (*Item si quis muleris visceribus vim intulerit quo partum abegerit, tenetur*, 408).

18. William Hawkins, *Treatise of the Pleas of the Crown*, vol. 1, ed. John Curwood (London: Printed for S. Sweet, 1824), 107. William Blackstone likewise writes that "the offence of mayhem by castration" was a crime that "all our old writers held to be felony" on the pain of capital punishment, permanent banishment, or the forfeiture of all property, "and this, although the mayhem was committed upon the highest provocation" (*Commentaries on the Laws of England*, vol. 4 [Chicago: University of Chicago Press, 1979], 15.1).

19. Blackstone, *Commentaries on the Laws of England*, 4.15.I.

20. John Bulwer, *Anthropometamorphosis: Man Transform'd, or the Artificial Changeling* (London: Printed by William Hunt, 1653), 355–56.

21. Thomas Browne, *Pseudodoxia Epidemica*, vol. 1, ed. Robin Robbins (Oxford: Clarendon Press, 1981), 3.9.28–34. No one has a better handle on the complexities of testicularity than Jordan Windholz, who addresses the matter in "The Queer Testimonies of Male Chastity in *All's Well That Ends Well*," *Modern Philology* 116, no. 4 (2019): 322–49.

22. Edward Coke, *Institutes*, vol. 3 (London: Printed for W. Clarke, 1809), 118.

23. For accounts of this practice, see Alanna Skuse, "'One Stroak of His Razour': Tales of Self-Gelding in Early Modern England," *Social History of Medicine* 33, no. 2 (2020): 377–93.

24. William Shakespeare, *Richard II*, 1.3.65–66, and *The Winter's Tale*, 2.2.24–25, in *The Riverside Shakespeare*, 2nd ed., ed. G. Blakemore Evans (Boston, MA: Houghton Mifflin, 1997).

25. *Oxford English Dictionary*, 2nd ed., s.v. "Lusty, adj.," accessed December 1, 2020, https://www.oed.com/dictionary/lusty_adj?tab=meaning_and_use#38742909.

26. Ari Friedlander, *Rogue Sexuality in Early Modern English Literature: Desire, Status, Biopolitics* (New York: Oxford University Press, 2022). For an argument about the sexual regulation of the poor and, in particular, the "instrumentalization and exploitation" of transfeminine people "for the benefit of the state" in the pamphlets of Henry Neville, see Madison Wolfert, "The Racial Biopolitics of Sex in the Work of Henry Neville," forthcoming in *English Literary Renaissance* (Fall 2024).

27. On biopolitics and the crip philology of impotence, see Ari Friedlander's dazzling essay "Impotence," forthcoming in *Logomotives: The Words That Changed Early Modern Culture*, eds. Marjorie Rubright and Stephen Spiess (Edinburgh: University of Edinburgh Press, 2024).

28. Thomas Taylor, *A Commentarie vpon the Epistle of S. Paul Written to Titus* (Cambridge: Printed by Cantrell Legge, 1612), 1.15.

29. Jasbir Puar, *The Right to Maim: Debility, Capacity, Disability* (Durham, NC: Duke University Press, 2017).

30. Michel Foucault, *The History of Sexuality: An Introduction*, vol. 1, trans. Robert Hurley (New York: Vintage Books, 1990), 101.

31. John Milton, *The Complete Poetry and Essential Prose of John Milton*, eds. William Kerrigan, John Rumrich, and Stephen M. Fallon (New York: Modern Library, 2007), 1089. All references to Milton are from this volume.

32. As Timothy Harrison notes, Adam "feels drawn into the world" by his "life processes," what we might call his virtues, capacities, or lusty energies ("Adamic Awakening and the Feeling of Being Alive in *Paradise Lost*," *Milton Studies* 54 (2013), 29–57, at 42).

33. On the absence of Samson's mother, see Amy Boesky, "Samson and Surrogacy," in *Milton and Gender*, ed. Catherine Gimelli Martin (New York: Cambridge University Press, 2009), 153–66.

34. Hannah Arendt, *The Human Condition*, 2nd ed. (Chicago: University of Chicago Press, 1958), 9.

35. Blackstone, *Commentaries on the Laws of England*, 4.15.I.

36. Coke, *Institutes*, 3.12, 288a.

37. Kevin Curran, "What Was Personhood?," in *Renaissance Personhood: Materiality, Taxonomy, Process*, ed. Kevin Curran (Edinburgh: Edinburgh University Press, 2020), 3.

38. Klaus Reinhardt, "The Texts of the 'Bible of Saint Louis,'" in *The Bible of Saint Louis*, vol. 2, ed. Ramon Gonzalvez Ruiz (Barcelona: M. Moleiro, 2004), 288. Use of the Biblical Philistines as a byword for foreignness as such persisted into the twentieth century, as did the false etymology holding that the term "Philistine" meant "wanderer" or "immigrant" (see Carl Theophilus Odhner, *Correspondences of Canaan: A Study of the Spiritual Geography and History of the Land and Nations of the World* [Bryn Athyn, PA: Academy Book Room, 1911], 95).

39. On the Crusading trope that pitted Christian warriors against Muslim "new Philistines," see Penny Cole, "'O God, the Heathen Have Come into Your Inheritance' (Ps. 78.1): The Theme of Religious Pollution in Crusade Documents, 1095–1188," in *Crusaders and Muslims in Twelfth-Century Syria*, ed. Maya Shatzmiller (New York: Brill, 1993), 106–7. On the racial logic behind casting Muslim nations as the "new Philistines," see Debra Higgs Strickland, *Saracens, Demons, and Jews: Making Monsters in Medieval Art* (Princeton, NJ: Princeton University Press, 2003), 171–72. Innocent III, organizer of the Fourth Crusade, denounced the Muslim armies defending Jerusalem as "barbarian battle-lines of Philistines" and "battle-lines of Saracens" (quoted in Giulio Cipollone, "From Intolerance to Tolerance: The Humanitarian Way, 1187–1216," in *Tolerance and Intolerance: Social Conflict in the Age of the Crusades*, eds. Michael Gervers and James M. Powell [Syracuse, NY: Syracuse University Press, 2001], 350). Marcus Bull notes that Andrew of Fleury's *Miracles of St. Benedict* calls the "Spanish 'Saracens'" of the Caliphate of Cordoba "new Philistines" because they, like their scriptural referents, were "simultaneously effeminate and aggressive, blindly trusting in their large numbers to bring about [their] military success" ("Muslims and Jerusalem in Miracle Stories," in *The Experience of Crusading*, eds. Marcus Graham Bull, Norman Housely, P. W. Edbury, and Jonathan Phillips [New York: Cambridge University Press, 2003], 36).

40. Charlotte Colding Smith notes that the twelve tyrants of the Old Testament, including the Philistine champion Goliath, were routinely portrayed in the "exotic"

costume of "the Ottoman Turk" (*Images of Islam, 1435–1600: Turks in Germany and Central Europe* [New York: Routledge, 2014], 86).

41. On the pleasures and anxieties mapped onto Muslim-coded clothing in this period, see Barbara Fuchs, *Exotic Nation: Maurophilia and the Construction of Early Modern Spain* (Philadelphia: University of Pennsylvania Press, 2009); and Javier Irigoyen-Garcia, *Moors Dressed as Moors: Clothing, Social Distinction and Ethnicity in Early Modern Iberia* (Toronto: University of Toronto Press, 2017).

42. The place of Islamophobia within the histories of white supremacy and anti-blackness has been the subject of decades worth of crucial, foundational scholarship in early modern studies, including work by Kim F. Hall, *Things of Darkness: Economies of Race and Gender in Early Modern England* (Ithaca, NY: Cornell University Press, 2018); Nabil I. Matar, *Islam in Britain, 1558–1685* (New York: Cambridge University Press, 1998); Dennis Britton, *Becoming Christian: Race, Reformation, and Early Modern English Romance* (New York: Fordham University Press, 2014); Benedict Robinson, *Islam and Early Modern English Literature: The Politics of Romance from Spenser to Milton* (New York: Palgrave Macmillan, 2007); Geraldine Heng, *The Invention of Race in the European Middle Ages* (New York: Cambridge University Press, 2018); Ambereen Dadabhoy, "Two Faced: The Problem of Othello's Visage," in *Othello: The State of Play*, ed. Lena Cowen Orlin (London: Bloomsbury, 2014), 121–47; and Nedda Mehdizadeh, "The Petrification of Rostam: Thomas Herbert's Revision of Persia in *A Relation of Some Yeares Travaile*," in *Remapping Travel Narratives, 1000–1700: To the East and Back Again*, ed. Montserrat Piera (Leeds: Arc Humanities Press, 2018), 111–28.

43. Walter S. H. Lim, "John Milton, Orientalism, and the Empires of the East in Paradise Lost," in *The English Renaissance, Orientalism, and the Idea of Asia*, eds. Debra Johanyak and Walter S. H. Lim (New York: Palgrave Macmillan, 2010), 224.

44. This conceptual move is especially insidious since, as Rachel Trubowitz argues, it elides distinctions between Israelites and Philistines to demonize both groups according to a rationale that is both Islamophobic and anti-Semitic. Samson appropriates for England "the sacred space of difference that the biblical Israel once occupied, but which it voluntarily gave up when it gave in to the natural inclination to slavery that makes Hebrews into Asians—and all fallen peoples into Judeo-Orientals." See "'The People of Asia and with Them the Jews': Israel, Asia, and England in Milton's Writings," in *Milton and the Jews*, ed. Douglas A. Brooks (New York: Cambridge University Press, 2008), 172.

45. 1 Samuel 5: 4–9. All Biblical quotations are from *Geneva Bible: A Facsimile of the 1560 Edition*, ed. Lloyd E. Berry (Madison: University of Wisconsin Press, 1969).

46. Aren Maeir draws on archaeological evidence to argue that 1 Sam. 5:6 should be translated "as 'Strike them in their penises'" ("A New Interpretation of the Term *'opalim* (עפלים) in the Light of Recent Archaeological Finds from Philistia," *Journal for the Study of the Old Testament* 32, no. 1 [2007], 23, 32).

47. Josephus, *Jewish Antiquities*, vol. 2, trans. H. Thackeray and Ralph Marcus (Cambridge, MA: Harvard University Press, 1998), 6.1.

48. Rashi, *The Book of Shmuel I*, ed. Avraham Davis (Lakewood, NJ: Metsudah Publications, 1999).

49. On *qere-ketiv*, see Yosef Ofer, *The Masora on Scripture and Its Methods* (Boston, MA: Walter de Gruyter, 2019). For help with the Hebrew and guidance concerning *qere-ketiv*, my thanks to Rabbi Becky Silverstein.

50. Megilla 25b.15. "The Sages taught in a *baraita*: All of the verses that are written in the Torah in a coarse manner are read in a refined manner. For example, the term 'shall lie with her [*yishgalena*]' (Deuteronomy 28:30) is read as though it said *yishkavena*, which is a more refined term. The term 'with hemorrhoids [*bafolim*]' (Deuteronomy 28:27) is read *bateḥorim*. The term 'doves' dung [*ḥiryonim*]' (II Kings 6:25) is read *divyonim*. The phrase 'to eat their own excrement [*ḥoreihem*] and drink their own urine [*meimei shineihem*]' (II Kings 18:27) is read with more delicate terms: To eat their own excrement [*tzo'atam*] and drink their own urine [*meimei ragleihem*]."

51. Robert Mills, *Seeing Sodomy in the Middle Ages* (Chicago: University of Chicago Press, 2015), 70, 73.

52. J. Compton Burnett, *The Medicinal Treatment of Diseases of the Veins* (London: Homeopathic Publishing Company, 1881), 134.

53. Mitchell Hart, "'They Dedicated Themselves to the Abominable Idol': Ancient Hebrew Sexuality and Modern Medical Diagnosis," *Jewish Social Studies* 21, no. 3 (Spring/Summer 2016): 72–90, at 78.

54. John Milton, "On the Morning of Christ's Nativity," in *John Milton: Complete Poems and Major Prose*, ed. Merritt Y. Hughes (Upper Saddle River, NJ: Prentice Hall, 1957), 199.

55. Sharon Achinstein, "Milton's Political Ontology of the Human," *ELH* 84, no. 3 (Fall 2017): 591–616, at 592.

56. John Baret, *An Aluearie, or, Triple Dictionary in Englishe, Latin, and French* (London: Henry Denham, 1574), B719.

57. Urvashi Chakravarty, "Race, Labour, and the Future of the Past: *King Lear*'s 'True Blank,'" *postmedieval* 11, nos. 2–3 (2020): 204–11, at 206. For the complex interplay between the technologies of writing and racialization, see especially Miles P. Grier, "Inkface: The Slave Stigma in England's Early Imperial Imagination," in *Scripturalizing the Human: The Written as the Political*, ed. Vincent L. Wimbush (New York: Routledge, 2015), 193–220. On the connection between "blanks" and the material history of the book, see Peter Stallybrass, "'Little Jobs': Broadsides and the Printing Revolution," in *Agent of Change: Print Culture Studies after Elizabeth L. Eisenstein*, eds. Sabrina Alcorn Baron, Eric N. Lindquist, and Eleanor F. Shevlin (Amherst: University of Massachusetts Press, 2007), 315–41; and Derek Dunne, "Filling in the Blanks in Early Modern Drama," *Huntington Library Quarterly* 85, no. 2 (Summer 2022): 259–87.

58. Imtiaz Habib, *Black Lives in the English Archives, 1500–1677: Imprints of the Invisible* (New York: Routledge, 2008), 60.

59. On idolatry and armor, see Nicolette Zeeman, "Theory Transposed: Idols, Knights and Identity," in *What Is an Image in Medieval and Early Modern England?*, eds. Antoinina Bevan Zlatar and Olga Timofeeva (Tubingen: Naar Francke Attempto Verlag, 2017), 39–80.

60. On artifice and idolatry within a framework of media studies that is altogether aligned with the account of prosthesis at work here, see Jennifer Waldron, "Dead Likenesses and Sex Machines: Shakespearean Media Theory," in *The Oxford Handbook of*

*Shakespeare and Embodiment: Gender, Sexuality, and Race*, ed. Valerie Traub (Oxford: Oxford University Press, 2016), 611–27.

61. Richard Godden, "Prosthetic Ecologies: Vulnerable Bodies and the Dismodern Subject in *Sir Gawain and the Green Knight*," *Textual Practice* 30, no. 7 (2016): 1273–90, at 1274.

62. Jeremy J. Citrome, "Bodies that Splatter: Surgery, Chivalry, and the Body in the Practica of John Arderne," *Exemplaria* 13, no. 1 (2001): 137–72.

63. Gordon Teskey, *Delirious Milton: The Fate of the Poet in Modernity* (Cambridge, MA: Harvard University Press, 2009), 195. Jonathan Goldberg discusses Miltonists' collective discomfort with these falling foreskins and the temptation to retreat to figurality in "Samson Uncircumcised," in *Political Theology and Early Modernity*, eds. Graham Hammill and Julia Reinhard Lupton (Chicago: University of Chicago Press, 2012), 282–98.

64. Michael Lieb, "'A Thousand Fore-Skins': Circumcision, Violence, and Selfhood in Milton," *Milton Studies* 38 (2000): 198–219, at 210.

65. "And Saul said, This wise shal ye say to Dauid, The king desireth no dowrie, but an hu[n]dreth foreskinnes of the Philistims, to be auenged of the Kings enemies: for Saul thoght to make Dauid fall into the hands of the Philistims . . . Afterwarde Dauid arose with his men, and went and slewe of the Philistims two hundreth men: and David broght their foreskinnes, and the gaue them wholy to the King that he might be the Kings sonne in lawe: therefore Saul gaue him Michal his daughter to wife. Then Saul sawe, & vnderstode that the Lord *was* with Dauid." (1 Sam. 18:25–28)

66. In the Trinity College manuscript, Milton listed Dinah as a possible subject for a tragedy, along with "Sodom," going so far as to draw up a *dramatis personae*. On this manuscript, see William Poole, "Milton, Dinah, and Theodotus," *Milton Quarterly* 47, no. 2 (May 2013): 65–71. Recently, Alex Lewis has ingeniously argued that Milton did in fact retell the Dinah story in *A Mask Presented at Ludlow Castle*, "Comus in Canaan: Milton's Masque and the Rape of Dinah," *Milton Studies* 63, no. 2 (2021): 157–87.

67. What exactly is meant by "defiling" has been the matter of considerable debate: it might mean rape, or it might refer to an exogamous sexual encounter. On the question of consent in the Dinah narrative, see especially Lyn M. Bechtel, "What if Dinah Is Not Raped? (Genesis 34)," *Journal for the Study of the Old Testament* 19, no. 62 (1994): 19–36.

68. Calvin also understands the passage as a warning against intermarriage, since "at this day also, our baptisme doth separate us from unbeleeuers, insomuch that he bringeth shame and reproche to him selfe, which ioyneth with them." See *A Commentarie of Iohn Caluine, vpon the First Booke of Moses called Genesis* (London: [By Henry Middleton] for Iohn Harison and George Bishop, 1578), 698.

69. Julia Reinhard Lupton, *Citizen-Saints: Shakespeare and Political Theology* (Chicago: University of Chicago Press, 2005), 190.

70. Calvin, *Commentarie*, 697.

71. John Milton, "A Treatise on Civil Power," in *Milton: Complete Poems and Major Prose*, ed. Hughes, 845–46.

72. Goldberg, "Samson Uncircumcised," 284.

73. Stanley Fish, "Question and Answer in *Samson Agonistes*," *Critical Quarterly* 11, no. 3 (1969): 237–65, at 242.

74. Mary S. Weinkauf, "Dalila: The Worst of All Possible Wives," *Studies in English Literature, 1500–1900* 13, no. 1 (1973): 135–47, at 147. For psychoanalytic explanations of Samson's disclosure, see Jackie DiSalvo, "Intestine Thorn: Samson's Struggle with the Woman Within," in *Milton and the Idea of Woman*, ed. Julia M. Walker (Chicago: University of Illinois Press, 1988), 211–29; and John Guillory, "Dalila's House: *Samson Agonistes* and the Sexual Division of Labor," in *Rewriting the Renaissance: The Discourses of Sexual Difference in Early Modern Europe*, eds. Margaret W. Ferguson, Maureen Quilligan, and Nancy J. Vickers (Chicago: University of Chicago Press, 1986), 106–22. John Shawcross also suspects that Samson is simply oversexed, and that he "revealed his secret only for sexual intercourse"; see *The Uncertain World of* Samson Agonistes (Cambridge: D. S. Brewer, 2001), 115.

75. On Milton rehabilitating Samson's intelligence, see John Mulryan, "The Heroic Tradition of Milton's *Samson Agonistes*," *Milton Studies* 18 (1983): 217–34.

76. Andrea Long Chu, *Females: A Concern* (New York: Verso, 2019), 78.

77. Hil Malatino, *Trans Care* (Minneapolis: University of Minnesota Press, 2020), 3.

78. Malatino, *Trans Care*, 3.

79. Patricia Parker, "Barbers and Barbary: Early Modern Cultural Semantics," *Renaissance Drama* 33 (2004): 201–44; and Greta LaFleur, *The Natural History of Sexuality* (Baltimore, MD: Johns Hopkins University Press, 2018), 63–102.

80. Will Fisher, *Materializing Gender in Early Modern English Literature and Culture* (New York: Cambridge University Press, 2007), 87.

81. John Milton, "The Doctrine and Discipline of Divorce," in *Milton: Complete Poems and Major Prose*, ed. Hughes, 712.

82. Quoted in Jeffrey Shoulson, *Milton and the Rabbis: Hebraism, Hellenism, and Christianity* (New York: Columbia University Press, 2010), 254.

83. For work on care in disability studies from an explicitly queer or trans perspective, see Leah Lakshmi Piepzna-Samarasinha, *Care Work: Dreaming Disability Justice* (Vancouver: Arsenal Pulp Press, 2018); Eli Clare, *Brilliant Imperfection: Grappling with Cure* (Durham, NC: Duke University Press, 2017).

84. DiSalvo, "Intestine Thorn," 217.

85. Tobin Siebers, *Disability Theory* (Ann Arbor: University of Michigan Press, 2005), 65–66.

86. Lisa Marie Cacho addresses how racialized disability serves as a metric to determine which populations are "ineligible for personhood" (6) in "Beyond Ethical Obligation," ch. 2 of *Social Death: Racialized Rightlessness and the Criminalization of the Unprotected* (New York: New York University Press, 2012), 61–69.

87. Jennifer Terry, *Attachments to War: Biomedical Logics and Violence in Twenty-First-Century America* (Durham, NC: Duke University Press, 2017), 25.

88. Clare, *Brilliant Imperfection*, 14.

89. On the complexities of the amputee-devotee relation, see Alison Kafer, "Desire and Disgust: My Ambivalent Adventures in Devoteeism," in *Sex and Disability*, eds. Robert McRuer and Anna Mollow (Durham, NC: Duke University Press, 2012), 331–54.

90. A significant body of scholarly work reframes *Samson Agonistes* in light of September 11. See, among others, John Carey, "A Work in Praise of Terrorism? September 11 and *Samson Agonistes*," *Times Literary Supplement*, September 6, 2002, 15–16; Feisal G. Mohamed, "Confronting Religious Violence: Milton's 'Samson Agonistes,'" *PMLA* 120, no. 2 (March 2005): 327–40; and the essays collected in *Milton in the Age of Fish: Essays on Authorship, Text, and Terrorism*, eds. Michael Lieb and Albert C. Labriola (Pittsburgh, PA: Duquesne University Press, 2006).

91. On this dynamic, see, among many others, Precarity Lab, ed., *Technoprecarious* (London: Goldsmiths Press, 2020).

92. Cameron Awkward-Rich, "'She of the Pants and No Voice:' Jack Bee Garland's Disability Drag," *Transgender Studies Quarterly* 7, no. 1 (February 2020): 20–36, at 22.

93. Jean-Thomas Tremblay, "Feminist Breathing," *differences* 30, no. 3 (2019): 92–117, at 94.

94. For this line as an echo of Psalm 43, see Mary Ann Radzinowicz, *Toward* Samson Agonistes: *The Growth of Milton's Mind* (Princeton, NJ: Princeton University Press, 2015), 209.

## EPILOGUE

1. North Dakota House Bill 1476 (January 2021).

2. See, for instance, the Ninth Circuit decision *Edmo v. Corizon, Inc.*, which held that refusing to provide a prisoner with gender-affirming surgery was a violation of her Eighth Amendment protections against cruel and unusual punishment. The court cited the endorsement of transitional care by "the American Medical Association, the American Medical Student Association, the American Psychiatric Association, the American Psychological Association, the American Family Practice Association, the Endocrine Society, the National Association of Social Workers, the American Academy of Plastic Surgeons, the American College of Surgeons, Health Professionals Advancing LGBTQ Equality, the HIV Medicine Association, the Lesbian, Bisexual, Gay and Transgender Physician Assistant Caucus, and Mental Health America." *Edmo v. Corizon, Inc.*, 935 F. 3d 757 (9th Cir. 2019), 769.

3. On the transphobia of self-professed "freethinkers," see Kathryn Lofton, "The Pulpit of Performative Reason," *Transgender Studies Quarterly* 9, no. 3 (August 2022): 443–59.

4. West Virginia House Bill 2976 (2023). Notably, this bill uses language identical to the North Dakota anti-trans bill, including its definition of "secular humanism" as a "faith-based worldview."

5. Jules Gill-Peterson, "The Anti-Trans Lobby's Real Agenda," *Jewish Currents*, April 21, 2021.

6. Just this year, North Dakota has passed measures that ban trans people from using public bathrooms, showers, and changing rooms (House Bill 1473 [2023]); not one but two bills banning trans students from participating in school sports (HB 1249 and HB 1489 [2023]); two bills prohibiting name and gender marker changes on birth certificates (HB 1139 [2023] and HB 1297 [2023]); a ban on drag performance, where "drag" is defined broadly enough to include trans people simply existing in public space (HB 1333 [2023]); a bill prohibiting government entities from adopting policies that penalize

misgendering trans people, and requiring teachers to inform parents immediately if they discover that a student is trans (HB 1522 [2023]); and, most chillingly, an update to the criminal code that makes the provision of gender-affirming care to minors a felony punishable by ten years in prison.

7. On the role of Christian legal organizations in anti-trans legislation, see S. J. Crasnow, "The Legacy of 'Gender Ideology': Anti-Trans Legislation and Conservative Christianity's Ongoing Influence on US Law," *Religion and Gender* 11, no. 1 (2021): 67–71; and Hannah Dick, "Advocating for the Right: Alliance Defending Freedom and the Rhetoric of Christian Persecution," *Feminist Legal Studies* 29 (2021): 375–97.

8. After significant public protest, the title "Millstone Act" was dropped, and the revised bill (Oklahoma SB 613 [2023]) settled on defining "minor" as including only those under the age of eighteen.

9. Carl Schmitt, *The Leviathan in the State Theory of Thomas Hobbes: Meaning and Failure of a Political Symbol*, trans. George Schwab and Erna Hilfstein (Westport, CT: Greenwood Press, 1996).

10. Richard Wolin, "Carl Schmit, Political Existentialism, and the Total State," *Theory and Society* 19, no. 4 (August 1990): 389–416, at 392.

11. For a timely reconsideration of Hirschfeld and his politics, see Laurie Marhoefer's pathbreaking *Racism and the Making of Gay Rights: A Sexologist, His Student, and the Empire of Queer Love* (Toronto: University of Toronto Press, 2022). On the complex position of transition under the Nazi regime, see Zavier Nunn, "Trans Liminality and the Nazi State," *Past and Present* 260, no. 1 (2023): 123–57.

12. For a precise, measured, and devastating history of this phenomenon, see Beans Velocci, *Binary Logic: The Power of Incoherence in American Sex Science* (Durham, NC: Duke University Press, forthcoming).

# Bibliography


Achinstein, Sharon. "Milton's Political Ontology of the Human." *ELH* 84, no. 3 (Fall 2017): 591–616.

Adair, Cassius. "Licensing Citizenship: Anti-Blackness, Identification Documents, and Transgender Studies." *American Quarterly* 71, no. 2 (June 201): 569–94.

Adair, Cassius, and Aren Aizura. "'The Transgender Craze Seducing Our [Sons]'; Or, All the Trans Guys Are Just Dating Each Other." *Transgender Studies Quarterly* 9, no. 1 (2022): 44–64.

Adelman, Janet. *Blood Relations: Christian and Jew in* Merchant of Venice. Chicago: University of Chicago Press, 2008.

Agamben, Giorgio. *The Open: Man and Animal.* Translated by Kevin Attell. Stanford, CA: Stanford University Press, 2004.

Aizura, Aren Z. *Mobile Subjects: Transnational Imaginaries of Gender Reassignment.* Durham, NC: Duke University Press, 2018.

Akhimie, Patricia. "Bruised with Adversity: Reading Race in *The Comedy of Errors*." In *The Oxford Handbook of Shakespeare and Embodiment*, edited by Valerie Traub, 186–96. New York: Oxford University Press, 2016.

Akhimie, Patricia. *Shakespeare and the Cultivation of Difference: Race and Conduct in the Early Modern World.* New York: Routledge, 2018.

Almond, Philip C. *Adam and Eve in Seventeenth-Century Thought.* New York: Cambridge University Press, 1999.

Amin, Kadji. "Glands, Eugenics, and Rejuvenation in *Man into Woman*: A Biopolitical Genealogy of Transsexuality." *Transgender Studies Quarterly* 5, no. 4 (2018): 589–605.

Amin, Kadji. "Taxonomically Queer? Sexology and New Queer, Trans, and Asexual Identities." *GLQ* 29, no. 1 (2023): 91–107.

Amin, Kadji. "We Are All Nonbinary: A Brief History of Accidents." *Representations* 158, no. 1 (2022): 106–19.

Andreadis, Harriette. *Sappho in Early Modern England: Female Same-Sex Literary Erotics, 1550–1714.* Chicago: University of Chicago Press, 2001.

Arendt, Hannah. *The Human Condition.* Chicago: University of Chicago Press, 1958.

Aristotle. *Generation of Animals.* Translated by A. L. Peck. Cambridge, MA: Harvard University Press, 1942.

Aristotle. *Parts of Animals.* Translated by A. L. Peck. Cambridge, MA: Harvard University Press, 2014.

Arvas, Abdulhamit. "Early Modern Eunuchs and the Transing of Gender and Race." *Journal for Early Modern Cultural Studies* 19, no. 4 (Fall 2019): 116–36.

Ashley, Florence. *Banning Transgender Conversion Practices: A Legal and Policy Analysis*. Chicago: University of Chicago Press, 2022.

Ashley, Florence. "A Critical Commentary on 'Rapid-Onset Gender Dysphoria.'" *Sociological Review* 68, no. 4 (2020): 779–99.

Augustine. *The City of God, Books XVII-XXII.* Translated by Gerald G. Walsh, S. J., and Daniel J. Honan. Washington, DC: Catholic University of America Press, 1954.

Augustine. *On the Trinity*. Edited by Gareth B. Matthews and translated by Stephen McKenna. New York: Cambridge University Press, 2002.

Awkward-Rich, Cameron. "Bodies with New Organs: Becoming Trans, Becoming Disabled." In Jasbir Puar, *The Right to Maim: Debility, Capacity, Disability*, 33–62. Durham, NC: Duke University Press, 2017.

Awkward-Rich, Cameron. "'She of the Pants and No Voice': Jack Bee Garland's Disability Drag." *Transgender Studies Quarterly* 7, no. 1 (February 2020): 20–36.

Awkward-Rich, Cameron. *The Terrible We: Thinking with Trans Maladjustment*. Durham, NC: Duke University Press, 2022.

Bailey, Amanda. *Flaunting: Style and the Subversive Male Body in Renaissance England.* Toronto: University of Toronto Press, 2007.

Bailey, J. Michael, and Suzanna Diaz (pseud.). "Rapid Onset Gender Dysphoria: Parent Reports on 1655 Possible Cases." *Archives of Sexual Behavior* 52 (2023): 1031–43. (Retracted).

Bald, R. C. *John Donne: A Life*. Oxford: Clarendon Press, 1970.

Bambach, Carmen C. *Drawing and Painting in the Italian Renaissance Workshop: Theory and Practice, 1300–1600*. New York: Cambridge University Press, 1999.

Bambach, Carmen C. "Leonardo, Tagliente, and Dürer: 'La scienza del far di groppi.'" *Achademia Leonardi Vinci* 4 (1991): 72–95.

Bamforth, Stephen, ed. *Histoires prodigieuses: MS 136 Wellcome Library*. Milano: Franco Maria Ricci, 2000.

Barad, Karen. "Transmaterialities: Trans*/Matter/Realities and Queer Political Imaginings." *GLQ* 21, nos. 2–3 (June 2015): 387–422.

Baret, John. *An Aluearie, or, Triple Dictionary in Englishe, Latin, and French*. London: Henry Denham, 1574.

Barker, Roberta. "The Duchess High and Low: A Performance History of *The Duchess of Malfi*." In *The Duchess of Malfi: A Critical Guide*, edited by Christina Luckyj, 42–65. New York: Continuum Books, 2011.

Bauer, Mattias, and Angelika Zirker. "Sites of Death as Sites of Interaction in Donne and Shakespeare." In *Shakespeare and Donne: Generic Hybrids and the Cultural Imaginary*, edited by Judith H. Anderson and Jennifer C. Vaught, 17–37. New York: Fordham University Press, 2013.

Baxandall, Michael. *Painting and Experience in the Fifteenth Century: A Primer in the Social History of Pictorial Style*. 2nd ed. New York: Oxford University Press, 1972.

Bechtel, Lyn M. "What if Dinah Is Not Raped? (Genesis 34)." *Journal for the Study of the Old Testament* 19, no. 62 (1994): 19–36.

Belsey, Catherine. "Emblem and Antithesis in *The Duchess of Malfi*." *Renaissance Drama* 11 (1980): 115–34.

Benjamin, Harry. *The Transsexual Phenomenon*. New York: Ace Publishing, 1966.

Bennett, Jane. *Vibrant Matter: A Political Ecology of Things*. Durham, NC: Duke University Press, 2010.

Benvenuto, Christine. *Sex Changes: A Memoir of Marriage, Gender, and Moving On*. New York: St. Martin's Press, 2012.

Benz, Ernst. *Adam, Der Mythus vom Urmenschen*. Munchen-Planegg: Otto-Wilhelm-Barth Verlag, 1955.

Berry, Edward. *Shakespeare and the Hunt: A Cultural and Social Study*. New York: Cambridge University Press, 2001.

Berry, Thomas, and Brian Swimme. *The Universe Story: From the Primordial Flaring Forth to the Ecozoic Era—A Celebration of the Unfolding of the Cosmos*. San Francisco, CA: HarperSanFrancisco, 1992.

Betancourt, Roland. *Byzantine Intersectionality: Sexuality, Gender, and Race in the Middle Ages*. Princeton, NJ: Princeton University Press, 2020.

Bey, Marquis. "Black Fugitivity Un/Gendered." *Black Scholar* 49, no. 1 (2019): 55–62.

Bey, Marquis. *Black Trans Feminism*. Durham, NC: Duke University Press, 2022.

Biberman, Matthew. *Masculinity, Anti-Semitism and Early Modern English Literature: From the Satanic to the Effeminate Jew*. New York: Routledge, 2004.

Binda, Hilary. "'My Name Engrav'd Herein': John Donne's Sacramental Temporality." *Exemplaria* 23, no. 4 (Winter 2011): 390–414.

Blackstone, William. *Commentaries on the Laws of England*. Vol. 4. Chicago: University of Chicago Press, 1979.

Boaistuau, Pierre. *Certaine Secrete Wonders of Nature Containing a Descriptio[n] of Sundry Strange Things, Seming Monstrous*. London: Henry Bynneman, 1569.

Bodin, Jean. *On the Demon-Mania of Witches*. Translated by Randy A. Scott. Toronto: Centre for Reformation and Renaissance Studies, 2001.

Boesky, Amy. "Samson and Surrogacy." In *Milton and Gender*, edited Catherine Gimelli Martin, 153–66. New York: Cambridge University Press, 2009.

Boff, Leonardo. *Ecology and Poverty: Cry of the Earth, Cry of the Poor*. Translated by Phillip Berryman. Maryknoll, NY: Orbis Books, 1997.

Bong, Sharon A. "Not Only for the Sake of Man: Asian Feminist Theological Responses to *Laudato Si'*." In *Planetary Solidarity: Global Women's Voices on Christian Doctrine and Climate Justice*, edited by Grace Ji-Sun Kim and Hilda P. Koster, 81–96. Minneapolis, MN: Fortress Press, 2017.

Booth, Stephen, ed. *Shakespeare's Sonnets*. New Haven, CT: Yale University Press, 1977.

Borck, C. Ray. "Negligent Analogies." *Transgender Studies Quarterly* 4, nos. 3–4 (November 2017): 679–84.

Boswell, John. *Christianity, Social Tolerance, and Homosexuality: Gay People in Western Europe from the Beginning of the Christian Era to the Fourteenth Century*. Chicago: University of Chicago Press, 1980.

Boyarin, Daniel. *Carnal Israel: Reading Sex in Talmudic Culture*. Berkeley: University of California Press, 1993.

Boyd, David Lorenzo, and Ruth Mazo Karras. "The Interrogation of a Male Transvestite Prostitute in Fourteenth-Century London." *GLQ* 1 (1995): 459–65.

de Bracton, Henry. *Bracton on the Laws and Customs of England*. Translated by Samuel E. Thorne. Cambridge, MA: Belknap Press, 1968.

de Bracton, Henry. *De Legibus et Consuetudinibus Angliae*. London: Miles Flesher and Robert Young, 1640.

Braidotti, Rosi. *Metamorphoses: Towards a Materialist Theory of Becoming*. Malden, MA: Polity, 2002.

Bray, Alan. *The Friend*. Chicago: University of Chicago Press, 2003.

Bredbeck, Gregory. *Sodomy and Interpretation: Marlowe to Milton*. Ithaca, NY: Cornell University Press, 1991.

Brilmyer, S. Pearl, Filippo Trentin, and Zairong Xiang. "The Ontology of the Couple: Or, What Queer Theory Knows about Numbers." *GLQ* 25, no. 2 (2019): 223–55.

*Britton*. Vol. 1. Translated by Francis Morgan Nichols. Cambridge: Clarendon Press, 1865.

Britton, Dennis Austin. *Becoming Christian: Race, Reformation, and Early Modern English Romance*. New York: Fordham University Press, 2014.

Brown, Pamela Allen. *The Diva's Gift to the Shakespearean Stage: Agency, Theatricality, and the Innamorata*. New York: Oxford, 2021.

Brown, Peter. *The Body and Society: Men, Women, and Sexual Renunciation in Early Christianity*. New York: Columbia University Press, 1988.

Browne, Thomas. *Pseudodoxia Epidemica*. Vol. 1. Edited by Robin Robbins. New York: Oxford University Press, 1981.

Bull, Marcus. "Muslims and Jerusalem in Miracle Stories." In *The Experience of Crusading*, edited by Marcus Graham Bull, Norman Housely, P. W. Edbury, and Jonathan Phillips, 13–38. New York: Cambridge University Press, 2003.

Bulmer, James C., ed. *Shakespeare Re-Dressed: Cross-Gender Casting in Contemporary Performance*. Cranbury, NJ: Associated University Presses, 2008.

Bulwer, John. *Anthropometamorphosis: Man Transform'd, or the Artificial Changeling*. London: Printed by William Hunt, 1653.

Burns, William E. *An Age of Wonders: Prodigies, Politics and Providence in England, 1657–1727*. New York: Manchester University Press, 2002.

Burt, Richard. "When Our Lips Synch Together: The Transvestite Voice, the Virtuoso, Speed, and Pumped-Up Volume in Some Over-Heard Shakespeares." In *Unspeakable ShaXXXspeares: Queer Theory and American Kiddie Culture*, 159–202. New York: St. Martin's Press, 1998.

Burt, Stephanie. "The Body of the Poem: On Transgender Poetry." *Los Angeles Review of Books*, November 17, 2013.

Bushnell, Rebecca. *Tragedies of Tyrants: Political Thought and Theater in the English Renaissance*. Ithaca, NY: Cornell University Press, 1990.

Bychowski, Gabrielle. "On Genesis: Transgender and Sub-Creation." *Transgender Studies Quarterly* 6, no. 3 (2019): 442–47.

Bychowski, Gabrielle. "Reconstructing the Pardoner: Transgender Skin Operations in Fragment VI." In *Writing on Skin in the Age of Chaucer*, edited by Nicole Nyffenegger and Katrin Rupp, 221–50. Boston, MA: Walter de Gruyter, 2018.

Bychowski, Gabrielle. "The Transgender Turn: Eleanor Rykener Speaks Back." In *Trans Historical: Gender Plurality before the Modern*, edited by Greta LaFleur, Masha Raskolnikov, and Anna Klosowska, 95–113. Ithaca, NY: Cornell University Press, 2021.

Bynum, Caroline Walker. "The Body of Christ in the Later Middle Ages: A Reply to Leo Steinberg." *Renaissance Quarterly* 39, no. 3 (Autumn 1986): 399–439.

Bynum, Caroline Walker. *Fragmentation and Redemption: Essays on Gender and the Human Body in Medieval Religion*. New York: Zone Books, 2012.

Bynum, Caroline Walker. *Holy Feast and Holy Fast: The Religious Significance of Food to Medieval Women.* Berkeley: University of California Press, 1987.

Bynum, Caroline Walker. *Jesus as Mother: Studies in the Spirituality of the High Middle Ages.* Berkeley: University of California Press, 1982.

Bynum, Caroline Walker. *Resurrection of the Body in Western Christianity, 200–1336.* New York: Columbia University Press, 1995.

Byrne, Janet S. "Patterns by Master F." *Metropolitan Museum Journal* 14 (1979): 103–38.

Cacho, Lisa Marie. *Social Death: Racialized Rightlessness and the Criminalization of the Unprotected.* New York: New York University Press, 2012.

Cain, Tom. "John Donne and the Ideology of Colonization." *English Literary Renaissance* 31, no. 3 (2001): 440–76.

Callaghan, Dympna. *Shakespeare without Women: Representing Gender and Race on the Renaissance Stage.* New York: Routledge, 2000.

Calvert, Thomas. *The Blessed Jew of Marocco: Or, a Blackmoor Made White.* York: T. Broad, 1648.

Calvin, John. *A Commentarie of Iohn Caluine, vpon the First Booke of Moses called Genesis.* London: [By Henry Middleton] for Iohn Harison and George Bishop, 1578.

Campagna, Ryan. "White World-Making in Early Modern England: Ideological and Phenomenological Constructions of Racial Whiteness from Shakespeare to Milton." PhD diss., University of Chicago, anticipated 2024.

Canetti, Elias. *Crowds and Power.* Translated by Carol Stewart. New York: Farrar, Straus and Giroux, 1984.

Carbine, Rosemary P. "Imagining and Incarnating an Integral Ecology: A Critical Ecofeminist Public Theology." In *Planetary Solidarity: Global Women's Voices on Christian Doctrine and Climate Justice,* edited by Grace Ji-Sun Kim and Hilda P. Koster, 45–66. Minneapolis, MN: Fortress Press, 2017.

cárdenas, micha. *Poetic Operations: Trans of Color Art in Digital Media.* Durham, NC: Duke University Press, 2022.

Carey, John. *John Donne: Life, Mind, and Art.* London: Faber and Faber, 1981.

Carey, John. "A Work in Praise of Terrorism? September 11 and *Samson Agonistes.*" *Times Literary Supplement,* September 6, 2002, 15–16.

Carr, Helen. "Donne's Masculine Persuasive Force." In *Jacobean Poetry and Prose: Rhetoric, Representation and the Popular Imagination,* edited by Clive Bloom, 96–118. London: Macmillan Press, 1988.

Casey, Damien. "The Spiritual Valency of Gender in Byzantine Society." In *Questions of Gender in Byzantine Society,* edited by Bronwen Neil and Lynda Garland, 167–82. New York: Routledge, 2016.

Céard, Jean. *La nature et les prodiges: l'insolite au 16e siècle, en France.* Geneva: Droz, 1977.

Cefalu, Paul. *English Renaissance Literature and Contemporary Theory: Sublime Objects of Theology.* New York: Palgrave Macmillan, 2007.

Cefalu, Paul. *The Johannine Renaissance in Early Modern English Literature and Theology.* New York: Oxford University Press, 2017.

Chakravarty, Urvashi. *Fictions of Consent: Slavery, Servitude, and Free Service in Early Modern England.* Philadelphia: University of Pennsylvania Press, 2022.

Chakravarty, Urvashi. "Race, Labour, and the Future of the Past: *King Lear*'s 'True Blank.'" *postmedieval* 11, nos. 2–3 (2020): 204–11.

Chakravarty, Urvashi. "Race, Natality, and the Biopolitics of Early Modern Political Theology." *Journal for Early Modern Cultural Studies* 18, no. 2 (Spring 2018): 140–66.

Chalk, Brian. "Webster's 'Worthyest Monument': The Problem of Posterity in *The Duchess of Malfi*." *Studies in Philology* 108, no. 3 (Summer 2011): 379–402.

Chamberlain, John. *The Letters of John Chamberlain*. Edited by Norman Egbert McClure. Philadelphia, PA: American Philosophical Society, 1939.

Chapman, Matthieu. *Anti-Black Racism in Early Modern English Drama: The Other "Other."* New York: Routledge, 2017.

Chatterjee, Shraddha. "Transgender Shifts: Notes on Resignification of Gender and Sexuality in India." *Transgender Studies Quarterly* 5, no. 3 (August 2018): 311–20.

Chen, Jian Neo, and micha cárdenas. "Times to Come: Materializing Trans Times." *Transgender Studies Quarterly* 6, no. 4 (2019): 472–80.

Chen, Mel. *Animacies: Biopolitics, Racial Mattering, and Queer Affect*. Durham, NC: Duke University Press, 2012.

Cheney, Patrick. "Jonson's *The New Inn* and Plato's Myth of the Hermaphrodite." *Renaissance Drama* 14 (1983): 173–94.

Chess, Simone. "Male Femininity and Male-to-Female Crossdressing in Shakespeare's Plays and Poems." In *Queer Shakespeare: Desire and Sexuality*, edited by Goran Stanivukovic, 227–43. New York: Bloomsbury Arden Shakespeare, 2017.

Chess, Simone. *Male-to-Female Crossdressing in Early Modern English Literature: Gender, Performance, and Queer Relations*. New York: Routledge, 2016.

Chess, Simone. "Queer Residue: Boy Actors' Adult Careers in Early Modern England." *Journal for Early Modern Cultural Studies* 19, no. 4 (2019): 242–64.

Chess, Simone. *Shakespeare in the Trans Archives*. New York: Routledge, forthcoming.

Chess, Simone, Colby Gordon, and Will Fisher, eds. "Early Modern Trans Studies." Special issue of *Journal for Early Modern Cultural Studies* 19, no. 4 (2019).

Chu, Andrea Long. *Females: A Concern*. Brooklyn, NY: Verso, 2019.

Cipollone, Giulio. "From Intolerance to Tolerance: The Humanitarian Way, 1187–1216." In *Tolerance and Intolerance: Social Conflict in the Age of the Crusades*, edited by Michael Gervers and James M. Powell, 28–40. Syracuse, NY: Syracuse University Press, 2001.

Cirillo, A. R. "The Fair Hermaphrodite: Love-Union in the Poetry of Donne and Spenser." *Studies in English Literature* 9, no. 1 (Winter 1969): 81–95.

Citrome, Jeremy J. "Bodies that Splatter: Surgery, Chivalry, and the Body in the Practica of John Arderne." *Exemplaria* 13, no. 1 (2001): 137–72.

Clare, Eli. *Brilliant Imperfection: Grappling with Cure*. Durham, NC: Duke University Press, 2017.

Clark, Robert, and Claire Sponsler. "Queer Play: The Cultural Work of Crossdressing in Medieval Drama." *New Literary History* 28, no. 2 (Spring 1997): 319–44.

Clements, Arthur L. *Poetry of Contemplation: John Donne, George Herbert, Henry Vaughan, and the Modern Period*. Albany: State University of New York Press, 1990.

Coakley, Sarah. "The Eschatological Body: Gender, Transformation, and God." *Modern Theology* 16, no. 1 (January 2000): 61–73.

Coddon, Karin S. "*The Duchess of Malfi*: Tyranny and Spectacle in Jacobean Drama." In *Madness in Drama*, edited by James Redwell, 1–17. New York: Cambridge University Press, 1993.

Cohen, Adam. *Imbeciles: The Supreme Court, American Eugenics, and the Sterilization of Carrie Buck*. New York: Penguin Press, 2016.

Coke, Edward. *The First Part of the Institutes of the Laws of England; Or, a Commentary upon Littleton*, Vol. 1. London: Printed for J. and W. T. Clarke, 1832.

Coke, Edward. *The First Part of the Institutes of the Laws of England; Or, a Commentary upon Littleton*, Vol. 2. London: Printed for E. and R. Brooke, 1794.

Coke, Edward. *Institutes of the Laws of England*. Vol. 3. London: Printed for W. Clarke, 1809.

Cole, Bruce. *The Renaissance Artist at Work: From Pisano to Titian*. New York: Harper and Row, 1983.

Cole, Penny. "'O God, the Heathen Have Come into Your Inheritance' (Ps. 78.1): The Theme of Religious Pollution in Crusade Documents, 1095–1188." In *Crusaders and Muslims in Twelfth-Century Syria*, edited by Maya Shatzmiller, 84–111. New York: Brill, 1993.

Coman, Jonah. "Queering Christ: *Habitus* Theology as Trans-Embodied Incarnation in Late Medieval Culture." PhD diss., Glasgow School of Art, 2019. https://radar.gsa.ac.uk/7437/1/2020_Coman_Jonah_PhD.pdf.

Compton Burnett, J. *The Medicinal Treatment of Diseases of the Veins*. London: Homeopathic Publishing Company, 1881.

Cooper, Cecilio M. "Fallen: Generation, Postlapsarian Verticality + the Black Chthonic." *Rhizomes: Cultural Studies in Emerging Knowledge* 38 (2022).

Corbeill, Anthony. *Sexing the World: Grammatical Gender and Biological Sex in Ancient Rome*. Princeton, NJ: Princeton University Press, 2015.

Corbeill, Anthony. "Weeping Statues, Weeping Gods and Prodigies from Republican to Early-Christian Rome." In *Tears in the Graeco-Roman World*, edited by Thorsten Fögen, 297–310. Berlin: Walter de Gruyter, 2009.

Corthell, Ronald. *Ideology and Desire in Renaissance Poetry: The Subject of Donne*. Detroit, MI: Wayne State University Press, 1997.

Cotten, Trystan. "Surgery." *Transgender Studies Quarterly* 1, nos. 1–2 (May 2014): 205–7.

Council on Biblical Manhood and Womanhood. "Nashville Statement." Accessed November 25, 2019. https://cbmw.org/nashville-statement/.

Crasnow, S. J. "'Becoming' Bodies: Affect Theory, Transgender Jews, and the Rejection of the Coherent Subject." *CrossCurrents* 71, no. 1 (2021): 49–62.

Crasnow, S. J. "The Legacy of 'Gender Ideology': Anti-Trans Legislation and Conservative Christianity's Ongoing Influence on US Law." *Religion and Gender* 11, no. 1 (2021): 67–71.

Crasnow, S. J. "On Transition: Normative Judaism and Trans Innovation." *Journal of Contemporary Religion* 32, no. 3 (2017): 403–15.

Crawford, Julie. "The Case of Lady Anne Clifford; Or, Did Women Have a Mixed Monarchy?" *PMLA* 121, no. 5 (October 2006): 1682–89.

Crawford, Julie. *Marvelous Protestantism: Monstrous Births in Post-Reformation England*. Baltimore, MD: Johns Hopkins University Press, 2005.

Crawford, Julie. "Transubstantial Bodies in *Paradise Lost* and *Order and Disorder*." *Journal for Early Modern Cultural Studies* 19, no. 4 (Fall 2019): 75–93.

Crawford, Julie. "Women's Secretaries." In *Queer Renaissance Historiography*, edited by Vin Nardizzi, Stephen Guy-Bray, and Will Stockton, 111–34. Burlington, VT: Ashgate, 2009.

Cressy, David. "Gender Trouble and Cross-Dressing in Early Modern England." *Journal of British Studies* 35, no. 4 (1996): 438–65.

Crewe, Jonathan. "In the Field of Dreams: Transvestism in *Twelfth Night* and *The Crying Game*." *Representations* 50 (Spring 1995): 101–21.

Crofton, Henry Thomas. "The Former Costume of the Gypsies." *Romani Studies* 2 (1908): 207–31.

Cunitz, Edouard, Johann-Wilhelm Baun, and Eduard Reuss, eds. *Calvini Opera*. Vol. 41. Brunsvigae: C. A. Schwetschke, 1853.

Currah, Paisley. *Sex Is as Sex Does: Governing Transgender Identity*. New York: New York University Press, 2022.

Curran, Kevin. "What Was Personhood?" In *Renaissance Personhood: Materiality, Taxonomy, Process*, edited by Kevin Curran, 1–20. Edinburgh: Edinburgh University Press, 2020.

Dadabhoy, Ambereen. "Two Faced: The Problem of Othello's Visage." In *Othello: The State of Play*, edited by Lena Cowen Orlin, 121–47. London: Bloomsbury, 2014.

Daniel, Drew. *Joy of the Worm: Suicide and Pleasure in Early Modern English Literature*. Chicago: University of Chicago Press, 2022.

Daniel, Drew. *The Melancholy Assemblage: Affect and Epistemology in the English Renaissance*. New York: Fordham University Press, 2013.

Daniel, Drew. "A Political Necrology of God." *Journal for Early Modern Cultural Studies* 13, no. 3 (Summer 2013): 105–25.

Daston, Lorraine, and Katharine Park. "The Hermaphrodite and the Orders of Nature: Sexual Ambiguity in Early Modern France." *GLQ* 1 (1995): 419–38.

Daston, Lorraine J., and Katherine Park. *Wonders and Other Orders of Nature, 1150–1750*. New York: Zone Books, 1998.

Daube, David. *The New Testament and Rabbinic Judaism*. London: Athlone Press, 1956.

Debes, Remy, ed. *Dignity: A History*. New York: Oxford University Press, 2017.

DeVun, Leah. "The Jesus Hermaphrodite: Science and Sex Difference in Premodern Europe." *Journal of the History of Ideas* 69, no. 2 (April 2008): 193–218.

DeVun, Leah. *The Shape of Sex: Nonbinary Gender from Genesis to the Renaissance*. New York: Columbia University Press, 2021.

DeVun, Leah, and Zeb Tortorici. "Trans, Time, and History." *Transgender Studies Quarterly* 5, no. 4 (2018): 518–39.

Dick, Hannah. "Advocating for the Right: Alliance Defending Freedom and the Rhetoric of Christian Persecution." *Feminist Legal Studies* 29 (2021): 375–97.

DiGangi, Mario. *The Homoerotics of Early Modern Drama*. New York: Cambridge University Press, 1997.

DiGangi, Mario. *Sexual Types: Embodiment, Agency, and Dramatic Character from Shakespeare to Shirley*. Philadelphia: University of Pennsylvania Press, 2011.

DiPasquale, Theresa M. "From Here to Aeviternity: Donne's Atemporal Clocks." *Modern Philology* 110, no. 2 (2012): 226–52.

DiPasquale, Theresa M. *Refiguring the Sacred Feminine: The Poems of John Donne, Aemilia Lanyer, and John Milton*. Pittsburgh, PA: Duquesne University Press, 2008.

DiSalvo, Jackie. "Intestine Thorn: Samson's Struggle with the Woman Within." In *Milton and the Idea of Woman*, edited by Julia M. Walker, 211–29. Chicago: University of Illinois Press, 1988.

Docherty, Thomas. *John Donne, Undone*. New York: Routledge, 2014.

Dolan, Frances. "Taking the Pencil out of God's Hand: Art, Nature, and the Face-Painting Debate in Early Modern England." *PMLA* 108, no. 2 (March 1993): 224–39.

Dollimore, Jonathan. "Shakespeare Understudies: The Sodomite, the Prostitute, the

Transvestite and their Critics." In *Political Shakespeare: Essays in Cultural Materialism*, edited by Jonathan Dollimore and Alan Sinfield, 129–53. Ithaca, NY: Cornell University Press, 1994.

Donne, John. *John Donne: Selected Letters*. Edited by P. M. Oliver. New York: Routledge, 2002.

Donne, John. *John Donne: The Satires, Epigrams, and Verse Letters*. Edited by Wesley Milgate. Oxford: Clarendon Press, 1967.

Donne, John. *John Donne's* Devotions upon Emergent Occasions, *together with* Death's Duel. Ann Arbor: University of Michigan Press, 1959.

Dowd, Michelle M. "Delinquent Pedigrees: Revision, Lineage, and Spatial Rhetoric in *The Duchess of Malfi*." *English Literary Renaissance* 39, no. 3 (2009): 499–526.

Drew-Bear, Annette. *Painted Faces on the Renaissance Stage: The Moral Significance of Face-Painting Conventions*. Lewisburg, PA: Bucknell University Press, 1994.

Dubrow, Heather. *Echoes of Desire: English Petrarchism and Its Counterdiscourses*. Ithaca, NY: Cornell University Press, 2018.

Dunne, Derek. "Filling in the Blanks in Early Modern Drama." *Huntington Library Quarterly* 85. no. 2 (Summer 2022): 259–87.

Dunning, Benjamin H. *Specters of Paul: Sexual Difference in Early Christian Thought*. Philadelphia: University of Pennsylvania Press, 2011.

Dusinberre, Juliet. "Squeaking Cleopatras: Gender and Performance in *Antony and Cleopatra*." In *Shakespeare, Theory, and Performance*, edited by James C. Bulman, 46–67. New York: Routledge, 1996.

Dusinberre, Juliet. "Women and Boys Playing Shakespeare." In *A Feminist Companion to Shakespeare*, 2nd ed., edited by Dympna Callaghan, 269–80. Malden, MA: John Wiley and Sons, 2016.

Duval, Jacques. *Traité des hermaphrodits*. Paris: Isidore Liseux, 1880.

Easton, Martha. "The Wound of Christ, the Mouth of Hell: Appropriations and Inversions of Female Anatomy in the Later Middle Ages." In *Tributes to Jonathan J.G. Alexander: The Making and Meaning of Illuminated Medieval and Renaissance Manuscripts, Art and Architecture*, edited by Susan L'Engle and Gerald B. Guest, 395–414. London: Harvey Miller, 2006.

Eliot, T. S. "Lancelot Andrewes." In *Selected Essays*, 299–311. New York: Harcourt, Brace and World, Inc., 1964.

Elledge, C. D. *Resurrection of the Dead in Early Judaism, 200 BCE-CE 200*. New York: Oxford University Press, 2017.

Elliott, Dyan. *Fallen Bodies: Pollution, Sexuality, and Demonology in the Middle Ages*. Philadelphia: University of Pennsylvania Press, 1999.

Elliott, Dyan. "Tertullian, the Angelic Life, and the Bride of Christ." In *Gender and Christianity in Medieval Europe*, edited by Lisa M. Bitel and Felice Lifshitz, 16–33. Philadelphia: University of Pennsylvania Press, 2010.

Ellison, Treva, Kai M. Green, Matt Richardson, and C. Riley Snorton, eds. "We Got Issues: Toward a Black Trans*/Studies." *Transgender Studies Quarterly* 4, no. 2 (May 2017): 162–69.

Empson, William. "Donne the Space Man." In *William Empson: Essays on Renaissance Literature*, vol., 1, edited by John Haffenden, 78–128. New York: Cambridge University Press, 1993.

Enterline, Lynn. "'Hairy on the In-side': *The Duchess of Malfi* and the Body of Lycanthropy." *Yale Journal of Criticism* 7 (1994): 85–129.

Espinoza, Roberto Che. *Activist Theology*. Minneapolis, MN: Fortress Press, 2019.

Ettinghausen, Henry. *Noticias del siglo XVII: relaciones españolas de sucesos naturales y sobrenaturales*. Barcelona: Puvill Libros, 1995.

Eusebius. *Ecclesiastical History*. Translated by Roy J. Deferrari. Washington, DC: Catholic University of America Press, 1955.

Feder, Sam, dir. *Disclosure*. Streaming documentary. Los Gatos, CA: Netflix, 2020.

Fenton, Geoffrey. *Monophylo*. London: printed by Henry Denham for William Seres, 1572.

Ferry, Anne. *The "Inward" Language: Sonnets of Wyatt, Sidney, Shakespeare, Donne*. Chicago: University of Chicago Press, 1983.

Festa, Thomas. "The Metaphysics of Labor in John Donne's Sermon to the Virginia Company." *Studies in Philology* 106, no. 1 (2009): 76–99.

Fish, Stanley. "Masculine Persuasive Force: Donne and Verbal Power." In *Soliciting Interpretation: Literary Theory and Seventeenth-Century English Poetry*, edited by Elizabeth D. Harvey and Katharine Eisaman Maus, 223–52. Chicago: University of Chicago Press, 1990.

Fish, Stanley. "Question and Answer in *Samson Agonistes*." *Critical Quarterly* 11, no. 3 (1969): 237–65.

Fisher, Will. *Materializing Gender in Early Modern English Literature and Culture*. New York: Cambridge University Press, 2007.

Fisk, Norman M. "Gender Dysphoria Syndrome." *Western Journal of Medicine* 120, no. 5 (May 1974): 386–91.

*Fleta*. Vol. 2. Edited and translated by G. O. Sayles and H. G. Richardson. London: B. Quaritch, 1955.

Foucault, Michel. *Abnormal: Lectures at the College de France, 1974–1975*. Translated by Graham Burchell. New York: Picador, 1999.

Foucault, Michel. *The History of Sexuality: An Introduction*. Vol. 1. Translated by Robert Hurley. New York: Vintage Books, 1990.

Francis, Pope. *Amoris Laetitia: Post-Synodal Apostolic Exhortation on Love in the Family*. Vatican City: Libreria Editrice, 2016.

Francis, Pope. "Dialogo del Santo Padre con i Vescovi della Polonia." February 8, 2016. http://press.vatican.va/content/salastampa/it/bollettino/pubblico/2016/08/02/0568/01265.html#en.

Francis, Pope. *Encyclical Letter Laudato Si' of the Holy Father Francis on Care for Our Common Home*. Rome: Libreria Editrice Vaticana, 2015.

Francis, Pope. *"Male and Female He Created Them": Towards a Path of Dialogue on the Question of Gender Theory in Education*. Vatican City: Congregation for Catholic Education, 2019.

Francis, Pope. *The Name of God is Mercy*. Translated by Oonagh Stransky. New York: Random House, 2016.

Freccero, John. "Donne's 'Valediction: Forbidding Mourning.'" *ELH* 30, no. 4 (1963): 335–76.

Friedlander, Ari. "Impotence." In *Logomotives: The Words That Changed Early Modern Culture*, edited by Marjorie Rubright and Stephen Spiess. Edinburgh: Edinburgh University Press, forthcoming 2024.

Friedlander, Ari. "Introduction: Desiring History and Historicizing Desire." *Journal for Early Modern Cultural Studies* 16, no. 2 (Spring 2016): 1–20.

Friedlander, Ari. *Rogue Sexuality in Early Modern English Literature: Desire, Status, Biopolitics*. New York: Oxford University Press, 2022.

Friedman, Jerome. *The Battle of Frogs and Fairford's Flies: Miracles and the Pulp Press During the English Revolution*. Cambridge, MA: Harvard University Press, 1961.

Friedman, Jerome. "Jewish Conversion, the Spanish Pure Blood Laws and Reformation: A Revisionist View of Racial and Religious Antisemitism." *Sixteenth Century Journal* 18, no. 1 (1987): 3–30.

Friedman, John Block. *The Monstrous Races in Medieval Art and Thought*. Cambridge, MA: Harvard University Press, 1981.

Frith, Mary. *The Life and Death of Mrs. Mary Frith*. Edited by Randall S. Nakayama. New York: Garland Publishing, Inc., 1993.

Fritz, Melanie, and Nat Mulkey. "The Rise and Fall of Gender Identity Clinics in the 1960s and 1970s." *Bulletin of the American College of Surgeons*, April 1, 2021.

Fuchs, Barbara. *Exotic Nation: Maurophilia and the Construction of Early Modern Spain*. Philadelphia: University of Pennsylvania Press, 2009.

Fudge, Erica. "Learning to Laugh: Children and Being Human in Early Modern Thought." *Textual Practice* 17, no. 2 (2003): 277–94.

Fudge, Erica. *Perceiving Animals: Humans and Beasts in Early Modern English Culture*. New York: St. Martin's Press, 2000.

Fujita, Minoru, and Michael Shapiro, eds. *Transvestism and the Onnagata Traditions in Shakespeare and Kabuki*. Boston, MA: Brill, 2006.

Galarte, Francisco J. *Brown Trans Figurations: Rethinking Race, Gender, and Sexuality in Chicanx/Latinx Studies*. Austin: University of Texas Press, 2021.

Gander, Kashmira. "Academic Says Trans Women Are Parasites for 'Occupying the Bodies of the Oppressed.'" *Newsweek*, March 15, 2018.

Garber, Marjorie. "Logic of the Transvestite: *The Roaring Girl* (1608)." In *Staging the Renaissance: Reinterpretations of Elizabethan and Jacobean Drama*, edited by David Scott Kastan and Peter Stallybrass, 221–34. New York: Routledge, 1991.

Garber, Marjorie. *Vested Interests: Cross-Dressing and Cultural Anxiety*. New York: Routledge, 1992.

*Geneva Bible: A Facsimile of the 1560 Edition*. Edited by Lloyd E. Berry. Madison: University of Wisconsin Press, 1969.

Gil, Daniel Juan. *Fate of the Flesh: Secularization and Resurrection in the Seventeenth Century*. New York: Fordham University Press, 2021.

Gilbert, Ruth. *Early Modern Hermaphrodites: Sex and Other Stories*. New York: Palgrave, 2002.

Gill-Peterson, Jules. "The Anti-Trans Lobby's Real Agenda." *Jewish Currents*, April 21, 2021.

Gill-Peterson, Jules. *Histories of the Transgender Child*. Minneapolis: University of Minnesota Press, 2018.

Godden, Richard H. "Prosthetic Ecologies: Vulnerable Bodies and the Dismodern Subject in *Sir Gawain and the Green Knight*." *Textual Practice* 30, no. 7 (2016): 1273–90.

Godden, Richard H., and Asa Simon Mittman, eds. *Monstrosity, Disability, and the Posthuman in the Medieval and Early Modern World*. Cham: Palgrave Macmillan, 2019.

Goldberg, Jonathan. "Samson Uncircumcised." In *Political Theology and Early Modernity*, edited by Graham Hammill and Julia Reinhard Lupton, 282–98. Chicago: University of Chicago Press, 2012.

Goldstein Lehnert, Sandra. "Self-Knowing Parts: Materialism and Trans History." PhD diss., CUNY Graduate Center, anticipated 2026.

Goldwyn, Robert M. "History of Attempts to Form a Vagina." *Plastic and Reconstructive Surgery* 59, no. 3 (March 1977): 319–29.

Goodrich, Micah. "Maimed Limbs and Biosalvation: Rehabilitation Politics in *Piers Plowman*." In *Trans Historical: Gender Plurality before the Modern*, edited by Greta LaFleur, Masha Raskolnikov, and Anna Klosowska, 267–96. Ithaca, NY: Cornell University Press, 2021.

Goodrich, Micah. "Trans Animacies and Premodern Alchemies." In *Medieval Mobilities: Gendered Bodies, Spaces, and Movements*, edited by Basil Arnould Price, Jane Elizabeth Bonsall, and Meagan Khoury, 199–223. New York: Palgrave Macmillan, 2023.

Goodrich, Micah. "*Ycrammed Ful of Cloutes and of Bones*: Chaucer's Queer Cavities." In *Medieval Futurity: Essays for the Future of a Queer Medieval Studies*, edited by Will Rogers and Christopher Michael Roman, 153–79. Boston, MA: Walter de Gruyter, 2021.

Gordon, Colby. "Hew." In *Logomotives: The Words That Changed Early Modern Culture*, edited by Marjorie Rubright and Stephen Spiess. Edinburgh: Edinburgh University Press, forthcoming 2024.

Gordon, Colby. "'The Sign You Must Not Touch': Trans Confession and Lyric Obscurity in John Donne." *postmedieval* 11, no. 2 (2020): 195–203.

Gordon, Colby. "A Woman's Prick: Trans Technogenesis in Sonnet 20." In *Shakespeare/Sex*, edited by Jennifer Drouin, 268–89. New York: Bloomsbury Arden Shakespeare, 2020.

Gossett, Che. "We Will Not Rest in Peace: AIDS Activism, Black Radicalism, Queer and/or Trans Resistance." In *Queer Necropolitics*, edited by Jin Haritaworn, Adi Kunstman, and Silvia Posocco, 31–50. New York: Routledge, 2014.

Grant, Robert M. "The Resurrection of the Body." *Journal of Religion* 28, no. 2 (April 1948): 120–30.

Gray, Erik. "Severed Hair from Donne to Pope." *Essays in Criticism* 47 (1997): 220–39.

Green, Richard. *The Sissy Boy Syndrome: The Development of Homosexuality*. New Haven, CT: Yale University Press, 1987.

Greenblatt, Stephen. *Shakespearean Negotiations: The Circulation of Social Energy in Renaissance England*. Berkeley: University of California Press, 1988.

Gregory of Nyssa. *De hominis opificio*. In *A Select Library of Nicene and Post-Nicene Fathers of the Christian Church*, edited by Philip Schaff and Henry Wace and translated by William More and Henry Austin Wilson. New York: Christian Literature Company, 1892.

Gregory of Nyssa. "On the Soul and Resurrection." In *Saint Gregory of Nyssa: Ascetical Works*, translated by Virginia Woods Callahan, 195–274. Washington, DC: Catholic University of America Press, 1967.

Grier, Miles P. "Inkface: The Slave Stigma in England's Early Imperial Imagination." In *Scripturalizing the Human: The Written as the Political*, edited by Vincent L. Wimbush, 193–220. New York: Routledge, 2015.

Grierson, H. J. C., ed. *The Poems of John Donne*. London: Oxford University Press, 1929.

Griffin-Gracy, Miss Major. "Miss Major Griffin-Gracy, interview by A.J. Lewis." By A. J. Lewis. *New York Public Library Community Oral History Project: NYC Trans Oral*

*History Project* (December 16, 2017). https://nyctransoralhistory.org/interview/miss-major/.

Guibbory, Achsah. "'Oh, Let Mee Not Serve So': The Politics of Love in Donne's *Elegies*." *English Literary History* 57, no. 4 (1990): 811–33.

Guibbory, Achsah. *Returning to John Donne*. Burlington, VT: Ashgate, 2015.

Guillory, John. "Dalila's House: *Samson Agonistes* and the Sexual Division of Labor." In *Rewriting the Renaissance: The Discourses of Sexual Difference in Early Modern Europe*, edited by Margaret W. Ferguson, Maureen Quilligan, and Nancy J. Vickers, 106–22. Chicago: University of Chicago Press, 1986.

Gutt, Blake. "Holy Queer and Holy Cure: Sanctity, Disability, and Transgender Embodiment in *Tristan de Nanteuil*." In *Trans and Genderqueer Subjects in Medieval Hagiography*, edited by Blake Gutt and Alicia Spenser-Hall, 223–44. Amsterdam: Amsterdam University Press, 2021.

Gutt, Blake, and Alicia Spencer-Hall, eds. *Trans and Genderqueer Subjects in Medieval Hagiography*. Amsterdam: Amsterdam University Press, 2021.

Guy-Bray, Stephen. *Loving in Verse: Poetic Influence as Erotic*. Toronto: University of Toronto Press, 2006.

Haber, Judith. "'My Body Bestow upon My Women': The Space of the Feminine in 'The Duchess of Malfi,'" *Renaissance Drama* 28 (1997): 133–59.

Habib, Imtiaz. *Black Lives in the English Archives, 1500–1677: Imprints of the Invisible*. New York: Routledge, 2008.

Haimson, Oliver L., Avery Dame-Griff, Elias Capello, and Zahari Richter. "Tumblr Was a Trans Technology: The Meaning, Importance, History, and Future of Trans Technologies." *Feminist Media Studies* 21, no. 3 (2019): 345–61.

Halberstam, Jack. *In a Queer Time and Place: Transgender Bodies, Subcultural Lives*. New York: New York University Press, 2005.

Hall, Kim F. "'These Bastard Signs of Fair': Literary Whiteness in Shakespeare's Sonnets." In *Post-Colonial Shakespeares*, edited by Ania Loomba and Martin Orkin, 64–83. New York: Routledge, 1998.

Hall, Kim F. *Things of Darkness: Economies of Race and Gender in Early Modern England*. Ithaca, NY: Cornell University Press, 2018.

Hall, Marcia B. *The Power of Color: Five Centuries of European Painting*. New Haven, CT: Yale University Press, 2019.

Halley, Janet E. "Textual Intercourse: Anne Donne, John Donne, and the Sexual Poetics of Textual Exchange." In *Seeking the Woman in Late Medieval and Renaissance Writings: Essays in Feminist Contextual Criticism*, edited by Sheila Fisher and Janet E. Halley, 187–206. Knoxville: University of Tennessee Press, 1989.

Halpern, Richard. *Shakespeare's Perfume: Sodomy and Sublimity in the Sonnets, Wilde, Freud, and Lacan*. Philadelphia: University of Pennsylvania Press, 2002.

Hamilton, Alastair. *The Apocryphal Apocalypse: The Reception of the Second Book of Esdras (4 Ezra) from the Renaissance to the Enlightenment*. New York: Oxford University Press, 1999.

Hamlin, Kimberly A. "The 'Case of a Bearded Woman': Hypertrichosis and the Construction of Gender in the Age of Darwin." *American Quarterly* 63, no. 4 (2011): 955–81.

Hammill, Graham. "Epilogue: The Solecism of Power." *Studies in English Literature, 1500–1900* 58, no. 1 (Winter 2018): 193–204.

Hammill, Graham. *The Mosaic Constitution: Political Theology and Imagination from Machiavelli to Milton*. Chicago: University of Chicago Press, 2011.

Hand, Molly. "Animality, Disability, and the Drama of Early Modern Witchcraft." In *Early Modern Witch Plays: A Critical Reader*, edited by Eric Pudney. London: Arden, forthcoming 2024.

Hansen, Mark. "Media Theory." *Theory, Culture and Society* 23, nos. 2–3 (2006): 297–306.

Hardwick, Charles. *A History of the Articles of Religion*. London: George Bell, 1876.

Harpster, Grace. "The Color of Salvation: The Materiality of Blackness in Alonso de Sandoval's *De insauranda Aethiopum salute*." In *Envisioning Others: Race, Color, and the Visual in Iberia and Latin America*, edited by Pamela A. Patton, 104–10. Boston, MA: Brill, 2016.

Harrison, Timothy. "Adamic Awakening and the Feeling of Being Alive in *Paradise Lost*." *Milton Studies* 54 (2013): 29–57.

Harrison, Timothy. "John Donne, the Instant of Change, and the Time of the Body." *ELH* 85, no. 4 (Winter 2018): 909–39.

Hart, Mitchell. "'They Dedicated Themselves to the Abominable Idol': Ancient Hebrew Sexuality and Modern Medical Diagnosis." *Jewish Social Studies* 21, no. 3 (Spring/Summer 2016): 72–90.

Hartwig, Joan. "Horses and Women in 'The Taming of the Shrew.'" *Huntington Library Quarterly* 45, no. 4 (Autumn 1982): 285–94.

Harvey, Elizabeth D. "Flesh Colors and Shakespeare's Sonnets." In *A Companion to Shakespeare's Sonnets*, ed. Michael Schoenfeldt, 314–28. Malden, MA: Blackwell Publishing, 2007.

Harvey, Elizabeth D. *Ventriloquized Voices: Feminist Theory and English Renaissance Texts*. New York: Routledge, 1992.

Hawkins, William. *Treatise of the Pleas of the Crown*. Vol. 1. Edited by John Curwood. London: Printed for S. Sweet, 1824.

Hayles, N. Katherine. *How We Think: Digital Media and Technogenesis*. Chicago: University of Chicago Press, 2012.

Hayward, Eva. "Lessons from a Starfish." In *Queering the Non-Human*, edited by Noreen Giffney and Myra J. Hird (Burlington, VT: Ashgate, 2008): 249–64.

Hayward, Eva, and Jami Weinstein. "Tranimalities in the Age of Trans* Life." *Transgender Studies Quarterly* 2, no. 2 (May 2015): 195–208.

Heaney, Emma, ed. *Feminism against Cisness*. Durham, NC: Duke University Press, forthcoming 2024.

Heng, Geraldine. *The Invention of Race in the European Middle Ages*. New York: Cambridge University Press, 2018.

Hentschell, Roze. "Treasonous Textiles: Foreign Cloth and the Construction of Englishness." *Journal of Medieval and Early Modern Studies* 32, no. 3 (Fall 2002): 543–70.

Herbert, George. *George Herbert: The Complete English Poems*. Edited by John Tobin. New York: Penguin, 1991.

Herbert, George. *The Latin Poems of George Herbert*. Translated by Mark McCloskey and Paul R. Murphy. Athens: Ohio University Press, 1965.

Herzig, Tamar. *Christ Transformed into a Virgin Woman: Lucia Brocadelli, Heinrich Institoris, and the Defense of the Faith*. Rome: Edizioni di Storia e Letteratura, 2013.

Herzig, Tamar. "Genuine and Fraudulent Stigmatics in the Sixteenth Century." In *Dissimulation and Deceit in Early Modern Europe*, eds. Miriam Eliav-Feldon and Tamar Herzig, 142–64. New York: Palgrave Macmillan, 2015.

Hester, M. Thomas. "Donne's (Re)Annunciation of the Virgin(ia Colony) in 'Elegy XIX.'" *South Central Review* 4, no. 2 (Summer 1987): 49–64.

Hirsch, Brett D. "Lycanthropy in Early Modern England: The Case of John Webster's *The Duchess of Malfi*." In *Diseases of the Imagination and Imaginary Disease in the Early Modern Period*, edited by Yasmin Haskell, 301–40. Turnhout: Brepols Publishers, 2011.

Hirsch, Brett D. "The Taming of the Jew: Spit and the Civilizing Process in *The Merchant of Venice*." In *Staged Transgression in Shakespeare's England*, edited by Rory Loughnane and Edel Semple, 136–52. New York: Palgrave Macmillan, 2013.

Hirschfeld, Magnus. *Transvestites: The Erotic Drive to Cross-Dress*. Translated by Michael A. Lombardi-Nash. Buffalo, NY: Prometheus Books, 1991 [1910].

Hock, Jessie. *The Erotics of Materialism: Lucretius and Early Modern Poetics*. Philadelphia: University of Pennsylvania Press, 2021.

Hodgson, Elizabeth M. A. *Gender and the Sacred Self in John Donne*. Newark: University of Delaware Press, 1999.

Holinshed, Raphaell. *Holinshed's Chronicles, England, Scotland, and Ireland*. Vol. 2. New York: Routledge, 1965.

Holsinger, Bruce. "The Color of Salvation: Desire, Death, and the Second Crusade in Bernard of Clairvaux's *Sermons on the Song of Songs*." In *The Tongue of the Fathers: Gender and Ideology in Twelfth-Century Latin*, edited by David Townsend and Andrew Taylor, 156–86. Philadelphia: University of Pennsylvania Press, 1998.

Homza, Lu Ann, ed. *Spanish Inquisition, 1478–1614: An Anthology of Sources*. Indianapolis, IN: Hackett Publishing Co., 2006.

Horak, Laura. "Trans on YouTube: Intimacy, Visibility, Temporality." *Transgender Studies Quarterly* 1, no. 4 (2014): 572–85.

Horbury, Ezra. "Early Modern Transgender Fairies." *Transgender Studies Quarterly* 8, no. 1 (February 2021): 75–95.

Horbury, Ezra, and Christine "Xine" Yao. "Empire and Eugenics: Trans Studies in the United Kingdom." *Transgender Studies Quarterly* 7, no. 3 (August 2020): 445–54.

Horowitz, Elliott. "The Jews and the Cross in the Middle Ages: Towards a Reappraisal." In *Philosemitism, Antisemitism, and "The Jews": Perspectives from the Middle Ages to the Twentieth Century*, edited by Tony Kushner and Nadia Valman, 114–31. Burlington, VT: Ashgate, 2004.

Howard, Jean. *The Stage and Social Struggle in Early Modern England*. New York: Routledge, 1994.

Howard, Scott (pseud.). *The Transgender Industrial Complex*. Montgomery County, PA: Antelope Hill Press, 2020.

Hutson, Lorna. "On Not Being Deceived: Rhetoric and the Body in *Twelfth Night*." *Texas Studies in Literature and Language* 38, no. 2 (Summer 1996): 140–74.

Imirizaldu, Jesús. *Monjas y Beatas Embaucadores*. Madrid: Editora Nacional, 1977.

Institoris, Heinrich. *Malleus Maleficarum*. Frankfurt am Main: apud Nicolaum Bassaeum, 1580.

Irigoyen-Garcia, Javier. *Moors Dressed as Moors: Clothing, Social Distinction and Ethnicity in Early Modern Iberia*. Toronto: University of Toronto Press, 2017.

Isidore of Seville. *The Etymologies of Isidore of Seville*. Translated by Stephen A. Barney, W. J. Lewis, J. A. Beach, and Oliver Berghof. New York: Cambridge University Press, 2009.

Jackson, Ken, and Arthur F. Marotti, "The Turn to Religion in Early Modern English Studies." *Criticism* 46, no. 1 (2004): 167–90.

Jacques-Lefevre, Nicole. "Such an Impure, Cruel, and Savage Beast . . . : Images of the Werewolf in Demonological Works." In *Werewolves, Witches, and Wandering Spirits: Traditional Belief and Folklore in Early Modern Europe*, edited by Kathryn A. Edwards, 181–97. Kirksville, MO: Truman State University Press, 2002.

Jankowski, Theodora A. "Defining/Confining the Duchess: Negotiating the Female Body in John Webster's 'The Duchess of Malfi.'" *Studies in Philology* 87, no. 2 (Spring 1990): 221–45.

Jardine, Lisa. "Boy Actors, Female Roles, and Elizabethan Eroticism." In *Staging the Renaissance: Reinterpretations of Elizabethan and Jacobean Drama*, edited by David Scott Kastan and Peter Stallybrass, 57–67. New York: Routledge, 1991.

Jardine, Lisa. *Reading Shakespeare Historically*. New York: Routledge, 1996.

Jardine, Lisa. *Still Harping on Daughters: Women and Drama in the Age of Shakespeare*. Brighton: Harvester Press Ltd., 1983.

Jeffreys, Sheila. *Gender Hurts: A Feminist Analysis of the Politics of Transgenderism*. New York: Routledge, 2014.

Jones, Ann Rosalind, and Peter Stallybrass. *Renaissance Clothing and the Materials of Memory*. New York: Cambridge University Press, 2000.

Jonson, Ben. *The New Inne. Or, The Light Heart*. London: printed by Thomas Harper for Thomas Alchorne, 1631.

Jorgensen, Christine. *Christine Jorgensen: A Personal Autobiography*. New York: Bantam Books, 1967.

Josephus. *Jewish Antiquities*. Vol. 2. Translated by H. Thackeray and Ralph Marcus. Cambridge, MA: Harvard University Press, 1998.

Joynt, Chase, and Kristen Schilt, dirs. *Framing Agnes*. New York: Kino Lorber, 2023.

Kafer, Alison. "Desire and Disgust: My Ambivalent Adventures in Devoteeism." In *Sex and Disability*, edited by Robert McRuer and Anna Mollow, 331–54. Durham, NC: Duke University Press, 2012.

Kahn, Victoria. *The Future of Illusion: Political Theology and Early Modern Texts*. Chicago: University of Chicago Press, 2014.

Kaplan, M. Lindsay. "Jessica's Mother: Medieval Constructions of Jewish Race and Gender in 'The Merchant of Venice.'" *Shakespeare Quarterly* 58, no. 1 (2007): 1–30.

Karant-Nunn, Susan C. "'Fragrant Wedding Roses': Lutheran Wedding Sermons and Gender Definition in Early Modern Germany." *German History* 17, no. 1 (1999): 25–40.

Karim-Cooper, Farah. *Cosmetics in Shakespearean and Renaissance Drama*. Edinburgh: Edinburgh University Press, 2006.

Keegan, Cáel M. "On the Necessity of Bad Trans Objects." *Film Quarterly* 75, no. 3 (2022): 26–37.

Kemp, Sawyer. "'In That Dimension Grossly Clad': Transgender Rhetoric, Representation, and Shakespeare." *Shakespeare Studies* 47 (2019): 120–27.

Kemp, Sawyer. "Two Othellos: Transitioning Anti-Blackness: A Dialogue with Skyler Cooper." *Shakespeare Bulletin* 39, no. 4 (2021): 651–65.

Keown, John. *Abortion, Doctors and the Law: Some Aspects of the Legal Regulation of Abortion in England from 1803–1982*. New York: Cambridge University Press, 1988.

Kesson, Andy. "Trying Television by Candlelight: Shakespeare's Globe's The Duchess of Malfi on BBC4." *Shakespeare Bulletin* 33, no. 4 (Winter 2015): 609–21.

Kier, Bailey. "Interdependent Ecological Transsex: Notes on Re/Production, 'Transgender' Fish, and the Management of Populations, Species, and Resources." *Women and Performance* 20, no. 3 (2010): 299–319.

Kingsbury, Susan Myra, ed. *The Records of the Virginia Company*. Vol. 3. Washington, DC: Government Printing Office, 1933.

Kitzes, Adam H. "Paradoxical Donne: *Biathanatos* and the Problems with Political Assimilation." *Prose Studies* 24, no. 3 (2001): 1–17.

Klawitter, George. *Andrew Marvell, Sexual Orientation, and Seventeenth-Century Poetry*. Madison, WI: Fairleigh Dickinson University Press, 2017.

Klawitter, George. "Verse Letters to TW from John Donne." *Journal of Homosexuality* 23, nos. 1–2 (1992): 85–102.

Kline, Wendy. *Building a Better Race: Gender, Sexuality, and Eugenics from the Turn of the Century to the Baby Boom*. Berkeley: University of California Press, 2001.

Kneidel, Gregory. *Rethinking the Turn to Religion in Early Modern English Literature: The Poetics of All Believers*. New York: Palgrave Macmillan, 2008.

Koch-Rein, Anson. "Trans-lating the Monster: Transgender Affect and Frankenstein." *Lit: Literature Interpretation Theory* 30, no. 1 (2019): 44–61.

Korda, Natasha. *Labors Lost: Women's Work and the Early Modern English Stage*. Philadelphia: University of Pennsylvania Press, 2011.

Korda, Natasha. *Shakespeare's Domestic Economies: Gender and Property in Early Modern England*. Philadelphia: University of Pennsylvania Press, 2002.

Kuchar, Gary. "Embodiment and Representation in John Donne's *Devotions upon Emergent Occasions*." *Prose Studies* 24, no. 2 (2001): 15–40.

Kunin, Aaron. *Love Three*. Seattle, WA: Wave Books, 2019.

Kunin, Aaron. "Shakespeare's Preservation Fantasy." *PMLA* 124, no. 1 (January 2009): 92–106.

Kunzel, Regina. "The Flourishing of Transgender Studies." *Transgender Studies Quarterly* 1, nos. 1–2 (May 2014): 285–97.

Kvam, Kristen, Linda Schearing, and Valarie Ziegler, eds. *Eve and Adam: Jewish, Christian, and Muslim Readings on Genesis and Gender*. Bloomington: Indiana University Press, 1999.

Ladin, Joy. *The Soul of the Stranger: Reading God and Torah from a Transgender Perspective*. Waltham, MA: Brandeis Press, 2019.

LaFleur, Greta. *The Natural History of Sexuality in Early America*. Baltimore, MD: Johns Hopkins University Press, 2018.

LaFleur, Greta. "Trans Feminine Histories, Trans Feminist Historiographies." Forthcoming in *Feminism against Cisness*, ed. Emma Heaney (Durham, NC: Duke University Press, 2024).

LaFleur, Greta, and Serena Bassi, eds. "Trans-Exclusionary Feminisms and the Global New Right." Special issue of *Transgender Studies Quarterly* 9, no. 3 (2022).

LaFleur, Greta, Masha Raskolnikov, and Anna Klosowska, eds. *Trans Historical: Gender Plurality before the Modern*. Ithaca, NY: Cornell University Press, 2021.

Lamb, W. R. M., ed. and trans. *Lysis, Symposium, Gorgias*. Cambridge, MA: Harvard University Press, 1925.

Lambert, Erin. "The Reformation and the Resurrection of the Dead." *Sixteenth Century Journal* 47, no. 2 (Summer 2016): 351–70.

Laqueur, Thomas. *Making Sex: Body and Gender from the Greeks to Freud*. Cambridge, MA: Harvard University Press, 1990.

Larson, Scott. "'Indescribable Being': Theological Performances of Genderlessness in the Society of the Publick Universal Friend, 1776–1819." *Early American Studies* 12, no. 3 (Fall 2014): 576–600.

Lavery, Daniel M. *Something That May Shock and Discredit You*. New York: Simon and Schuster, Inc., 2020.

Lavery, Grace. "Egg Theory's Early Style." *Transgender Studies Quarterly* 7, no. 3 (August 2020): 383–98.

Lavery, Grace. "The King's Two Anuses: Trans Feminism and Free Speech." *differences* 30, no. 3 (2019): 119–51.

Lavery, Grace. *Pleasure and Efficacy: Of Pen Names, Cover Versions, and Other Trans Techniques*. Princeton, NJ: Princeton University Press, 2023.

Lawee, Eric. "The Reception of Rashi's 'Commentary on the Torah' in Spain: The Case of Adam's Mating with the Animals." *Jewish Quarterly Review* 97, no. 1 (Winter 2007): 33–66.

Levine, Laura. *Men in Women's Clothing: Anti-Theatricality and Effeminization, 1579–1642*. New York: Cambridge University Press, 1994.

Lewis, Alex. "Comus in Canaan: Milton's Masque and the Rape of Dinah." *Milton Studies* 63, no. 2 (2021): 157–87.

Lewis, C. S. *A Preface to Paradise Lost*. New York: Oxford University Press, 1961.

Lezra, Jacques. *Wild Materialism: The Ethic of Terror and the Modern Republic*. New York: Fordham University Press, 2010.

Lieb, Michael. "'A Thousand Fore-Skins': Circumcision, Violence, and Selfhood in Milton." *Milton Studies* 38 (2000): 198–219.

Lieb, Michael, and Albert C. Labriola. *Milton in the Age of Fish: Essays on Authorship, Text, and Terrorism*. Pittsburgh, PA: Duquesne University Press, 2006.

Light, Ellis Amity. "Fluxing Fellowship: Bodily Fluids and Forms of Community in Medieval Devotional Literature." PhD diss., Fordham University, 2023. https://media.proquest.com/media/hms/PFT/2/reNdR?_s=E%2Frpp1KwXx67qQxPkq%2B2GA%2BTR2g%3D.

Light, Ellis Amity. "Trans Activisms and Interspecies Entanglement in the Middle English *Patience*," forthcoming in the "Trans Natures" special issue of *Medieval Ecocriticisms*, edited by Aylin Malcolm and Nat Rivkin (2024).

Lim, Walter S. H. "John Milton, Orientalism, and the Empires of the East in Paradise Lost." In *The English Renaissance, Orientalism, and the Idea of Asia*, edited Debra Johanyak and Walter S. H. Lim, 203–37. New York: Palgrave Macmillan, 2010.

Littman, Lisa. "Parent Reports of Adolescents and Young People Perceived to Show Signs of a Rapid Onset of Gender Dysphoria." *PLOS ONE* 13, no. 8 (2018). (Retracted).

Lochrie, Karma. "Mystical Acts, Queer Tendencies." In *Constructing Medieval Sexuality*, edited by Karma Lochrie, Peggy McCracken, and James A. Schultz, 180–200. Minneapolis: University of Minnesota Press, 1997.

Lodine-Chaffey, Jennifer. "'Beyond Death': John Webster's *The Duchess of Malfi* and Posthumous Influence." *Ben Jonson Journal* 26, no. 1 (2019): 113–32.

Loftis, Sonya Freeman. "Lycanthropy and Lunacy: Cognitive Disability in *The Duchess* of Malfi." In *Monstrosity, Disability, and the Posthuman in the Medieval and Early Modern World*, edited by Richard H. Godden and Asa Simon Mittman, 209–25. Cham: Palgrave Macmillan, 2019.

Lofton, Kathryn. "The Pulpit of Performative Reason." *Transgender Studies Quarterly* 9, no. 3 (August 2022): 443–59.

Long, Kathleen. *Hermaphrodites in Renaissance Europe*. Burlington, VT: Ashgate, 2006.

Love, Heather. *Underdogs: Social Deviance and Queer Theory*. Chicago: University of Chicago Press, 2021.

Ludlow, Morwenna. *Gregory of Nyssa, Ancient and (Post)modern*. New York: Oxford University Press, 2007.

Lupton, Julia Reinhard. *Citizen-Saints: Shakespeare and Political Theology*. Chicago: University of Chicago Press, 2005.

Lupton, Julia Reinhard. "Creature Caliban." *Shakespeare Quarterly* 51, no. 1 (April 2000): 1–23.

Lupton, Julia Reinhard. *Shakespeare Dwelling: Designs for the Theater of Life*. Chicago: University of Chicago Press, 2018.

Lupton, Julia Reinhard. *Thinking with Shakespeare: Essays on Politics and Life*. Chicago: University of Chicago Press, 2011.

Lupton, Julia Reinhard, and Graham Hammill, eds. *Political Theology and Early Modernity*. Chicago: University of Chicago Press, 2012.

Luther, Martin. "Explanation of the Ninety-Five Theses." In *Luther's Works*, vol. 31. Translated by Harold J. Grimm and Helmut T. Lehmann, 79–252. Philadelphia, PA: Muhlenberg Press and Fortress Press, 1957.

Luu, Lien Bich. *Immigrants and the Industries of London, 1500–1700*. New York: Routledge, 2005.

Lykosthenes, Konrad. *The Doome Warning All Men to the Iudgemente wherein Are Contained for the Most Parte all the Straunge Prodigies Hapned in the Worlde*. London: Ralphe Nubery, 1581.

MacBain, Bruce. *Prodigy and Expiation: A Study in Religion and Politics in Republican Rome*. Bruxelles: Latomus, 1982.

MacDonald, Dennis. "Corinthian Veils and Gnostic Androgynes." In *The Image of the Feminine in Gnosticism*, edited by Karen L. King, 276–92. Harrisburg, PA: Trinity Press, 1988.

MacDonald, Dennis. *There Is No Male and Female: The Fate of a Dominical Saying in Paul*. Philadelphia, PA: Fortress Press, 1987.

Maeir, Aren. "A New Interpretation of the Term *'opalim* (עפלים) in the Light of Recent Archaeological Finds from Philistia." *Journal for the Study of the Old Testament* 32, no. 1 (2007): 23–40.

Maitland, F. W. "The Deacon and the Jewess; Or, Apostasy at Common Law." *Law Quarterly Review* 2, no. 2 (1886): 153–65.

Malatino, Hil. "Future Fatigue: Trans Intimacies and Trans Presents (or How to Survive the Interregnum)." *Transgender Studies Quarterly* 6, no. 4 (2019): 635–58.

Malatino, Hil. *Queer Embodiment: Monstrosity, Medical Violence, and Intersex Experience*. Lincoln: University of Nebraska Press, 2019.

Malatino, Hil. *Trans Care*. Minneapolis: University of Minnesota Press, 2020.

Marchal, Joseph A. *Appalling Bodies: Queer Figures before and after Paul's Letters*. New York: Oxford University Press, 2020.

Marchiano, Lisa. "Outbreak: On Transgender Teens and Psychic Epidemics." *Psychological Perspectives: A Quarterly Journal of Jungian Thought* 60, no. 3 (2017): 345–66.

Marhoefer, Laurie. *Racism and the Making of Gay Rights: A Sexologist, His Student, and the Empire of Queer Love*. Toronto: University of Toronto Press, 2022.

Marotti, Arthur. *John Donne, Coterie Poet*. Eugene, OR: Wipf and Stock Publishers, 1986.

Matar, Nabil I. *Islam in Britain, 1558–1685*. New York: Cambridge University Press, 1998.

Matar, Nabil I. *Turks, Moors, and Englishmen in the Age of Discovery*. New York: Columbia University Press, 1999.

Matthew of Paris. *Chronica Majora*. Edited by Henry Richards Luard. London: Longman and Co., 1876.

Matthew of Paris. *Historia Anglorum*. Edited by Frederic Madden. London: Longmans, Green, Reader, and Dyer, 1866.

Maus, Katharine Eisaman. *Inwardness and Theater in the English Renaissance*. Chicago: University of Chicago Press, 1995.

Maxwell, Lynn. "Wax Magic and *The Duchess of Malfi*." *Journal for Early Modern Cultural Studies* 14, no. 3 (Summer 2014): 31–54.

McLuskie, Kathleen. "The Act, the Role, and the Actor: Boy Actresses on the Elizabethan Stage." *New Theatre Quarterly* 3, no. 10 (1987): 120–30.

McManus, Clare. *Women on the Renaissance Stage: Anna of Denmark and Female Masquing in the Stuart Court (1590–1619)*. New York: Manchester University Press, 2002.

Meeks, Wayne. "The Image of the Androgyne: Some Uses of a Symbol in Earliest Christianity." *History of Religions* 13, no. 3 (February 1974): 165–208.

Mehdizadeh, Nedda. "The Petrification of Rostam: Thomas Herbert's Revision of Persia in *A Relation of Some Yeares Travaile*." In *Remapping Travel Narratives, 1000–1700: To the East and Back Again*, edited by Montserrat Piera, 111–28. Leeds: Arc Humanities Press, 2018.

Melanchthon, Philipp, and Martin Luther. *Of Two Woonderful Popish Monsters to Wyt, of a Popish Asse Which Was Found at Rome in the Riuer of Tyber, and of a Monkish Calfe, Calued at Friberge in Misne*. Translated by John Brooke. London: Thomas East, 1579.

Merlet, Janine. *Venus et Mercure*. Paris: Editions de la Vie Moderne, 1931.

Merlin, Virginie. "L'homme qui change le sexe." *Paris Match* 1300 (April 1974): 37–39.

Metzler, Irina. *Disability in Medieval Europe: Thinking about Physical Impairment during the High Middle Ages*. New York: Routledge, 2006.

Meyerowitz, Joanne. *How Sex Changed: A History of Transsexuality in the United States*. Cambridge, MA: Harvard University Press, 2002.

Mikesell, Margaret Lael. "Catholic and Protestant Widows in *The Duchess of Malfi*." *Renaissance and Reformation* 7, no. 4 (November 1983): 265–79.

Miller, Justin, and Gordon Dean. "Liability of Physicians for Sterilization Operations." *American Bar Association Journal* 16, no. 3 (March 1930): 158–61.

Miller, Nichole E. *Violence and Grace: Exceptional Life between Shakespeare and Modernity*. Evanston, IL: Northwestern University Press, 2014.

Mills, Robert. *Seeing Sodomy in the Middle Ages*. Chicago: University of Chicago Press, 2015.

Milton, John. *The Complete Poetry and Essential Prose of John Milton*. Edited by William Kerrigan, John Rumrich, and Stephen M. Fallon. New York: Modern Library, 2007.

Milton, John. *John Milton: Complete Poems and Major Prose*. Edited by Merritt Y. Hughes. Upper Saddle River, NJ: Prentice Hall, 1957.

Milton, John. "Tetrachordon." In *The Divorce Tracts of John Milton*, edited by Sara J. van den Berg and Howard Scott, 239–360. Pittsburgh, PA: Duquesne University Press, 2010.

Minty, Leonard le Marchant. "Unlawful Wounding; Will Consent Make It Legal?" *Medico-Legal Journal* 24, no. 2 (1956): 54–62.

Miranda, Deborah. "Extermination of the Joyas: Gendercide in Spanish California." *GLQ* 16, no. 102 (2010): 253–84.

Mitchell, Dianne. "John Donne's Poetics of Mediation." *Journal for Early Modern Cultural Studies* 18, no. 4 (Fall 2018): 73–99.

Mohamed, Feisal G. "Confronting Religious Violence: Milton's 'Samson Agonistes.'" *PMLA* 120, no. 2 (March 2005): 327–40.

Morris, Jan. *Conundrum*. London: Faber, 1974.

Moulton, Ian. *Before Pornography: Erotic Writing in Early Modern England*. New York: Oxford University Press, 2000.

Mueller, Janel. "'This Dialogue of One': A Feminist Reading of Donne's 'Exstasie.'" *ADE Bulletin* 81 (Fall 1985): 39–42.

Mueller, Janel. "Women among the Metaphysicals: A Case, Mostly, of Being Donne For." *Modern Philology* 87, no. 2 (November 1989): 142–58.

Muessig, Carolyn. *The Stigmata in Medieval and Early Modern Europe*. New York: Oxford University Press, 2020.

Mulryan, John. "The Heroic Tradition of Milton's *Samson Agonistes*." Milton Studies 18 (1983): 217–34.

Namaste, Viviane. *Invisible Lives: The Erasure of Transsexual and Transgendered People*. Chicago: University of Chicago Press, 2000.

Nardizzi, Vin. "Shakespeare's Trans*plant* Poetics: Vegetable Blazons and the Seasons of Pyramus's Face." *Journal for Early Modern Cultural Studies* 19, no. 4 (Fall 2019): 156–77.

Ndiaye, Noémie. *Scripts of Blackness: Early Modern Performance Culture and the Making of Race*. Philadelphia: University of Pennsylvania Press, 2022.

Niccoli, Ottavia. *Prophecy and People in Renaissance Italy*. Translated by Lydia G. Cochrane. Princeton, NJ: Princeton University Press, 1990.

Nunn, Zavier. "Trans Liminality and the Nazi State." *Past and Present* 260, no. 1 (2023): 123–57.

Odhner, Carl Theophilus. *Correspondences of Canaan: A Study of the Spiritual Geography and History of the Land and Nations of the World*. Bryn Athyn, PA: Academy Book Room, 1911.

Ofer, Yosef. *The Masora on Scripture and Its Methods*. Boston, MA: Walter de Gruyter, 2019.

Ordover, Nancy. *American Eugenics: Race, Queer Anatomy, and the Science of Nationalism*. Minneapolis: University of Minnesota Press, 2003.

Orgel, Stephen. *Impersonations: The Performance of Gender in Shakespeare's England*. New York: Cambridge University Press, 1996.

Orgel, Stephen. "The Renaissance Artist as Plagiarist." *ELH* 48, no. 3 (Autumn 1981): 476–95.

Origen. *Homilies on Genesis and Exodus*. Translated by Ronald E. Heine. Washington, DC: Catholic University of America Press, 1981.

Origen. *Origen's Treatise on Prayer*. Translated by Eric George Jay. London: SPCK, 1954.

Orlin, Lena Cowen. "Three Ways to Be Invisible in the Renaissance: Sex, Reputation, and Stitchery." In *Renaissance Culture and the Everyday*, edited by Patricia Fumerton and Simon Hunt, 183–203. Philadelphia: University of Pennsylvania Press, 1999.

Owens, Margaret E. "John Webster, Tussaud Laureate: The Waxworks in *The Duchess of Malfi*." *ELH* 79 (2012): 851–77.

Paré, Ambroise. *On Monsters and Marvels*. Translated by Janis L. Pallister. Chicago: University of Chicago Press, 1982.

Paré, Ambroise. *The Workes of That Famous Chirurgion Ambrose Parey Translated out of Latine and Compared with the French*. Translated by Thomas Johnson. London: Th. Cotes and R. Young, 1634.

Parker, Courtney Bailey. *Spectrums of Shakespearean Crossdressing: The Art of Performing Women*. New York: Routledge, 2020.

Parker, Patricia. "Barbers and Barbary: Early Modern Cultural Semantics." *Renaissance Drama* 33 (2004): 201–44.

Parker, Roszika. *The Subversive Stitch: Embroidery and the Making of the Feminine*. New York: Routledge, 1989.

Parr, Johnstone. "The Horoscope in Webster's *The Duchess of Malfi*." *PMLA* 60, no. 3 (September 1945): 760–65.

Parris, Benjamin. "Seizures of Sleep in Early Modern Literature." *Studies in English Literature* 58, no. 1 (Winter 2018): 51–76.

Pastoureau, Michel. "La Réforme et la coleur." *Bulletin de la Société de l'Histoire du Protestantisme Français* 138 (1992): 323–42.

Pelikan, Jaroslav, ed. *Luther's Works*. Vol. 1. St. Louis, MO: Concordia Publishing House, 1958.

Pendergraft, Mary. "'Thou Shalt Not Eat the Hyena:' A Note on 'Barnabas' Epistle 10.7." *Vigiliae Christianae* 46, no. 1 (March 1992): 75–79.

Pequigney, Joseph. *Such Is My Love: A Study of Shakespeare's Sonnets*. Chicago: University of Chicago Press, 1985.

Person, Ethel. "Harry Benjamin: Creative Maverick." *Journal of Gay and Lesbian Mental Health* 12, no. 3 (2008): 259–75.

Pescatori, Rossella. "The Myth of the Androgyne in Leone Ebreo's *Dialogues of Love*." *Comitatus* 38, no. 1 (2007): 115–28.

Philo. *Allegorical Interpretation of Genesis 2 and 3*. In *Philo*, vol. 1, edited and translated by F. H. Colson and G. H. Whitaker. Cambridge, MA: Harvard University Press, 1929.

Philo. *De opificio mundi*. In *Philo*, vol. 1, edited and translated by F. H. Colson and G. H. Whitaker. Cambridge, MA: Harvard University Press, 1929.

Pico della Mirandola. *Heptaplus, or Discourse on the Seven Days of Creation*. Translated by Jessie Brewer McGaw. New York: Philosophical Library, 1977.

Piepzna-Samarasinha, Leah Lakshmi. *Care Work: Dreaming Disability Justice*. Vancouver: Arsenal Pulp Press, 2018.

Poitevin, Kimberly. "Inventing Whiteness: Cosmetics, Race, and Women in Early Modern England." *Journal for Early Modern Cultural Studies* 11, no. 1 (Spring/Summer 2011): 59–89.

Poole, William. "Milton, Dinah, and Theodotus." *Milton Quarterly* 47, no. 2 (May 2013): 65–71.

Power, Terri. *Shakespeare and Gender in Practice*. New York: Palgrave, 2016.

Precarity Lab, ed. *Technoprecarious*. London: Goldsmiths Press, 2020.

Preciado, Paul B. *Testo Junkie: Sex, Drugs, and Biopolitics in the Pharmacopornographic Era*. Translated by Bruce Benderson. New York: Feminist Press at CUNY, 2013.

Prosser, Jay. *Second Skins: The Body Narratives of Transsexuality*. New York: Columbia University Press, 1998.

Prosser, Jay. "Transsexuals and the Transsexologists: Inversion and the Emergence of Transsexual Subjectivity." In *Sexology in Culture: Labelling Bodies and Desires*, edited by Lucy Bland and Laura Doan, 116–32. Chicago: University of Chicago Press, 1998.

Puar, Jasbir. *The Right to Maim: Debility, Capacity, Disability*. Durham, NC: Duke University Press, 2017.

Pye, Christopher, ed. *Political Aesthetics in the Era of Shakespeare*. Evanston, IL: Northwestern University Press, 2020.

Raber, Karen. *Animal Bodies, Renaissance Culture*. Philadelphia: University of Pennsylvania Press, 2013.

Rackin, Phyllis. "Androgyny, Mimesis, and the Marriage of the Boy Heroine on the English Renaissance Stage." *PMLA* 102, no. 1 (1987): 29–41.

Rackin, Phyllis. *Shakespeare and Women*. New York: Oxford University Press, 2005.

Radzinowicz, Mary Ann. *Toward* Samson Agonistes: *The Growth of Milton's Mind*. Princeton, NJ: Princeton University Press, 2015.

Rambuss, Richard. *Closet Devotions*. Durham, NC: Duke University Press, 1998.

Rambuss, Richard. *Spenser's Secret Career*. New York: Cambridge University Press, 1993.

Rashi. *The Book of Shmuel I*. Edited by Avraham Davis. Lakewood, NJ: Metsudah Publications, 1999.

Rasmussen, Susanne. *Public Portents in Republican Rome*. Rome: L'Erma di Bretschneider, 2003.

Raun, Tobias. *Out Online: Trans Self-Representation and Community Building on YouTube*. New York: Routledge, 2016.

Raymond of Capua. *The Life of St. Catherine of Siena*. Translated by George Lamb. New York: 1960.

Reinhardt, Klaus. "The Texts of the 'Bible of Saint Louis.'" In *The Bible of Saint Louis*, vol. 2, edited by Ramon Gonzalvez Ruiz, 269–321. Barcelona: M. Moleiro, 2004.

Resnick, Irven M. "Medieval Roots of the Myth of Jewish Male Menses." *Harvard Theological Review* 93, no. 3 (July 2000): 241–63.

Restar, A. J. "Methodological Critique of Littman's (2018) Parental-Respondents Accounts of 'Rapid-Onset Gender Dysphoria.'" *Archives of Sexual Behavior* 49, no. 1 (2020): 61–66.

de Reuck, Jennifer. "'Plagued in Art': The Fashioning of an Aesthetics of Sacrifice in *The Duchess of Malfi*." *Shakespeare in Southern Africa* 27 (2015): 25–32.

Richards, Renée, with John Ames. *Second Serve: The Renée Richards Story*. New York: Stein and Day, 1983.

Robinson, Benedict. *Islam and Early Modern English Literature: The Politics of Romance from Spenser to Milton*. New York: Palgrave Macmillan, 2007.

Roller, Lynn. *In Search of God the Mother: The Cult of Anatolian Cybele*. Berkeley: University of California Press, 1999.

Rose, Mary Beth. *The Expense of Spirit: Love and Sexuality in English Renaissance Drama*. Ithaca, NY: Cornell University Press, 1988.

Rosenberg, Jordy. "The Molecularization of Sexuality: On Some Primitivisms of the Present." *Theory and Event* 17, no. 2 (2014).

Rosenberger, Veit. *Gezähmte Götter: Das Prodigienwesen der römischen Republik*. Stuttgart: Franz Steiner Verlag, 1998.

Rosenblatt, Jason P., and Winfried Schleiner. "John Selden's Letter to Ben Jonson on Cross-Dressing and Bisexual Gods." *English Literary Renaissance* 29, no. 1 (1999): 44–74.

Rothstein, Marian. *The Androgyne in Early Modern France: Contextualizing the Power of Gender*. New York: Palgrave, 2015.

Rubright, Marjorie. "Becoming Scattered: The Case of Iphis's Trans*Version and the Archipelogic of John Florio's *Worlde of Wordes*." In *Ovidian Transversions: 'Iphis and Ianthe', 1300–1650*, edited by Valerie Traub, Patricia Badir, and Peggy McCracken, 118–49. Edinburgh: Edinburgh University Press, 2019.

Rubright, Marjorie. "Transgender Capacity in *The Roaring Girl*." *Journal for Early Modern Cultural Studies* 19, no. 4 (Fall 2019): 45–74.

Rüff, Jakob. *The Expert Midwife, or, An Excellent and Most Necessary Treatise of the Generation and Birth of Man*. London: E. G[riffin] for S. B[urton], 1637.

Ruscelli, Girolamo. *The Secrets of Alexis: Containing Many Excellent Remedies against Divers Diseases*. London: Printed by William Stansby, 1615.

Rust, Jennifer. *The Body in Mystery: The Political Theology of the* Corpus Mysticum *in the Literature of Reformation England*. Evanston, IL: Northwestern University Press, 2014.

Sabine, Maureen. *Feminine Engendered Faith: The Poetry of John Donne and Richard Crashaw*. New York: Palgrave, 1992.

Salih, Sarah. *Versions of Virginity in Late Medieval England*. Rochester, NY: D. S. Brewer, 2001.

Sanchez, Melissa. "Colonial Cacophony and Early Modern Trans Studies: Spenser with Julia Serano." *Spenser Studies* 27 (2023): 317–44.

Sanchez, Melissa. "Transdevotion: Race, Gender, and Christian Universalism." *Journal for Early Modern Cultural Studies* 19, no. 4 (Fall 2019): 94–115.

Santner, Eric. *On Creaturely Life: Rilke, Benjamin, Sebald*. Chicago: University of Chicago Press, 2006.

Santner, Eric. *The Royal Remains: The People's Two Bodies and the Endgames of Sovereignty*. Chicago: University of Chicago Press, 2011.

Sauer, Michelle M. "Queer Time and Lesbian Temporality in Medieval Women's Encounters with the Side Wound." In *Medieval Futurity: Essays for the Future of Queer Medieval Studies*, edited by Will Rogers and Christopher Michael Roman, 199–220. Boston, MA: Walter de Gruyter, 2021.

Saunders, Ben. *Desiring Donne: Poetry, Sexuality, Interpretation*. Cambridge, MA: Harvard University Press, 2006.

Schmitt, Carl. *The Leviathan in the State Theory of Thomas Hobbes: Meaning and Failure of a Political Symbol*. Translated by George Schwab and Erna Hilfstein. Westport, CT: Greenwood Press, 1996.

Schoenfeldt, Michael. *Prayer and Power: George Herbert and Renaissance Courtship*. Chicago: University of Chicago Press, 1991.

Schutte, Anne Jacobson. "'Such Monstrous Births': A Neglected Aspect of the Antinomian Controversy." *Renaissance Quarterly* 38, no. 1 (Spring 1985): 85–106.

Scot, Reginald. *The Discoverie of Witchcraft*. New York: Dover, 1972.

Seid, Danielle M. "The Reveal." *Transgender Studies Quarterly* 1, nos. 1–2 (May 2014): 176–77.

Setzer, Claudia. *Resurrection of the Body in Early Judaism and Early Christianity: Doctrine, Community, and Self-Definition*. Leiden: Brill, 2004.

Sexon, Sophie. "Gender-Querying Christ's Wounds." In *Trans and Genderqueer Subjects in Medieval Hagiography*, edited by Blake Gutt and Alicia Spencer-Hall, 133–54. Amsterdam: Amsterdam University Press, 2021.

Sexon, Sophie. "Seeing Mobility in Static Images: Tools for Non-Binary Identification in Late Medieval Sources." In *Medieval Mobilities: Gendered Bodies, Spaces, and Movements*, edited by Basil Arnould Price, Jane Elizabeth Bonsall, and Meagan Khoury, 77–108. New York: Palgrave Macmillan, 2023.

Seymour, Nicole. *Strange Natures: Futurity, Empathy, and the Queer Ecological Imagination*. Chicago: University of Illinois Press, 2013.

Shakespeare, William. *Hamlet*. Edited by G. R. Hibbard. New York: Oxford University Press, 1987.

Shakespeare, William. *Macbeth*. Edited by Nicholas Brooke. New York: Oxford University Press, 1990.

Shakespeare, William. *The Riverside Shakespeare*. 2nd ed. Edited by G. Blakemore Evans. Boston, MA: Houghton Mifflin, 1997.

Shannon, Laurie. *The Accommodated Animal: Cosmopolity in Shakespearean Locales*. Chicago: University of Chicago Press, 2013.

Shannon, Laurie. *Sovereign Amity: Figures of Friendship in Shakespearean Contexts*. Chicago: University of Chicago Press, 2002.

Shapiro, Michael. *Gender in Play on the Shakespearean Stage: Boy Heroines and Female Pages*. Ann Arbor: University of Michigan Press, 1994.

Shawcross, John. *The Uncertain World of* Samson Agonistes. Cambridge: D. S. Brewer, 2001.

Shelton, Stephanie. "The Influences of Barad's 'Transmaterialities' on Queer Theories and Methods." *GLQ* 25, no. 1 (2019): 119–24.

Shoulson, Jeffrey. *Milton and the Rabbis: Hebraism, Hellenism, and Christianity*. New York: Columbia University Press, 2010.

Shuger, Debora. *The Renaissance Bible: Scholarship, Sacrifice, and Subjectivity*. Berkeley: University of California Press, 1994.

Shuger, Debora. "The Title of Donne's *Devotions*." *English Language Notes* 22, no. 4 (1985): 39–40.

Shuger, Debora K. *Political Theologies in Shakespeare's England: The Sacred and the State in* Measure for Measure. New York: Palgrave, 2001.

shuster, stef m. *Trans Medicine: The Emergence and Practice of Treating Gender*. New York: New York University Press, 2021.

Siebers, Tobin. *Disability Theory*. Ann Arbor: University of Michigan Press, 2005.

Simon, Elliott M. "Pico, Paracelsus, and Dee: The Magical Measure of Human Perfectibility." In *Gender and Scientific Discourse in Early Modern Culture*, 2nd ed., edited by Kathleen P. Long, 13–41. New York: Routledge, 2016.

Simpson, Evelyn M., and George R. Potter, eds. *The Sermons of John Donne*. Berkeley: University of California Press, 1956.

Sinfield, Alan. *Shakespeare, Authority, Sexuality: Unfinished Business in Cultural Materialism*. New York: Routledge, 2006.

Skuse, Alanna. "'One Stroak of His Razour': Tales of Self-Gelding in Early Modern England." *Social History of Medicine* 33, no. 2 (2020): 377–93.

Smith, Charlotte Colding. *Images of Islam, 1435–1600: Turks in Germany and Central Europe*. New York: Routledge, 2014.

Smith, Ian. *Race and Rhetoric in the Renaissance: Barbarian Errors*. New York: Palgrave Macmillan, 2009.

Smith, John. *The Mysterie of Rhetorique Unveil'd*. London: Printed by E. Cotes for George Eversden, 1665.

Smith, Megan Kathleen. "Reading It Wrong to Get It Right: Sacramental and Excremental Encounters in Early Modern Poems about Hair Jewelry." *Philological Quarterly* 94, no. 4 (2015): 353–75.

Snodin, Michael, and Maurice Howard. *Ornament: A Social History Since 1450*. New Haven, CT: Yale University Press, 1996.

Snorton, C. Riley. *Black on Both Sides: A Racial History of Trans Identity*. Minneapolis: University of Minnesota Press, 2017.

Soergel, Philip M. *Miracles and the Protestant Imagination: The Evangelical Wonder Book in Reformation Germany*. New York: Oxford University Press, 2012.

Song, Eric. *Love against Substitution: Seventeenth-Century English Literature and the Meaning of Marriage*. Stanford, CA: Stanford University Press, 2022.

Spade, Dean. "Mutilating Gender." In *The Transgender Studies Reader*, vol. 1, edited by Susan Stryker and Stephen Wittle, 315–32. New York: Routledge, 2013.

Spade, Dean. *Normal Life: Administrative Violence, Critical Trans Politics, and the Limits of Law*. Durham, NC: Duke University Press, 2015.

Speelberg, Femke. "Fashion and Virtue: Textile Patterns and the Print Revolution 1520–1620." *Metropolitan Museum of Art Bulletin* 73, no. 2 (Fall 2015): 1–48.

Sperry, Eileen. "Decay, Intimacy, and the Lyric Metaphor in Jon Donne." *Studies in English Literature* 59, no. 2 (2019): 45–66.

Spillers, Hortense. "Mama's Baby, Papa's Maybe: An American Grammar Book." *diacritics* 17, no. 2 (1987): 65–81.

Spinoza, Benedict de. *Ethics Proved in Geometrical Order*. Edited by Matthew J. Kisner. Translated by Michael Silverthorne and Matthew J. Kisner. New York: Cambridge University Press, 2018.

Springborg, Patricia. "Hobbes, Donne and the Virginia Company: *Terra Nullius* and 'The Bulimia of Dominium.'" *History of Political Thought* 36, no. 1 (Spring 2015): 113–64.

Stallybrass, Peter. "'Little Jobs': Broadsides and the Printing Revolution." In *Agent of Change: Print Culture Studies after Elizabeth L. Eisenstein*, edited by Sabrina Alcorn Baron, Eric N. Lindquist, and Eleanor F. Shevlin, 315–41. Amherst: University of Massachusetts Press, 2007.

Stallybrass, Peter. "Transvestism and the 'Body Beneath': Speculating on the Boy Actor." In *Erotic Politics: Desire on the Renaissance Stage*, edited by Susan Zimmerman, 64–83. New York: Routledge, 1992.

Stanley, Eric. *Atmospheres of Violence: Structuring Antagonism and the Trans/Queer Ungovernable*. Durham, NC: Duke University Press, 2021.

Steinbock, Eliza, Marianna Szczygielska, and Anthony Clair Wagner, eds. *Tranimacies: Intimate Links between Animal and Trans* Studies*. New York: Routledge, 2021.

Stephens, Walter. "Witches Who Steal Penises: Impotence and Illusion in *Malleus Maleficarum*." *Journal of Medieval and Early Modern Studies* 28, no. 3 (Fall 1998): 495–529.
Stern, Alexandra Minna. *Eugenic Nation: Faults and Frontiers of Better Breeding in Modern America*. Berkeley: University of California Press, 2016.
Stevenson, Walter. "The Rise of Eunuchs in Greco-Roman Antiquity." *Journal of the History of Sexuality* 5, no. 4 (April 1995): 495–511.
Stiegler, Bernard. *Technics and Time: The Fault of Epimetheus*. Vol. 1. Translated by Richard Beardsworth and George Collins. Stanford, CA: Stanford University Press, 1998.
Stoller, Robert. "Boyhood Gender Aberrations: Treatment Issues." *Journal of the American Psychoanalytic Association* 26, no. 3 (1978): 541–58.
Stoller, Robert. *Sex and Gender: The Development of Masculinity and Femininity*. London: H. Karnac Ltd., 1968.
Stone, Lawrence. *The Family, Sex and Marriage in England, 1500–1800*. New York: Harper and Row, 1977.
Strassfeld, Max. *Trans Talmud: Androgynes and Eunuchs in Rabbinic Literature*. Oakland: University of California Press, 2022.
Strassfeld, Max. "Transing Religious Studies." *Journal of Feminist Studies in Religion* 34, no. 1 (2018): 37–53.
Strassfeld, Max, and Roberto Che Espinoza. "Introduction: Mapping Trans Studies in Religion." *Transgender Studies Quarterly* 6, no. 3 (2019): 283–84.
Strickland, Debra Higgs. *Saracens, Demons, and Jews: Making Monsters in Medieval Art*. Princeton, NJ: Princeton University Press, 2003.
Stryker, Susan. "My Words to Victor Frankenstein above the Village of Chamounix: Performing Transgender Rage." *GLQ* 1, no. 3 (1994): 237–54.
Stryker, Susan. *Transgender History: The Roots of Today's Revolution*. Berkeley, CA: Seal Press, 2017.
Tanner, Norman P., ed. *Decrees of the Ecumenical Council: Trent to Vatican II*. Vol. 2. London: Sheed and Ward, 1990.
Targoff, Ramie. "Facing Death." In *The Cambridge Companion to John Donne*, edited by Achsah Guibbory, 217–32. New York: Cambridge University Press, 2006.
Targoff, Ramie. *John Donne, Body and Soul*. Chicago: University of Chicago Press, 2008.
Tarnoff, Maura. "Sewing Authorship in John Skelton's 'Garlande or Chapelet of Laurell.'" *ELH* 75, no. 2 (Summer 2008): 415–38.
Taylor, Charles. *A Secular Age*. Cambridge, MA: Harvard University Press, 2007.
Taylor, John. *The Needles Excellency*. London: Printed for Iames Boler, 1631.
Taylor, Thomas. *A Commentarie vpon the Epistle of S. Paul Written to Titus*. Cambridge: Printed by Cantrell Legge, 1612.
de Terreros y Pando, Esteban. *Diccionario Castellano*. Vol. 2. Madrid: Viuda de Ibarra, Hijos y Compañia, 1787.
Terry, Jennifer. *Attachments to War: Biomedical Logics and Violence in Twenty-First-Century America*. Durham, NC: Duke University Press, 2017.
Teskey, Gordon. *Delirious Milton: The Fate of the Poet in Modernity*. Cambridge, MA: Harvard University Press, 2009.
Thomas, J. H., ed. *Systematic Arrangement of Lord Coke's First Institute of the Laws of England*. Philadelphia, PA: Alexander Toward, 1876.

Thornton, Max. "Trans/Criptions: Gender, Disability, and Liturgical Experience." *Transgender Studies Quarterly* 6, no. 3 (2019): 358–67.

Tietze, Hans. "Master and Workshop in the Venetian Renaissance." *Parnassus* 11, no. 8 (December 1939): 34–45.

Tornelli, Andrea, and Giacomo Galeazzi. *This Economy Kills: Pope Francis on Capitalism and Social Justice*. Collegeville, MN: Liturgical Press, 2015.

Tougher, Shaun. *The Roman Castrati: Eunuchs in the Roman Empire*. New York: Bloomsbury, 2022.

Tourmaline, Eric A. Stanley, and Johanna Burton, eds. *Trap Door: Trans Cultural Production and the Politics of Visibility*. Cambridge, MA: MIT Press, 2017.

Traub, Valerie. "Desire and the Difference It Makes." In *The Matter of Difference: Materialist Feminist Criticism of Shakespeare*, edited by Valerie Wayne, 81–114. Ithaca, NY: Cornell University Press, 1991.

Traub, Valerie. *The Renaissance of Lesbianism in Early Modern England*. New York: Cambridge University Press, 2002.

Traub, Valerie. "Sex without Issue: Sodomy, Reproduction, and Signification in Shakespeare's Sonnets." In *Shakespeare's Sonnets: Critical Essays*, edited by James Schiffer, 431–54. New York: Garland Publishing, 1999.

Tremblay, Jean-Thomas. "Feminist Breathing." *differences* 30, no. 3 (2019): 92–117.

Trexler, Richard C. "Gendering Jesus Crucified." In *Iconography at the Crossroads*, edited by Brendan Cassidy, 107–20. Princeton, NJ: Index of Christian Art, 1993.

Trigg, Christopher. "The Racial Politics of Resurrection in the Eighteenth-Century Atlantic World." *Early American Literature* 55, no. 1 (2020): 47–84.

Trubowitz, Rachel. "'The People of Asia and with Them the Jews': Israel, Asia, and England in Milton's Writings." In *Milton and the Jews*, edited by Douglas A. Brooks, 151–77. New York: Cambridge University Press, 2008.

*A True Relation of the Birth of Three Monsters in the City of Namen in Flanders*. London: Printed by Simon Stafford, for Richard Bunnian, 1608.

Tuke, Thomas. *Discourse against the Painting and Tincturing of Women*. London: By Thomas Creede and Bernard Alsop for Edward Marchant, 1616.

Turner, Henry S. *The Corporate Commonwealth: Pluralism and Political Fictions in England, 1516–1651*. Chicago: University of Chicago Press, 2016.

Ulrichs, Karl Heinrich. *Memnon: Die Geschlectsnature des mannliebenden Urnings*. Schleiz: C. Hübscher, 1868.

Ursell, Michael. "Interinanimation and Lifelessness in John Donne's Book Studies." *Studies in English Literature* 56, no. 1 (Winter 2016): 71–92.

Vaccaro, Jeanne. "Feelings and Fractals: Woolly Ecologies of Transgender Matter." *GLQ* 21, nos. 2–3 (2015): 273–93.

Vaccaro, Jeanne. "Felt Matters." *Women and Performance* 20, no. 3 (2010): 253–66.

Valentine, David. *Imagining Transgender: An Ethnography of a Category*. Durham, NC: Duke University Press, 2007.

Van Arsdall, Anne, Helmut W. Klug, and Paul Blanz. "The Mandrake Plant and Its Legend: A New Perspective." In *Old Names—New Growth: Proceedings of the 2nd ASPNS Conference*, edited by Peter Bierbauner and Helmut W. Klug, 285–46. Frankfurt/Main: Lang, 2009.

Van der Lugt, Maaike. "Sex Difference in Medieval Theology and Canon Law." *Medieval Feminist Forum* 46, no. 1 (2010): 101–21.

Vasari, Giorgio. *Lives of the Artists*. Translated by Julia Conaway Bonadella. New York: Oxford University Press, 1991.

Velasco, Sherry. *The Lieutenant Nun: Transgenderism, Lesbian Desire, and Catalina de Erauso*. Austin: University of Texas Press, 2000.

Velissariou, Aspasia. "Neither a Devil nor a Man: D'Amville in Tourneur's *The Atheist's Tragedy*." *Early Modern Literary Studies* 20, no. 2 (2018): 1–20.

Velocci, Beans. *Binary Logic: The Power of Incoherence in American Sex Science*. Durham, NC: Duke University Press, forthcoming.

Velocci, Beans. "Standards of Care: Uncertainty and Risk in Harry Benjamin's Transsexual Classifications." *Transgender Studies Quarterly* 8, no. 4 (November 2021): 462–80.

Vendler, Helen. *The Art of Shakespeare's Sonnets*. Cambridge, MA: Harvard University Press, 1997.

Vincent, Nicholas. "Two Papal Letters on the Wearing of the Jewish Badge, 1221 and 1229." *Jewish Historical Studies* 34 (1994–96): 209–24.

Wade, Peter, and Patrick Reis. "CPAC Speaker Calls for Eradication of 'Transgenderism.'" *Rolling Stone*, March 6, 2023.

Waldron, Jennifer. "Dead Likenesses and Sex Machines: Shakespearean Media Theory." In *Oxford Handbook of Shakespeare and Embodiment*, edited by Valerie Traub, 611–27. New York: Oxford University Press, 2016.

Waldron, Jennifer. "Of Stones and Stony Hearts: Desdemona, Hermione, and Post-Reformation Theatre." In *The Indistinct Human in Renaissance Literature*, edited by Jean E. Feerick and Vin Nardizzi, 205–27. New York: Palgrave, 2012.

Wall, Wendy. *Staging Domesticity: Household Work and English Identity in Early Modern Drama*. New York: Cambridge University Press, 2002.

Wall-Randell, Sarah. "The Proper False: *Twelfth Night* and 'Original Practices,' 2002–2022." In *Twelfth Night: The State of Play*, edited by Emma Smith. London: Arden, forthcoming 2024.

Watson, Robert. *The Rest is Silence: Death as Annihilation in the English Renaissance*. Berkeley: University of California Press, 1994.

Weaver, Harlan. "Monster Trans: Diffracting Affect, Reading Rage." *Somatechnics* 3, no. 2 (2013): 287–306.

Weaver, Harlan. "Trans Species." *Transgender Studies Quarterly* 1, nos. 1–2 (2014): 253–54.

Weber, Max. *The Protestant Ethic and the Spirit of Capitalism*. New York: Routledge, 1992.

Webster, John. *The Duchess of Malfi*. Edited by Michael Neill. New York: Norton, 2015.

Weinkauf, Mary S. "Dalila: The Worst of All Possible Wives." *Studies in English Literature, 1500–1900* 13, no. 1 (1973): 135–47.

Whigham, Frank. "Sexual and Social Mobility in *The Duchess of Malfi*." *PMLA* 100, no. 2 (March 1985): 167–86.

Windholz, Jordan. "The Queer Testimonies of Male Chastity in *All's Well That Ends Well*." *Modern Philology* 116, no. 4 (2019): 322–49.

Wiseman, S. J. "Hairy on the Inside: Metamorphosis and Civility in English Werewolf Texts." In *Renaissance Beasts: Of Animals, Humans, and Other Wonderful Creatures*, edited by Erica Fudge, 50–69. Urbana: University of Illinois Press, 2004.

Wolfert, Madison. "The Racial Biopolitics of Sex in the Work of Henry Neville." Forthcoming in *English Literary Renaissance* (Fall 2024).

Wolfthal, Diane. "Beyond Human: Visualizing the Sexuality of Abraham Bosse's Mandrake." In *Renaissance Posthumanism*, edited by Joseph Campana and Scott Maisano, 211–52. New York: Fordham University Press, 2016.

Wolin, Richard. "Carl Schmit, Political Existentialism, and the Total State." *Theory and Society* 19, no. 4 (August 1990): 389–416.

Woodbridge, Linda. *Women and the English Renaissance: Literature and the Nature of Womankind, 1540 to 1620*. Urbana: University of Illinois Press, 1984.

Wülker, Ludwig. *Die geschichtliche Entwicklung des Prodigienwesens*. Leipzig: Universität Leipzig, 1903.

Yavneh, Naomi. "The Spiritual Eroticism of Leone's Hermaphrodite." In *Playing with Gender: A Renaissance Pursuit*, edited by Jean Brink, Maryanne Horovitz, and Allison Courdet, 85–98. Chicago: University of Illinois Press, 1991.

Yonge, James. *Currus triumphalis, e terebintho*. London: Printed for J. Martyn, 1679.

Young, R. V. "Love, Poetry, and John Donne in the Love Poetry of John Donne." *Renascence* 52, no. 4 (2000): 250–73.

Zeeman, Nicolette. "Theory Transposed: Idols, Knights and Identity." In *What Is an Image in Medieval and Early Modern England?*, edited by Antoinina Bevan Zlatar and Olga Timofeeva, 39–80. Tubingen: Naar Francke Attempto Verlag, 2017.

Žižek, Slavoj, Eric Santner, and Kenneth Reinhard, eds. *The Neighbor: Three Inquiries in Political Theology*. Chicago: University of Chicago Press, 2005.

# Index